TAKING SIDES

Clashing Views
on Controversial
Psychological Issues

7th edition

Clashing Views
on Controversial
Psychological Issues

7th edition

Edited, Selected, and with Introductions by

Brent Slife
Baylor University

and

Joseph Rubinstein
Purdue University

The Dushkin Publishing Group, Inc.

To my three garrulous sons, Conor,
Nathan, and Jacob (B. S.)

For my teachers in dialogues: Morris
and Bessie (J. R.)

BF
149
.T34
1992

Library of Congress Catalog Card Number:
91–76396

Manufactured in the United States of America

Seventh Edition, First Printing

ISBN: 1–56134–058–8

 Printed on Recycled Paper

 The Dushkin Publishing Group, Inc.
SluiceDock, Guilford, CT 06437
DPG *Innovative Publishing Since 1971*

PREFACE

Critical thinking skills are a significant component of a meaningful education, and this book is specifically designed to stimulate critical thinking and
initiate lively and informed dialogue on psychological issues. In this book we
present 38 selections, arranged in pro and con pairs, that address a total of 19
different controversial issues in psychology. The opposing views demonstrate that even experts can derive conflicting conclusions and opinions from
the same body of information.

A dialogue approach to learning is certainly not new. The ancient Greek
philosopher Socrates engaged in it with his students some 2,400 years ago.
His point-counterpoint procedure was termed a *dialectic*. Although Socrates
and his companions hoped eventually to know the "truth" by this method,
they did not see the dialectic as having a predetermined end. There were no
right answers to know or facts to memorize. The emphasis in this learning
method is on how to evaluate information—on developing reasoning skills.

It is in this dialectical spirit that *Taking Sides: Clashing Views on Controversial
Psychological Issues* was originally compiled, and it has guided us through this
seventh edition as well. To encourage and stimulate discussion and to focus
the debates in this volume, each issue is expressed in terms of a single
question and answered with two points of view. But certainly the reader
should not feel confined to adopt only one or the other of the positions
presented. There are positions that fall between the views expressed, or
totally outside them, and we encourage you to fashion your own conclusions.

Some of the questions raised in this volume go to the very heart of what
psychology as a discipline is all about and the methods and manner in which
psychologists work. Others address newly emerging concerns. In choosing
readings we were guided by the following criteria: the readings had to be
understandable to newcomers to psychology; they had to have academic
substance; and they had to express markedly different points of view.

Plan of the book Each issue in this volume has an issue *introduction*,
which points out significant quotes from each author and defines each
author's position. Also provided is a set of point-counterpoint statements
that pertain to the issue—they should help get the dialogue off the ground.
Each issue concludes with *challenge questions* to provoke further examination
of the issue. The introduction and challenge questions are designed to assist
the reader in achieving a critical and informed view on important psychological issues. At the back of the book is a listing of all the *contributors to this
volume*, which gives information on the psychologists, psychiatrists, philosophers, professors, and social critics whose views are debated here.

i

Changes to this edition This new edition has been significantly updated. There are 10 completely new issues: *Should Psychologists Study Memory Through Controlled Laboratory Experiments?* (Issue 2); *Can Experiments Using Animals Be Justified?* (Issue 3); *Do Gender Differences Originate From Biological Factors?* (Issue 10); *Are Children of Divorced Parents at Greater Risk?* (Issue 12); *Should Adolescents Be Allowed to Make Decisions About Abortion Without Parental Involvement?* (Issue 13); *Should Psychotherapists Allow Suicide?* (Issue 14); *Should Psychotherapy Include Religious Values?* (Issue 16); *Is Electroconvulsive Therapy Safe?* (Issue 17); *Should Psychologists Be Allowed to Prescribe Drugs?* (Issue 18); and *Would Legalizing Drugs Have Beneficial Effects on Society?* (Issue 19). Although Issue 2 is new, the YES reading has been retained from an issue that appeared in the previous edition, because of its effectiveness. The issues that were dropped from the previous edition were done so on the recommendation of professors who let us know what worked and what could be improved. In all, there are 19 new selections.

Supplements There is an *Instructor's Manual with Test Questions* (multiple-choice and essay), which is available through the publisher. A general guidebook, called *Using Taking Sides in the Classroom*, which discusses methods and techniques for integrating the pro/con approach into any classroom setting, is also available.

Acknowledgments In working on this revision we received useful suggestions from many of the users of the previous edition, and we were able to incorporate many of their recommendations for new issues and new readings. We particularly wish to thank the following professors:

Nusha Askari
San Jose State University

Lois Bonnell
Kean College of New Jersey

Marvin Brodsky
University of Manitoba

Alane S. Brown
Fort Lewis College

Nancy A. Busch
Fordham University

Susan Delaney
Pacific University

Marion Eppler
Middlebury College

Edward Fajardo
Oakton Community College

Austin Flint
American International College

Gordon Hammerle
Adrian College

James W. Hammond
Columbia Union College

Harold A. Herzog
Western Carolina University

Henry L. Roediger, III
Rice University

Daniel L. Johnson
Radford University

Duane Kauffmann
Goshen College

Karl N. Kelley
North Central College

John S. Klein
Castleton State College

Mark Krejci
Concordia College, Moorhead

R. Eric Landrum
University of Wisconsin,
Platteville

John M. Lembo
Millersville University

Ralph J. McKenna
Hendrix College

Janet Morahan-Martin
Bryant College

Edgar C. O'Neal
Tulane University

Bob Osborne
Middlebury College

Christine M. Panyard
Mercy College of Detroit

Allen D. Potthoff
California State University,
Fullerton

Anne E. Powell
Smith College

Thomas P. Pusateri
Loras College

Lisa Razzano
De Paul University

John J. Rearden
Eastern Illinois University

Miguel Roig
St. John's University

Nancy Sauerman
Kirkwood Community College

Donald Spring
Union College

Bruce C. Stockin
Westmont College

Elmer A. Sundby
University of Wisconsin,
Eau Claire

T. Gale Thompson
Bethany College

Mary Thomsen
Los Angeles Pierce College

Charles Verschoor
Miami-Dade Community
College

Special thanks to Mimi Egan, program manager of the Taking Sides series at the Dushkin Publishing Group, for her perspicacity.

Brent D. Slife
Hewitt, Texas

Joseph Rubinstein
West Lafayette, Indiana

CONTENTS IN BRIEF

CONTENTS

Professor of psychology Stanley Milgram makes his case for the suspension
of normal ethical standards when a social scientist is seeking to benefit
society. Research associate Thomas H. Murray holds that social scientists
must consider the costs of deception to the individual scientist, the subject,
and the society at large, and determine if the information produced is worth
those costs.

Cognitive psychologists Mahzarin R. Banaji and Robert G. Crowder argue
that laboratory studies under controlled conditions are the best means of
understanding the general principles of memory. Cognitive psychologist
Ulric Neisser contends that memory researchers need to study the practical
problems of memory in the natural settings in which these problems occur.

Anthropologist John R. Cole argues that although animal research has
declined in recent years, some animal research is still necessary and beneficial to society. Attorney Steven Zak asserts that animals have the right to not
be treated like instruments for the betterment of humankind and that legal
barriers should be erected to prevent animal exploitation.

Forensic neurologist Richard Restak interprets physiological research as suggesting that free will is a delusion; therefore, biological processes control behaviors. Noted humanistic psychologist Joseph F. Rychlak contends that when the concepts of free will and determinism are fully understood, physiological research generally supports the existence of free will.

Professor of philosophy Herbert Fingarette proposes that the concept of alcoholism as a disease is a myth that has been generated and is currently sustained by those whose own economic interests are served by the myth. Professor of anthropology William Madsen alleges that Fingarette's assertions are based on unscientific research and misunderstanding and are harmful in the long run to alcoholics and to society.

Bernard Dixon, an editor and writer who specializes in science and health issues, presents a series of studies that show the relationship between our state of mind and the workings of our immune system. Free-lance writer Ellen Switzer, who specializes in medicine, psychology, and law, asserts that there is no credible evidence for the claims that the course of a serious illness can be altered by the state of mind of an individual afflicted with a disease.

Sociologist Steven Goldberg contends that the biological differences between men and women explain any psychological differences observed in behavior, emotion, or attitude. Sociologist Cynthia Fuchs Epstein counters Goldberg's claim by citing empirical evidence and recent social developments that she feels indicate the cultural origins of gender differences.

Burton L. White, educator and researcher, contends that the absence of a primary caretaker during a child's first few years produces serious emotional and psychological debilitation. Joanne Curry O'Connell, a professor of educational psychology, asserts that child development investigators have found no consistent adverse effects of out-of-home child day care.

Clinician and researcher Judith S. Wallerstein contends that children of divorced parents are at greater risk than children of intact families for mental and physical problems. Sociologists David H. Demo and Alan C. Acock question the idea that intact, two-parent families are always best for children, and they argue that divorce often includes many positive changes.

A committee of psychologists affiliated with the American Psychological Association (APA) argues that empirical research shows that adolescents are competent enough to make their own decisions concerning abortion. Psychologist Everett L. Worthington, Jr., et al. summarize research that they feel evidences the benefits of adolescents involving the family in decisions such as abortion.

Psychiatrist and psychoanalyst Thomas Szasz considers the patients of psychotherapists to be moral agents who are able to decide for themselves whether or not suicide is a viable option. Psychologist and suicide researcher George A. Clum views suicidal behavior as temporary and impulsive, and he argues that suicidal patients need external restraint to reduce the danger.

Psychologist D. L. Rosenhan describes an experiment that, he contends, demonstrates that once a patient is labeled as schizophrenic, his behavior is seen as such by mental health workers regardless of the true state of the patient's mental health. Psychiatrist Robert L. Spitzer argues that diagnostic labels are necessary and valuable and that Rosenhan's experiment has many flaws.

Clinical psychologist and researcher Allen E. Bergin advocates injecting theistic religious values into the psychotherapeutic context. Albert Ellis, president of the Institute for Rational-Emotive Therapy, feels that extreme religiosity leads to emotional disturbance, and he advances values that are based upon a humanistic-atheistic system of beliefs.

Psychiatrist Raymond R. Crowe argues that ECT is not only safe and
effective, but it also acts quickly after many other treatments have failed.
Former ECT patient Leonard Roy Frank asserts that ECT only seems effective
and that many practitioners of ECT underestimate its risks.

PART 6 SOCIAL ISSUES   323

Clinical psychologist Ronald E. Fox argues that prescription privileges for
psychologists is a logical extension of psychological practice. Clinical psychologist Garland Y. DeNelsky argues that such privileges would make psychology a medical specialty and remove psychology's uniqueness as a discipline.

Richard J. Dennis, chairman of the Advisory Board of the Drug Policy
Foundation, argues that legalizing most drugs would reduce crime, save
money, and not increase the number of addicts. Professor of management
and public policy James Q. Wilson feels that legalizing drugs would lead to
an increase in use, accidents, and drug-related violence.

INTRODUCTION

Ways of Looking at Psychological Issues
Brent Slife

Joseph Rubinstein

In a sense, all of life may be viewed as a trial. We are all members of the jury called upon to participate in decisions that will affect the lives of friends, neighbors, family, and ourselves. Somewhere along the line, even though we cannot be certain about what is "true," we must make a decision that calls for some sort of action. We must take a side.

People who are alert to social issues frequently ask specific questions to help them in their search for evidence. After gathering evidence from various points of view, they deliberate and make decisions. But, as any involved citizen is keenly aware, knowing the "facts" often is not enough to make useful decisions. It is seeing relationships after examining evidence from all sides and the development of personal insights that makes it worthwhile to gather "facts."

YOUR LIFE IS IN YOUR HANDS—IF YOU CHOOSE

The issues that stimulate heated controversy usually do so because they touch our lives and because there is no final proof or fully objective answer. Although it may not always be obvious how they do it, issues have the potential to command our personal destinies, as people who wish to have a say in their future are well aware.

The process of our personal deliberation about these questions and attempts to find answers constitutes, in large measure, our role in the world in which we live. If we choose *not* to explore, we are placing major decisions about our lives in the hands of parents, teachers, salespeople, government officials, and others in our local community, state, and nation. On the other hand, a concern for exploring these issues can be a prelude to active community involvement and to taking a vital part in fashioning our future.

How some of the psychological issues in this anthology affect you, especially if you have no prior knowledge of them, may not be immediately apparent. However, coming to grips with questions such as *Is Our State of Mind Responsible for Our State of Health?* (Issue 6) is very likely to provide personal direction in your own life.

DISTINGUISHING TYPES OF INFORMATION

In the exploration of public issues, there are certain skills that lead to constructive resolutions. Chief among these is the ability to distinguish among the various types of information we all use to arrive at conclusions. We become lost in a discussion when we cannot distinguish between fact and opinion or between evidence based on data and evidence based on values. When we can sort out types of information, we are prepared for an orderly discussion based on a combination of objective evidence and personal values. In the process, we frequently find out more about ourselves and what we really consider important in life.

In order to help you develop the ability to make these distinctions, several types of information are described below. A definition for each term is in italics.

Hypothesis

A statement of how at least two events or conditions may be related. Hypotheses are stated as though they are answers to questions, but they are actually guesses. The reason for stating a hypothesis is to make clear what events or conditions must be investigated. The definitions for the terms in a hypothesis are very often at the heart of the problem being discussed. Participants in a discussion may be arguing without getting anywhere simply because they each have a different meaning for the same term and do not realize it. A research investigation is done in order to determine whether a hypothesis should be accepted or rejected.

Data

The recorded observations and measurements collected in a research study. The data in some cases may be simply a collection of numbers. They indicate what the results of the study are *before* any conclusions are made.

Evidence

The application of data to confirm or reject a hypothesis that has been previously stated. This involves a use of the data to make conclusions.

Conclusions

The final inferences concerning what the evidence allows us to assume.

Fact

Information that we take to be true because it is widely accepted. Facts are the trickiest kinds of information. In a court of law, the jury's responsibility is to decide what the "facts" are. The court's responsibility is to decide what is meant by the law. It is common in science for new facts to change old facts. In some cases, it can be done by a simple vote. Mental disorders, or "abnormalities," are officially designated and classified by a committee of the

American Psychiatric Association. Trustees of the association vote to approve or disapprove of the committee's classifications. Since these experts agree that schizophrenia is abnormal, it is therefore a "fact."

Opinion
A judgment made by an individual who interprets the data in terms of what makes personal sense. Opinions are often confused with objective evidence.

Values
Ideas held by an individual or a group about the way things ought to be. Values are extremely important determinants of how we live our lives and make decisions. We all have values, but we are often not clear about them until we think about them or discuss issues with other people.

FREE WILL AND DETERMINISM

Underlying many public issues dealing with the scientific study of humans is a fundamental question that philosophers have asked for centuries: "Do people have *free will* to exert control over their own destinies, or are their destinies completely *determined* by forces outside their control?

If you are a strong believer in *free will*, then when reading the issues here, you may take the position that we are always free to make a decision that will change the future.

If you are an advocate of *determinism*, then you will believe that what we are is already locked up in our genetic structures and that how we behave is fully determined by a combination of our past experiences and our environmental circumstances.

When scanning the questions in the table of contents, you will note that some of them are specifically concerned with the extent to which certain characteristics, such as intelligence, are inherited. Others are concerned with the value of using psychological knowledge to control the behavior of other people.

To find out why people are as they are, psychologists assume that there are reasons for people being as they are. In other words, our biology determines what we are, and conditions and events determine how we will behave.

One scientific strategy accepted by many psychologists in their search for causes assumes that human nature is lawful and ordered by conditions and events. We attempt to predict the fate of humans by studying the forces acting upon them and within them. The responsibility of a scientist is to find as many cause-and-effect relationships and explanations as possible.

The idea that things cause us to be what we are has been quite fruitful. It has helped us discover some highly predictable relationships. For example, if certain areas of the brain are destroyed, a person will not be able to remember events that happen after the brain injury. But what are the limitations of predictability? Would knowing everything about the brain enable us to predict everything about the person? This scientific strategy assumes that there are *no* limitations to predictability. According to this notion, *everything* is caused by *something*.

This is primarily the premise of determinism. It keeps psychologists looking for causes that determine human affairs. It is not necessarily a "fact" or a "truth." In discussing these issues, you will soon begin to appreciate the difference between making assumptions about truth and making assumptions for strategic reasons.

While psychologists may appear to take the strict determinist position in the search for causes, they are, nevertheless, very likely to take the free will position that we must accept personal responsibility for our conduct.

PSYCHOLOGICAL APPROACHES

In making sense of information, we all use a framework to put it all together. As individuals, we are not always aware of our own frameworks. They are hard to recognize because we may change our way of looking at information from time to time. You may view the same information in a variety of ways, depending upon whether it comes from your boyfriend or girlfriend, your mother or father, your teacher, or today's newspaper.

The more we engage in specific attempts to put information together, the more likely we are to achieve personal insights and to believe that we know who we are and what we are like. This development of a sense of personal identity is a part of the excitement of discussing issues.

Just as we personally develop frameworks for putting information together, so do specialists in human behavior. In the brief history of psychology, specialists have developed a variety of scientific approaches. Several modern perspectives have evolved from these and are easily recognizable today. They may be roughly categorized as follows.

Biological
In its extreme form, this point of view suggests that if we fully understood all there is to know about the human body and how all of its parts operate, we would understand all we wish to know about our emotions, creative urges, and social behavior. In this extreme form, we are just mechanisms. Prediction and control of human behavior may be achieved by fine technicians just as prediction and control of automobile performance may be achieved by fine engineers and mechanics.

If we knew enough, according to this view, we could eliminate fighting by cutting it out of the brain, or we could combat the "blues" by swallowing pills to change our personal chemistry.

Psychodynamic
This point of view emphasizes that the behavior we are aware of in ourselves and in others stems from forces within us that we are not normally aware of—that we are born with an inventory of drives and instincts that respond

to life's experiences. These hidden inner forces are considered to be responsible for the way we feel, think, and behave. To understand these forces is to understand human nature, according to this school of thought.

Behavioral
This perspective contends that we need only observe how a person responds to stimuli in the environment; all that we would ever want to know about a person can be described in terms of the individual's behavior. If we achieve control over the environment, we achieve control over the individual.

You may have noticed how obvious the deterministic assumption is in these frameworks. Humans are acted upon by their inherited nature, by the environment, or by a combination of both. The following two frameworks lean more toward the direction of free will, with humans taking an active role in decision-making.

Cognitive
Human beings receive information about the world in which they live, and then they do something with it. From the cognitive viewpoint, we are active agents in choosing which information we will receive. After receiving information, we process it in some personally meaningful way and then either use it or put it away in the form of memories for later use. Here, consideration for the active selection and personal processing of information implies that we are not merely passive responders.

Humanistic
This point of view grew specifically out of a reaction against other psychological perspectives that emphasize the forces determining human destiny. The humanistic orientation places emphasis on our *human* nature, rather than our mechanistic nature. It emphasizes how we see and think about ourselves, rather than what we do. It is a concern for our striving to become more than we are at this moment, a striving to fill our potentials.

There is yet another orientation: the eclectic one. An eclectic orientation chooses whatever seems to work best from any of the many existing frameworks for understanding human nature. An eclectic psychologist may take a biological point of view when researching and theorizing, a psychodynamic point of view when trying to understand his children, a behaviorist point of view when training his experimental subjects to perform certain tasks, a cognitive point of view when teaching, and a humanistic point of view in his general way of dealing with people. You may best understand this if you think about the different ways you might answer the question, "What have you been doing lately?" when asked by your best friend, your kid sister, your mother, or your chemistry professor.

IN CONCLUSION

As the editors of this volume, we respect all these points of view. We see the fruitfulness of scientific strategies that seek the determining causes of behavior. In that sense, we appreciate a deterministic orientation. Nevertheless, we are unwilling to ask you to sit back and take a passive role in these issues. We firmly believe that your active involvement in these issues will help you develop the skills that give you increasing control over your own destiny. In that sense, we emphasize your freedom of will.

In order to have an impact on your world, you must learn, deliberate, discuss, decide, and act. To do this effectively, you should know the difference between what the objective evidence tells you and what your values tell you. And you should be able to distinguish between "truth" and "strategy" when you take sides.

WHO Photo by E. Schwab

PART 1

The Study of Psychology

Scientific research in any field poses serious ethical and procedural questions, and psychology is no exception. The issues in this part deal with a variety of concerns among psychological researchers.

Can Deception in Research Be Justified?

Should Psychologists Study Memory Through Controlled Laboratory Experiments?

Can Experiments Using Animals Be Justified?

ISSUE 1

Can Deception in Research Be Justified?

YES: Stanley Milgram, from "Subject Reaction: The Neglected Factor in the Ethics of Experimentation," *Hastings Center Report* (October 1977)

NO: Thomas H. Murray, from "Learning to Deceive," *Hastings Center Report* (April 1980)

ISSUE SUMMARY

YES: Professor of psychology Stanley Milgram makes his case for the suspension of normal ethical standards when a social scientist is seeking to benefit society, especially when safeguards are employed to ensure that no harm is done to the subject.
NO: Research associate Thomas H. Murray holds that social scientists must consider the costs of deception to the individual scientist, the subject, and the society at large, and determine if the information produced is worth those costs.

What is there about human beings that enables them to harm others so callously? Why do so many people often harbor prejudices, blindly follow the orders of malicious authority, or conform to the behavior of others with little consideration for the consequences? How can people look away when others nearby are in desperate need of help? Why do war and injustice exist?

These are questions of paramount interest to social psychologists. They seek answers that go beyond the conventional "wisdom" that derives from tales about the "bad guys."

Psychology, defined as the science of behavior and mental processes, is largely dedicated to methods of investigation that are objective and capable of precisely isolating variables. The information the psychologists discover in the research laboratory about how people behave and how they think and feel about their behavior affects us all. When these research results become known, they influence the way we think about ourselves and others and frequently influence lawmakers responsible for legislation and public policy.

If social psychologists seek laboratory answers to the important but unpleasant questions about human beings in extraordinary situations, there must be some pretense in setting up the situations and some deception in presenting them to the subjects of the research—at least that is what many researchers have believed. But how does the deception affect the people involved—the subjects and the researchers themselves? Do the results of the scientific studies outweigh in importance any potential harm to the subjects that may result from the deceptive methods?

Stanley Milgram is the researcher primarily responsible for our understanding of the conditions under which most people obey an authority figure, even at the risk of inflicting serious harm to others. His research was stimulated by the questionable ethics of Nazi officers who excused themselves by claiming they were "just following orders." Ironically, this research has led to his being called upon time and again to explain his own ethics. He points out that suspension of normal ethics is commonplace when specific professional expertise is involved. He maintains that the same suspension is due the social scientist who seeks to benefit society, especially when the subjects are properly debriefed and report no dissatisfaction with the procedures.

Thomas H. Murray chronicles his own disillusionment when, as a graduate student attracted by the important questions researched by social scientists, he decided to join their ranks. He found that the lofty principles of research do not necessarily protect the researcher from becoming unprincipled in behavior. He indicates that he and his colleagues sometimes treated subjects in a way that placed the value of the research over the well-being of individuals. Murray contends that "we need to consider the costs of deception research to the individual scientists and his or her professional community."

POINT	COUNTERPOINT
• "Technical illusions" are short-term and are followed by debriefing.	• It is too easy for the researcher to continue lying, even when debriefing.
• Temporary stress is part of real life and, therefore, should be a part of scientific research.	• In real life, people usually have more opportunity to protect their self-esteem.
• When deceptive research is properly done, those who take part in it judge their participation to be acceptable.	• Regardless of what participants report, there is probably serious damage to the self-esteem of many.
• There is no evidence that deceptive research carried out in a professional fashion has caused participants any harm.	• There is probably harm done to researchers when they become "professional liars" and view people as "easy, foolish, and not especially nice."

YES
Stanley Milgram

SUBJECT REACTION: THE NEGLECTED FACTOR IN THE ETHICS OF EXPERIMENTATION

Social psychology is concerned with the way in which individual behavior, thoughts, and action are affected by the presence of other people. Although experimentation is not the only way of garnering knowledge in the discipline, it is a major tool of inquiry. As experiments in social psychology typically involve human subjects, they necessarily raise ethical issues, some of which I will discuss here.

INFORMED CONSENT

Many regard informed consent as the cornerstone of ethical practice in experimentation with human subjects. Yet social psychology has until now been unable to assimilate the principle into its routine experimental procedures. Typically, subjects are brought into an experiment without being informed of its true purpose. Indeed, sometimes subjects are misinformed. Is such a procedure ever justifiable?

Herbert Kelman[1] has distinguished two quite different explanations for not informing the potential subject of the nature of the experiment in which he is to take part. One might term the first the motivational explanation; that is, if one told the subject what the experiment was to be like, he might refuse to participate in it. Misinforming people to gain their participation appears a serious violation of the individual's rights, and cannot routinely constitute an ethical basis for subject recruitment.

The second, more typical, reason for not informing a subject is that many experiments in social psychology cannot be carried out if the subject knows about the experiment beforehand.

Consider in this connection Solomon Asch's classic study[2] of group pressure and conformity. The subject is told that he is to take part in a study on the perception of lines. He is asked to make a judgment as to which of three lines is equivalent in length to a standard line, but he does so in the presence of other individuals who, unknown to him, are working for the experimenter and give wrong answers. The experimenter's purpose is to see whether the subject will go along with the erroneous group information or resist the group and give the correct answer.

Clearly the subject is misinformed in several respects. He is to take part in an experiment on perception rather than group pressure. He is not informed that the others present are working for the experimenter, but is led to believe that they have the same relationship to the experimenter as he. It is apparent that if a subject were informed of the true purpose before participating in the study, he could not experience the psychological conflict that is at the crux of Asch's study. The subject is not denied the information because the experimenter fears he would not participate in the study, but for strictly epistemological reasons, that is, for somewhat the same reason the author of a murder mystery does not reveal to the reader who the culprit is: to do so would undermine the psychological effects of the reading experience.

A majority of the experiments carried out in social psychology use some degree of misinformation. Such practices have been denounced as "deception" by critics, and the term "deception experiment" has come to be used routinely, particularly in the context of discussions concerning the ethics of such procedures. But in such a context, the term "deception" somewhat biases the issue. It is preferable to use morally neutral terms such as "masking," "staging," or "technical illusions" in describing such techniques, because it is not possible to make an objective ethical judgment on a practice unless it is described in terms that are not themselves condemnatory.

Is the use of technical illusions ever justified in experiments? The simplest response, and the one that is most socially and ethically comfortable, is to assert unequivocally that they are not. We all know that honesty and a fully informed relationship with the subject is highly desirable and should be implemented whenever possible. The problem is that many people also believe strongly in the value of inquiry into social psychology, of its potential to enlighten us about human social behavior, and ultimately to benefit us in important ways. Admittedly, this is a faith, but one which impels us to carefully examine whether the illusions and misinformation required by experiments have any claim to legitimacy. We know that illusions are accepted in other domains without affronting our moral sensibilities. To use a simple-minded example, on radio programs, sound-effects of prancing horses are typically created by a sound-effects man who uses split coconut shells; rainfall is created by sand falling on metal sheets, and so forth. A certain number of listeners know about this, some do not; but we do not accuse such programs of deceiving their listeners. Rather we accept the fact that these are technical illusions used in support of a dramatic effect.

Most experiments in social psychology, at least the good ones, also have a dramatic component. Indeed, in the best experiments the subjects are brought into a dramaturgical situation in which the script is only partially written: it is the subject's actions that complete the script, providing the information sought by the investigator. Is the use of technical illusions to be permitted in radio programs, but not scientific inquiry?

There are many instances in everyday life in which misinformation is tolerated or regarded as legitimate. We do not cringe at the idea of giving children misinformation about Santa Claus, because we feel it is a benign illusion, and common sense tells us it is not harmful. Furthermore, the practice is legitimized by tradition. We may give someone misinformation that takes him to a surprise party. The absolutists may say that this is an immoral act, that in doing so one has lied to another person. But it is more important to focus on the person who is the recipient of this information. Does he find it a demeaning experience, or a delightful treat?

One thing is clear: masking and technical illusions ought never to be used unless they are indispensable to the conduct of an inquiry. Honesty and openness are the only desirable basis of transaction with people generally. This still leaves open the question of whether such devices are permissible when they cannot be avoided in a scientific inquiry.

There is another side to this issue. In the exercise of virtually every profession there may be some exemption from general moral practice which permits the profession to function. For example, although a citizen who has witnessed a murder has a moral obligation to come forth with this information, lawyers have a right—indeed an obligation—of "privileged communication." A lawyer may know that his client has committed a murder, and is obligated not to tell the authorities. In other words, a generally accepted moral obligation is suspended and transformed in the case of legal practice, because in the long run we consider this exemption beneficial to society.

Similarly, it is generally impermissible to examine the genitals of strange women. But it is a technical requirement for the practice of obstetrics and gynecology. Once again, for technical reasons, we suspend a general moral rule in the exercise of a profession, because we believe the profession is beneficial to society.

The question arises: is there any comparable exemption due the social scientist because of technical requirements in the kind of work he does, which in the long run, we believe will benefit society? It is true that most often the individual participant in an experiment is not the beneficiary. Rather it is society as a whole that benefits, or at least, that is the supposition of scientific inquiry.

Still another side to the staging by social psychologists is frequently overlooked. The illusions employed by most experiments are usually short-term. They are sustained only insofar as they are required for the purpose of the experiment. Typically, the subject is informed of the experiment's true character immediately after he has participated in it. If for thirty minutes the experimenter holds back on the truth, at the conclusion he reaffirms his confidence in the subject by extending his trust to him by a full revelation of the purpose and procedures of the experiment. It is odd how rarely critics of social psychology experiments mention this characteristic feature of the experimental hour.

From a formal ethical standpoint, the question of misinformation in social psychology experiments is important, because dissimulation subverts the possibility of informed consent. Indeed, the emphasis on "deception" has virtually preempted discussion of ethics among social psychologists. Some feel it is a misplaced emphasis. Support is given to this

view by a recent study by Elinor Mannucci.[3] She questioned 192 laymen concerning their reaction to ethical aspects
of psychology experiments, and found
that they regarded deception as a relatively minor issue. They were far more
concerned with the quality of the experience they would undergo as subjects. For
example, despite the "deceptive" elements in the Asch experiment the great
majority of respondents in Mannucci's
study were enthusiastic about it, and
expressed admiration for its elegance
and significance. Of course, the layman's
view need not be the final word, but it
cannot be disregarded, and my general
argument is that far more attention
needs to be given to the experiences and
views of those who actually serve as
subjects in experiments.

NEGATIVE EFFECTS

Is an experiment that produces some sort
of negative, aversive, or stressful effect in
the subject ever justified? In this matter,
two parameters seem critical: first, the
intensity of the negative experience, and
second, its duration. Clearly, the discussion that follows refers to effects that do
not permanently damage a subject, and
which most typically do not exceed in
intensity experiences which the subject
might encounter in ordinary life.

One thing is clear. If we assert categorically that negative emotions can
never ethically be created in the laboratory, then it follows that highly significant domains of human experience are
excluded from experimental study. For
example, we would never be able to
study stress by experimental means; nor
could we implicate human subjects in
experiments involving conflict. In other
words, only experiments that aroused

neutral or positive emotions would be
considered ethical topics for experimental investigation. Clearly, such a stricture
would lead to a very lopsided psychology, one that caricatured rather than accurately reflected human experience.

Moreover, historically, among the most
deeply informative experiments in social
psychology are those that examine how
subjects resolve conflicts, for example:
Asch's study of group pressure studies
the conflict between truth and conformity; Bibb Latané and John Darley's bystander studies[4] create a conflict as to
whether the subject should implicate
himself in other peoples' troubles or not
get involved; my studies of obedience[5]
create a conflict between conscience and
authority. If the experience of conflict is
categorically to be excluded from social
psychology, then we are automatically
denying the possibility of studying such
core human issues by experimental
means. I believe that this would be an
irreparable loss to any science of human
behavior.

My own studies of obedience were
criticized because they created conflict
and stress in some of the subjects. Let me
make a few comments about this. First,
in this experiment I was interested in
seeing to what degree a person would
comply with an experimental authority
who gave orders to act with increasing
harshness against a third person. I
wanted to see when the subject would
refuse to go on with the experiment. The
results of the experiment showed first
that it is more difficult for many people
to defy the experimenter's authority than
was generally supposed. The second
finding is that the experiment often
places a person in considerable conflict.
In the course of the experiment subjects
sometimes fidget, sweat, and break out

in nervous fits of laughter. I have dealt with some of the ethical issues of this experiment at length elsewhere,[6] but let me make a few additional remarks here.

SUBJECT REACTION: A NEGLECTED FACTOR

To my mind, the central moral justification for allowing my experiment is that it was judged acceptable by those who took part in it. Criticism of the experiment that does not take account of the tolerant reaction to the participants has always seemed to me hollow. I collected a considerable amount of data on this issue, which shows that the great majority of subjects accept this experiment, and call for further experiments of this sort. The table below shows the overall reaction of participants to this study, as indicated in responses to a questionnaire. On the whole, these data have been ignored by critics or even turned against the experimenter, as when critics claim that "this is simply cognitive dissonance. The more subjects hated the experiment, the more likely they are to say they enjoyed it." It becomes a "damned-if-they-like-it and damned-if-they-don't" situation. Critics of the experiment fail to come to grips with what the subject himself says. Yet, I believe that the subject's viewpoint is of extreme importance, perhaps even paramount. Below I shall present some approaches to ethical problems that derive from this view.

Some critics assert that an experiment such as mine may inflict a negative insight on the subject. He or she may have diminished self-esteem because he has learned he is more submissive to authority than he might have believed. First, I readily agree that the investigator's responsibility is to make the laboratory session as constructive an experience as possible, and to explain the experiment to the subject in a way that allows his performance to be integrated in an insightful way. But I am not at all certain

Table 1

Excerpt from Questionnaire
Used in a Follow-up Study of the Obedience Research

Now that I have read the report, and all things considered . . .	Defiant	Obedient	All
1. I am very glad to have been in the experiment	40.0%	47.8%	43.5%
2. I am glad to have been in the experiment	43.8%	35.7%	40.2%
3. I am neither sorry nor glad to have been in the experiment	15.3%	14.8%	15.1%
4. I am sorry to have been in the experiment	0.8%	0.7%	0.8%
5. I am very sorry to have been in the experiment	0.0%	1.0%	0.5%

THE OBEDIENCE EXPERIMENTS

In order to take a close look at the act of obeying, I set up a simple experiment at Yale University. Eventually, the experiment was to involve more than a thousand participants and would be repeated at several universities, but at the beginning, the conception was simple. A person comes to a psychological laboratory and is told to carry out a series of acts that come increasingly into conflict with conscience. The main question is how far the participant will comply with the experimenter's instructions before refusing to carry out the actions required of him.

But the reader needs to know a little more detail about the experiment. Two people come to a psychology laboratory to take part in a study of memory and learning. One of them is designated as a "teacher" and the other a "learner." The experimenter explains that the study is concerned with the effects of punishment on learning. The learner is conducted into a room, seated in a chair, his arms strapped to prevent excessive movement, and an electrode attached to his wrist. He is told that he is to learn a list of word pairs; whenever he makes an error, he will receive electric shocks of increasing intensity.

The real focus of the experiment is the teacher. After watching the learner being strapped into place, he is taken into the main experimental room and seated before an impressive shock generator. Its main feature is a horizontal line of thirty switches, ranging from 15 volts to 450 volts, in 15-volt increments. There are also verbal designations which range from SLIGHT SHOCK to DANGER—SEVERE SHOCK. The teacher is told that he is to administer the learning test to the man in the other room. When the learner responds correctly, the teacher moves on to the next item; when the other man gives an incorrect answer, the teacher is to give him an electric shock. He is to start at the lowest shock level (15 volts) and to increase the level each time the man makes an error, going through 30 volts, 45 volts, and so on.

The "teacher" is a genuinely naive subject who has come to the laboratory to participate in an experiment. The "learner," or victim, is an actor who actually receives no shock at all. The point of the experiment is to see how far a person will proceed in a concrete and measurable situation in which he is ordered to inflict increasing pain on a protesting victim. At what point will the subject refuse to obey the experimenter?

Conflict arises when the man receiving the shock begins to indicate that he is experiencing discomfort. At 75 volts, the "learner" grunts. At 120 volts he complains verbally; at 150 he demands to be released from the experiment. His protests continue as the shocks escalate, growing increasingly vehement and emotional. At 285 volts his response can only be described as an agonized scream.

Observers of the experiment agree that its gripping quality is somewhat obscured in print. For the subject, the situation is not a game; conflict is intense and obvious. On the one hand, the manifest suffering of the learner presses him to quit. On the other, the experimenter, a legitimate authority to whom the subject feels some commitment, enjoins him to continue. Each time the subject hesitates to administer shock, the experimenter orders him to continue. To extricate himself from the situation, the subject must make a clear break with authority. The aim of this investigation was to find when and how people would defy authority in the face of a clear moral imperative.

From *Obedience to Authority: An Experimental View* by Stanley Milgram. Copyright © 1974 by Stanley Milgram. Reprinted by permission of Harper & Row, Publishers, Inc.

that we should hide truths from subjects, even negative truths. Moreover, this would set experimentation completely apart from other life experiences. Life itself often teaches us things that are less than pleasant, as when we fail an examination or do not succeed in a job interview. And in my judgment, participation in the obedience experiment had less effect on a participant's self-esteem than the negative emotions engendered by a routine school examination. This does not mean that the stress of taking an examination is good, any more than the negative effects of the obedience experiments are good. It does mean that these issues have to be placed in perspective.

I believe that it is extremely important to make a distinction between biomedical interventions and those that are of a purely psychological character, particularly the type of experiment I have been discussing. Intervention at the biological level prima facie places a subject "at risk." The ingestion of a minute dose of a chemical or the infliction of a tiny surgical incision has the potential to traumatize a subject. In contrast, in all of the social psychology experiments that have been carried out, there is no demonstrated case of resulting trauma. And there is no evidence whatsoever that when an individual makes a choice in a laboratory situation—even the difficult choices posed by the conformity or obedience experiments—any trauma, injury, or diminution of well-being results. I once asked a government official, who favored highly restrictive measures on psychology experiments, how many cases of actual trauma or injury he had in his files that would call for such measures. He indicated that not a single such case was known to him. If this is true, then much of the discussion about the need to impose government restrictions on the conduct of psychology experiments is unrealistic.

Of course, one difficulty in dealing with negative effects is the impossibility of proving their nonexistence. This is particularly true of behavioral or psychological effects. It seems that no matter what procedures one follows—interviewing, questionnaires, or the like—there is always the possibility of unforeseen negative effects, even if these procedures do not uncover them. Therefore, in an absolute sense, one can never establish the absence of negative effects. While this is logically correct, we cannot use this as a basis for asserting that such effects necessarily follow from psychological experimentation. All we can do is rely on our best judgment and assessment procedures in trying to establish the facts, and to formulate our policies accordingly.

IS ROLE PLAYING A SOLUTION?

Given these problems and the particular requirements of experiments in social psychology, is there any way to resolve these issues so that the subject will be protected, while allowing experimentation to continue? A number of psychologists have suggested that role playing may be substituted for any experiment that requires misinformation. Instead of bringing the subject into a situation whose true purpose and nature were kept from him, the subject would be fully informed that he was about to enter a staged situation, but he would be told to act as if it were real. For example, in the obedience experiment subjects would be told: "pretend you are the subject performing an experiment and you are giving shocks to another person." The subject would enter the situation knowing the "victim" was not receiving shocks, and he would go through his paces.

I do not doubt that role playing has a certain utility. Indeed, every good experimenter employs such role playing when he is first setting up his laboratory situation. He and his assistants often go through a dry run to see how the procedure flows. Thus, such simulation is not new, but now it is being asked to serve as the end point, rather than the starting point of an experimental investigation. However, there is a major scientific problem. Even after one has had a subject role play his way through an experimental procedure, we still must wonder whether the observed behavior is the same as that which a genuine subject would produce. So we must still perform the crucial experiment to determine whether role-played behavior corresponds to nonrole-played behavior.

Nor is role playing free of ethical problems. A most striking simulation in social psychology was carried out by Philip Zimbardo at Stanford University.[7] Volunteers were asked to take part in a mock prison situation. They were to simulate either the role of prisoner or guard with the roles chosen by lot. They were picked up at their homes by local police cars, and delivered to Zimbardo's mock prison. Even in the role-playing version of prison, the situation became rather ugly and unpleasant, and mock guards acted cruelly toward the mock prisoners. The investigator called off the simulation after six days, instead of the two weeks for which it had been planned. Moreover, the simulation came under very heavy ethical criticism. The ethical problems that simulation was designed to solve did not all disappear. The more closely role-playing behavior corresponds to real behavior, the more it gen-

erates real emotions, including aversive states, hostile behavior, and so on. The less real emotions are present, the less adequate the simulations. From the standpoint of the aversive emotions aroused in a successful simulation, ethical problems still exist.

Kelman aptly summarized the state of simulation research when he stated that simulation is not so useless a tool of investigation as its critics first asserted, nor as free of ethical problems as its proponents believed.[8]

PRESUMPTIVE CONSENT

Recall that the major technical problem for social psychology research is that if subjects have prior knowledge of the purposes and details of an experiment they are often, by this fact, disqualified from participating in it. Informed consent thus remains an ideal that cannot always be attained. As an alternative, some psychologists have attempted to develop the doctrine of presumptive consent. The procedure is to solicit the view of a large number of people on the acceptability of an experimental procedure. These respondents would not themselves serve in the experiment, having been "spoiled" in the very process of being told the details and purposes of the experiment. But we could use their expressed views about participation as evidence of how people in general would react to participation. Assuming the experiment is deemed acceptable, new subjects would be recruited for actual participation. Of course, this is, ethically, a far weaker doctrine than that which relies on informed consent of the participant. Even if a hundred people indicate that they would be willing to take part in an experiment, the person actually chosen for participation might find it objectionable. Still, the doctrine of the "presumed consent of a reasonable person" seems to me better than no consent at all. That is, when for epistemological purposes the nature of a study cannot be revealed beforehand, one would try to determine in advance whether a reasonable person would consent to being a subject in the study and use that as a warrant either for carrying out the investigation or as a basis for modifying it.

Perhaps a more promising solution is to obtain prior general consent from subjects in advance of their actual participation. This is a form of consent that would be based on subjects' knowing the general types of procedures used in psychological investigations, but without their knowing what specific manipulations would be employed in the particular experiment in which they would take part. The first step would be to create a pool of volunteers to serve in psychology experiments. Before volunteering to join the pool people would be told explicitly that sometimes subjects are misinformed about the purposes of an experiment, and that sometimes emotional stresses arise in the course of an experiment. They would be given a chance to exclude themselves from any study using deception or involving stress if they so wished. Only persons who had indicated a willingness to participate in experiments involving deception or stress would, in the course of the year, be recruited for experiments that involved these elements. Such a procedure might reconcile the technical need for misinformation with the ethical problem of informing subjects.

Finally, since I emphasize the experience of the person subjected to procedures as the ultimate basis for judging whether an experiment should continue or not, I wonder whether participants in such experiments might not routinely be given monitoring cards which they would fill out and submit to an independent monitoring source while an experiment is in progress. An appropriate monitoring source might be a special committee of the professional organization, or the human subjects' committee of the institution where the experiment is carried out. Such a procedure would have the advantage of allowing the subject to express reactions about an experiment in which he has just participated, and by his comments the subject himself would help determine whether the experiment is allowable or not. In the long run, I believe it is the subject's reaction and his experience that needs to be given its due weight in any discussion of ethics, and this mechanism will help achieve this aim.

NOTES

1. Herbert Kelman, "Remarks Made at the American Psychological Association," New Orleans, 1974.
2. Solomon E. Asch, Social Psychology (New York: Prentice Hall, 1952).
3. Elinor Mannucci, Potential Subjects View Psychology Experiments: An Ethical Inquiry. Unpublished Doctoral Dissertation. The City University of New York, 1977.
4. Bibb Latané and John Darley, The Unresponsive Bystander: Why Doesn't He Help? (New York: Appleton, 1970).
5. Stanley Milgram, Obedience to Authority: An Experimental View (New York: Harper and Row, 1974).
6. Stanley Milgram, "Issues in the Study of Obedience: A Reply to Baumrind," American Psychologist 19 (1964), 848-52.
7. Philip Zimbardo, "The Mind Is a Formidable Jailer: A Pirandellian Prison," The New York Times Magazine (April 8, 1973), p. 38.
8. Kelman, "Remarks."

NO   Thomas H. Murray

LEARNING TO DECEIVE

In 1968 Paul Goodman, the radical social critic, came to Temple University, introduced himself as a social psychologist, and spoke eloquently against the war in Vietnam. None of this is surprising except for Goodman's self-identification as a social psychologist. Perhaps it should have struck a discordant note in the minds of his audience, but to those of us whose image of social psychology came from the uncritical textbooks of the sixties, a person of Goodman's commitments fits our image of what a social psychologist ought to be. To unsophisticated undergraduates social psychology seemed to be *the* relevant discipline. What other groups of scientists devoted their lives to research on prejudice, conformity, obedience to destructive authority, propaganda, conflict resolution, or any of a multitude of topics that seemed to penetrate to the heart of war, injustice, and other evils?

It was only natural for a college graduate in that same year, idealistic and naive, to enter a graduate program in social psychology as a way to honor simultaneously intellect and justice. I enrolled, filled with enthusiasm and hope. Enlightenment, in the form of disillusionment, came slowly. In a discipline like social psychology that values "hands-on" research, the real education takes place not in the seminar room but in the laboratory. There the skills of the profession are transmitted, the real work done, and the appropriate views learned. It is those practiced views, and their impact on those who adopt them, that I want to explore here.

THE GROWTH OF DISCIPLINE

The history of social psychology offers some clues as to how it reached its stance on laboratory work. The widely acknowledged founder of experimental social psychology was Kurt Lewin, whose career spanned the twenties to the fifties. In his vision of the science, social progress would advance hand in hand with social theory. His famous adage, "There is nothing so practical as a good theory," soon came to be translated into something more like "Take care of theory and practical matters will take care of themselves." The

From Thomas H. Murray, "Learning to Deceive," *Hastings Center Report*, vol. 10, no. 2 (April 1980). Copyright © 1980 by the Institute of Society, Ethics, and the Life Sciences. Reprinted by permission of The Hastings Center.

emphasis was on doing good, respectable science; and the sine qua non of scientific respectability was the experimental method and its historical setting, the laboratory.

So dawned the age of the social laboratory and its pinnacle—the highly charged, dramatic, deception experiment.

An important part of the socialization of a professional is exposure to examples of excellence. Some of the examples offered to graduate students in my program (a representative one, I think) were Stanley Schachter's experiments on emotionality, Leonard Berkowitz on aggression, Bibb Latané and John Darley on helping in emergencies.[1] What these research programs and their kin had in common beside the fact that they were unusually well done were at least two things: the experiences of the subjects of the studies were intense and dramatic; and the deceptions employed were elaborate and skillfully managed.

By the sixties social psychologists had grown wary of Lewin's boundless faith in democracy, and were less worried about the immediate practicality of their research; but they remembered one lesson above all—whatever you do, do it with style and flair. Within the discipline the suspicion was growing that the acclaim a study received might have as much to do with the ingenuity and panache of the deception as with the importance of the scientific question. The tendency to choose flash over substance became so serious that a respected social psychologist, Kenneth Ring, took the discipline to task for what he called "frivolous values."[2] But these worries were largely ignored. Deception was securely entrenched as a methodology; not the only one certainly, but predominant in a number of research areas.* This was the state of the discipline in the mid-1960s, though one would not have known it from the typical undergraduate textbook.

Perhaps my description of the discipline suggests an image of the deception researcher as a cool manipulator, utterly insensitive to the feelings of his or her subjects. That description fits very few social psychologists. The individuals with whom I worked closely were principled and responsible people, concerned with doing the right things. Their behavior would be much easier to understand, and much less interesting, had they been callous and cynical. Certainly I met the latter type, but I never worked with them directly.

Consider the problem this way: explain how otherwise good people, at least no worse than the run of academics, come routinely to frighten, provoke, insult, depress, and generally lie to the subjects of their experiments. And what is the impact of their views in practice on themselves and on their conception of human nature outside of the laboratory? To my knowledge, there are no authoritative studies on the personalities of social psychologists, their values, or their beliefs about human nature—a curious gap for a discipline so interested in behavior and motivation.

*Studies of the incidence of deception research are difficult to interpret. They typically take a sample of journals known to publish mostly social psychological research and classify the studies into those that employ deception as a major part of the procedure, and those that do not. Results vary widely, depending on the journals sampled and the criteria for classifying a procedure as a "deception." For the sixties they range from 16 percent to 38 percent. But in some research areas—conformity and attitude change studies, for example—deception was used in 81 percent and 72 percent of the studies, respectively. These areas, and related ones, also carried with them the highest prestige within the discipline.

The question then is: does deception research harm the researcher? All forms of work have their hazards. Are there any hazards unique to or especially acute for the scientist who routinely deceives as a part of his or her profession? Perhaps a "case history"—an autobiographical one in this instance—can illuminate the kinds of harms that arise in deception research, without of course testifying to their extent. As just this sort of "case history," I offer my own experience as a graduate student and neophyte deception researcher.

A STUDY IN HELPING BEHAVIOR

The first deception study in which I participated was on helping behavior in emergencies. We played out an elaborate scenario for each individual subject with minor variations. The variations allowed us to create five separate conditions or "treatments" within the experiment, varying in the likelihood that they would inhibit helping responses. Our subjects were greeted by a phony "experimenter," taken through an elaborate cover story (one that by all the usual criteria worked very well), and asked to sit in a tiny booth watching a TV monitor. Within a very few minutes, they witnessed the "experimenter," apparently alone in another room, receive what looked like a severe electric shock and collapse on the floor, out of camera range. My job was to time the subjects—how long would it take them to call for help or otherwise come to the "experimenter's" aid? If they made no move to seek help within six minutes, I retrieved them from their booths. Then, with the study essentially over, I began my real work—"debriefing" the subject.

Whether or not the person "helped"—

in the vernacular of the research report— I "revealed the true purpose of the study, answered all questions honestly, and remained with the subject until all negative effects of participation had been removed." Not quite. While I did reveal the true purpose of the study, I did not always answer all questions honestly; and I seriously doubt that I, or anyone else, could have removed all negative effects of participation.

Those people who offered help—almost always in the first two minutes— were a pleasure to talk with afterwards. They praised the experiment, my cleverness, and social psychology in general. But why shouldn't they? They had been put to the test, and they had passed! When another human being was in need, they responded. They left the debriefing confident.

However, my experiences with subjects who did not respond within six minutes was another matter. I quickly began to dread the movement of the stopwatch hands. I knew that when the six minutes had passed I would have to face someone who might be trembling, who might have trouble talking, and who would probably have fabricated some fantastic explanation of what had happened to the "victim." Among the 99 subjects I put through the procedure, I saw individuals whose faces were drained of color, who were reduced to stuttering, or who could barely force words through their clenched teeth. These subjects had many versions of what had happened: the "victim" had sneezed, or tripped, or just maybe there was something wrong. Virtually every subject who had not responded showed some anxiety.

Of course, I had to explain the study. What do you tell people who sat idly by, or at least who felt that they had done so, while another human being was in possible danger? When I told many of the people who did not help that they were in an experimental condition designed to inhibit helping, it seemed to make them feel better. However, when I debriefed subjects who had failed to help even though they were not in a condition designed to inhibit helping, I found myself lying, saying that they were in a help-inhibiting situation.

When they congratulate you for running such an ingenious and significant experiment, as they invariably do, you try to forget the uncertainty in their handshakes. You try to convince yourself that, yes, all harmful effects have been removed. But I did not believe it then, and I do not today. If your experiment is good, according to the canons of experimental design in social psychology, it is realistic. If you are not getting people's "real" responses to your simulations of reality, then you have no claim to be doing good science. The more skillful you are at simulating reality, the more accurately your subjects can infer how they are likely to act in the larger social world from the way they have acted in your laboratory. To the extent that my simulated emergency was realistic, my nonresponding subjects could make the inference that they were not the sort of person who acts courageously to help others in a crisis. And I doubt that my attempts to reassure them, including my willingness to encourage their rationalizations, could really undo all the damage to their self-esteem.

The social psychologist who wants to study some humanly significant area of human behavior with a deception paradigm comes squarely up against a paradox: the more "real"—hence, valuable—the study,

the greater the likelihood that someone's self-image will be altered unfavorably. This paradox appears as a moral problem only if you believe that there is something ethically objectionable about social scientists, in Diana Baumrind's phrase, "inflicting insight" on their unwitting subjects. Others, Stanley Milgram for one, see this as merely telling subjects some truth about themselves.[3] But this already presumes that the scientist knows in just what respects the study is "real," and can explain it fully to the subjects, so that the subjects do not assume better—or worse—of themselves than is warranted. The first presumption is virtually impossible to satisfy; and there is evidence that the second may be wrong. That I might be making some individuals, volunteers in innocence and ignorance, judge themselves cowardly or callous, troubled me deeply. Before I began the work, I was warned that debriefing subjects after a procedure like the one we used would be like six weeks of psychotherapy packed into a half-hour. I had no idea how appropriate the warning would be.

One further incident brought home to me the potential effects of deception manipulations on subjects. Sometime after the helping research, I attended a meeting to discuss a proposed research project which was to use the now notorious "self-esteem manipulation." It is an extremely clever use of a principle well known to fortune-tellers—that within very wide limits, people will believe almost anything reported to them about themselves, as long as it comes from an "authoritative" source with some special claim to knowledge. Subjects take a phony personality test supposedly in the final stage of validation. When they return a couple of weeks later, they are handed an envelope containing a report of their "results." There are only two reports—one favorable, one unfavorable—and they are handed out on a random basis. What you do on the "test" has absolutely no relationship to the profile you receive. If you receive the positive profile, you read a flattering set of comments on the warmth of your personality, the depth of your friendships, your sincerity, honesty, maturity, and integrity. It ends with a sentence like: "On the whole, this is one of the most favorable profiles we have ever encountered." If, by chance, you receive the negative profile, you read about your coldness, shallowness, insincerity, lack of principle, immaturity, and lack of integration. It concludes with: "On the whole, this is one of the most unfavorable profiles we have ever encountered."

The purpose of this charade is to manipulate the individual's self-esteem in a controlled fashion, so that the effects of high vs. low self-esteem on some other variables can be systematically studied. To my knowledge, this manipulation is no longer in use, but a decade ago it was popular. At that time I protested. I argued that its scientific validity was suspect: it was at least plausible that the sort of "self-esteem" affected by the manipulation was different in action from the normal underlying level of self-esteem; that what was really being studied by the "self-esteem manipulation" was the effect of being told you were a complete loser. No wonder that people with experimentally induced "low self-esteem" then performed poorly on a wide range of tasks! My methodological objections carried little weight. My ethical objection—that it was wrong to fraudulently alter, even temporarily, a person's self-

perception—carried no weight at all. It was irrelevant.

For years I felt my misgivings about deception research were the product of an overly scrupulous mind. The weight of opinion in my profession rested clearly on the side of deception research, though there were notable exceptions even then.[4] But deception research has come under increasingly strong attack in recent years. And I now find myself not so alone.

My case is undoubtedly extreme. But it is not unprecedented. There are examples of virulent attacks on deception research by former social psychologists, for example, Thorne Shipley[5] and Donald Warwick.[6] There are also an unknown number of would-be social psychologists who quietly retired from the field because they were unable to put their wholehearted efforts into deception research, and unwilling or unable to develop other research methods. Even though Alan Elms, a graduate student who assisted Milgram in his now famous research on "obedience," defends the use of deception, he has foresworn it in his own research.[7] How many young and idealistic graduate students have found themselves choosing between lying to a subject and adding to the anxiety caused by a deception, between becoming a professional liar and taking up a new profession? And what compromises must be made to allow a person to deceive in the name of science?

It should not be hard for the reader to empathize with the social psychologist contemplating the use of deception. You want to study some pressing problem; you believe that the controlled laboratory setting is the best place to disentangle the complex threads of social phenomena and get at the truth; and the only way you know of duplicating the real world in your laboratory is through elaborate deceptions. Nowhere in your reasoning does callousness or cynicism appear; nowhere do you think of your subjects as "marks" or dupes. You want to do good, science is the surest road to knowledge; therefore, you are doing good. Since the problem you want to study is likely some socially troublesome issue, by studying it, and thereby contributing to its resolution, you are doing doubly good. How could anyone have the temerity to accuse you of harming your subjects, when your intentions are so obviously laudable?

Social psychologists, like psychoanalysts, have specialized in the study of rationalization and self-justification. They, more than anyone, ought to be able to recognize the powerful pressures on them to justify deception research. To adjure deception research now would be tantamount to confessing to past sins; it would be abandoning the tool many know best; it would make impossible many of the most interesting and impressive (and most highly rewarded) studies. It would require surrender of the singularly unique contribution of social psychology to the catalogue of social research methods.

The argument over the future of deception research must begin with a clear-headed assessment of the reality and importance of intrusions on subjects' well-being and substantive rights. Ultimately, the victor will be decided by government regulations. But beyond that we need to consider the costs of deception research to the individual scientist and his or her professional community.

To begin with the latter, I find it difficult to believe that social psychologists are proud of their image as the tricksters of science. (There is even a tape of selected vignettes from the "Candid Camera" show especially designed to illustrate social psychological principles. Both the television show and the discipline have specialized in getting people to reveal their foibles through elaborately staged and carefully recorded scenarios.) The word has certainly gotten around on campuses so that a large percentage of students expect to be deceived in psychology experiments, although they do not necessarily consider deception bad.[8] Some regard that appraisal as a warrant for the continued use of deception; others, myself included, as a warning. I have heard social psychology spoken of scornfully by other scientists and by humanists. But these are all externalities. What psychic price does the individual social psychologist pay?

I know too many principled people who are social psychologists to make any hasty generalizations. And perhaps the mild cynicism they exhibit is no worse than the typical academic's. But do any of the values and presumptions they live with in their identity as researcher spill over into the rest of their lives? In trying to make our laboratory so much like the world, do we sometimes succeed in making our world like the laboratory? When we learn to stage events and manage impressions, are we led to do the same with our other relationships? Do we eventually come to see people as so easily duped outside the laboratory as inside it? And if our research induces people to behave inhumanely, do we come to believe that that is indeed the way people are? Because so much of social psychological research leads people to behave irrationally (if they behaved reasonably and rationally, what need would there be for the science?), do we come to see people as fundamentally irrational? In short, do we come to see people in general as easily manipulable, foolish, and not especially nice, as a result of our characteristic procedures?

The deception researcher's personal dilemma is this: either one successfully dissociates the carefully crafted manipulativeness that characterizes the relationship with research subjects from relationships with people outside the laboratory, or one does not. In the first case, we should worry about the impact of the inauthentic relationship on the subject, and about the researcher's learning to systematically shut off ethically central aspects of his or her personality, as for example, learning to lie with a completely straight face and a clear conscience. The very ability to dissociate completely parts of one's life would seem to threaten one's psychological integration as well as one's personal integrity. In the second case, it follows analytically that one's relationships outside the laboratory are colored by the way one treats subjects. Neither option looks morally attractive.

It could be said that I have misrepresented the nature of the subject-experimenter relationship; specifically, I have left out the debriefing where the two people face each other honestly, and try to confront the feelings aroused by what each has done. Indeed, I suspect this does happen with some extraordinary researchers, deepening their humanity and their strength as moral actors. But I think it is the rare exception to the discouraging rule. The vast majority of social psychologists receive only the most superficial training on how to conduct a compassionate debriefing. Debriefings are more often viewed as discharging a responsibility (often an unpleasant one),

an opportunity to collect additional data, or even as a chance for a further manipulation! Deception researchers are not trained to recognize signs of anxiety in their subjects, nor to deal with them should they appear. Any special sensitivity of researcher to subject is likely to be the result of individual talent, or of clinical training which is not routinely part of a social psychologist's graduate experience.

One final cost of deception research requires discussion. What kind of science can grow from a discipline that relies on systematically deceiving its subjects? Here I am not questioning its moral value but rather its scientific value. Defenders of deception research regularly argue that if you were to tell subjects what you were really studying, then their responses would be somehow "unnatural." It is a point well taken, although the realm to which it is applicable may be smaller than originally thought. But, implicit in that very argument is the understanding that human subjects are not the passive recipients of external manipulations; that their responses are mediated by meanings and expectations.

And if, as is demonstrably the case, many, perhaps the majority, of our subjects expect to be deceived, do we have a science of "how-people-behave-when-they-don't-trust-the-authority-figure-who-is-telling-them-what-is-what" and no more? The people who become our "subjects" do not surrender their curiosity when they enter the lab. Nor do they lose their interest in interpersonal relationships, including that potential one with the experimenter. To assume that they do either, or that by employing deception we are somehow escaping the complex task of understanding the role of setting, expectations, and other persons, is naive and in the long run destructive to our goal of developing a robust science.

How might social psychology adapt were its practitioners to abandon or severely curtail the use of deception, or if we were to accept more complex models of persons-as-subjects? I believe the results would be intellectually invigorating as well as morally defensible. In my criticism of the received wisdom I am certainly not suggesting that we don rose-colored spectacles. Rather I am arguing that we may now be wearing dark glasses. Deception research may be neither good for the science nor good for the scientist.

NOTES

1. For Schachter's early work on emotionality see S. Schachter and J. W. Singer, "Cognitive, Social, and Physiological Determinants of Emotional State," *Psychological Review* 69 (1962), 379–99; and S. Schachter and L. Wheeler, "Epinephrine, Chlorpromazine and Amusement," *Journal of Abnormal and Social Psychology* 65 (1962), 121–28. An influential work by Berkowitz was L. Berkowitz, *Aggression: A Social Psychological Analysis* (New York: McGraw-Hill, 1962). Latané and Darley's work is summarized in B. Latané and J. M. Darley, *The Unresponsive Bystander: Why Doesn't He Help?* (New York: Appleton Century-Crofts, 1970).

2. Kenneth Ring, "Experimental Social Psychology: Some Sober Questions About Some Frivolous Values," *Journal of Experimental Social Psychology* 3 (1967), 113–23.

3. For Baumrind's latest thoughts on the matter see Diana Baumrind, "IRGBs and Social Science Research: The Costs of Deception," *IRB: A Review of Human Subjects Research* 1 (October 1979), 1–4. For a recent statement of Milgram's views see Stanley Milgram, "Subject Reaction: The Neglected Factor in the Ethics of Experimentation," *Hastings Center Report* 7 (October 1977), 19–23.

4. Herbert Kelman, "The Human Use of Human Subjects," *Psychological Bulletin* 67 (1967), 1–11.

5. Thorne Shipley, "Misinformed Consent: An Enigma in Modern Social Science Research," *Ethics in Science and Medicine* 4 (1977), 93–106.

6. Donald P. Warwick, "Deceptive Research: Social Scientists Ought to Stop Lying," *Psychology Today* (February 1975), pp. 38, 40, 105.

7. Alan Elms, "Deception in Social Science Research: Under What Conditions Is It Justifiable?" Paper presented at a conference on "Ethical Issues in Social Science Research" at the Joseph and Rose Kennedy Institute of Ethics, Georgetown University, Washington, D.C., September 27–29, 1979.

8. Y. M. Epstein, P. Suedfeld, and S. J. Silverstein, "Subjects' Expectations of and Reactions to Some Behaviors of Experimenters," *American Psychologist* 28 (1973), 212–21.

CHALLENGE QUESTIONS

Can Deception in Research Be Justified?

1. Do you think it is especially important to know the circumstances under which good people do bad things?

2. If you have ever participated in research, did you expect to be deceived? If so, do you think the expectation changed your behavior in any way? How might this affect the results of the research?

3. What do you think about the concepts of *role playing*, *presumptive consent*, and *prior general consent*? What are the advantages and disadvantages for the subject? For the research?

4. Much of Murray's objections to deception in research originated in his disillusionment with his own behavior as a researcher. Do you think most other researchers are likely to behave the same way? If so, would they feel any differently about their own behavior than Murray did?

ISSUE 2

Should Psychologists Study Memory Through Controlled Laboratory Experiments?

YES: Mahzarin R. Banaji and Robert G. Crowder, from "The Bankruptcy of Everyday Memory," *American Psychologist* (September 1989)

NO: Ulric Neisser, from "A Case of Misplaced Nostalgia," *American Psychologist* (January 1991)

ISSUE SUMMARY

YES: Cognitive psychologists Mahzarin R. Banaji and Robert G. Crowder argue that laboratory studies under controlled conditions are the best means of understanding the general principles of memory.
NO: Cognitive psychologist Ulric Neisser contends that memory researchers need to study the practical problems of memory in the natural settings in which these problems occur.

The importance of understanding memory seems undeniable. In fact, people use memory so much that they often take it for granted, such as for communication, knowledge gathering, and facial recognition. It is doubtful that you could understand the words on this page without memory. You would probably not even recognize that they *are* words without memory.

How should this crucial mental function be studied? Historically, psychologists have gone about this task through controlled laboratory experiments. They felt that this approach allowed them to understand the basic principles of memory. Controlled experiments weeded out what was considered to be the less relevant aspects of memory, such as the everyday settings in which the memories took place. The underlying "laws" of these memories could then be more easily discerned.

In a provocative article in 1978, Ulric Neisser voiced his regret over his field's reliance upon controlled laboratory experimentation. He felt that most of the research at that point had been devoted to less important aspects of memory, because these were the most easily subjected to laboratory controls. The situation was akin to the legendary drunk who kept looking for his money under the steetlamp, even though he had lost it some 20 yards away. When asked why he was doing this curious thing, he pointed out that the light was better where he was looking. Neisser's 1978 indictment of cognitive research is that his own field was like the drunk—looking only under the light of laboratory experimentation, when the "money," or the more important aspects of memory, was elsewhere.

To find the cognitive "money," Neisser advocated a naturalistic study of memory, which involves research performed in the field with relatively few controls. Just as the naturalistic study of animal behavior has helped biologists, so could the naturalistic study of memory help psychologists. Psychologists could study the "everyday" aspects of memory: memory for classroom lectures, political speeches, and parental instructions, for example. These studies would have *ecological validity*, because they would be valid in the real-life setting (or ecology) of the memory function being studied.

In the next 10 years or so, this type of research seemed to gain momentum, accumulating several ecologically valid studies to be considered by the field as a whole. Would such investigations become the mainstay of memory research? Mahzarin R. Banaji and Robert G. Crowder answer this question negatively. They contend that the movement toward everyday memory has proven itself to be "largely bankrupt" and that it endangers the "genuine accomplishments" of a young cognitive psychology. They feel that naturalistic observations may include unnoticed, uncontrolled factors that are actually responsible for the effects being observed. Hence, the only way to discover what really happens is to move to the laboratory where the various factors can be controlled and systematically examined.

In his reply, Ulric Neisser claims that since his 1978 article, all sorts of naturalistic research have been conducted, much of which has been quite productive. Neisser then challenges Banaji and Crowder's argument that psychology should seek "context-free laws," advocating, instead, a naturalistic analysis patterned after biology.

POINT	COUNTERPOINT
• Everyday memory research has produced no important results.	• Four lines of research have produced significant findings.
• Memory researchers should seek context-free laws like physicists do.	• Memory researchers should seek naturalistic functions like biologists do.
• Research findings need to be generalizable.	• Research findings need to be ecologically valid.
• Controlled laboratory study is the best means of research.	• Even "traditional" studies have become more ecologically valid.

YES

Mahzarin R. Banaji and
Robert G. Crowder

THE BANKRUPTCY
OF EVERYDAY MEMORY

ABSTRACT: *A new approach to the study of memory has emerged recently, characterized by a preoccupation with natural settings and with the immediate applicability of research findings. In contrast, the laboratory study of memory relies on experimental techniques for theory testing and is concerned with the discovery of generalizable principles. Although both approaches share the goal of generalizability, they differ sharply in the evaluation of how that goal is best accomplished. In this article, we criticize the everyday memory approach, arguing that ecologically valid methods do not ensure generalizability of findings. We discuss studies high in ecological validity of method but low in generalizability, and others low in ecological validity of method but high in generalizability. We solidly endorse the latter approach, believing that an obsession with ecological validity of method can compromise genuine accomplishments.*

Once upon a time, when chemistry was young, questions of ecological validity were earnestly raised by well-respected chemists and were debated at scientific meetings and in scholarly journals. We understand from a colleague (who is a distinguished historian of science but modestly asked not to be named) that partisans of one point of view called themselves the "everyday chemistry movement." They pointed out that the world offered many vivid examples of chemical principles at work in our daily lives—the rising of pastry dough, the curdling of sauces (the great chef Brillat-Savarin was then laying the foundation for the principles of applied chemistry thereafter called French cuisine), the smelting of metal alloys, the rusting of armor, and the combustion of gunpowder. Why not, they asked, study chemical principles in these ecologically faithful settings rather than in tiresome laboratories with their unnatural test tubes, burners, and finicky rules of measurement? The normal world around us, they said, has no end of

From Mahzarin R. Banaji and Robert G. Crowder, "The Bankruptcy of Everyday Memory," *American Psychologist*, vol. 44, no. 9 (September 1989). Copyright © 1989 by the American Psychological Association. Reprinted by permission.

YES Banaji and Crowder / 25

interesting and virtually unstudied manifestations of chemistry. One scholar, who was famous for his contributions to the new science, even commented that he thought one thing was certain: "If X is an interesting or socially significant aspect of chemistry, then chemists have hardly ever studied X." (Some advocates were actually abusive in their statements; we cite one of the nicer ones.)

Of course this parable is apocryphal. Its purpose is to make the point that the other sciences would have been hopelessly paralyzed if they had been deprived of the methods of science during their evolution. Imagine astronomy being conducted with only the naked eye, biology without tissue cultures, physics without vacuums, or chemistry without test tubes! The everyday world is full of principles from these sciences in action, but do we really think their data bases should have been those everyday applications? Of course not. Should the psychology of memory be any different? We think not.

There has been more than a decade of passionate rhetoric claiming that important questions about memory could be tackled if only researchers looked to the "real world" for hypothesis validation. Yet, no delivery has been made on these claims: No theories that have unprecedented explanatory power have been produced; no new principles of memory have been discovered; and no methods of data collection have been developed that add sophistication or precision. In this article, we argue that the movement to develop an ecologically valid psychology of memory has proven itself largely bankrupt and, moreover, that it carries the potential danger of compromising genuine accomplishments of our young endeavor. . . .

A CHALLENGE TO THE EXPERIMENTAL SCIENCE OF MEMORY

We proceed by presenting some issues raised by Neisser (1978) in a chapter that is widely cited as the vision of an ecological approach to the study of memory, assuming for now that such a goal is possible in psychology, unlike astronomy, for example. (We take it to be beyond question, here and elsewhere, that we do not mean to personalize the controversy by citing Neisser repeatedly. Some of his pronouncements, besides being influential, are especially articulate and thus are inviting pegs on which to hang our arguments. Indeed, his most recent statement [Neisser, 1988] is considerably less severe in its indictment of laboratory techniques in the study of memory.)

The Thundering Silence

The first conference on practical aspects of memory (Gruneberg et al., 1978) began with a talk titled "Memory: What Are the Important Questions?" in which Neisser rebuked psychology's "thundering silence" about questions of great interest, such as how one remembers sources of information, arguments, or material that is relevant to one's current thought. He also pointed to the embarrassment of discovering that we psychologists have no answers for our layperson friend who eagerly poses innocent questions such as the following: Why are there limitations on memories for early childhood? Why is it difficult to remember appointments? Why is it easy to find one's way around one's hometown after a 30-year absence? Why did I forget what I had for breakfast this morning?

Neisser's (1978) lament was that psychologists are not interested in such questions because they do not believe them to be truly important. This allegation has at least two answers: First, it is a misrepresentation. Psychologists have no delusions that laboratory techniques are their own justification. Rather, many of us believe that the way in which questions about memory can best be answered is through the empirical discovery of facts about memory that have *generalizability*, and not by the use of tasks that carry an illusion of ecological validity by testing memory in everyday contexts. By analogy, our apocryphal chemist might well retain an interest in why cake dough rises during baking but decide that controlled experimentation on yeast or the reactions of moist baking powder to heat would pay off more than loitering in professional bakeries and taking careful notes. (This issue will receive fuller discussion in a later section.)

Second, no embarrassment is in order when a psychologist is confronted with a layperson asking so-called interesting questions about memory. Science is an acquired taste, and scientific priorities may or may not continue to respect the mundane definition of what is "interesting." What other science, we ask, has established that its students should decide on the importance of questions by checking first with Aunt Martha or the expressway toll-taker? Why, and with what value, should the science of memory be singled out among the other sciences and burdened with this absurd criterion of legitimacy? If one wished to maintain that psychology has an inherently different responsibility from those of the other sciences, namely, the responsibility to provide the everyday public with everyday explanations, then one would need to explain why this peculiar demand is attached to psychology. That philosophical analysis is missing from the literature in our judgment, but to refute it here would take us far afield of our agenda.

Counterintuition as a Criterion of Good Science

Another issue in research on memory concerns the findings themselves. Neisser pointed out that enduring principles of memory, such as the effects of meaningfulness, practice, savings at relearning, and so on, are painfully obvious to students (and even to kindergartners!). According to Neisser, this should be yet another embarrassment to psychologists, who discover that the pinnacle of 100 years of slaving in the laboratory is a string of simplistic, intuitive effects. Again, there are several answers to the accusation.

It is our experience that students in introductory courses are often surprised and intrigued when they are introduced to experimental findings about memory, one example being the serial position curve. In fact, one of us has routinely asked her introductory psychology class a question before conducting the well-known classroom demonstration: "I am going to read a list of words to you, such as Apple, Mug, Square, etc. At the end of reading that list, I will ask you to write down as many of the words as you can remember. Before I do that, however, can you tell me which of these words you think you will remember?" Of the many and interesting hypotheses students have generated, rarely has one borne resemblance to the correct answer. Contrary to Neisser's claim, students do not always know these findings before they hear our lectures.

However, even if laypersons do find out that our experimental data only reaffirm their preconceived theories about how memory works, that confirmation should not be a source of embarrassment to us as Neisser has proclaimed. The belief that objects that are thrown up will fall down also corresponds to intuition and everyday observation. Needless to say, if the principle of counterintuition were applied to decisions of scientific worth, Isaac Newton might easily have ignored inventing the calculus. Risking the embarrassment of stating the obvious and intuitive, we say that the question to the scientist is not only that an effect occurs, but why it occurs. That a wise undergraduate can predict that a recency effect will be obtained unless the subject is assigned to an immediate distractor condition cannot belittle the efforts of a scientist interested in the nature of short-term memory.

Myths About Memory

Our students and laypersons in general "know" many things about memory that are complete nonsense. One is that slow learners show less forgetting than faster learners (Underwood, 1964). Another is that rote repetition increases the probability of later recall (Craik & Watkins, 1973; Rundus, 1977). A third is that some lucky adults have photographic memories (see Klatzky, 1984, Chap. 6, for other examples of "commonsense" principles of memory that are just silly in light of evidence that we have). As with intuitive physics (McCloskey, 1983), a systematic body of knowledge is needed for people to sort out which of their many beliefs are worth holding on to and which are worthless.

Intuitive psychology, below the surface, is just as fraught with ignorance as intuitive physics (McCloskey, 1983). If the growth of memory performance with repeated practice is a boring, Ebbinghausian platitude, painfully obvious to the laity, then so is the growth of recall under conditions of maintenance rehearsal. The latter belief, however, is dead wrong. Folk wisdom embraces many correct intuitions, but it also embraces many ideas that are utter nonsense. Our great grandparents knew for sure that mushrooms were poisonous, but they also "knew" that tomatoes were poisonous. A systematic body of knowledge about memory needs to be accumulated in order to separate the myths from the facts, and our experimental techniques will serve well to accomplish this goal.

A TWO-BY-TWO ARRAY OF APPROACHES

The attitude reflected in Neisser's (1978) commentary is based on at least one fundamental confusion, that the use of lifelike methods guarantees generality of conclusions to real-life situations. We argue that ecological validity of the methods as such is unimportant and can even work against generalizability.

This theme can be clarified by the construction of a two-dimensional array of scientific approaches. One dimension is the ecological validity of the methodology. The other is the external generalizability of the conclusions permitted by the research. For simplicity, these may be imagined as a two-by-two array (Figure 1), although in reality we think of them as dimensions. Now, nobody would deny that, other things being equal, the cell in which ecologically valid methods are used to achieve generalizable results is the best situation in which to find oneself. Nor could it possibly be denied that the combination of contrived, artificial methods and conclusions with no external validity produces a sorry state. The only real debates focus on the other two cells, where a cost-benefit analysis must be applied, and it is these two cells that we scrutinize in the rest of the article.

Figure 1

A Two-by-Two Array of Approaches to Science

Ecological Validity of Method

		High	Low
Generalizability of results	High		
	Low		

We come down solidly in favor of accepting contrived methods as long as the payoff in generality of conclusions is great enough. Gathering from a survey of the sources cited, we conclude that others of our colleagues in the study of memory would opt for the other cell, lifelike methods at all costs. That strategy, we fear, would lead the psychology of memory into the same stultification as studying backyard astronomy with the naked eye, chemistry in the kitchen, and biology with a walk through the forest. We have nothing against backyards, kitchens, or forests, but they are not ideal settings for the practice of science, and neither is everyday memory. We question whether the principles of learning discovered in the animal laboratory (see Rescorla, 1988) would have emerged if behaviorists had been dedicated to following rats around their natural urban habitats, craning their necks peering into upturned manhole covers.

Of course, some sciences absolutely require naturalistic observation and description in order to define the phenomena under study. Certain areas of ethology, and perhaps primate social behavior, are good examples of areas that depend on naturalistic observation, but we deny that a case has been made for this approach in the study of memory. The method of naturalistic observation can succeed in a science that has developed precise techniques for translating observations into a formal language such that the operations of invariant mechanisms can be shown obviously. For example, even before the theory of problem solving embodied in General Problem Solver (Newell & Simon, 1972) was developed, Duncker (1945) had used verbal protocol data to study problem solving. The difference, besides the availability of tape-recording equipment, was that Newell and Simon were able to cast their "naturalistic" observations into a formal language (i.e., IPL-V, LISP) allowing the construction of formal theories of cognitive processes.

Returning to our discussion of the ecological validity of method, an example will illustrate how such a concern can impede progress in resolving questions of legitimate concern. A classic unresolved controversy concerns the affect-memory relationship. The following question was posed by several clinical and cognitive psychologists: What is the influence of the affective nature of information on memory for that information? Early research on this topic (see Rapaport, 1942/1971) sometimes showed an affective asymmetry effect (better memory for affectively pleasant than unpleasant information) and at other times showed an affective intensity effect (better memory for both pleasant and unpleasant information than for neutral information). In retrospect, it appeared that the experimenters who typically found the asymmetry effect used "real-life" memories (in particular, memories from Christmas vacation), whereas the ones that found an intensity effect had tested for memory of laboratory constructed pleasant and unpleasant information.

In the 1930s and 1940s, the ecologically valid procedure was popular partly because of the "realness" of everyday memories and also because results supported the popular psychodynamic construct of repression. It appeared not to matter much that results of research using real-life memories were not free of interpretive confounds. The most obvious confound was that pleasant and unpleasant memories may be linked to extraneous variables (such as greater spontaneous rehearsal of real-life pleasant memories) that are responsible for the observed difference rather than the affective nature of the memories per se. . . .

The procedures employed by everyday memory researchers are similar to those used in early investigations of affect and memory and, we think, are equally prone to the hazards of employing real-world settings. . . .

Complexity of Phenomena: The Example of Social Psychology

The nature of forgetting is a particularly troublesome question for everyday memory researchers. For instance, Neisser (1978) commented that just as it is no longer meaningful to ask questions about the causes of crime because there are so many different and complex types of crime, "forgetting is an equally incoherent notion" (p. 10). In response, we have another fundamental disagreement with believers in everyday memory methods. Our view is that the more complex a phenomenon, the greater the need to study it under controlled conditions, and the less it ought to be studied in its natural complexity. To borrow examples from social psychology, about which concerns of external validity were debated some years ago, it is because the nature of obedience to authority in Nazi Germany was known to be complex that Milgram chose to demonstrate its vicissitudes in the laboratory (Milgram, 1963). It is because the nature of bystander nonintervention in the Kitty Genovese case was complex that laboratory experiments with the power of systematic manipulations of independent variables were performed to understand it (Latane & Darley, 1970). Several of these studies incorporated laboratory manipulations that mimicked the real world and concurrently maintained the control necessary to infer a causal relationship.

In the study of memory, laboratory stimuli that approximate the real world have been frequently used. Probably the most striking examples are studies of eyewitness memory (Loftus, 1979; McCloskey & Zaragoza, 1985) in which a little red Datsun, a can of Pepsi, and hammers and wrenches are appropriate stimuli to study memory for objects of the kind an eyewitness may easily be called on to testify. However, it was because these researchers followed scientific protocol that the results have generalizability. In our view, the complexity of a phenomenon is a compelling reason to seek, not abandon, the laboratory.

The above references to social psychological experiments are reminders that the everyday memory movement's disenchantment with the laboratory is not unprecedented. An example is what came to be known in the early 1970s as the "crisis in social psychology." The crisis referred to the sentiment among many social psychologists, as well as the informed public, that social psychology had renounced its mission by being an experimental science. Who cares about the college sophomore observed through a one-way mirror filling out a 7-point scale? Social psychology, they argued in a curiously familiar voice, must be concerned with real events and real people if it is to comment on the nature of social behavior. For several years the debate continued in social psychology, but if current research procedures are any indication, the controversy was settled in favor of hypothesis derivation from theory and hypothesis testing in the laboratory.

CONCLUSION

In summary, we students of memory are just as interested as anybody else in why we forget where we left the car in the morning or in who was sitting across the table at yesterday's meeting. Precisely for this reason we are driven to laboratory experimentation and away from naturalistic observation. If the former method has been disappointing to some after about 100 years, so should the latter approach be disappointing after about 2,000. Above all, the superficial glitter of everyday methods should not be allowed to replace the quest for truly generalizable principles.

REFERENCES

Craik, F. I. M., & Watkins, M. J. (1973). The role of rehearsal in short-term memory. *Journal of Verbal Learning and Verbal Behavior, 12*, 599–607.

Duncker, K. (1945). On problem-solving. *Psychological Monograph 58*, No. 5, (Whole No. 270).

Gruneberg, M. M., Morris, P. E., & Sykes, R. N. (1978). *Practical aspects of memory*. London: Academic Press.

Klatzky, R. L. (1984). *Memory and awareness: An information processing perspective*. New York: Freeman.

Latane, B., & Darley, J. M. (1970). *The unresponsive bystander: Why doesn't he help?* New York: Appleton-Century-Crofts.

Loftus, E. F. (1979). The malleability of human memory. *American Scientist, 67*, 312–320.

McCloskey, M. (1983). Intuitive physics. *Scientific American, 248*, 122–130.

McCloskey, M., & Zaragoza, M. (1985). Misleading postevent information and memory for events: Arguments and evidence against memory impairment hypotheses. *Journal of Experimental Psychology: General, 114*, 1–14.

Milgram, S. (1963). Behavioral study of obedience. *Journal of Abnormal and Social Psychology, 67*, 371–378.

Neisser, U. (1978). Memory: What are the important questions? In M. M. Gruneberg, P. E. Morris, & R. N. Sykes (Eds.), *Practical aspects of memory* (pp. 3–24). London: Academic Press.

Neisser, U. (1988). New vistas in the study of memory. In U. Neisser & E. Winograd (Eds.), *Remembering reconsidered: Ecological and traditional approaches to the study of memory* (pp. 1–10). Cambridge, England: Cambridge University Press.

Newell, A., & Simon, H. A., (1972). *Human problem solving*. Englewood Cliffs, NJ: Prentice-Hall.

Rapaport, D. (1971). *Emotions and memory*. New York: International Universities Press. (Original work published 1942).

Rescorla, R. A. (1988). Pavlovian conditioning: It's not what you think it is. *American Psychologist, 43*, 151–160.

Rundus, D. (1977). Maintenance rehearsal and single-level processing. *Journal of Verbal Learning and Verbal Behavior, 16*, 665–681.

Underwood, B. J. (1964). Degree of learning and the measurement of forgetting. *Journal of Verbal Learning and Verbal Behavior, 3*, 112–129.

NOTES

We thank Bob Abelson, R. Bhaskar, Denise Dellarosa, Matt Erdelyi, Tony Greenwald, Beth Loftus, Mike Lynn, Jack Mayer, Roddy Roediger, Peter Salovey, and the Memory Lunch Group at Yale for valuable comments and discussions. Inclusion in this list does not necessarily imply agreement with our position.

Preparation of this article was supported in part by a grant from the Social Science Faculty Research Fund at Yale University to M. Banaji and by Grant GB 8608344 from the National Science Foundation to R. G. Crowder.

Correspondence concerning this article should be addressed to Mahzarin R. Banaji or Robert G. Crowder, Department of Psychology, Yale University, P. O. Box 11A, Yale Station, New Haven, CT 06520-7447.

NO

Ulric Neisser

A CASE OF MISPLACED NOSTALGIA

To counter Banaji and Crowder's (1989) claim that the naturalistic study of memory has not been productive, this reply cites four significant lines of research: Ross's (1989) theory of bias in recalling personal traits, Nelson's (1986) studies of children's event representations, Bahrick's (1984) long-term follow-up of school learning, and new work on "flashbulb memories" by Neisser and Harsch. Banaji and Crowder's analogy to chemistry is misleading: In biology, a more appropriate model, the importance of field studies is taken for granted. And not all the progress of the last 12 years has been on the ecological side; "traditional" memory research has now gone well beyond the limitations noted by Neisser (1978), and both approaches are now moving ahead together.

I have bad news for Banaji and Crowder (September 1989). It's too late: The good old days are gone, the genie is out of the bottle. The situation I described and deplored in 1978 ("If X is an interesting or socially significant aspect of memory, then psychologists have hardly ever studied X," Neisser, 1978, p. 4) will never return, however much they may long for it. The present state of affairs is nearly the opposite. Nowadays, if X is an ecologically common or socially significant domain of memory, somebody is probably studying it intensively. Estimates of one's own traits at earlier points in time, memory in young children (and recollections of childhood), retrieval of material learned in school, recall of unusual or emotional experiences—these are only a few of the naturalistic domains in which important findings have recently appeared. The psychologists who made those findings will surely go on with their work; no amount of nostalgic grumbling about the proper methods of science is likely to deter them. This being rather obviously the case, two questions present themselves: (a) Why does it bother Banaji and Crowder so much? (b) How does it fit into the study of memory as a whole?

But perhaps it is not the case. Banaji and Crowder (1989) simply denied it. According to them, the study of *everyday memory* (an awkward phrase, I think) has not produced any important results at all. That claim must be

From Ulric Neisser, "A Case of Misplaced Nostalgia," *American Psychologist*, vol. 46, no. 1 (January 1991). Copyright © 1991 by the American Psychological Association. Reprinted by permission.

refuted before we proceed; otherwise my argument would rest on shaky ground. Luckily, Banaji and Crowder phrased it so sweepingly that refutation is easy:

> No delivery has been made on these claims: No theories that have unprecedented explanatory power have been produced; no new principles of memory have been discovered; and no methods of data collection have been developed that add sophistication or precision. (p. 1185; all italics added)

A single counterexample would suffice to refute null hypotheses like these: I will list four for good measure. To be sure, there is something arbitrary about any such list; other students of memory in natural contexts have their own favorite studies, and I do not claim any unique privilege for mine. Some of the studies mentioned here combine theory and data in a way that should appeal even to Banaji and Crowder; others have produced results that would never have emerged from standard laboratory studies. One (which, of course, I like especially) is partly my own work. Four should be enough.

1. People often have occasion to recall what they were like at some earlier point in time. How bad were my headaches last week? How fast did I read before I took this study-skills course? Was I happy in my college days? Michael Ross (1989) developed a systematic theory of such estimates. In his view they are largely derived from the trait's *present* value (my pain today, my reading speed now, my current happiness), taken together with an implicit hypothesis about its stability or change over time. If I have no reason to believe that my headaches have changed, for example, then recall of last week's pain will be biased toward today's level. If I have just been through

a treatment program, however, recall of pain levels before it began will be biased upward from today's level—after all, the program must have done some good! In a recent issue of *Psychological Review*, Ross (1989) reported about a dozen studies, covering a wide range of personally significant traits, that support his theory. (An independent measure of the original trait was available in each case.) This work, which offers unexpected and yet systematic insights into a commonplace use of memory, meets every standard methodological criterion.

2. The use of everyday events as targets may be optional in studying adult memory, but it is essential with young children. Using naturalistic methods, Katherine Nelson (1986) and her associates showed that recall of familiar routines as well as of specific episodes can be elicited from two-year-olds, and perhaps even (Nelson, 1988) from one-year-olds. Such recall is quite sketchy at first, but interestingly, it is rarely wrong. It takes an increasingly rich narrative form during development, as parents instruct their children in the social uses of memory (Hudson, in press). Some characteristics of young children's memory—its dependence on external cueing; its focus on things that adults would take for granted—may help to explain the "childhood amnesia" that will overtake their recall later (Fivush & Hamond, in press).

3. Harry Bahrick's (1984) studies of memory for school-learned material are now well-known. By locating people who had studied Spanish at various times in the past (and controlling other variables with covariance techniques), Bahrick was able to trace out 50-year forgetting functions. Although some aspects of those functions were predictable from traditional theories of memory

(e.g., effects of the level of original learning), others were not: The rate of forgetting dropped to zero after 5 years or so, producing a 25-year plateau in performance. These data, which could not have been obtained by standard laboratory methods, have obvious theoretical and practical significance.

4. Banaji and Crowder (1989) believe that so-called *flashbulb memories*, such as recalling how one first heard the news of the explosion of the space shuttle *Challenger*, "present nothing unexpected to conventional laboratory work on memory" (p. 1190). They probably mean that although such memories are roughly accurate, no special memory mechanism is involved. That is the view of McCloskey, Wible, and Cohen (1988), whose study they cited. But recent work suggests that the real puzzle about flashbulb memories is quite different: Why do people so often have vivid recollections that are entirely incorrect? Nicole Harsch and I asked Emory University freshmen, on the morning after the *Challenger* disaster, how they had heard the news the day before (Harsch & Neisser, 1989; Neisser & Harsch, in press). Three years later, 44 of them were asked to recall it again. Most gave very plausible and confident accounts, but about one third of those accounts were dead wrong. Although errors do often occur in eyewitness testimony (Loftus, 1979), neither folk psychology nor conventional theories of memory had led us to expect so many utterly false reports. Not all forms of everyday memory are prone to such errors. For example, they do not occur in recall of randomly selected events (Brewer, 1988). Clarification of these issues will probably require continued naturalistic research: The strong emotions and long retention intervals characteristic of flash-bulb memories are not easily established under laboratory conditions.

WHY DOES IT BOTHER BANAJI AND CROWDER?

Banaji and Crowder's (1989) use of analogies from chemistry and physics is no accident. Despite a rather curious disclaimer (p. 1191), they obviously believe, as almost everyone once did, that psychology should seek universal context-free laws like those of the classical sciences. But physics is no longer the unchallenged model of science. Modern biology has demonstrated the enormous power of functional analysis coupled with naturalistic observation. Banaji and Crowder asked their readers, mockingly, to imagine doing chemistry without laboratory controls. Can they imagine evolutionary biology, or ecology, or ethology, without field studies? Without some analysis of the function of body parts and behavior patterns?

Perhaps they can; certainly they have no conception of function in psychology. Discussions of what mechanisms are "good for" leave them frankly puzzled (Banaji & Crowder, 1989, p. 1191). Fortunately, other psychologists have found the concept less mysterious. Modern interest in functional and ecological analysis is not confined to memory alone; it has already influenced research on perception (Gibson, 1979), conceptualization (Medin & Wattenmaker, 1987; Mervis, 1987; Rosch, 1978), development (Ceci & Bronfenbrenner, 1985), and cognitive linguistics (Lakoff, 1987). Instead of merely recombining the elements and testing the hypotheses of a traditional mental chemistry, as Banaji and Crowder would apparently recommend, such investigators try to study variables that play functional roles in natural settings. It is hard to believe that we would be better off without the discoveries that they have made.

Anyway, that is not one of the options. The ecological approach is here to stay, in the study of memory as elsewhere in psychology. There are certain to be more and more naturalistic studies in the years to come. Many of them will be less than outstanding in quality, but that's part of science: No one rejects evolutionary biology out of hand just because some Darwinian studies are flawed. I understand Banaji and Crowder's (1989) impatience with weak studies. My own critique of traditional memory research (Neisser, 1978) was fueled by impatience of a similar kind. But it is inappropriate to react, as they did, by arguing that the only acceptable scientific protocol is that of the fully controlled laboratory study. There is more than one way to skin a phenomenon.

WHERE DOES IT FIT?

The ecological approach is not the only source of new ideas about remembering. The "traditional" study of memory itself has undergone radical changes since I characterized it so harshly in 1978. At that time it was chiefly focused on explicit recognition or recall of isolated items from lists. Today, a glance at the *Journal of Experimental Psychology: Learning, Memory, and Cognition* shows that such research has become almost an endangered species. Currently popular topics include implicit memory, mental imagery, motor skills, story schemata, social scripts, object recognition, and cognitive maps—many of them appreciably closer (than the old methods were) to the sorts of things people do everyday. Whether

laboratory study of such problems will produce what Banaji and Crowder (1989) called "truly generalizable principles" (p. 1192) remains to be seen—or rather, to be tested across the relevant ecological settings. (Taken by themselves, encapsulated laboratory experiments can never ensure true generalizability.) But even without such tests, some of these studies clearly meet what Eugene Winograd (1988) has called "the one requirement for scientific research we all implicitly follow: our understanding of memory is enhanced" (p. 18).

Much ecologically oriented work on memory also meets that test. The research described here is only a sample. There is not enough space to describe the many excellent studies of oral tradition, prospective remembering, conversational use of the past, personal recall, and eyewitness testimony that have also enhanced our understanding in the last few years. Far from "compromising genuine accomplishments of our young endeavor" (Banaji & Crowder, 1989, p. 1185), this work is an integral part of those accomplishments. No serious student of memory can afford to ignore it.

REFERENCES

Bahrick, H. P. (1984). Semantic memory content in permastore: Fifty years of memory for Spanish learned in school. *Journal of Experimental Psychology: General, 113,* 1–29.

Banaji, M. R., & Crowder, R. G. (1989). The bankruptcy of everyday memory. *American Psychologist, 44,* 1185–1193.

Brewer, W. F. (1988). Memory for randomly sampled autobiographical events. In U. Neisser & E. Winograd (Eds.), *Remembering reconsidered: Ecological and traditional approaches to the study of memory* (pp. 21–90). New York: Cambridge University Press.

Ceci, S. J., & Bronfenbrenner, U. (1985). Don't forget to take the cupcakes out of the oven: Strategic time-monitoring, prospective memory, and context. *Child Development, 56,* 175–190.

Fivush, R., & Hamond, N. R. (in press). Autobiographical memory across the preschool years: Toward reconceptualizing childhood amnesia. In R. Fivush & J. A. Hudson (Eds.), *Knowing and remembering in young children.* New York: Cambridge University Press.

Gibson, J. J. (1979). *The ecological approach to visual perception.* Boston: Houghton Mifflin.

Harsch, N., & Neisser, U. (1989, November). *Substantial and irreversible errors in flashbulb memories of the* Challenger *explosion.* Poster presented at the meeting of the Psychonomic Society, Atlanta, GA.

Hudson, J. A. (in press). The emergence of autobiographic memory in mother–child conversation. In R. Fivush & J. A. Hudson (Eds.), *Knowing and remembering in young children.* New York: Cambridge University Press.

Lakoff, G. (1987). *Women, fire, and dangerous things: What categories reveal about the mind.* Chicago: Chicago University Press.

Loftus, E. (1979). *Eyewitness testimony.* Cambridge MA: Harvard University Press.

McCloskey, M., Wible, C. G., & Cohen, N. J. (1988). Is there a special flashbulb memory mechanism? *Journal of experimental psychology: General, 117,* 171–181.

Medin, D. L., & Wattenmaker, W. D. (1987). Category cohesiveness, theories, and cognitive archaeology. In U. Neisser (Ed.), *Concepts and conceptual development: Ecological and intellectual factors in categorization* (pp. 25–62). New York: Cambridge University Press.

Mervis, C. B. (1987). Child-basic object categories and early lexial development. In U. Neisser (Ed.), *Concepts and conceptual development: Ecological and intellectual factors in categorization* (pp. 201–233). New York: Cambridge University Press.

Neisser, U. (1978). Memory: What are the important questions? In M. M. Gruneberg, P. E. Morris, & R. N. Sykes (Eds.), *Practical aspects of memory* (pp. 3–24). London: Academic Press.

Neisser, U., & Harsch, N. (in press). Phantom flashbulbs: False recollections of hearing the news about *Challenger.* In E. Winograd & U. Neisser (Eds.), *Flashbulb memories: Recalling the "Challenger" explosion and other disasters.* New York: Cambridge University Press.

Nelson, K. (1986). *Event knowledge: Structure and function in development.* Hillsdale, NJ: Erlbaum.

Nelson, K. (1988). The ontogeny of memory for real events. In U. Neisser & E. Winograd (Eds.), *Remembering reconsidered: Ecological and traditional approaches to the study of memory* (pp. 244–276). New York: Cambridge University Press.

Rosch, E. (1978). Principles of categorization. In E. Rosch & B. B. Lloyd (Eds.), *Cognition and categorization* (pp. 27–48). Hillsdale, NJ: Erlbaum.

Ross, M. (1989). Relation of implicit theories to the construction of personal histories. *Psychological Review, 96,* 341–357.

Winograd, E. (1988). Continuities between ecological and laboratory approaches to memory. In U. Neisser & E. Winograd (Eds.), *Remembering reconsidered: Ecological and traditional approaches to the study of memory* (pp. 11–20). New York: Cambridge University Press.

CHALLENGE QUESTIONS

Should Psychologists Study Memory Through Controlled Laboratory Experiments?

1. How might a psychologist go about doing naturalistic observations of people? Give two examples and describe some of the difficulties that may be encountered.

2. Banaji and Crowder claim that more than a decade of research has been conducted on everyday memory, and that this research has not been all that fruitful. Find some of this research yourself, and write whether or not you feel that Banaji and Crowder are correct and why.

3. Think of an "everyday memory" issue that the authors do not mention. Describe how you might go about investigating it.

4. Banaji and Crowder state that many students are surprised by the findings about memory. Consider what you knew about memory before you read this issue, and describe those findings that surprised you as well as those findings you may have discovered in the readings.

ISSUE 3

Can Experiments Using Animals Be Justified?

YES: John R. Cole, from "Animal Rights and Wrongs," *The Humanist* (July/August 1990)

NO: Steven Zak, from "Ethics and Animals," *The Atlantic* (March 1989)

ISSUE SUMMARY

YES: Anthropologist John R. Cole argues that although animal research has declined in recent years due to newly developed alternatives, some animal research is still necessary and beneficial to society.

NO: Attorney Steven Zak asserts that animals have the right to not be treated like instruments for the betterment of humankind and that legal barriers should be erected to prevent animal exploitation.

Until recently, humans were thought to be distinctly different from lower animals. Only humans were considered to have self-consciousness, rationality, and language. Today, however, these distinctions appear to have become blurred by modern research. Many scientists, for example, believe that chimpanzees use language symbols and that many animals have some type of consciousness.

This apparent lack of hard-and-fast distinctions between humans and other animals have many implications, one of which concerns the use of animals in experimental research. For hundreds of years animals have been considered by humans to be tools of research. In fact, research ethics has demanded that most experimental treatments be tested on animals before they are tested on humans. Another view, however, has come to the fore. Because there is no clear distinction between lower and higher animals, this new view asserts that the lower animals should be accorded the same basic rights as humans. Animal experimentation, from this perspective, cannot be taken for granted; it must be justified on the same moral and ethical grounds as research on humans. This perspective has recently gained considerable momentum as supporters have become politically organized.

In the following selections, John R. Cole argues that animal rights groups are too extremist in their positions. One can promote animal protection against abuse without also banning animal research. Cole contends that scientists have the right to improve the life of humans through research.

Animal research was instrumental in the development of vaccines, antibiotics, antidepressants, tranquilizers, insulin, cancer treatments, and most surgical procedures, just to name a few. He notes that few animal rights activists refuse to undergo medical procedures that were developed through animal research. Moreover, the use of animals in research is declining, as changing cultural attitudes and the development of experimental alternatives (such as tissue cultures and computer models) have lowered the rate of animal research.

Steven Zak discusses the activities and beliefs of several animal rights activist groups, such as True Friends, the Animal Liberation Front, and the Royal Society for the Prevention of Cruelty to Animals. He states that "the animal rights advocates' position is that animal research is an ethical travesty that justifies extraordinary, and even illegal, measures." Animal rights efforts have been a catalyst for needed reforms in animal rights laws, but these reforms do not go far enough in protecting the rights of animals. Opponents of animal rights argue that animals do not live by moral rules and therefore are not entitled to the same rights as humans. Zak contends that living beings do not have to be qualitatively the same to be worthy of equal respect.

POINT	COUNTERPOINT
• To claim that animals have the same rights as people is an elitist stance.	• Animals have rights, and these should be protected by the Constitution.
• Animal research has achieved major benefits for both humans and animals.	• The interests of human beings should not overwhelm the interests of animals.
• Animal research is declining, but it is still necessary and justified for some uses.	• Animal research is an ethical travesty that justifies extraordinary and even illegal measures to prevent it.
• Less invasive animal research procedures have been developed and are being used in animal research.	• If researchers were not allowed to use animals in research, more alternative research methods would be explored.
• There are laws and research guidelines that protect animals that are used in research.	• Animal protection laws should be replaced by a rights act that would prohibit the use of any animals to their detriment.

YES

John R. Cole

ANIMAL RIGHTS AND WRONGS

According to Chris DeRose, head of Last Chance for Animals: "A life is a life. If the death of one rat cured all diseases it wouldn't make any difference to me. In the scheme of life we're equal."

According to Cardinal John O'Connor, speaking on Earth Day 1990 (and endorsing some environmental concerns other than the "non-truth" of overpopulation as a problem): "The earth exists for the human person, not vice versa." (O'Connor was taking his cue from Genesis 1:29, which issues the following command: "Fill the earth, and subdue it, and rule over . . . all the living creatures that move on the earth.")

Finally, in the words of a leading national science figure whose position requires diplomatic anonymity: "The animal rights issue is anti-intellectualism, know-nothingism. It's the single biggest threat to American science education today."

These comments may represent easily attacked extremes but, unfortunately, they are not straw-man arguments. Neither the animal rights movement, its more militant animal *liberationist* wing, nor its critics are monolithic, although both sides sometimes portray each other (or themselves) as if they were. To argue that science and commerce require the use of animals is not an argument for animal abuse. To advocate animal protection, one need not go so far as to argue that other animals have the "right" to exploit each other but that humans somehow do not without standing accused of speciesism. (What about *kingdomism?* Animalia can be hard to distinguish from Plantae—hence the recognition of Fungi, Monera, and Protista as kingdoms. Some of these have at least something like rudimentary nervous systems, and they are built from the same basic kinds of cells as monkeys, rats, and people. Since plants, fungi, protista, and monera are more numerous than animals, are experiments with them acceptable? And in this scheme of things, where do we put viruses?)

Turn the argument around one hundred and eighty degrees. Since humans are animals, should not people have certain rights, too? The primitive hunter who felt a kinship with his prey and apologized for killing when

From John R. Cole, "Animal Rights and Wrongs," *The Humanist*, vol. 50, no. 4 (July/August 1990). Copyright © 1990 by the American Humanist Association. Reprinted by permission.

necessary but went ahead and did it anyway was, I suggest, displaying more natural humanism than today's extremist advocate of absolute animal rights. So, too, are the scientists concerned with improving the lot of our own and fellow species through their research.

To decide what is acceptable and what is not requires values clarification. What is the value of life, and how is that value determined? When, if ever, are animal—and human—experiments ethical and worth the sacrifice? (Sacrifice *is* the term used by experimenters.)

TO CLAIM THAT ANIMALS HAVE THE SAME rights as people (perhaps more) is an oddly elitist stance which would shock almost anyone in the Third World. Who other than a few masochistic fundamentalists can argue in good conscience that suffering is desirable in itself? One would think any argument insisting that animals should not suffer unduly in the laboratory could be extended to say that humans and other animals should not suffer unduly *outside* the lab, either. Telling a Tanzanian farmer stricken with malaria or schistosomiasis or polio to "lie back and enjoy it" is as inhuman and arrogant (if not more so) as applying that callous phrase to rape victims. It would make no sense whatever to most people if you told them that they or their children could not be cured of disease because it would require experimenting on monkeys or rats or fertilized duck eggs. Anyone not comfortably ensconced in a well-fed, upper- or upper-middle-class sanctuary in Western culture would find it especially absurd. I may be mistaken, but I would guess that virtually everyone arguing for a total ban on animal experimentation has already had their shots (or is not living in a vulnerable area) and

goes to a doctor who has dissected monkey and human cadavers whose real tissues do not look (and cannot feel) like a computer-screen simulation. Put another way, what training or research would *not* be acceptable to the parents of a child needing serious medical or surgical treatment? Who decides?

Animal research has developed vaccines (for such diseases as typhoid, diphtheria, and polio, to name but a few), antibiotics, local anesthetics, steroids and hormone treatments, insulin, antihypertensives, diuretics and Beta blockers, leukemia and cancer therapies, tranquilizers, antidepressants, and most surgical procedures, from transplants to suturing to blood typing. Even an abbreviated and strictly medical list like this is impressive. It can be argued that some of these are only partially due to animal experimentation or that some, in retrospect, could have been developed using other techniques such as *in vitro* tissue cultures, but the picture is not a simple litany of horrors.

IT IS OFTEN ARGUED BY ANIMAL RIGHTS activists that all species are unique, so that animal experiments are not really applicable to humans. This is really a "scientific" creationist argument and simply untrue. Even though humans and other animals are not biologically or genetically identical, they are similar enough that many aspects of animal research are applicable to humans. While there was already a strong linkage between smoking and lung disease, for example, the case was not made airtight until countless rats were sacrificed to prove it. One can regret that the rats suffered at all and hope that they were sacrificed humanely, but it is hard to get around the fact that *potentially* unnecessary experiments were necessary, after all.

After sixty years of growth, the number of animals used in research—at least in America—has declined sharply in recent years. One reason is the increased concern for animal welfare on the part of researchers; another is the drastically increased costs of animal research; and yet a third is the growing availability of alternatives such as *in vitro* tissue cultures and computer modeling. Animal welfare reformers, ethicists, and changing cultural attitudes all deserve some of the credit for this change; so, too, do the scientists who have developed experimental alternatives and mastered many of the earlier trial-and-error experiences of biology moving beyond its rudimentary stage of development. There has also been a shift away from the use of such procedures as the Draize test for rabbit eye sensitivity to cosmetics as noninvasive tests become available. Thus, one major use of animals that has widely been considered frivolous is being phased out.

We know now that some earlier lines of experimentation were dead ends, but hindsight is always clearer. Similarly, every high-school science class in the country does not have to replicate every well-established experiment, and the National Association of Biology Teachers has established fairly thorough guidelines for classroom instruction in the United States and Canada.

However, selective replication of experiments is needed in order to test variants of earlier hypotheses or new procedures. The major aspects of animal experimentation are controlled by federal and state laws, National Institutes of Health and other guidelines monitored by peer review committees, humane societies such as the International Primate Protection League, and disciplinary codes of ethics in medicine and the sciences. Universities and animal research laboratories are required by law to have review committees to approve research proposals and to monitor experiments and the treatment of animals. They are legally required to include neutral public representatives, not just science insiders. This does not mean that everything is now perfect or that tension and disagreement will soon go away or even *should* go away. Even though it needs to be strengthened and clarified, I suggest that this matrix of protection and sensitivity to the issues involved is too often ignored or dismissed by animal rights activists who imply that there is only one side to the story and that all experimenters are sadistic or ignorant or both, plying a brutal trade for mindless profit and glory.

Trauma injury research is traumatic by definition. The University of Pennsylvania experiments which involved inflicting head injuries on baboons and other animals resulted in raids by animal liberationists, who destroyed records and stole and later publicized videotapes of the experiments. These tapes *are* horrifying; on the other hand, a tape of a rally of children and adults supporting this research has had little publicity. People saved by surgical and recuperative techniques developed in these experiments felt that they owed their lives to the controversial scientific research—and to the baboons who died in the process.

Currently, protests have halted a long-term United States Army project in Texas in which goats were shot and then treated by Army physicians and medics. The Army claims that the work was vital training for people who will have to treat battlefield injuries uncommon in everyday life or in medical schools; animal rights activists argue that animals are being harmed for no good reason. They do not seem to oppose *all* military research on the classic pacifist grounds that preparing for war makes it more likely or "thinkable"; the question seems to involve only the animals' right not to be shot, not the question of whether young people sent to war should suffer unduly.

Pound dogs have been collected by the U.S. Surgical Corporation, a Connecticut company, and used to train salesmen in how to sell their new suturing staple technique to surgeons. Does this constitute a waste of thousands of dogs' lives if they are used for sales—not medical—training? At the risk of insulting its clients, the company might respond that practicing doctors in fact get most of their ongoing training from salespeople, and that the dogs were doomed anyway. Is surgical training limited to classrooms? To computer simulations? I personally do not know the answers.

Is there an intellectual justification for the proliferation of laws banning experiments on pound animals, or is it simply another case of American romanticism about pets? Does it devalue life to extract some use from it—as painlessly as possible—at or near death? These questions are not easy to answer, I hope, nor are they meant to be.

When seemingly horrible experiments are actually looked at in context, they may prove to have been very useful to humans and other animals. On the other hand, many experiments are poorly designed and do not achieve their goals, whether or not they employ animals. Can the process be made more humane *and* better scientifically without actual prohibition?

A "good end" certainly does not justify all means of animal experimentation, but it is worth bearing in mind. Seen in the context of their real or potential gains versus their cost in animal life, some experiments look better at second glance. For example, sticking tubes into horses' hearts one hundred and fifty years ago was rather grisly, but it answered basic questions about anatomy. Moreover, catheterization is now a major part of the treatment and relief of many illnesses. Re-enacting such experiments today without anesthesia should be judged differently than we judge the original experiment—or current research. An AIDS vaccine might be desirable enough that colonies of monkeys or chimpanzees bred for scientific use should be sacrificed in its development. At the same time, we should, in my opinion, avoid further endangering dwindling populations living in the wild.

We cannot simply equate painlessness with acceptability; rather, we need to recognize that some pain or discomfort (or at least inconvenience) accompanies most experiments, even if long-term suffering is avoided via euthanasia. Now that pain can be considerably controlled, it may be tempting to think that it can be abolished. As anyone who has ever had surgery or even a tooth filling can testify, anesthesia is not perfect, so its mere availability should not be the only factor considered in judging invasive animal research. This does not justify doing things in other than the least painful way possible, but it is a reminder that experimental goals often cannot be reached magically and painlessly. Researchers must now consciously decide that benefits will outweigh drawbacks, rather than falling back on the idea that animals cannot suffer. This realization has already cut down on animal experimentation, even among people who reject the antivivisectionist argument that virtually *no* experiments are conscionable.

On Earth Day, I was approached by a man asking for petition signatures. One petition called for the outlawing of animal breeding and genetic records, and the other aimed at banning leashes and other animal "movement and activity restrictions" such as fences. (I was there disseminating information about research on acid rain causes and effects, I might add.) I refused to sign on the grounds that the petitions were both harmful and silly. "Won't more animals—and people—be killed or injured in traffic if restrictions are forbidden?" I asked. "Are farmers and geneticists better off unaware of genetics and left to folk wisdom, at best?" He accused me of being like Nazi "experimenter" Josef Mengele and told me that acid rain might be the Earth Mother's revenge on humans for mistreating her creatures. (Did Mother Nature build dirty power plants and devastate clean and economical mass transit in favor of automobile sales and poisoned fish?) He had quit college to work on his cause, and he accused me of being an "intellectual" bought and paid for by the university before moving on to a possibly more receptive audience at the adjacent crystal power exhibit. Given his supposedly humane objective, this person was, I submit, simply wrongheaded and counterproductive. The general public is greatly concerned about the slaughter of cute baby seals or giant pandas but not as worried about the welfare of frogs and bats which, arguably, serve more vital functions in the world ecosystem. Virtually no one is militant about protecting flies, mosquitoes, or other slimy, crawly things. The extinction of smallpox is not widely bemoaned. A few people

argue that plagues like AIDS are desirable checks on population, but this shows their poor understanding of human demographics—the response to wars, plagues, and so forth has always been an *intensification* of reproduction and other pressures upon the environment. Carried a step further, a few people misinterpret the Gaia hypothesis to suggest that the earth is actually sentient and would like to be rid of its human "infection," but this is a naive application of nineteenth century Spencerism, not modern Gaiaist systems theory.

It is tempting for people who get their meat from plastic packages to ignore the fact that it came from a living cow, sheep, or whatever. Is the person who kills or butchers an animal any less human than the one who eats the packaged result? Or do people who hunt and slaughter their own food have just as much humanity—if not more, since they accurately see the connections between life, suffering, and death? Are people who take polio vaccines consisting of weakened or murdered viruses more humane than the people who painstakingly developed the vaccines, consciously harming some animals (as well as viruses) in the process? There are some absolutists who could answer all of these questions easily. And while many people recognize that the earth is not a human toy to be used and thrown away—that the earth would get along quite well without us and our fantasies of being the pinnacle of perfection and goal of evolution—most people (certainly most scientists) believe that a more feasible and desirable middle way exists for relating to our environment.

ANIMAL LIBERATIONISTS RESENT BEING branded "terrorists" by their critics. As the saying goes, one person's terrorist is another person's freedom fighter, and in any case it should be noted that most people in the movement oppose "terrorizing" people or animals, even though extreme civil disobedience can be threatening. Some do not disavow property damage, however, and some condone destroying laboratories and research records and "liberating" lab animals, even though the latter is hardly humane; the animals are usually unable to live on their own because of the experiments conducted on them or the mere fact of having been raised in captivity.

The absolutist true believer, either animal rights activist or animal experimentation advocate, takes a rather easy path—the first claiming that no harm or perhaps even inconvenience to animals is ever justified, the second that virtually all experiments are conscionable and that "civilians" should stay out of the way. The truth is never so cut-and-dried, however. For example, many people opposed to abortion do not demand that the practice be made illegal for all people no matter what the circumstance, but until recently they have been outshouted by an extremely narrow leadership cadre. The animal rights movement has had a similar history of drowning out its own potentially widely acceptable concerns and constructive viewpoints with a barrage of militant oversimplification.

Many scientists are repelled by arguments equating human rights or civil rights with animal rights because these arguments demean people more than they elevate the status of animals. Understandably, many African-Americans resented the 1960s song "Woman is the Nigger of the World," noting that white women were better off than poor people of color of either gender. Similarly, Third World people today—most of whom have fewer rights and a lower standard of living than American household pets—will be hard pressed to understand the industrial world's growing concern over the rights of animals.

NO   Steven Zak

ETHICS AND ANIMALS

In December of 1986 members of an "animal-liberation" group called True Friends broke into the Sema, Inc., laboratories in Rockville, Maryland, and took four baby chimpanzees from among the facility's 600 primates. The four animals, part of a group of thirty being used in hepatitis research, had been housed individually in "isolettes"—small stainless-steel chambers with sealed glass doors. A videotape produced by True Friends shows other primates that remained behind. Some sit behind glass on wire floors, staring blankly. One rocks endlessly, banging violently against the side of his cage. Another lies dead on his cage's floor.

The "liberation" action attracted widespread media attention to Sema, which is a contractor for the National Institutes of Health [NIH], the federal agency that funds most of the animal research in this country. Subsequently the NIH conducted an investigation into conditions at the lab and concluded that the use of isolettes is justified to prevent the spread of disease among infected animals. For members of True Friends and other animal-rights groups, however, such a scientific justification is irrelevant to what they see as a moral wrong; these activists remain frustrated over conditions at the laboratory. This conflict between the NIH and animal-rights groups mirrors the tension between animal researchers and animal-rights advocates generally. The researchers' position is that their use of animals is necessary to advance human health care and that liberation actions waste precious resources and impede the progress of science and medicine. The animal-rights advocates' position is that animal research is an ethical travesty that justifies extraordinary, and even illegal, measures.

The Sema action is part of a series that numbers some six dozen to date and that began, in 1979, with a raid on the New York University Medical Center, in which members of a group known as the Animal Liberation Front (ALF) took a cat and two guinea pigs. The trend toward civil disobedience is growing. For example, last April members of animal-rights groups demonstrated at research institutions across the country (and in other countries, including Great Britain and Japan), sometimes blocking entrances to them by forming human chains. In the United States more than 130 activists were arrested, for offenses ranging from blocking a doorway and trespassing to burglary.

To judge by everything from talk-show programs to booming membership enrollment in animal-rights groups (U.S. membership in all groups is estimated at 10 million), the American public is increasingly receptive to the animal-rights position. Even some researchers admit that raids by groups like True Friends and the ALF have exposed egregious conditons in particular labs and have been the catalyst for needed reforms in the law. But many members of animal-rights groups feel that the recent reforms do not go nearly far enough. Through dramatic animal-liberation actions and similar tactics, they hope to force what they fear is a complacent public to confront a difficult philosophical issue: whether animals, who are known to have feelings and psychological lives, ought to be treated as mere instruments of science and other human endeavors. . . .

Animal-rights activists feel acute frustration over a number of issues, including hunting and trapping, the destruction of animals' natural habits, and the raising of animals for food. But for now the ALF considers animal research the most powerful symbol of human dominion over and exploitation of animals, and it devotes most of its energies to that issue. The public has been ambivalent, sometimes cheering the ALF on, at other times denouncing the group as "hooligans." However one chooses to characterize the ALF, it and other groups like it hold an uncompromising "rights view" of ethics toward animals. The rights view distinguishes the animal-protection movement of today from that of the past and is the source of the movement's radicalism.

"THEY ALL HAVE A RIGHT TO LIVE"

Early animal-protection advocates and groups . . . seldom talked about rights. They condemned cruelty—that is, acts that produce or reveal bad character. In early-nineteenth-century England campaigners against the popular sport of bull-baiting argued that it "fostered every bad and barbarous principle of our nature." Modern activists have abandoned the argument that cruelty is demeaning to human character ("virtue thought") in favor of the idea that the lives of animals have intrinsic value ("rights thought"). Rights thought doesn't necessarily preclude the consideration of virtue, but it mandates that the measure of virtue be the foreseeable consequences to others of one's acts.

"Michele" is thirty-five and works in a bank in the East. She has participated in many of the major ALF actions in the United States. One of the missions involved freeing rats, and she is scornful of the idea that rats aren't worth the effort. "These animals feel pain just like dogs, but abusing them doesn't arouse constituents' ire, so they don't get the same consideration. They all have a right to live their lives. Cuteness should not be a factor."

While most people would agree that animals should not be tortured, there is no consensus about animals' right to live (or, more precisely, their right not to be killed). Even if one can argue, as the British cleric Humphrey Primatt did in 1776, that "pain is pain, whether it be inflicted on man or on beast," it is more difficult to argue that the life of, say, a dog is qualitatively the same as that of a human being. To this, many animal-rights activists would say that every morally relevant characteristic that is lacking in all animals (rationality might be one, according to some ways of defining that term) is also lacking in some "marginal" human beings, such as infants, or the senile, or the severely retarded. Therefore, the activists argue, if marginal human beings have the right to live, it is arbitrary to hold that animals do not. Opponents of this point of view often focus on the differences between animals and "normal" human beings, asserting, for instance, that unlike most human adults, animals do not live by moral rules and therefore are not part of the human "moral community."

The credibility of the animal-rights viewpoint, however, need not stand or fall with the "marginal human beings" argument. Lives don't have to be qualitatively the same to be worthy of equal respect. One's perception that another life has value comes as much from an appreciation of its uniqueness as from the recognition that it has characteristics that are shared by one's own life. (Who would compare the life of a whale to that of a marginal human being?) One can imagine that the lives of various kinds of animals differ radically, even as a result of having dissimilar bodies and environments—that being an octopus feels different from being an orangutan or an oriole. The orangutan cannot be redescribed as the octopus minus, or plus, this or that mental characteristic; conceptually, nothing could be added to or taken from the octopus that would make it the equivalent of the oriole. Likewise, animals are not simply rudimentary hu-

man beings, God's false steps, made before He finally got it right with us.

Recognizing differences, however, puts one on tentative moral ground. It is easy to argue that likes ought to be treated alike. Differences bring problems: How do we think about things that are unlike? Against what do we measure and evaluate them? What combinations of likeness and difference lead to what sorts of moral consideration? Such problems may seem unmanageable, and yet in a human context we routinely face ones similar in kind if not quite in degree: our ethics must account for dissimilarities between men and women, citizens and aliens, the autonomous and the helpless, the fully developed and the merely potential, such as children or fetuses. We never solve these problems with finality, but we confront them. . . .

Both advocates and opponents of animal rights also invoke utilitarianism in support of their points of view. Utilitarianism holds that an act or practice is measured by adding up the good and the bad consequences—classically, pleasure and pain—and seeing which come out ahead. There are those who would exclude animals from moral consideration on the grounds that the benefits of exploiting them outweigh the harm. Ironically, though, it was utilitarianism, first formulated by Jeremy Bentham in the eighteenth century, that brought animals squarely into the realm of moral consideration. If an act or practice has good and bad consequences for animals, then these must be entered into the moral arithmetic. And the calculation must be genuinely disinterested. One may not baldly assert that one's own interests count for more. Animal researchers may truly believe that they are impartially weighing all interests when they conclude that human interests overwhelm those of animals. But a skeptical reader will seldom be persuaded that they are in fact doing so. . . .

Even true utilitarianism is incomplete, though, without taking account of rights. For example, suppose a small group of aboriginal tribespeople were captured and bred for experiments that would benefit millions of other people by, say, resulting in more crash-worthy cars. Would the use of such people be morally acceptable? Surely it would not, and that point illustrates an important function of rights thought: to put limits on what can be done to individuals, even for the good of the many. Rights thought dictates that we cannot kill one rights-holder to save another—or even more than one other—whether or not the life of the former is "different" from that of the latter.

Those who seek to justify the exploitation of animals often claim that it comes down to a choice: kill an animal or allow a human being to die. But this claim is misleading, because a choice so posed has already been made. The very act of considering the taking of life X to save life Y reduces X to the status of a mere instrument. Consider the problem in a purely human context. Imagine that if Joe doesn't get a new kidney he will die. Sam, the only known potential donor with a properly matching kidney, himself has only one kidney and has not consented to give it—and his life—up for Joe. Is there really a choice? If the only way to save Joe is to kill Sam, then we would be unable to do so—and no one would say that we chose Sam over Joe. Such a choice would never even be contemplated.

In another kind of situation there *is* a choice. Imagine that Joe and Sam both need a kidney to survive, but we have only one in our kidney bank. It may be that we should give the kidney to Joe, a member of our community, rather than to Sam, who lives in some distant country (though this is far from clear—maybe flipping a coin would be more fair). Sam (or the loser of the coin flip) could not complain that his rights had been violated, because moral claims to some resource—positive claims—must always be dependent on the availability of that resource. But the right not to be treated as if one were a mere resource or instrument—negative, defensive claims—is most fundamentally what it means to say that one has rights. And this is what members of the ALF have in mind when they declare that animals, like human beings, have rights.

Where, one might wonder, should the line be drawn? Must we treat dragonflies the same as dolphins? Surely not. Distinctions must be made, though to judge definitively which animals must be ruled out as holders of rights may be impossible even in principle. In legal or moral discourse we are virtually never able to draw clear lines. This does not mean that drawing a line anywhere, arbitrarily, is as good as drawing one anywhere else.

The line-drawing metaphor, though, implies classifying entities in a binary way: as either above the line, and so entitled to moral consideration, or not. Binary thinking misses nuances of our moral intuition. Entities without rights may still deserve moral consideration on other grounds: one may think that a dragonfly doesn't quite qualify for rights yet believe that it would be wrong to crush one without good reason. And not all entities with rights need be treated in precisely the same way. This is apparent when one compares animals over whom we have assumed custody with wild animals. The former, I think, have rights to our affirmative aid, while the latter have such rights only in certain circumstances. Similar distinctions can be made among human beings, and also between human beings and particular animals. For example, I recently spent $1,000 on medical care for my dog, and I think he had a right to that care, but I have never given such an amount to a needy person on the street. Rights thought, then, implies neither that moral consideration ought to be extended only to the holders of rights nor that all rights-holders must be treated with a rigid equality. It implies only that rights-holders should never be treated as if they, or their kind, didn't matter.

ANIMALS, REFRIGERATORS, AND CAN OPENERS

The question of man's relationship with animals goes back at least to Aristotle, who granted that animals have certain senses—hunger, thirst, a sense of touch—but who held that they lack rationality and therefore as "the lower sort [they] are by nature slaves, and . . . should be under the rule of a master." Seven centuries later Saint Augustine added the authority of the Church, arguing that "Christ himself [teaches] that to refrain from the killing of animals . . . is the height of superstition, for there are no common rights between us and the beasts. . . ." Early in the seventeenth century René Descartes argued that, lacking language, animals cannot have thoughts or souls and thus are machines.

One may be inclined to dismiss such beliefs as archaic oddities, but even today some people act as if animals were unfeeling things. I worked in a research lab for several summers during college, and I remember that it was a natural tendency to lose all empathy with one's animal subjects. My supervisor seemed actually to delight in swinging rats around by their tails and flinging them against a concrete wall as a way of stunning the animals before killing them. Rats and rabbits, to those who injected, weighed, and dissected them, were little different from cultures in a petri dish: they were just things to manipulate and observe. Feelings of what may have been moral revulsion were taken for squeamishness, and for most of my lab mates those feelings subsided with time.

The first animal-welfare law in the United States, passed in New York State in 1828, emphasized the protection of animals useful in agriculture. It also promoted human virtue with a ban on "maliciously and cruelly" beating or torturing horses, sheep, or cattle. Today courts still tend to focus on human character, ruling against human beings only for perpetrating the most shocking and senseless abuse of animals. . . .

Most states leave the regulation of medical research to Washington. In 1966 Congress passed the Laboratory Animal Welfare Act, whose stated purpose was not only to provide humane care for animals but also to protect the owners of dogs and cats from theft by proscribing the use of stolen animals. (Note the vocabulary of property law; animals have long been legally classified as property.) Congress then passed the Animal Welfare Act [AWA] of 1970, which expanded the provisions of the 1966 act to include more species of animals and to regulate more people who handle animals. The AWA was further amended in 1976 and in 1985.

The current version of the AWA mandates that research institutions meet certain minimum requirements for the handling and the housing of animals, and requires the "appropriate" use of pain-killers. But the act does not regulate research or experimentation itself, and allows researchers to withhold anesthetics or tranquilizers "when scientifically necessary." Further, while the act purports to regulate dealers who buy animals at auctions and other markets to sell to laboratories, it does little to protect those animals. . . .

The 1985 amendments to the AWA were an attempt to improve the treatment of animals in laboratories, to improve enforcement, to encourage the consideration of alternative research methods that use fewer or no animals, and to minimize duplication in experiments. One notable change is that for the first time, research institutions using primates must keep them in environments conducive to their psychological well-being; however, some animal-rights activists have expressed skepticism, since the social and psychological needs of primates are complex, and the primary concern of researchers is not the interests of their animal subjects. Last September [1988] a symposium on the psychological well-being of captive primates was held at Harvard University. Some participants contended that we lack data on the needs of the thirty to forty species of primates now used in laboratories. Others suggested that the benefits of companionship and social life are obvious.

The U.S. Department of Agriculture is responsible for promulgating regulations under the AWA and enforcing the law. Under current USDA regulations the cages of primates need only have floor space equal to three times the area occupied by the animal "when standing on four feet"—in the words of the USDA, which has apparently forgotten that primates have hands. The 1985 amendments required the USDA to publish final revised regulations, including regulations on the well-being of primates, by December of 1986. At this writing the department has yet to comply, and some activists charge that the NIH and the Office of Management and Budget have delayed the publication of the new regulations and attempted to undermine them.

One may believe that virtue thought—which underlies current law—and rights thought should protect animals equally. After all, wouldn't a virtuous person or society respect the interests of animals? But virtue thought allows the law to disregard these interests, because virtue can be measured by at least two yardsticks: by the foreseeable effects of an act on the interests of an animal or by the social utility of the act. The latter standard was applied in a 1983 case in Maryland in which a researcher appealed his conviction for cruelty to animals after he had performed experiments that resulted in monkeys' mutilating their hands. Overturning the conviction, the Maryland Court of Appeals wrote that "there are certain normal human activities to which the infliction of pain to an animal is purely incidental"—thus the actor is not a sadist—and that the state legislature had intended for these activities to be exempt from the law protecting animals.

The law, of course, is not monolithic. Some judges have expressed great sympathy for animals. On the whole, though, the law doesn't recognize animal rights. Under the Uniform Commercial Code, for instance, animals—along with refrigerators and can openers—constitute "goods."

ALTERNATIVES TO
US-VERSUS-THEM

Estimates of the number of animals used each year in laboratories in the United States range from 17 million to 100 million: 200,000 dogs, 50,000 cats, 60,000 primates, 1.5 million guinea pigs, hamsters, and rabbits, 200,000 wild animals, thousands of farm animals and birds, and millions of rats and mice. The conditions in general—lack of exercise, isolation from other animals, lengthy confinement in tiny cages—are stressful. Many experiments are painful or produce fear, anxiety, or depression. For instance, in 1987 researchers at the Armed Forces Radiobiology Research Institute reported that nine monkeys were subjected to whole-body irradiation; as a result, within two hours six of the monkeys were vomiting and hypersalivating. In a proposed experiment at the University of Washington pregnant monkeys, kept in isolation, will be infected with the simian AIDS virus; their offspring, infected or not, will be separated from the mothers at birth.

Not all animals in laboratories, of course, are subjects of medical research. In the United States each year some 10 million animals are used in testing products and for other commercial purposes. For instance, the United States Surgical Corporation, in Norwalk, Connecticut, uses hundreds of dogs each year to train salesmen in the use of the company's surgical staple gun. In 1981 and 1982 a group called Friends of Animals brought two lawsuits against United States Surgical to halt these practices. The company successfully argued in court that Friends of Animals lacked "standing" to sue, since no member of the organization had been injured by the practice; after some further legal maneuvering by Friends of Animals both suits were dropped. Last November [1988] a New York City animal-rights advocate was arrested as she planted a bomb outside United States Surgical's headquarters.

In 1987, according to the USDA, 130,373 animals were subjected to pain or distress unrelieved by drugs for "the purpose of research or testing." This figure, which represents nearly seven percent of the 1,969,123 animals reported to the USDA that year as having been "used in experimentation," ignores members of species not protected by the AWA (cold-blooded animals, mice, rats, birds, and farm animals). Moreover, there is reason to believe that the USDA's figures are low. For example, according to the USDA, no primates were subjected to distress in the state of Maryland, the home of Sema, in any year from 1980 to 1987, the last year for which data are available.

Steps seemingly favorable to animals have been taken in recent years. In addition to the passage of the 1985 amendments to the AWA, the Public Health Service [PHS], which includes the NIH, has revised its "Policy on Humane Care and Use of Laboratory Animals," and new legislation has given legal force to much of this policy. Under the revised policy, institutions receiving NIH or other PHS funds for animal research must have an "institutional animal care and use committee" consisting of at least five members, including one nonscientist and one person not affiliated with the institution.

Many activists are pessimistic about these changes, however. They argue that the NIH has suspended funds at noncompliant research institutions only in response to political pressure, and assert that the suspensions are intended as a token gesture, to help the NIH regain lost credibility. They note that Sema, which continues to keep primates in isolation cages (as regulations permit), is an NIH contractor whose principal investigators are NIH employees. As to the makeup of the animal-care committees, animal-rights advocates say that researchers control who is appointed to them. In the words of one activist, "The brethren get to choose."

However one interprets these changes, much remains the same. For example, the AWA authorizes the USDA to confiscate animals from laboratories not in compliance with regulations, but only if the animal "is no longer required . . . to carry out the research, test or experiment"; the PHS policy mandates pain relief "unless the procedure is justified for scientific reasons." Fundamentally, the underlying attitude that animals may appropriately be used and discarded persists.

If the law is ever to reflect the idea that animals have rights, more-drastic steps—such as extending the protection of the Constitution to animals—must be taken. Constitutional protection for animals is not an outlandish proposition. The late U.S. Supreme Court Justice William O. Douglas wrote once, in a dissenting opinion, that the day should come when "all of the forms of life . . . will stand before the court—the pileated woodpecker as well as the coyote and bear, the lemmings as well as the trout in the streams."

Suppose, just suppose, that the AWA were replaced by an animal-rights act, which would prohibit the use by human beings of any animals to their detriment. What would be the effect on medical research, education, and product testing? Microorganisms; tissue, organ, and cell cultures; physical and chemical systems that mimic biological functions; computer programs and mathematical models that simulate biological interactions; epidemiologic data bases; and clinical studies have all been used to reduce the number of animals used in experiments, demonstrations, and tests. A 1988 study by the National Research Council, while finding that researchers lack the means to replace all animals in labs, did conclude that current and prospective alternative techniques could reduce the number of animals—particularly mammals—used in research.

Perhaps the report would have been more optimistic if scientists were as zealous about conducting research to find alternatives as they are about animal research. But we should not be misled by discussions of alternatives into thinking that the issue is merely empirical. It is broader than just whether subject A and procedure X can be replaced by surrogates B and Y. We could undergo a shift in world view: instead of imagining that we have a divine mandate to dominate and make use of everything else in the universe, we could have a sense of belonging to the world and of kinship with the other creatures in it. The us-versus-them thinking that weighs animal suffering against human gain could give way to an appreciation that "us" includes "them." That's an alternative too.

Some researchers may insist that scientists should not be constrained in their quest for knowledge, but this is a romantic notion of scientific freedom that never was and should not be. Science is always constrained, by economic and social priorities and by ethics. Sometimes, paradoxically, it is also freed by these constraints, because a barrier in one direction forces it to cut another path, in an area that might have remained unexplored.

Barriers against the exploitation of animals ought to be erected in the law, because law not only enforces morality but defines it. Until the law protects the interests of animals, the animal-rights movement will by definition be radical. And whether or not one approves of breaking the law to remedy its shortcomings, one can expect such activities to continue. "I believe that you should do for others as you would have done for you," one member of the ALF says. "If you were being used in painful experiments, you'd want someone to come to your rescue."

CHALLENGE QUESTIONS

Can Experiments Using Animals Be Justified?

1. Can you personally justify the use of animals in medical and psychological research? How and where would you draw the line on the use of animals in other types of research? Is the use of animals justifiable in cosmetics research? Why or why not?

2. Cole contends that even extremists in the animal rights movement do not reject the medical benefits resulting from animal research. Assuming you were against all instances of animal research, would you turn down medical procedures for yourself or your children because they were developed at the expense of animals? Would there be exceptions, such as vaccinations for your children or a life-threatening illness?

3. Cole makes the case that experimentation with animals has produced many important medical and psychological findings. Can you think of other benefits? How can this research be justified in light of the current controversy?

4. Zak asserts that animal research is an ethical travesty that justifies extraordinary and even illegal measures to prevent it. Do you think illegal methods are justified in protecting the rights of animals?

5. Zak claims that animals deserve to have their rights protected by the Constitution. Do you agree with this position? Why or why not? Should this extend to insects and nonanimal species as well? Where would you draw the line in the recognition of such rights?

UN PHOTO 153344/JANE SCHREIBMAN

PART 2

Biological Processes

The biological foundations of experience and behavior are a critical part of psychology. Here we debate issues that focus on the relationship between biology and behavior.

Is Our Behavior Primarily Determined by Biological Processes?

Is the "Disease" of Alcoholism a Myth?

Is Our State of Mind Responsible for Our State of Health?

ISSUE 4

Is Our Behavior Primarily Determined by Biological Processes?

YES: Richard Restak, from "Is Free Will a Fraud?" *Science Digest* (1983)

NO: Joseph F. Rychlak, from "Free Will: 'Doing Otherwise, All Circumstances Remaining the Same,' " *An Original Essay Written for This Volume*

ISSUE SUMMARY

YES: Forensic neurologist Richard Restak interprets physiological research as suggesting that free will is a delusion; therefore, biological processes control behaviors.

NO: Noted humanistic psychologist Joseph F. Rychlak contends that when the concepts of free will and determinism are fully understood, physiological research generally supports the existence of free will.

Most people will agree that it makes sense to think of ourselves as biological organisms. After all, there is a lot of commonsensical evidence to support the view that biology is important in determining our behavior. Alterations in biochemistry, with various drugs for example, affect mental and behavioral processes. And psychological functioning often seems to change with brain injury.

Most people, however, will *also* say that they have the freedom of will to make choices and decisions. They will argue, for example, that they are not *forced* to choose vanilla over chocolate ice cream or to decide upon one vacation destination over another. Although most people may consistently make one choice or decision over another, they will nevertheless assert that they *could* have done otherwise. Indeed, some will say that the very meaningfulness of their lives depends on their abilities to make their own choices, to act of their own accord, and to *not* be ruled by forces beyond their voluntary control.

There are psychologists and biologists who would argue that our behavior cannot be both biologically determined *and* freely chosen. Richard Restak, in arguing against free will, frames this issue by first describing the degree of free will exercised in "three seemingly unconnected scenarios." He argues that the degree of freedom depicted in these scenarios would "traditionally be explained on the basis of the extent of conscious awareness behind [one's] actions." However, he claims that much of the work of the mind is conducted "utterly outside of our awareness." "In fact, it is possible—just possible—that consciousness does not exist at all." He cites experimental evidence on the brain that suggests that an act of will "is nothing more than an intellectual face-saving measure." Instead of weighing the options, choosing one, and *then* acting on the choice, research indicates that "we have already acted at the moment when we are supposed to be weighing options." He admits that most conventional concepts of free will do not have to be "scrapped," but they do "have to be modified."

Joseph F. Rychlak asserts the importance and possibility of free will. He laments the lack of a clear definition for free will, and he challenges several "misleading ideas about free will." These misleading ideas include: free will is escape from constraints on behavior; free will only "occurs through conscious deliberation"; and free will is "only an aspect of behavior *before* it takes place." He then offers his own definition of the phenomenon and illustrates the implications of free will and determinism in a dating situation. Rychlak contends that "natural laws themselves are not set in stone." One does not have to assume that a billiard-ball organization of events is the *only* logical point of view of the biological data. He goes on to cite several leading brain researchers as supportive of this free will view, including Penfield, Sperry, and Libet. Interestingly, this last researcher was also cited by Restak as supporting *his* position.

POINT	COUNTERPOINT
• The degree of freedom is the extent of consciousness.	• Free will does not require consciousness.
• Physiological research suggests that free will is a delusion.	• Physiological research is quite consistent with free will.
• Free will means that options are weighed before acting upon them.	• Free will does not have to go before behavior.
• Brain research shows that many actions may not follow from choices.	• The research data can be interpreted in ways other than billiard-ball determinism.
• Experiments on brain surgery question conventional notions of conscious awareness.	• A famous neurosurgeon concluded that the mind was not the brain.
• Persons receive nonconscious stimulations to act from brain mechanisms.	• This may be so, but research indicates that these persons can control whether the act occurs.

YES

Richard Restak

IS FREE WILL A FRAUD?

• You buy a lottery ticket on a Monday, place it in a drawer and promptly forget about it. That Friday you find that the ticket has won you $500. Your friends phone to offer congratulations.

• On the tennis court you go after a ball that is unplayable by your usual standards. To everyone's surprise—notably your own—you fire back a brilliant return.

• You are a judge at a murder trial. You are familiar with every detail of the case. When the jury returns a verdict of guilty, you review the evidence one last time and sentence the prisoner to death.

Three seemingly unconnected scenarios; three seemingly unconnected outcomes. But in each case, there is a parallel: An act of free will was exercised—a choice was made, a measure taken.

There, however, the similarity ends. For the three scenarios differ—and differ dramatically—in the degree of volition involved.

In the first instance, you merely purchased a ticket and did nothing more; everything that followed happened according to the rules of chance alone.

In the second case, you probably couldn't duplicate your brilliant return no matter how hard you tried. The shot *was* volition, in a way. But since you don't know how you did what you did, how can you take credit for it?

In the third scenario, the matter of a freely chosen decision seems more clear-cut. After listening to all of the evidence and taking the jury's verdict into account, you deliberately decided to impose the maximum sentence. But how do you know that this reasoned and conscious act wasn't just as automatic as winning the lottery or executing your impossible tennis shot?

The degree of freedom that exists in these situations would traditionally be explained on the basis of the extent of conscious awareness behind your actions. Beyond buying your ticket, the lottery situation doesn't involve any conscious awareness at all. Similarly, on the tennis court, there is precious little time to weigh options. You can only react instantaneously, and, on the basis of your previous training and skill, you may or may not be able to manage the shot.

But when we come to the courtroom situation, most people would accept this as a conscious, carefully deliberated decision—clearly an example of free will.

Fine. So where in the brain does this will reside? Which lobes, which cortices, which hemispheres are involved when we make a "deliberate" or "conscious" choice?

Most believe that the portions of the brain responsible for conscious awareness and will are the cerebral hemispheres. These are the regions that are specialized for reading, writing, language and all those activities that distinguish us from our primate cousins. But things are not quite that simple. The cerebral hemispheres in fact *don't* seem to govern the state of conscious awareness. Indeed, large portions of both hemispheres can be damaged by stroke or disease or even surgically removed and still the individual remains conscious, aware and capable of acting volitionally. It is more likely that the cerebral hemispheres *enhance* rather than *create* conscious awareness.

Wrote Bertrand Russell, "Suppose you are out walking on a wet day, and you see a puddle and avoid it. You are not likely to say to yourself: 'There is a puddle. It would be advisable not to step into it.' But if somebody said, 'Why did you suddenly step aside?' you would answer 'Because I didn't wish to step into that puddle.' You know retrospectively that you had a visual perception... and you express this knowledge in words. But what would you have known, and in what sense, if your attention had not been called to the matter by the questioner?"

Apparently, the work of the mind is often conducted quite outside our awareness. The unconscious hums along efficiently and incessantly, becoming apparent to us only when we deliberately choose to examine its operation.

Consciousness, by contrast, is a somewhat more sophisticated state of mind—a special form of awareness that is tied up with our ability to concretize thoughts, pictures and words. Without such a talent for symbolizing, there can be awareness, but not consciousness. This is the principal reason why few of us are able to remember many experiences from before the second or third year of life. This common amnesia probably has nothing to do with sexual repression or other Freudian notions. Rather, it is because the immaturity of our symbol formation and language capabilities at that time left us no bridge between the self we are now and the self we were then.

OUTSIDE OUR AWARENESS

But even well beyond childhood, it seems that much of the activity that churns ceaselessly through our minds does so utterly outside of our awareness. Though we may be loath to admit it, the mind appears to operate perfectly well without our use of conscious coaching or intervention.

Though descriptions such as this make it tempting to conclude that consciousness operates as a sort of on-off intellectual mechanism, it might be a mistake to regard it as such. In fact, it is possible—just possible—that consciousness does not exist at all. This most vaunted of human traits could be an illusion.

Experiments conducted during brain surgery lend support to this arresting theory. Since the human brain isn't capable of registering pain on direct stimulation or manipulation, patients are often operated on while they are fully awake. This provides the neurosurgeon with the opportunity to check on his patient's progress simply by leaning over the operating table and asking, "How are you doing?" It also makes possible a number of experiments that require the patient's conscious cooperation and willing participation.

In 1969, Benjamin Libet, a neurophysiologist at Mount Zion Hospital in San Francisco, reported on a series of such operating room studies he carried out in cooperation with neurosurgeon Bertram Feinstein. In one notable experiment, Libet and Feinstein measured the time it took for a touch stimulus on the patient's skin to reach the brain as an electrical signal. The patient was also requested to signal the arrival of the stimulus by pushing a button. Libet and Feinstein found that the first detectable electrical signal on the brain's surface occurred in 10 milliseconds. The patient's response — the button pushing — took place in one-tenth of a second. But strangely, the patient didn't report being consciously aware of the stimulus and response for close to half a second. Remarkably, the data indicated that the patient's conscious actions were somehow referred back in time so that they helped create the comforting delusion that the stimulus *preceded* action instead of the other way around.

The experiment suggests that, at least in some cases, an act of will is nothing more than an intellectual face-saving measure, designed to cover up the fact that we have already acted at the moment when we are supposed to be weighing options and making choices. Free will may thus be nothing more than a sort of ex post facto delusion.

The Libet experiments are by no means the only ones that have found evidence supporting this conclusion. One later study discovered that a full 1.5 seconds before we decide to engage in a simple act like lifting a finger, the brain has already begun generating waves and signals preparing for the event.

Compelling though experiments of this kind may be, one of the criticisms leveled at them is that they generally deal with matters both artificial and trivial. Who cares about pushing a button or raising a finger to please an experimenter? What has this to do with flesh and blood issues? The critics have a point. When it comes to matters that really matter—choosing a job, buying a home—we do spend whatever time is necessary to reach a conclusion that is both reasonable and sensible. But there are a number of reasons to believe that even complex and significant decisions may be directed by something other than cool deliberation.

In 1825, a French neurologist named Itard encountered a noblewoman, the Marquise of Dampierre, who was living as a recluse because of a series of peculiar and bizarre symptoms. Though she was well educated and traveled in the most refined circles, the Marquise was given on occasion to barking like a dog or shouting obscenities, behavior she claimed she was unable to control.

Fifty years later, another Frenchman, Georges Gilles de la Tourette, described nine more cases of individuals who demonstrated peculiar ticlike movements, grunting or barking noises and the irresistible impulse to shout obscenities. What made these people so fascinating to Tourette and other neurologists who have followed him was the patients' mental state. Tourette wrote:

"It is perfectly regular and normal: The subjects are reasonable, in no way do their acts resemble those of madmen, they are totally aware of their state, most are very intelligent. In all our patients, the general sensitivity was absolutely normal. . . . As for the physical, moral and mental state of the patient . . . it is excellent in all respects except, of course, for the disadvantages which such an abnormal state can create."

Joseph Bliss, a 64-year-old Tourette's patient who has battled the disorder his entire life, helps illuminate this paradox: "Contrary to the statements of patients with TS [Tourette's syndrome] and many other observers, the movement or sound is not the sole symptom.

RELENTLESS URGE

"Each movement is preceded by certain preliminary sensory signals and is, in turn, followed by sensory impressions at the end of the action. Each movement is the result of a voluntary capitulation to a demanding and relentless urge, accompanied by an extraordinarily subtle sensation that provokes and fuels the urge. Successively sharper movements build up to a climax, a climax that never comes.

"The TS movements are intentional bodily movements. The intention is to relieve a sensation, as surely as the movement to scratch an itch is to relieve the itch. If the itch was so subtle and fast that it escaped detection, would that make the act any less voluntary?"

Famous figures who are thought to have suffered from TS include Dr. Johnson, the eighteenth-century literary lion, and the Prince of Condé, who was one of Louis XIV's greatest generals.

One way of explaining the Tourette's phenomenon and other disorders might be to postulate that the brain always operates according to the purpose or goal that occupies the overall organism at any given moment. Generally, we walk, talk, sing, run, eat, sleep and so forth for very specific reasons. But sometimes such ordinarily

goal-oriented conduct can become disconnected by disease; suddenly, the victim is engaging in seemingly deliberate behavior with no discernible objective. Injury to a brain area known as the subthalamic nucleus, for example, can cause a victim to begin flailing his limbs suddenly and inexplicably, causing episodes that look quite intentional, but are in fact quite purposeless.

What emerges from most ongoing research into such phenomena is the notion that while most conventional concepts of free will and autonomy do not have to be scrapped, they do indeed have to be modified. Yes, we do chart our own intellectual and emotional course, but maybe not as independently as we think; yes, we are free to make complex choices and detailed decisions, but maybe not as often as we'd like.

The brain is a powerful organ that deals with getting a job done in any number of ways. If I pick up my pen, I can do it with the right hand or the left hand or I can lean over and pick it up with my teeth. Each of the different methods involves different muscles organized in different ways. While I can select the way I will pick up the pen, the mechanisms of exactly how the act will be performed must lie forever outside my conscious awareness. I can't "will" the particular configuration of muscle contractions that comes into play when I write my name. I can decide to write it, but the act will use its own inscrutable methods.

Brain research thus offers little hope of our achieving the Greek dictum "Know thyself." Rather, its emphasis is more in line with the Kierkegaardian doctrine of self-creation, "Choose thyself." Pick a goal, select an objective and then let your brain get the job done.

There is not a center in the human brain involved in the exercise of will any more than there is a center in the brain of the swan responsible for the beauty and complexity of its flight. Rather, the brains of all creatures are probably organized along the lines of multiple centers and various levels. If scientists insist on concluding otherwise, their efforts to understand the mind through the study of the brain will be forever frustrated. The first step toward solving the puzzle may be to realize that the distinctions between freedom of will and unthinking reflex are far more tentative than we've believed.

NO
Joseph F. Rychlak

FREE WILL: "DOING OTHERWISE, ALL CIRCUMSTANCES REMAINING THE SAME"

It would be hard to find a concept that has more confusion surrounding it than the concept of free will. This is in one sense curious, because almost everyone who takes the time to think about his or her behavior will admit that there is a sense of "freedom to choose" in many if not most of the things that we do. Yet, we are told by leading scientists that free will is an illusion (Skinner, 1971) or even a fraud (Restak, 1983). How can this be? What are we to believe?

Before we can answer such questions we have to get clearly in mind what is meant by the phrase "free will." This is a phrase used popularly rather than technically, so few people bother to clarify its precise meaning. It is not uncommon for a writer to use this phrase without defining it, as if we all understood what it meant. It pops into writings on behavioral determinism, the nature of mind, brain functioning, and the manipulations employed in doing a psychological experiment. In each of these contexts the precise meaning of the phrase is likely to be different. This is especially troublesome when the person using the phrase is denying that a freely-willed course of behavior can take place.

For example, a critic might say that if we believe in free will it means that we think people can escape constraints on their behavior, such as their physical limits, or the realities of their existence. People obviously cannot will to make their fingers bend backwards if they are not double-jointed to begin with. People cannot will to leap over tall buildings in a single bound. People cannot even will to be more intelligent, beautiful, or wealthy than they actually are, although they can hope to improve their status on each of the dimensions in due time.

Another misleading idea about free will is that it supposedly occurs through conscious deliberation, as if we first take everything possible into consideration, weigh alternatives carefully, and arrive at a logically precise reason on the basis of which to behave. Phrased this way, we would all have to admit that we certainly are lacking of free will because much of our behavior remains a mystery to us, and we usually advance in life in at least a partial state of confusion and wonderment. But free will does not depend on one's level of enlightenment and personal understanding.

Another erroneous belief is that free will is only an aspect of behavior *before* it takes place. Critics find it pointless to talk about freely-willed behaviors *after* a course of events has been enacted. Yet we all have experienced regret at having missed some past opportunity, or we harbor resentment over some past frustration. Our entire evening is ruined if we don't get really good seats at a concert, or we wonder and worry over the fact that our friend said something "strange" the last time we met. We tend to be "Monday morning quarterbacks" concerning the play of our favorite football team, and we would love to have known what we know today in our earlier lives. Wow! The opportunities we missed! Though such retrospective concerns and wishes may seem to be a fatefully unalterable outcome of our already "lived lives," the truth is that our concern about how things might have been different in the past is a reflection of the ongoing functioning of our free will.

Why do I say this? Because the central idea in free-willist theories is that an action carried on by a person is free if and only if that person "could have done otherwise, *all circumstances remaining the same*" (O'Connor, 1971, p. 82; see also Searle, 1984, p. 95 for the same definition). And about the only time this sort of concern arises is *after* a course of behavior is carried out.

We wonder, "Did I really have a choice in what happened?" or "Why did that bad thing have to happen to me?" or "If I could only live that incident over again, all circumstances remaining the same, I would surely handle it differently."

Our first problem is to clarify what "all circumstances remaining the same" means. As we discuss this meaning let us now think of Marcia, talking with Juan on the telephone, trying to decide whether or not to accept his invitation to go out on a date. She thinks over his looks, his general manner, his intelligence, possibly even his economic status as she ponders what to do. These qualities are among the circumstances she takes into consideration in making the decision "Will I go out with him or not?"

According to those who believe that there is no free will, Marcia's decision will be made based upon the workings of her brain physiology, in combination with past environmental shapings that have conditioned her mental mechanism to "work" or "function" the way it does today. Though she may appear to be deciding something, the outcome is a foregone conclusion. All the factors affecting her "decision" had already been in place well before Marcia appeared to be exercising free will.

In this view, the idea of "all circumstances remaining the same" involves these purely mechanical factors of her past life. As she ponders, Marcia may *appear* to be deciding something. However, all that is happening is a physical process taking time to carry its actions out to what appears to be a conclusion but is simply an ending. There is no "self" or "decider" initiating the direction of this process, or countering it to redirect its course.

The *free-will theorist* would suggest that in framing the list of characteristics for the sake of which she is evaluating Juan as a potential romantic involvement,

Marcia is actually an *agent* rather than a mechanism. "Agency" means that she, as a person, makes a difference in the outcome of the deliberation—which is not an iron-clad certainty by any means. Given the list of Juan's characteristics that she is using to contemplate her decision, Marcia is believed to be capable of behaving *either* way—to go out with Juan or to politely deny his request.

To the scientist who routinely thinks of determinism as *only* a physical action, the kind of thing that takes place when one billiard ball causes a second ball to roll by bumping into it, this ability claimed for Marcia to act or not to act seems to be a strike against (physical) nature. Physical acts occur lawfully, and they never occur in the sense of either "this way or that way." A leaf falling from a tree has no options as to the direction it will take in the descent. So, the claim would be made by this type of scientist that Marcia's final decision was *not* open to a true selection. She did what she did and that was all she could do. Juan is in the same situation. He called Marcia for the date because his behavior too was determined by natural laws influencing his behavior without the possibility of really deciding "this way or that way" in light of such laws.

What the free-willist realizes is that the natural laws themselves are not set in stone. One can look at the laws of nature from more than one logical point of view. For example, it is possible to view our universe as organized in either an earth-centered (geocentric, Ptolemaic) manner or a sun-centered (heliocentric, Copernican) manner. Science has established that the latter, sun-centered arrangement is the correct one, but for several centuries the former view was espoused by scientists. Even today, if we were willing

to accept some corrections in our mathematical tracings of the heavens, we *could* arrange our understanding of the universe in a geocentric manner. We could even predict nature's lawful events with precision, although we would have to make some adjustments in our calculations of planetary motion.

This teaches us that to speak of natural laws is not to settle the issue of determinism as simply that of billiard-ball bumpings of atoms, or whatever, moving events along. We must add in the determinism of the logically reasoning scientist who always takes a position on such billiard-ball regularities and in the process frames an assumption enabling us to understand such physical events. It was Einstein who taught us most dramatically that a logical rearrangement of our view of nature is possible by *opposing* our common sense understanding of natural processes to think about them in another way. There is more than one kind of determinism influencing a scientist's considerations in the understanding of nature.

So, how is Marcia framing her considerations? This is where we might expect to find free will in operation if we believe that she has personally chosen to frame Juan's potentials in light of certain characteristics, emphasizing some more than others, much in the way that our scientist chooses to construct a view of physical reality. The free-willist must believe that Marcia can actually judge these attributes in a like-dislike, good-bad, or yes-no fashion. That is, if Marcia's decisions were like a billiard ball, her brain would search out and find earlier shapings of her behavior stored in her memory. These recorded impulses would then be sent forward to her vocal apparatus, and so on. That is to say, Marcia would act in a *unidirectional* manner. She, as the billiard ball that was bumped, would roll in the direction her automatic brain processes would direct her. There are scientists who think this is exactly how our brains work (e.g., Bindra, 1976; Konorski, 1967; Restak, 1983). Cognition or thought is identical with brain activity in this view. Determinism is billiard-ball determinism, and no more.

On the other hand, the free-willist looks at Marcia as a person with alternative viewpoints from which to choose, just as the scientist chooses from among alternative ways of viewing lawfully flowing natural events from "this" or "that" point of view. But how is it feasible for Marcia to think either this way or that way, possibly countering what her past life has shaped her to think? That is, maybe Marcia will decide to go out with Juan for the very reason that she has always refused young men like him in the past. She might just act on a whim— "to see what the other side of the street looks like."

Well, to believe that she could act this way we must have some idea of an oppositional logic taking place in Marcia's thoughts, enabling a *bidirectionality* to arise within which a choice can be made. Usually, when we think of "logic" we think of a course of reasoning which is based on solitary grounds, which leads unidirectionally to one, and only one, true conclusion or decision. But there has been a form of logic evident in human reason for centuries, called by Aristotle (1952, p. 143) *dialectical* logical reasoning, that enables us to understand how it would be possible for all circumstances to remain the same in Marcia's deliberations and yet she could influence the course that events actually took. She can act this way because her logical (rule-following) reasoning is framed by oppositional meanings, forcing her to always take a position "this way" or "that way" on whatever is confronting her in life.

As agents, human beings cannot always consciously verbalize what they frame as their grounding assumptions concerning each personal "real" experience. If we were to ask Marcia how she made her decision, which probably took place in a matter of seconds, she may be unable to tell us much about it. In fact, she might not even acknowledge or admit to some of the grounds she used to select Juan or reject Juan. These could be characteristics regarding Juan's—and Marcia's—level of morality. We call these unadmitted grounds "unconscious." Free will is not dependent upon consciousness. People can be described as choosing and behaving intentionally even though they do not admit these choices and intentions to themselves "consciously."

People seem capable of contemplating dualities and contradictions in life, which suggests that the human cognitive outlook is more that of "taking a position" on what is occurring than it is of "responding to" what is taking place. When children are taught the Ten Commandments, they are not simply learning ten proper ways to behave. They are, of necessity, being taught ten sins as well. Their task is to take a position on the "good" side of the moral ledger, not on the "bad" side. Marcia is taking a position on Juan, given the characteristics that she has framed to understand him. Her dialectical intelligence might even confuse her at times, because some of his characteristics she likes, others she dislikes. Marcia cannot keep her likes and dislikes about herself out of the picture either. How satisfied has she been with her life recently? Maybe everything looks "great" in her life—too great! Maybe it is too exciting and she should now think about a more settled romantic life. Or, maybe things have been too settled and even dull.

The upshot is that Marcia can behave in a way opposite to her typical pattern. Marcia is still "being determined," but this determination is based on a logical process rather than a billiard-ball mechanism. In this sense, we might think of *free will* as personally influencing the grounds (reasons, assumptions, etc.) for the sake of which we will be determined.

But how well does this free-will explanation jibe with the kinds of evidence that the billiard-ball determinists rely on? This invariably comes down to brain researchers of one sort or another. Well, oddly enough, the drift of brain research is quite consistent with a view of the person as an agent (Gazzaniga, 1985; Granit, 1977; Penfield, 1975; Popper & Eccles, 1977; Sperry, 1985). I will take up two of the more interesting findings in brain research that I believe reflect dialectical or oppositional reasoning. They demonstrate that people are not simply being manipulated by physical brain mechanisms.

Wilder Penfield (1975), a famous neurosurgeon and brain scientist, conducted experiments in which he electrically stimulated the exposed cortex of epileptic patients during operations for the removal of cortical tissue involved with the disorder (p. 12). The cortex is not sensitive to pain from such stimulation, so electrical needles can be inserted without discomfort to the patient. Patients can also remain conscious during the operation in which a local analgesic is administered and a bone flap is then cut through the skull. Penfield was able to talk to his patients even as he stimulated their brains into action. What he found was remarkable. When the parietal region of a male patient's brain was stimulated, he moved his hand; but he did *not* sense this as a natural act. In fact, he reached over with his other hand to hold his moving hand still because he had not intended to move it (Ibid., p. 77).

Patients often told Penfield that "they" did not move their hand, "he" moved it (with the electrical stimulation). It was obvious that though their brain was mechanically working to cause actions, such patients were fully cognizant that they had not willed these actions into being. And, they could *oppose* themselves to these mechanical actions. When Penfield stimulated his patients' speech centers and they vocalized something, they quickly informed him that "they" were not talking, but merely having words pulled out by the electrical stimulation. In no instance did Penfield find it possible to stimulate the brain (frontal lobes, etc.) and get the patient to *believe* something, to take on an idea as if it were willfully his or her own. So compelling were his findings that Penfield concluded that the brain was *not* the mind, but that it was used by the mind much as a person directs the hardware of a computer through framing the software of a program (Ibid., p. 46).

There is evidence from another source that individuals can counter what their mechanical brain process is prompting them to do. I refer here to the interesting work of Benjamin Libet (1985) in which, through a highly creative research apparatus, he is able to relate cortical brain activity to a voluntary action (flexing a finger or moving a wrist) to see if there are any brain signals preceding the action. Such brain signals were indeed found. Libet called them "readiness potentials," because he found that roughly 400 ms. before a person spontaneously felt like flexing a finger, he or she had registered an electrophysiological brain signal of this type on Libet's apparatus. This sounds like the billiard ball determinism, as if the brain were (unconsciously) thinking for the person (consciously).

However, consistent with a view of oppositionality in human reasoning, Libet *also* found that his subjects were "free *not* to act out any given urge or initial decision to act; and each subject indeed reported frequent instances of such aborted intentions" (Ibid., p. 530). Libet concluded that subjects may spontaneously receive unconscious prompts to act from brain mechanisms, but that they always can select and control what will happen in their behavior "either by permitting or triggering the final motor outcome of the unconsciously initiated process *or by vetoing* the progression to actual motor activation" (Ibid., p. 529). This is highly similar to Penfield's findings and it supports my contention that oppositionality can be brought to bear in different circumstances, to throw the weight of the agent "this" way or "that" way, to follow a course of action underway or to negate it entirely—assuming that we are talking here about physical possibilities. We can never forget the matter of physical limitations discussed earlier.

Up to now there is no scientific basis on which to reject the idea that people can and do set the grounding beliefs, assumptions, or decisions for the sake of which their behavior will be determined. At least, they can do so in the sense of opposing what is being forced upon them by their biological equipment. The same can apply to pressure being exerted by other people, in a social context. The agent can behave in concurrence with such biological or social promptings, *but also in contradiction* to such promptings, redirecting events accordingly. This is not always a happy outcome, because people deny physical prompts as symptoms that can lead to their death if they are not treated by a physician. People can reject the social goodwill of others, leading to unhappiness for all concerned. But with free will comes the related issue of responsibility, something we would probably take more seriously today if we really believed that human beings were agents rather than mechanisms (see Rychlak, 1979).

We conclude, therefore, that Marcia *is* capable of free will, which means that she can make a choice based on how she arranges her grounding assumptions in thinking about Juan. She may not make the right choice, and on the evening of the date she may think "Why did I decide to go out with this 'jock'? He is a bore, and I knew better." Or, she may find her relationships with Juan very enjoyable and worthy of further cultivation. Whatever happens, Marcia is best understood as a behaving organism having capacities going beyond the billiard-ball determinations of a machine. Marcia is an organism who can influence through opposition and contrast the grounds for the sake of which she will be determined. When she arranges or modifies these grounds we speak of Marcia's "freedom" to behave and when she then carries out the course of her behavior determinately, we speak of "will." Free will is not an illusion or a fraud. It is simply the marvelous capacity that human beings have to behave differently, all circumstances remaining the same.

REFERENCES

Aristotle. (1952). *Topics.* In Vol. 8 of R. M. Hutchins (Ed.), *Great books of the western world.* Chicago: Encyclopedia Britannica.

Bindra, D. (1976). *A theory of intelligent behaviour.* London: John Wiley & Sons, Inc.

Gazzaniga, M. S. (1985). *The social brain: Discovering the networks of the mind.* New York: Basic Books, Inc.

Granit, R. (1977). The purposive brain. Cambridge, MA: The MIT Press.

Kagan, J. (1984). *The nature of the child.* New York: Basic Books, Inc.

Konorski, J. (1967). *Integrative activity of the brain.* Chicago: University of Chicago Press.

Libet, B. (1985). Unconscious cerebral initiative and the role of conscious will in voluntary action. *The Behavioral and Brain Sciences, 8,* 529–566.

O'Connor, D. J. (1971). *Free will.* Garden City, NY: Doubleday & Co.

Penfield, W. (1975). *The mystery of the mind.* Princeton, NJ: Princeton University Press.

Popper, K. R., & Eccles, J.C. (1977). *The self and its brain.* London: Springer-Verlag.

Restak, R. (1983). Is free will a fraud? *Science Digest,* October 1983, 82–84.

Rychlak, J. F. (1979). *Discovering free will and personal responsibility.* New York: Oxford University Press.

Rychlak, J. F. (1988). *The psychology of rigorous humanism* (2nd ed.). New York: New York University Press.

Searle, J. (1984). *Minds, brains and science.* Cambridge, MA: Harvard University Press.

Skinner, B. F. (1971). *Beyond freedom and dignity.* New York: Alfred A. Knopf.

Sperry, R. (1985). *Science and moral priority: Merging mind, brain, and human values.* New York: Praeger.

CHALLENGE QUESTIONS

Is Our Behavior Primarily Determined by Biological Processes?

1. Does the study of pathological or abnormal states (such as Restak's report of investigations of Tourette's syndrome) help in understanding normal behavior?

2. Restak and Rychlak cite different experimental investigations conducted by the same man, Benjamin Libet. Did this researcher intend for his research to be interpreted as it has? Find Libet's studies and describe the position he seems to have on the issue of free will and biological determinism.

3. If free will were a delusion, as Restak posits in the middle of his paper, what implications would this have for our system of laws and our codes of moral behavior?

4. Can free will be reconciled with science or scientific method?

ISSUE 5

Is the "Disease" of Alcoholism a Myth?

YES: Herbert Fingarette, from "Alcoholism: The Mythical Disease," *The Public Interest* (Spring 1988)

NO: William Madsen, from "Thin Thinking About Heavy Drinking," *The Public Interest* (Spring 1989)

ISSUE SUMMARY

YES: Professor of philosophy Herbert Fingarette proposes that the concept of alcoholism as a disease is a myth that has been generated and is currently sustained by those whose own economic interests are served by the myth.
NO: Professor of anthropology William Madsen alleges that Fingarette's assertions are based on unscientific research and misunderstanding and are harmful in the long run to alcoholics and to society.

Alcohol is one of many psychoactive (affecting the mind or behavior) drugs that influence consciousness, perceptions, and behavior through their effects on the central nervous system. In today's drug-ridden world, it continues to be among the most widely used and abused drugs. Alcohol is a central nervous system depressant; however, common initial short-term effects are loss of tension and inhibitions, which can lead to increased sociability. It is not surprising that alcohol abuse is common among high school and college students, since its use initially promises to help override some social shortcomings by helping individuals to relax in potentially stressful situations.

Increased usage may lead to psychological or physical dependence. Whereas psychological dependence is learned through the satisfaction of personal needs, physical dependence, or *addiction*, is more obviously physiological in nature. The generally accepted notion that the use of alcohol progresses through psychological to physical dependence is responsible for the "disease" concept of alcoholism. In recent years the idea of "disease" has been expanded to include many compulsive behaviors, such as gambling, child abuse, sex, shopping, and eating.

Herbert Fingarette asserts that there is a widely accepted myth that alcoholism involves physical dependence. This includes the belief that certain people have an allergy to alcohol, which means that once these people begin drinking, they start down a dangerous road that results in the need for ever-increasing doses of alcohol, cravings and pain when use is discontinued, and loss of control over drinking. This, he says, is the idea of disease that is promoted by the liquor industry to appeal to consumers who presumably are not allergic and by health professionals who stand to gain economically by treating the "disease."

Fingarette claims that there is no scientific foundation for this concept and that the studies supposedly providing evidence are seriously flawed. Pointing out that there are many biological phenomena *associated* with chronic heavy drinking, he indicates that many people confuse correlation and causation. Drinking behavior, he says, is more dependent upon personal beliefs, cultural styles, and specific situations than on physiological effects.

William Madsen questions Fingarette's understanding of medical issues and scientific literature. He maintains that the studies cited by Fingarette to support his claims are not scientifically valid, and he cites alternate studies to support his own claims that alcoholism is indeed a disease.

Madsen touches on the differences between medical, behavioral, and moral models of thinking about alcohol use and abuse, claiming that Fingarette is inappropriately using a moral model. He maintains that Fingarette's position is damaging and irresponsible.

POINT	COUNTERPOINT
• The probability of inheriting alcoholism is low.	• Scientific evidence indicates six inherited temperaments that predispose individuals to become alcoholics.
• Research shows that what alcoholics believe they are drinking affects their drinking behavior more than the actual presence of alcohol.	• Research on drinking behavior is artificial and based on research with rats.
• Studies show that alcoholics can control their drinking.	• Research shows that only 6% of treated alcoholics can ever return to normal drinking.
• The rate of improvement for alcoholics receiving treatment is no greater than for those not receiving treatment.	• Some treatment programs have recovery rates as high as 85%.

YES   Herbert Fingarette

ALCOHOLISM: THE MYTHICAL DISEASE

The idea that alcoholism is a disease is a myth, and a harmful myth at that. The phrase itself—"alcoholism is a disease"—is a slogan. It lacks definite medical meaning and therefore precludes one from taking any scientific attitude toward it, pro or con. But the slogan has political potency. And it is associated in the public consciousness with a number of beliefs about heavy drinking that do have meaning, and do have important consequences for the treatment of individuals and for social policy. These beliefs lack a scientific foundation; most have been decisively refuted by the scientific evidence.

This assertion obviously conflicts with the barrage of pronouncements in support of alcoholism's classification as a disease by health professionals and organizations such as the American Medical Association [AMA], by the explosively proliferating treatment programs, and by innumerable public-service organizations. So it may seem that a sweeping challenge to the disease concept can only be hyperbole, the sensationalist exaggeration of a few partial truths and a few minor doubts.

To the contrary: the public has been profoundly misled, and is still being actively misled. Credulous media articles have featured so many dramatic human-interest anecdotes by "recovering alcoholics," so many "scientific" pronouncements about medical opinion and new discoveries, that it is no wonder the lay public responds with trusting belief.

Yet this much is unambiguous and incontrovertible: the public has been kept unaware of a mass of scientific evidence accumulated over the past couple of decades, evidence familiar to researchers in the field, which radically challenges each major belief generally associated in the public mind with the phrase, "alcoholism is a disease." I refer not to isolated experiments or off-beat theories but to massive, accumulated, mainstream scientific work by leading authorities, published in recognized journals. If the barrage of "public service" announcements leaves the public wholly unaware of this contrary evidence, shouldn't this in itself raise grave questions about the credibility of those who assure the public that alcoholism has now been scientifically demonstrated to be a disease? . . .

From Herbert Fingarette, *Heavy Drinking: The Myth of Alcoholism as a Disease* (University of California Press, 1988, 1989), of which this article is a partial summary, omitting citations. Reprinted by permission of the author. This article first appeared in *The Public Interest*, no. 91 (Spring 1988).

Use of the word "disease" . . . shapes the values and attitudes of society. The selling of the disease concept of alcoholism has led courts, legislatures, and the populace generally to view damage caused by heavy drinkers as a product of "the disease and not the drinker." The public remains ambivalent about this, and the criminal law continues to resist excusing alcoholics for criminal acts. But the pressure is there, and, of more practical importance, the civil law has largely given in. Civil law now often mandates leniency or complete absolution for the alcoholic from the rules, regulations, and moral norms to which non-diseased persons are held legally or morally accountable. Such is the thrust of a current appeal to the U.S. Supreme Court by two veterans, who are claiming certain benefits in spite of their having failed to apply for them at any time during the legally specified ten-year period after discharge from the army. Their excuse: alcoholism, and the claim that their persistent heavy drinking was a disease entitling them to exemption from the regulations. The Court's decision could be a bellwether.

What seems compassion when done in the name of "disease" turns out, when the facts are confronted, to subvert the drinker's autonomy and will to change, and to exacerbate a serious social problem. This is because the excuses and benefits offered heavy drinkers work psychologically as incentives to continue drinking. The doctrine that the alcoholic is "helpless" delivers the message that he might as well drink, since he lacks the ability to refrain. As for the expensive treatments, they do no real good. Certainly our current disease-oriented policies have not reduced the scale of the problem; in fact, the number of chronic heavy drinkers reported keeps rising. (It is currently somewhere in the range of ten to twenty million, depending on the definitions one uses.)

In the remainder of this discussion I will set out the major beliefs associated with the disease concept of alcoholism, and then summarize the actual evidence on each issue. I will also sketch an alternative perspective on chronic heavy drinking that is warranted by the evidence we have today.

CONVENTIONAL WISDOM

Science, according to the conventional view, has established that there is a specific disease that is triggered by drinking alcoholic beverages. Not everyone is susceptible; most people are not. But (the argument continues) a significant minority of the population has a distinctive biological vulnerability, an "allergy" to alcohol. For these people, to start drinking is to start down a fatal road. The stages are well defined and develop in regular order, as with any disease, with the symptoms accumulating and becoming increasingly disabling and demoralizing. First comes what looks like normal social drinking, but then, insidiously and inevitably, come heavier and more frequent drinking, drunken bouts, secret drinking, morning drinking, and, after a while, "blackouts" of memory from the night before. It begins to take more and more liquor to get the same effect—physical "tolerance" develops—and any attempt to stop drinking brings on the unbearable and potentially life-threatening "withdrawal" symptoms. Eventually, the crucial symptom develops: "loss of control." At that point, whenever the person takes a drink the alcohol automatically triggers an inability to control the drinking, and drunken bouts become the rule. There follows an inevitable, deepening slavery to alcohol, which wrecks social life, brings ruin, and culminates in death. The only escape— according to this elaborate myth—is appropriate medical treatment for the disease.

The myth offers the false hope that as a result of recent "breakthroughs" in science we now basically understand what causes the disease—a genetic and neurophysiological defect. But fortunately, it is claimed, medical treatment is available, and generally produces excellent results. However, the argument continues, even after successful treatment the alcoholic can never drink again. The "allergy" is never cured; the disease is in remission, but the danger remains. The lifelong truth for the alcoholic is, as the saying goes, "one drink—one drunk." The possibility of a normal life depends on complete abstinence from alcohol. There are no "cured" alcoholics, only "recovering" ones.

That is the classical disease concept of alcoholism. As I have said, just about every statement in it is either known to be false or (at a minimum) lacks scientific foundation.

ORIGINS OF THE MYTH

. . . Alcoholics Anonymous [A.A.], founded in 1935, taught that alcohol was not the villain in and of itself, and that most people could drink safely. (In this way the great majority of drinkers and the beverage industry were mollified.) A minority of potential drinkers, however, were said to have a peculiar biological vulnerability; these unfortunates, it was held, are "allergic" to alcohol, so that their drinking activates the disease, which

then proceeds insidiously along the lines outlined earlier.

This contemporary version of the disease theory of alcoholism, along with subsequent minor variants of the theory, is often referred to now as the "classic" disease concept of alcoholism. Like the temperance doctrine, the new doctrine was not based on any scientific research or discovery. It was created by the two ex-alcoholics who founded A.A.: William Wilson, a New York stockbroker, and Robert Holbrook Smith, a physician from Akron, Ohio. Their ideas in turn were inspired by the Oxford religious movement, and by the ideas of another physician, William Silkworth. They attracted a small following, and a few sympathetic magazine articles helped the movement grow.

ALCOHOLISM AND SCIENCE

What A.A. still needed was something that would serve as a scientific authority for its tenets. After all, the point of speaking of a "disease" was to suggest science, medicine, and an objective malfunction of the body. The classic disease theory of alcoholism was given just such an apparent scientific confirmation in 1946. A respected scientist, E. M. Jellinek, published a lengthy scientific article, consisting of eighty-plus pages impressively filled with charts and figures. He carefully defined what he called the "phases of alcoholism," which went in a regular pattern, from apparently innocent social drinking ever downward to doom. The portrait, overall and in its detail, largely mirrored the A.A. portrait of the alcoholic. Jellinek's work and A.A. proselytizing generated an unfaltering momentum; the disease concept that they promulgated has never been publicly supplanted by the prosaic truth.

Jellinek's portrait of the "phases of alcoholism" was not an independent scientific confirmation of A.A. doctrine. For as Jellinek explicitly stated, his data derived entirely from a sampling of A.A. members, a small fraction of whom had answered and mailed back a questionnaire that had appeared in the A.A. newsletter. The questionnaire was prepared by A.A. members, not by Jellinek; Jellinek himself criticized it, finding it scientifically inadequate. In addition, many A.A. members did not even subscribe to the newsletter, and so had no opportunity to respond. Jellinek obtained only 158 questionnaires, but for various reasons could actually use just 98 of them. This was a grossly inadequate set of data, of course, but it was all Jellinek had to work with. . . .

By the 1970s there were powerful lobbying organizations in place at all levels of government. The National Council on Alcoholism (NCA), for example, which has propagated the disease concept of alcoholism, has been a major national umbrella group from the early days of the movement. Until 1982 the NCA was subsidized by the liquor industry, which had several representatives on its board. The alliance was a natural one: at the cost of conceding that a small segment of the population is allergic to alcohol and ought not to drink, the liquor industry gained a freer hand with which to appeal to the majority of people, who are ostensibly not allergic.

Health professionals further widened the net, and economic incentives came powerfully into play. Federal and local governments began to open their health budgets to providers of alcoholism treatment, and also to alcoholism researchers.

Insurance companies are increasingly required to do the same. Today, treatment aimed at getting alcoholics to stop drinking brings in over a billion dollars a year. Alcoholism researchers now rely on what is probably the second largest funding source after defense—government health funds. And by now there are hundreds of thousands of formerly heavy drinkers who feel an intense emotional commitment; they supply a large proportion of the staffs of treatment centers. . . .

BIOLOGICAL CAUSES?

What does it mean to say that alcoholism is a disease? In public discussions in the news media, it is usually taken to mean that alcoholism has a single biological cause. "I believe [alcoholics] have a genetic predisposition and a certain kind of biochemistry that dooms you to be an alcoholic if you use alcohol." This is a characteristic remark, with what in this domain is a familiar kind of specious authority. The statement was printed in an alcoholism bulletin issued under the aegis of a University of California Extension Division Alcoholism Program. It appears in an interview with Kevin Bellows, a lay activist heading an international organization fighting alcoholism.

Lay activists are not alone in pressing this theme. When I was on a network talk-show recently, the physician on the panel—a man high in government alcoholism advisory councils—devoted most of his time to running through a list of recent research discoveries about the biological peculiarities of alcoholics. His thesis was that alcoholism is unquestionably a disease, and he plainly implied that it has a biological cause. What the lay audience does not realize is that the newly discovered biological phenomena can rarely be regarded as *causes* of chronic heavy drinking; instead, they are merely *associated* with chronic heavy drinking, or with intoxication. Nevertheless, the audience is led to infer that they play a causal role; in fact, we know that there are *no* decisive physical causes of alcoholism.

Long-term heavy drinking is undoubtedly an important contributing cause of bodily ailments—including major organ, nerve, circulatory, and tissue disorders. The illness and mortality rates of heavy drinkers are far higher than those of the population generally. Chronic heavy drinking is rivaled only by habitual smoking as a major contributor to the nation's hospital and morgue populations. But all this is the *effect* of drinking; the drinking behavior itself is the cause. Stop the behavior and you stop its terrible physical effects.

Another abnormal physical condition associated with heavy drinking is the appearance of biological "markers." These metabolic and other physiological conditions—statistically abnormal but not necessarily ailments in and of themselves—may often be present among alcoholics. More significantly, some of them are present in persons who are not and have not been alcoholics, but who have been identified on independent grounds as being at higher-than-average risk of eventually becoming alcoholics. Such "markers" can serve as warning signs for those at higher risk. It has been hypothesized that some of these biological "markers" may play a causal role in bringing about alcoholic patterns of drinking. The question is: What kind and what degree of causality are at issue?

One much discussed metabolic "marker" is the difference in the way those who are independently identified as being at higher risk oxidize alcohol into acetaldehyde and in turn metabolize the acetaldehyde. The toxic effects of acetaldehyde in the brain have led to speculation that it might play a key causal role in inducing alcoholism. Analogous claims have been made about the higher level of morphine-like substances that alcoholics secrete when they metabolize alcohol. As it happens (so often in these matters), there are serious difficulties in measuring acetaldehyde accurately, and the reported results remain inadequately confirmed. But these confirmation problems are problems of technique, and not of fundamental importance.

The substantive point, generally obscured by the excitement of new discovery, is that even if the existence of any such metabolic processes were confirmed, they still would not cause alcoholic behavior, because the metabolism of alcohol takes place only when there is alcohol in the body. Therefore, these metabolic products cannot be present in alcoholics who have not been drinking for a period of time, and in whom the total metabolic process in question is not presently taking place. Yet by definition, these individuals return to drinking and do so recurrently, in spite of the intermittent periods of sobriety. The metabolic phenomena bear only on drinking that is done while in a state of intoxication; the key question about alcoholism, however, is why a sober person, with no significant toxic product remaining in the body, should resume drinking when it is known to have such harmful effects.

The story of biological discoveries concerning alcoholism is always the same: many unconfirmed results are unearthed, but no causal link to repetitive drinking is ever established. There is one exception, however: the recent discoveries in genetics. A study of these, and of how they have been reported to the public, is revealing.

ALCOHOLISM AND GENES

Several excellently designed genetic studies of alcoholism have recently come up with credible positive results; thus we have been hearing from activists, treatment-center staff members, and physicians that "alcoholism is a genetic disease." The reality—as revealed by the data—is very different from what this slogan suggests.

The course followed in these recent "decisive" studies has been simple: find children who were born of an alcoholic mother or father, who were put up for adoption very shortly after birth, and who thus spend little time with their biological parents. Then see whether this group of children shows a higher rate of alcoholism in later life than a comparable group of adoptees whose biological parents were not alcoholics. Controlling all other relevant conditions so that they are the same for both groups, one can infer that any eventual differences in the group rates of alcoholism is attributable to their heredity, the one respect in which they differ. In all these studies, the prevalence of alcoholism was significantly greater among the biological sons of alcoholics, especially the sons of alcoholic fathers. Doesn't this suggest that alcoholism is hereditary?

To answer this question, let us consider the first of these reports, a 1973 article by Donald Goodwin and his colleagues. They concluded that about 18 percent of the biological sons of an alcoholic parent themselves became alcoholics, whereas only 5 percent of the biological sons of non-alcoholic parents become alcoholics—a statistically significant ratio of almost four to one, which in all probability is ascribable to heredity. This is what we typically hear about in the media, with or without the precise numbers.

Now let's look at the same data from a different angle, and in a more meaningful context. As simple arithmetic tells us, if 18 percent of the sons of alcoholics do become alcoholics, then 82 percent— more than four out of five—do *not*. Thus, to generalize from the Goodwin data, we can say that the odds are very high— better than four to one—that the son born of an alcoholic parent will *not* become an alcoholic. Put differently, it is utterly false, and perniciously misleading, to tell people with a parental background of alcoholism that their heredity "dooms" them to become alcoholics, or even that their heredity makes it probable that they will become alcoholics. Quite the contrary. Their alcoholic heredity does make it more probable that they'll become alcoholics than if they had non-alcoholic parents, but the probability is still low. This is to say that life circumstances are far more important than genes in determining how many people in any group will become heavy drinkers.

There is yet another important implication: since 5 percent of the sons of non-alcoholic parents become alcoholics, and since there are far more non-alcoholic parents than alcoholic ones, that 5 percent ends up representing a far larger total number of alcoholic sons. This is consistent with what we know anyway— the great majority of alcoholics do not have alcoholic parents.

The most recent (and influential) adoptee genetic study, reported by Cloninger and his colleagues, concludes with these words: "The demonstration of the critical importance of sociocultural influences in most alcoholics suggests that major changes in social attitudes about drinking styles can change dramatically the prevalence of alcohol abuse regardless of genetic predisposition."

Given the possibly dramatic effect of social attitudes and beliefs, the media emphasis on genes as the cause of alcoholism has a pernicious, though unremarked, effect. As we have noted, only a minority of alcoholics have an alcoholic parent. Emphasis on heredity as the "cause" of alcoholism may give a false sense of assurance to the far greater number of people who are in fact in danger of becoming alcoholics, but who do not have an alcohlic parent. These potential alcoholics may feel free to drink heavily, believing themselves genetically immune to the "disease."

The Special Committee of the Royal College of Psychiatry put the matter in perspective by saying the following in its book-length statement on alcoholism: "It is common to find that some genetic contribution can be established for many aspects of human attributes or disorders (ranging from musical ability to duodenal ulcers), and drinking is unlikely to be the exception."

CAUSES OF ALCOHOLISM

There is a consensus among scientists that no single cause of alcoholism, biological or otherwise, has ever been scientifically established. There are many causal factors, and they vary from drinking pattern to drinking pattern, from drinker to drinker. We already know many of the predominant influences that evoke or shape patterns of drinking. We know that family environment plays a role, as does age. Ethnic and cultural values are also important: the Irish, Scandinavians, and Russians tend to be heavy drinkers; Jews do not. The French traditionally drank modest amounts at one sitting, but drank more regularly over the course of the day. Cultural norms have changed in France in recent decades and so have drinking styles.

We have interesting anthropological reports about the introduction of European styles of drinking into non-European tribal societies. Among the Chichicastenango Indians of Guatemala, for example, there are two different ways of drinking heavily. When drinking ceremonially, in the traditional way, men retain their dignity and fulfill their ceremonial duties even if they have drunk so much that they cannot walk unassisted. When they drink in the bars and taverns where secular and European values and culture hold sway, the men dance, weep, quarrel, and act promiscuously.

The immediate social setting and its cultural meaning are obviously important in our own society. The amount and style of drinking typically vary according to whether the drinker is in a bar, at a formal dinner party, a post-game party, or an employee get-together. It is known that situations of frustration or tension, and the desire for excitement, pleasure, or release from feelings of fatigue or social inhibitions, often lead people to drink. Much depends on what the individual has "learned" from the culture about the supposed effects of alcohol, and whether the person desires those particular effects at a particular moment.

But does any of this apply to alcoholics? The belief in a unique disease of alcoholism leads many to wonder whether the sorts of influences mentioned above can make much of a difference when it comes to the supposedly "overwhelming craving" of alcoholics. Once one realizes that there is no distinct group of "diseased" drinkers, however, one is less surprised to learn that no group of drinkers is immune to such influences or is vulnerable only to other influences.

DO ALCOHOLICS LACK CONTROL?

. . . [W]hen alcoholics in treatment in a hospital setting, for example, are told that they are not to drink, they typically follow the rule. In some studies they have been informed that alcoholic beverages are available, but that they should abstain. Having decided to cooperate, they voluntarily refrain from drinking. More significantly, it has been reported that the occasional few who cheated nevertheless did not drink to excess but voluntarily limited themselves to a drink or two in order to keep their rule violation from being detected. In short, when what they value is at stake, alcoholics control their drinking accordingly.

Alcoholics have been tested in situations in which they can perform light but boring work to "earn" liquor; their preference is to avoid the boring activity and forgo the additional drinking. When promised money if they drink only moderately, they drink moderately enough to earn the money. When threatened with denial of social privileges if they drink more than a certain amount, they drink moderately, as directed. The list of such experiments is extensive. The conclusions are easily confirmed by carefully observing one's own heavy-drinking acquaintances, provided one ignores the stereotype of "the alcoholic." . . .

A USEFUL LIE?

Even if the disease concept lacks a scientific foundation, mightn't it nevertheless be a useful social "white lie," since it causes alcoholics to enter treatment? This common—and plausible—argument suffers from two fatal flaws.

First, it disregards the effects of this doctrine on the large number of heavy drinkers who do not plan to enter treatment. Many of these heavy drinkers see themselves (often correctly) as not fitting the criteria of "alcoholism" under some current diagnostic formula. The inference they draw is that they are therefore not ill, and thus have no cause for concern. Their inclination to deny their problems is thus encouraged. This can be disastrous, since persistent heavy drinking is physically, mentally, and often socially destructive.

Furthermore, since most people diagnosable as alcoholics today do not enter treatment, the disease concept insidiously provides an incentive to keep drinking heavily. For those many alcoholics who do not enter treatment and who (by definition) want very much to have a drink, the disease doctrine assures them that they might as well do so, since an effort to refrain is doomed anyway.

Moreover, a major implication of the disease concept, and a motive for promoting it, is that what is labeled "disease" is held to be excusable because involuntary. Special benefits are provided alcoholics in employment, health, and civil-rights law. The motivation behind this may be humane and compassionate, but what it does functionally is to reward people who continue to drink heavily. This is insidious: the only known way to have the drinker stop drinking is to establish circumstances that provide a motivation to stop drinking, not an excuse to continue. The U.S. Supreme Court currently faces this issue in two cases before it. And the criminal courts have thus far resisted excusing alcoholics from criminal responsibility for their misconduct. But it's difficult to hold this line when the AMA insists the misconduct is involuntary.

The second flaw in the social "white lie" argument is the mistaken assumption that use of the word "disease" leads alcoholics to seek a medical treatment that works. In fact, medical treatment for alcoholism is ineffective. Medical authority has been abused for the purpose of enlisting public faith in a useless treatment for which Americans have paid more than a billion dollars. To understand why the treatment does no good, we should recall that many different kinds of studies of alcoholics have shown substantial rates of so-called "natural" improvement. As a 1986 report concludes, "the vast majority of [addicted] persons who change do so on their own." This "natural" rate of improvement, which varies according to class, age, socioeconomic status, and certain other psychological and social variables, lends credibility to the claims of success made by programs that "treat" the "disease" of alcoholism. . . .

A British report concludes that "it seems likely that treatment may often be quite puny in its powers in comparison to the sum of [non-treatment] forces."

The more pessimistic reading of the treatment-outcome data is that these elaborate treatments for alcoholism as a disease have no measurable impact at all. In a review of a number of different long-term studies of treatment programs, George Vaillant states that "there is compelling evidence that the results of our treatment were no better than the natural history of the disease." . . .

NEW APPROACHES

In recent years, early evaluation studies have been reexamined from a non-disease perspective, which has produced interesting results. For example, it appears that the heaviest and longest-term drinkers improve more than would be expected "naturally" when they are removed from their daily routine and relocated, with complete abstinence as their goal. This group is only a small subset of those diagnosable as alcoholics, of course. The important point, though, is that it is helpful to abandon the one-disease, one-treatment approach, and to differentiate among the many different patterns of drinking, reasons for drinking, and modes of helping drinkers.

Indeed, when we abandon the single-entity disease approach and view alcoholism pluralistically, many new insights and strategies emerge. For example, much depends on the criteria of success that are used. The disease concept focuses attention on only one criterion—total, permanent abstinence. Only a small percentage of alcoholics ever achieve this abolitionist goal. But a pluralistic view encourages us to value other achievements, and to measure success by other standards. Thus, marked improvement is quite common when one takes as measures of success additional days on the job, fewer days in the hospital, smaller quantities of alcohol drunk, more moderate drinking on any one occasion, and fewer alcohol-related domestic problems or police incidents. The Rand Report found that about 42 percent of heavy drinkers with withdrawal symptoms had reverted to somewhat more moderate drinking with no associated problems at the end of four years. Yet, as non-abstainers, they would count as failures from the disease-concept standpoint.

The newer perspective also suggests a different conception of the road to improvement. Instead of hoping for a medical magic bullet that will cure the disease, the goal here is to change the way drinkers live. One should learn from one's mistakes, rather than viewing any one mistake as a proof of failure or a sign of doom. Also consistent with the newer pluralistic, non-disease approach is the selection of specific strategies and tactics for helping different sorts of drinkers; methods and goals are tailored to the individual in ways that leave the one-disease, one-treatment approach far behind.

Much controversy remains about pluralistic goals. One of the most fiercely debated issues is whether so-called "controlled drinking" is a legitimate therapeutic goal. Some contend that controlled drinking by an alcoholic inevitably leads to uncontrolled drinking. Disease-concept lobbies, such as the National Council on Alcoholism, have tried to suppress scientific publications reporting success with controlled drinking, and have excoriated them upon publication. Some have argued that publishing such data can "literally kill alcoholics." Authors of scientific studies, such as Mark and Linda Sobell, have been accused of fraud by their opponents (though expert committees have affirmed the scientific integrity of the Sobells' work). Attacks like these have been common since 1962, when D. L. Davies merely reviewed the literature and summarized the favorable results already reported in a number of published studies—and was severely criticized for doing so. But since that time

hundreds of similar reports have appeared. One recent study concludes that most formerly heavy drinkers who are now socially adjusted become social drinkers rather than abstainers.

In any case, the goal of total abstinence insisted upon by advocates of the disease concept is not a proven successful alternative, since only a small minority achieves it. If doubt remains as to whether the controversy over controlled drinking is fueled by non-scientific factors, that doubt can be dispelled by realizing that opposition to controlled drinking (like support for the disease concept of alcoholism) is largely confined to the U.S. and to countries dominated by American intellectual influence. Most physicians in Britain, for example, do not adhere to the disease concept of alcoholism. And the goal of controlled drinking—used selectively but extensively—is widely favored in Canada and the United Kingdom. British physicians have little professional or financial incentive to bring problem drinkers into their consulting rooms or hospitals. American physicians, in contrast, defend an enormous growth in institutional power and fee-for-service income. The selling of the term "disease" has been the key to this vast expansion of medical power and wealth in the United States.

What should our attitude be, then, to the long-term heavy drinker? Alcoholics do not knowingly make the wicked choice to be drunkards. Righteous condemnation and punitive moralism are therefore inappropriate. Compassion, not abuse, should be shown toward any human being launched upon a destructive way of life. But compassion must be realistic: it is not compassionate to encourage drinkers to deny their power to change, to assure them that they are helpless and dependent on others, to excuse them legally and give them special government benefits that foster a refusal to confront the need to change. Alcoholics are not helpless; they can take control of their lives. In the last analysis, alcoholics must *want* to change and *choose* to change. To do so they must make many difficult daily choices. We can help them by offering moral support and good advice, and by assisting them in dealing with their genuine physical ailments and social needs. But we must also make it clear that heavy drinkers must take responsibility for their own lives. Alcoholism is not a disease; the assumption of personal responsibility, however, is a sign of health, while needless submission to spurious medical authority is a pathology.

NO

William Madsen

THIN THINKING
ABOUT HEAVY DRINKING

The conflict between the moral and medical approaches to alcoholism is being revived. The newest champion of the moral cause is Herbert Fingarette, who has argued in *The Public Interest* (Spring 1988) that "the idea that alcoholism is a disease" is a "myth" that is being pawned off on a gullible public by a coalition of avaricious doctors, cynical providers of ineffective "treatment," public officials eager to shirk their duties and millions of alcoholics who wish to avoid taking personal responsibility for their actions. Those who perpetuate the myth, Fingarette suggests, do so for the most venal reasons: physicians "defend an enormous growth in institutional power and fee-for-service income"; researchers seek government funds; legislators, judges, and bureaucrats lighten their work loads by compelling heavy drinkers to enter costly but ineffective treatment programs, as a show of addressing the social problems posed by alcohol abuse.

The perpetration of the myth that alcoholism is a disease, Fingarette further charges, has required that the public be "kept unaware of a mass of scientific evidence accumulated over the past couple of decades, evidence familiar to researchers in the field, which radically challenges each major belief generally associated in the public mind with the phrase, 'alcoholism is a disease.' "

But Fingarette's attempt to share the scientific truth with the heretofore deluded public is badly misconceived, because he himself—a layman in the field, lacking all scientific credentials—has completely misunderstood the medical issues and badly misrepresented the pertinent scientific literature. In what follows I will point out only a few of the most glaring defects in his arguments.

FINGARETTE'S CLAIM THAT ALCOHOLISM IS NOT A DISEASE IS SUPPOSEDLY BASED not on "isolated experiments or off-beat theories," but on "massive, accumulated, mainstream scientific work by leading authorities, published in recognized journals." But the hard scientific evidence from biology and medicine

From William Madsen, "Thin Thinking About Heavy Drinking," *The Public Interest*, no. 95 (Spring 1989), pp. 112-118. Copyright © 1989 by National Affairs, Inc. Reprinted by permission of the author.

offered by Fingarette is tiny and insignificant. His portrayal of the findings of psychology and sociology as hard scientific fact is unpersuasive, but constitutes practically all of the evidence for his erroneous arguments.

Thus Fingarette fails to recognize the obvious inadequacy of much experimentation done on alcoholics under highly artificial laboratory conditions. These experiments are based on simplistic models of "rat research" in laboratories in which all variables can supposedly be controlled. But as animal researchers realized long ago, laboratory research must be supplemented by observations of the behavior of animals in their normal environment. Fingarette accepts the results of these lab experiments as proof that alcoholics do not experience uncontrollable "craving" for a drink; he deduces that alcoholics can willfully control their drinking behavior, which in turn disproves the disease concept of alcoholism. One of these studies showed that when alcoholics are "promised money if they drink only moderately, they drink moderately enough to earn the money." Another demonstrated that if the alcoholic had to do something boring—like pushing a lever—to get a drink, the alcoholic would "avoid the boring activity and forgo the additional drinking." But it is ludicrous to think that data from such contrived experiments will bear any resemblance to the behavior of alcoholics in a normal environment. Outside a laboratory, alcoholics have been known to lie, steal, break into liquor stores, and even threaten to kill to obtain alcohol when they really craved it.

By fiat Fingarette then rejects the claim that alcoholism is a disease, claiming instead the "heavy drinkers" drink for reasons "that are not results of alcohol's chemical effect." He further tries to justify his dismissal of alcoholism as a disease by asserting that since drinking habits range from abstinence to chronic abuse, it is impossible to establish distinct categories of drinking. By this reasoning we should throw out the concept of "puberty" in growth studies, because the onset and termination of that condition are hard to mark and vary widely from individual to individual. Or perhaps because there is debate today over the demarcation between life, brain death, and biological death, the concept of death is invalid. Death would be for Fingarette a fabrication foisted on the public by money-mad morticians and by cadavers trying to avoid their responsibilities to the living. Fingarette's refusal to classify alcoholism as a disease rests on his opinion and nothing else.

Fingarette knows little about what constitutes a disease. Since no single cause has been discovered for alcoholism, he believes that it cannot be a disease. But by this standard many medically accepted diseases would be denied their classification, such as diabetes, chronic obstructive pulmonary disease, eczema, psoriasis, Alzheimer's disease, and schizophrenia.

Fingarette also seems to have trouble understanding that diseases are not static, but progress through a course. He is extremely critical of Jellinek's claim that the disease of alcoholism goes through "phases." It is true that Jellinek's claim was not completely supported by later studies. Nevertheless, Fingarette's critique is unpersuasive. In the first place, no individual case of a disease follows a generic model perfectly. Jellinek's research, moreover, was the first to produce a useful description of the disease's course, and subsequent progress has been based on his work.

Some scientific evidence is too strong for Fingarette to ignore, and so he dismisses it as irrelevant. The evidence derives from genetics: Fingarette admits that 18 percent of the sons of alcoholic parents become alcoholics, but sees little significance in this, since this means that 82 percent of them "do *not.*" Fingarette would do well to consider the implications of Mendel's classic pea-flower experiments. Seventy-five percent of his cross-bred flowers were red, but this does not mean that genetic factors played no role in causing 25 percent to be white. Fingarette has also ignored the vast and significant literature on genetics and personality. Of particular importance here is the research of neuropsychologist Ralph Tarter at the University of Pittsburgh School of Medicine, which indicates that there are six inherited "temperaments" that seem to predispose individuals to alcoholism.

Fingarette's sampling of the alcoholism literature, then, has been very limited. He ignores most of the significant biological research, such as that on alcoholic abnormalities in the P3 wave and in enzymes. The material he does cite was chosen prejudicially, and he lacks the background to discuss the physical aspects of the disease.

FINGARETTE ASSUMES THAT THE AMERICAN Medical Association [AMA]ratified the diagnosis of alcoholism as a physiological disease. Had he bothered to check the facts, he would have found that the AMA pronouncement in fact supports his own stance, rather than establishing the physiological model of alcoholism that he attacks. As Dr. Joseph Beasley pointed out in his book *Wrong Diagnosis, Wrong Treatment,* the AMA's official statement describes alcoholism primarily as a mental condition—the behavioral outcome of both conscious and unconscious psychological forces. In other words, the AMA recognizes alcoholism as a behavioral disorder. Furthermore, a behavioral model, as Dr. Margaret Bean demonstrates, is "often a disguised variant of the moral model." Thus, had he read widely enough in the literature, Fingarette could have claimed that the AMA supported his position. Although Fingarette denies that "punitive moralism" directed at the alcoholic is an appropriate response, he still strongly advocates the moral model. As Dr. Bean states, "The moral model assumes that alcoholism is a result of voluntarily chosen behavior (excessive drinking) which results from either immorality (not knowing or caring that one's behavior is bad) or defective will power (knowing but not behaving well) because of poor self-discipline or impulse control." Dr. Beasley cites Bean's work and other evidence to demonstrate that in fact the biological aspects of the disease of alcoholism have until recently been largely ignored. He concludes that alcoholism is a real disease, but "not a behavioral one." Thus Fingarette, who claims to be attacking an antiquated model of alcoholism as a physiological disease, is actually attacking a rather recent one, which has yet to be ratified by the AMA, but which is fully accepted by physicians today.

Having "disproved" the concept of "craving" (and the related concept of "loss of control") by misinterpreting their meaning and drawing on the results of slipshod research projects, Fingarette attempts to pursue his attack on the disease concept. He lets us in on the ultimate secret held back by proponents of the disease theory: "controlled drinking" (as opposed to total abstinence) is a legitimate therapeutic goal for alcoholics.

Although he claims that "hundreds of . . . reports" confirm this view, he never identifies them. He does refer to the 1962 work of D. L. Davies, who first reported successful "controlled drinking" that was accomplished without his knowledge, endorsement, or training. Fingarette does not mention that this "success" involved only seven individuals out of a sample of ninety-one. Had he really read the report, I do not see how he could think that even these seven had returned to normal drinking. One, for example, regularly relied on Antabuse when he had to be sure that no unpredictable drinking binge would interrupt some important activity. Nor does Fingarette mention that Davies strongly urges abstinence as the only valid therapeutic goal for alcoholics.

FINGARETTE CHIEFLY RESTS HIS CASE ON the 1972 report of Linda and Marc Sobell. Two ambitious graduate students with comparatively little experience, the Sobells were eager to arouse the interest of alcoholism researchers. Knowledgeable professionals with vast experience have rejected their study as a fraud. Whether or not this is the case, an evaluation of the evidence casts substantial doubt upon the study's validity.

The original grant that funded the Sobells' research was made to Dr. Halmuth Schaefer, then Chief of Research at Patton State Hospital in California. Schaefer had to leave for New Zealand and turned the grant over to the Sobells. They grossly enlarged Shaefer's original goals for the project and set out to make gamma alcoholics—that is, those who are biologically addicted — into "controlled drinkers."

The experimental subjects in the research were exposed to movies of themselves after drinking and were counseled. Seated at a realistic bar, they were free to order drinks as they pleased, but received a slight electric shock in one finger if they ordered straight liquor or drank too fast. Finally the subjects "graduated"; each was given an identity card stating that the bearer had been "trained as a SOCIAL DRINKER." These were signed by Marc Sobell as project director. Follow-up studies by the Sobells and by Glen Caddy and his associates announced that the experiment had been a success.

In 1982, however, *Science* published an article based primarily on a review of the Sobell evidence. The study was extremely difficult to do and the investigators are to be congratulated for overcoming obstacles put in their way by the Sobells. Irving M. Maltzman, one of the authors, has stated that these obstacles were "to my knowledge unprecedented within the scientific enterprise." The editor of *Science* also noted the Sobells' totally unprofessional attempts to block publication of the article. Maltzman openly accused the Sobells of fraud. Because of the seriousness of the charge, the Committee on Ethics of the American Psychological Association censured Dr. Maltzman; but the censure was withdrawn after a hearing in which Maltzman presented some of the evidence for his charges. As Maltzman says, "The Ethics Committee found that I had a reasonable basis for my beliefs." Nor was the *Science* report the only significant source to question the veracity of the claims made by the Sobells. Dr. Schaefer, who had originally turned the project funds over to the Sobells, demanded that his name be withdrawn from any association with the project, stating that "the data clearly show that social drinking is not an acceptable alternative."

The *Science* article, which was meticulous in its quest for accuracy, depicts anything but a successful experiment. Only sixteen of the twenty subjects were classified as gamma alcoholics when the project began. Of these, thirteen were hospitalized again within a year for alcohol-related complaints. Two others were using alcohol destructively during the same period. The sixteenth appeared to be drinking socially, but because of further research, Maltzman now believes that this person may not have been a genuine gamma alcoholic. Of the four experimental subjects who were alpha alcoholics (that is, psychologically dependent but not addicted), three reportedly drank to excess, were arrested on drunk-driving charges, and abused drugs other than alcohol. At best, then, one (possible) gamma alcoholic ended up drinking responsibly.

In 1983 a "60 Minutes" report concluded that the Sobell experiment failed tragically. By 1983 five of the experimental subjects had died alcohol-related deaths, all before reaching forty-two years of age. These facts point to grave ethical and legal problems. The Sobells encouraged individuals to ingest a substance that could and did prove lethal to them, while claiming the imprimatur of science. Their action was negligent and culpable in the extreme.

Fingarette blithely discounts the deaths following the Sobell experiment. In his book (*Heavy Drinking: The Myth of Alcoholism*, University of California Press, 1988) he claims that six subjects died in ten years in the control group that received abstinence-oriented psychotherapy. From this he concludes that controlled drinking "may prove to be a significantly more successful method than abstinence for at least some drinkers." It is true that psychotherapeutic approaches to alcoholism are seldom successful. I know from my experience as a consultant that abstinence programs run by psychotherapists can be disastrous. Once this is recognized, Fingarette's argument amounts to the claim that one inadequate program was successful because fewer experimental subjects died in it than in another inadequate program—odd reasoning at best.

FINALLY, FINGARETTE DISREGARDS ACCUmulated scientific research suggesting that no more than 1.6 percent of treated alcoholics can ever return to normal drinking. To urge alcoholics to try for a goal with a demonstrated failure rate of 98.4 percent is madness. Even the Sobells recommended abstinence as the primary goal in treating alcoholics. Despite Fingarette's claims, controlled drinking has been so disastrously ineffective as therapy that professionals in this country have totally abandoned it. Fingarette's critique of "the myth of alcoholism" comes tumbling down like a house of cards.

Fingarette's diatribe against Alcoholics Anonymous [AA] is also unpersuasive. Treatment programs based on AA principles, such as the Betty Ford Center, the Navy Alcohol Recovery Program, and the Employment Assistance Programs, have recovery rates up to 85 percent. It is true that AA reaches only a small percentage of alcoholics and is far from successful with all who join. But it is the best approach we have today; it merits support rather than attack from Fingarette and other self-designated "authorities."

When Fingarette criticizes the philosophical foundations of Alcoholics Anonymous, he lapses into caricature. Alcoholics Anonymous realizes quite as well as Fingarette that alcoholism has "psychological, social, cultural, economic, and even spiritual dimensions." In fact, every suggestion that Fingarette makes in his book for helping alcoholics recover is endorsed by Alcoholics Anonymous—with the lethal difference that AA recommends abstinence, while Fingarette advocates controlled drinking with tolerated binges. Although the members of AA believe that one drink may compel them to have another, they otherwise see alcoholism in the same terms as Fingarette—a fact Fingarette understandably chooses to disregard. In his excellent book, *The Alcoholics Anonymous Experience*, Milton Maxwell states that "AA sees alcoholism as an illness, symptomatic of a personality disorder. Its program is designed to get at the basic problem, that is, to bring about a change in personality." Years earlier, Bill Wilson, cofounder of AA, wrote that "anyone who knows the alcoholic personality by first-hand contact knows that no true 'alky' ever stopped drinking permanently without undergoing a profound personality change."

Finally, and perhaps most importantly, Fingarette's emphasis on the alcoholic's need to accept personal responsibility is platitudinous. "Alcoholics are not helpless; they can take control of their lives. In the last analysis, alcoholics must *want* to change and *choose* to change." Who would disagree? Not the medical profession and certainly not Alcoholics Anonymous—even though Fingarette accuses them of sanctioning the drinking of alcoholics by proclaiming their total lack of responsibility for their actions. Here again, Fingarette overwhelms the reader by his ability to misrepresent the truth.

DOCTORS ALWAYS EXPECT THAT PATIENTS who are not totally psychotic or comatose will take due responsibility for their own cures. Likewise, far from freeing alcoholics from accountability, Alcoholics Anonymous stresses that they must take full responsibility for their behavior. Alcoholics, far from being freed of responsibility for past performance, whether drunk or sober, are expected to make amends for the wrongs of the past. While the AA group gives all the help it can to each member, one of its most important sayings is, "We will walk with you but we can't walk for you." If Fingarette had simply made this valid and important point about public policy—that alcoholism should not serve as a legal defense in either civil or criminal actions—he would have discovered that virtually all recovering alcoholics agree with him. The AMA specifically states that alcoholism is properly not a valid defense for civil and criminal violations of the law.

Fingarette has no trouble demanding responsibility of others, both alcoholics and nonalcoholics. He claims in his book that private hosts "should be encouraged to assume some responsibility, moral if not legal, in serving alcohol to their guests." Do crusades like his, which seem to urge alcoholics to drink, show any responsibility at all? While claiming that alcoholism is a myth, Fingarette does concede that "alcoholism is . . . profoundly harmful, both to the drinkers themselves and to others." I am convinced that his crusade will increase the damage to which he rightly points.

CHALLENGE QUESTIONS

Is the "Disease" of Alcoholism a Myth?

1. How is it possible that vested interests can determine what is or is not considered a disease?

2. How might your personal experience with people who drink alcohol affect your position on this issue?

3. Fingarette claims that important words like *disease, control, craving,* and *success* are redefined to sell the public on a profitable way of thinking. Do you agree? How might *disease* be defined differently to fit medical, behavioral, and moral models?

4. Both of the authors in this issue disparage some research as unscientific and offer other research as more acceptable. What is your own view about their assessments of unacceptable and acceptable research?

ISSUE 6

Is Our State of Mind Responsible for Our State of Health?

YES: Bernard Dixon, from "Dangerous Thoughts," *Science86 Magazine*, a publication of the American Association for the Advancement of Science (April 1986)

NO: Ellen Switzer, from "Blaming the Victim," *Vogue* (September 1987)

ISSUE SUMMARY

YES: Bernard Dixon, an editor and writer who specializes in science and health issues, presents a series of studies that show the relationship between our state of mind and the workings of our immune system.
NO: Free-lance writer Ellen Switzer, who specializes in medicine, psychology, and law, asserts that there is no credible evidence for the claims that the course of a serious illness can be altered by the state of mind of an individual afflicted with a disease and that false claims are harmful to those that are ill.

In today's highly advanced scientific world, many are impressed with how well scientists understand the body's defensive response to microbial invasion. Is an understanding of the struggle between the invaders and the body's defenses enough to account for illness? Might there be something about our personalities that determines what illnesses we are most likely to contract and how we recover?

In his article, Bernard Dixon writes that "the mind can influence the body's vulnerability to infection in an insidious but potent way." He then introduces the reader to an alliance of psychiatrists, immunologists, neuroscientists, and microbiologists who work together in a field known variously as behavioral immunology, psychoimmunology, and neuroimmuno-modulation. He discusses some of the variables and research procedures used by investigators looking for relationships between mental states and health states. Among the most common bridges between mental and health states are:

1. *stress:* the biological response to any event, emotional or otherwise, that imposes unusual demands on the individual.

2. *anxiety:* a generalized state of tension and apprehension concerning some uncertain event.

Central to an understanding of Dixon's argument are recent studies on the physiological workings of the immune system, which reveal the following:

- *B cells* manufacture antibodies against microbes.
- *helper T cells* aid the B cells in making the right kind of antibodies.
- *killer T cells* wipe out invading organisms if there has been previous exposure to the organisms.
- *natural killer cells* (or lymphocytes) detect and destroy harmful cells regardless of prior exposure.

In an opposing view, Ellen Switzer argues that promoting the idea that sick individuals bear responsibility for their sickness is harmful. She presents the findings of a number of researchers and clinicians who, although they accept the role of stress and anxiety in aggravating illness, do not conclude that stress and anxiety *produce* illness. She also strives to separate out those researchers who advocate positive thinking to *improve* the quality of life from those who propose it as a way to *cure* disease.

Switzer's quarrel is with those who argue that people cause their own illnesses because of their attitudes and mental states, which biologically alter their ability to resist disease.

POINT	COUNTERPOINT
• Studies show that grief felt by men whose wives recently died resulted in lowered immune response.	• Physical changes in grieving men could have been brought about by changes in diet or other habits following the deaths of their wives.
• Stress, anxiety, depression, and feelings of helplessness all have been demonstrated to modify the immune system.	• Research does not show that any mind state can produce enough change in the immune system to influence the course of any disease.
• The feelings of stress can upset the body's defenses by revving up the immune system to the point at which it attacks healthy tissue.	• There is no scientific proof that changes in feelings and attitude can actually cure disease.

YES

Bernard Dixon

DANGEROUS THOUGHTS

HOW WE THINK AND FEEL CAN MAKE US SICK

Until recently, Ellen hadn't seen a physician in years. When other people got a bug, she was the one who invariably stayed healthy. But then her luck seemed to change. First she caught a bad cold in January, then had a bout of flu in February, followed by a nasty cough that still lingers. What an infuriating coincidence that these ailments hit as her career was faltering—months of unemployment following companywide layoffs.

But is it a coincidence? Intuition may suggest that we have fewer colds when we are content with our lives, more when we are under stress. That the mind can influence the body's vulnerability to infection in an insidious but potent way is a perennial theme of folklore and literature. Now even scientists are beginning to take that idea seriously. An alliance of psychiatrists, immunologists, neuroscientists, and microbiologists, specialists who rarely look beyond their own disciplines, are beginning to work together in a field so new that it goes under a variety of names, including behavioral immunology, psychoimmunology, and neuroimmunomodulation. Behind these polysyllables lies the challenge of understanding the chemical and anatomical connections between mind and body and eventually, perhaps, even preventing psychosomatic illness.

Just 10 years ago, most specialists in communicable disease would have scoffed at any suggestion that the mind can influence the body in this way. Textbooks portrayed infection as the simple, predictable outcome whenever a disease causing microbe encountered a susceptible host. Various factors such as old age, malnutrition, and overwork could make a disease more severe. But there was no place for the fanciful notion that elation, depression, contentment, or stress could affect the course of disease.

Today, that once-conventional wisdom is being revised by scientists around the world. Playing a major role in these investigations are researchers at England's Medical Research Council Common Cold Unit near Salisbury.

From Bernard Dixon, "Dangerous Thoughts," *Science86 Magazine*, a publication of the American Association for the Advancement of Science (April 1986). Copyright © 1986 by the American Association for the Advancement of Science. Reprinted by permission.

Their work shows that even this relatively trivial infection is affected by the psyche. And the lessons learned may apply to more serious diseases, including cancer.

For nearly four decades now, volunteers at the Common Cold Unit have helped test the efficacy of new antiviral drugs and have proven that colds are caused by rhinoviruses and a few related viruses. In 1975 psychologist Richard Totman at Nuffield College, Oxford, and Wallace Craig and Sylvia Reed of the Common Cold Unit conducted the first psychological experiments. The scientists infected 48 healthy volunteers by dribbling down their nostrils drops containing two common cold viruses. The researchers then offered 23 of their subjects the chance to take a new "drug," actually a placebo, that would presumably prevent colds. The investigators warned these subjects that if they accepted this treatment, they would have to have their gastric juices sampled with a stomach tube. The scientists had no intention of doing this; the warning was simply a ruse to put the volunteers under stress. The other half of the group was neither offered the drug nor cautioned about the stomach tube. Totman and his colleagues theorized that the 23 offered the placebo would experience either mild anxiety or regret, depending on the decision they made. This might cause them to allay their state of mind by justifying to themselves their decision—as a theory called cognitive dissonance predicts—which would result in greater bodily resistance and milder colds.

The experts were wrong. When an independent physician assessed the volunteers' symptoms, he found that the 23 offered the choice had cold symptoms that were significantly more severe than those given no option. Apparently anxiety generated by contemplating something unpleasant or refusing to help a worthy cause had a tangible influence on the course of the illness.

Totman's group also made some intriguing observations about the way stress affects people outside the laboratory. Volunteers were interviewed by a psychologist, received rhinoviruses, caught colds, and were monitored. Individuals who during the previous six months had experienced a stressful event, such as death of a loved one, divorce, or a layoff, developed worse colds than the others, and introverts had more severe colds than extroverts. Not only were the introverts' symptoms worse than those of their peers, their nasal secretions contained more rhinovirus, confirming that their illnesses were worse.

The Common Cold Unit is now trying to find out how stress affects people with strong social networks compared with their more introverted colleagues.

But how could an individual's mental state encourage or thwart the development of a cold? Research at several centers in the United States supports the most plausible explanation—that psychological stress impairs the effectiveness of the immune system, which has the dual role of recognizing and eliminating microbes from outside the body as well as cancer cells originating within.

The first line of defense of the immune system is the white blood cells called lymphocytes. These include B cells, which manufacture antibodies against microbes; helper T cells, which aid the B cells in making the right kind of antibodies; and killer T cells, which wipe out invading organisms if they have been exposed to them before. Another kind of lymphocyte, the natural killer cell, has received a lot of attention lately for its ability to detect and destroy harmful cells, including malignant ones, even if it hasn't encountered the invaders previously. Together with scavenging white blood cells that gobble up dead cells and debris, the various types of lymphocytes work in complex, coordinated ways to police the body's tissues.

Researchers can measure the efficiency of the immune system by measuring how well a patient's lymphocytes respond to foreign substances. For instance, they can grow the patient's lymphocytes in glassware and expose them to substances called mitogens, which mimic the behavior of microorganisms by stimulating the white cells to divide. Since a rapid increase in the number of white cells is a crucial early stage in the defense against invasion, patients whose white cells don't proliferate may have malfunctioning immune systems.

But most researchers are cautious about generalizing from the results obtained from a single technique of this sort, since the immune system has complicated backups to keep us healthy even when our lymphocytes aren't proliferating. Nevertheless, reports of stress reducing the efficiency of the immune system have been accumulating on such a scale—and with such variety—that it is becoming difficult to resist the conclusion that anxiety increases our vulnerability to disease.

In one landmark study, for example, Steven Schleifer and his colleagues at Mt. Sinai School of Medicine in New York sought help from spouses of women with advanced breast cancer. They persuaded 15 men to give blood samples every six to eight weeks during their wives' illnesses and for up to 14 months after the women died. While none of the men showed depressed lymphocyte response while their wives were ill, their white cell response was significantly lowered as early as two weeks after their wives died and for up to 14 months later. Schleifer believes he has shown, contrary to earlier studies, that it was bereavement, not the experience of the spouses' illness, that lowered immunity.

Prompted by his observations of the bereaved widowers, Schleifer wondered if serious, debilitating depression would also show up as weakened immunity. When he took blood samples from 18 depressed patients at Mt. Sinai and the Bronx Veterans Administration Hospital, he found their lymphocytes were significantly less responsive to mitogens than those of healthy individuals from the general population matched for age, sex, and race.

We sometimes think humans are uniquely vulnerable to anxiety, but stress seems to affect the immune defenses of lower animals too. In one experiment, for example, behavioral immunologist Mark Laudenslager and colleagues at the University of Denver gave mild electric shocks to 24 rats. Half the animals could switch off the current by turning a wheel in their enclosure, while the other half could not. The rats in the two groups were paired so that each time one rat turned the wheel it protected both itself and its helpless partner from the shock. Laudenslager found that the immune response was depressed below normal in the helpless rats but not in those that could turn off the electricity. What he has demonstrated, he believes, is that lack of control over an event, not the experience itself, is what weakens the immune system.

Other researchers agree. Jay Weiss, a psychologist at Duke University School of Medicine, has shown that animals who are allowed to control unpleasant stimuli don't develop sleep disturbances, ulcers, or changes in brain chemistry typical of stressed rats. But if the animals are confronted with situations they have no control over, they later behave passively when faced with experiences they can control. Such findings reinforce psychiatrists' suspicions that the experience or perception of helplessness is one of the most harmful factors in depression.

One of the most startling examples of how the mind can alter the immune response was discovered by chance. In 1975 psychologist Robert Ader at the University of Rochester School of Medicine and Dentistry conditioned mice to avoid saccharin by simultaneously feeding them the sweetener and injecting them with a drug that while suppressing their immune systems caused stomach upsets. Associating the saccharin with the stomach pains, the mice quickly learned to avoid the sweetener. In order to extinguish the taste aversion, Ader reexposed the animals to saccharin, this time without the drug, and was astonished to find that those rodents that had received the highest amounts of sweetener during their earlier conditioning died. He could only speculate that he had so successfully conditioned the rats that saccharin alone now served to weaken their immune systems enough to kill them.

If you can depress the immune system by conditioning, it stands to reason you can boost it in the same way. Novera Herbert Spector at the National Institute of Neurological and Communicative Disorders and Stroke in Bethesda, Maryland, recently directed a team at the University of Alabama, Birmingham, which confirmed that hypothesis. The researchers injected mice with a chemical that enhances natural killer cell activity while simultaneously exposing the rodents to the odor of camphor, which has no detectable effect on the immune system. After nine sessions, mice exposed to the camphor alone showed a large increase in natural killer cell activity.

What mechanism could account for these connections between the psyche and the immune system? One well-known link is the adrenal glands, which the brain alerts to produce adrenaline and other hormones that prepare the body to cope with danger or stress. But adrenal hormones cannot be the only link between mind and body. Research by a group under Neal Miller, professor emeritus of psychology at the Rockefeller University in New York City, has shown that even rats whose adrenal glands have been removed suffer depressed immunity after being exposed to electric shocks.

Anxiety, it seems, can trigger the release of many other hormones, including testosterone, insulin, and possibly even growth hormone. In addition, stress stimulates secretion of chemicals called neuropeptides, which influence mood and emotions. One class of neuropeptides known as endorphins kills pain and causes euphoria. Endorphins have another interesting characteristic: they fit snugly into receptors on lymphocytes, suggesting a direct route through which the mind could influence immunity.

This idea is borne out in the lab, where one of the natural pain-killers, beta-endorphin, can impair the response of lymphocytes in test tubes. Evidence from cancer studies shows that chemicals blocking the normal functions of endorphins can slow the growth of tumors. And other work suggests that tumor cells may be attracted to certain neuro-peptides, providing a route for cancer to spread all over the body.

Neuropeptides are turning out to be extraordinarily versatile in their interaction with the immune system. At the National Institutes of Health in Bethesda, Maryland, Michael Ruff has found neuropeptides that attract scavenging white cells called macrophages to the site of injured or damaged tissue. There the macrophages regulate and activate other immune cells as well as gobble up bacteria and debris. What is even more surprising, however, is that the macrophages themselves actually release neuropeptides. This has led Ruff to speculate that these scavenging white cells may also serve as free-floating nerve cells able to communicate with the brain.

But why should that two-way communication sometimes have the effect of allowing stress to upset the body's defenses? One answer may lie in evolution. When early man was attacked by a saber-toothed tiger, for example, it may have been more important from a survival standpoint for his immune system to turn off briefly. In its zeal to get rid of foreign matter and damaged tissue, a revved-up immune system can also attack healthy tissue. Shutting down the immune system for a short time would avert any damage to the body's healthy tissues and would cause no harm, since it takes a while for infection to set in. As soon as the danger had passed, the immune system was able to rebound—perhaps stronger than before—and go about its main business of fighting invading organisms. But the kind of stress we modern humans suffer is of a different kind: it is rarely life threatening and often lasts a long time, weakening our immune defenses for long periods and making us vulnerable to infections and cancer.

The immune system is extraordinarily complex, and the mind is even more so. As Nicholas Hall of George Washington University School of Medicine says, "We're putting together two kinds of black boxes and trying to make sense of what happens."

In the process, researchers are wrestling with three issues of scientific and social import. First, what can be done to protect people at vulnerable times in their lives from a potentially catastrophic failure of their immune defenses? Second, should counseling and psychological support become as important as traditional therapeutic measures in the treatment of disease? And finally, what are the corresponding benefits to health of the positive emotions of hope, affection, love, mirth, and joy?

NO   Ellen Switzer

BLAMING THE VICTIM

Are we psychologically responsible for our health—and illness? Experts point out that the cure to what ails us isn't always in our heads, our attitudes, or our ability to "visualize" it. Here, an unexpected take on the mind-over-medicine controversy.

Is cancer more likely to strike unhappy people than happy, well-adjusted ones? Can patients suffering from cancer or other life-threatening disease improve their chances of survival by learning to enjoy life more, thinking optimistically, giving or receiving "unconditional love," or learning to imagine sick cells being eaten away by healthy ones? Are heart attacks, peptic ulcers, inflammatory bowel disease, or arthritis consequences of having a certain personality type, and will changing that personality prevent or mitigate the course of such conditions?

Many surveys show that the vast majority of Americans will answer some or all of these questions with a resounding "yes." Too many of us have become convinced that there is scientific proof that our mental and emotional states or specific personality characteristics are the principal causes of *physical* illness, and that changes in attitude, outlook, and feelings can actually cure disease, not simply improve the quality of life for the patient.

The fact is that to date there is *no* scientific proof, either statistical or physiological, that any of these assumptions is true, according to *The New England Journal of Medicine*, one of the world's most prestigious medical publications. An editorial signed by Marcia Angell, M.D., the magazine's senior deputy editor, argues that many of our current beliefs are not only scientifically unjustified but damaging to a great many patients with serious disease. "The evidence for mental state as a cause and cure of today's scourges is not much better than it was for the afflictions of earlier centuries," she writes. "Most reports of such a connection are anecdotal. They usually deal with patients whose disease remitted after some form of positive thinking, and there is no attempt to determine the frequency of this occurrence and compare it with the frequency of remission without positive thinking. Other, more ambitious studies suffer from such serious flaws in design or analysis that bias is nearly inevitable."

Angell cites one frequently mentioned study that reports the death rate among those who have been recently widowed to be higher than among those still married: "Although the authors were cautious in their interpretation, others have been quick to ascribe the findings to grief, rather than to, say, a change in diet or other habits. Similarly, the known physiologic effects of stress on the adrenal glands are often over-interpreted so that it is a short leap to a view of stress as a cause of one disease or another."

But is there any harm in this belief apart from its lack of scientific substantiation? Angell believes that there definitely is. These assumptions may (and often do) lead lay persons and some physicians to blame the victim for (1) getting sick, and (2) not getting well: A patient gets cancer, it is assumed, because he or she is angry, is unable to give or to receive love, represses negative feelings, et cetera. Another is said to have had a heart attack because she is too driven, too obsessed with success to relax and smell the flowers. A third "needs" his illness to keep family members under control. And patients are said not to respond to treatment because they lack the will to live, are unable to exercise control over pain, or do not have the self-discipline to follow whatever mental therapy a "healer" has prescribed.

"The medical profession also participates in the tendency to hold the patient responsible for his progress," Angell adds. "In our desire to pay tribute to gallantry and grace in the face of hardship, we sometimes credit these qualities with cures, not realizing we may also be implying blame when there are reverses."

In the same issue of the *Journal* that contained this editorial, there was also a carefully researched study by Barrie R. Cassileth, Ph.D., and associates which concludes that there was no relationship between attitudes and survival or recurrence of cancer in 359 patients. According to Cassileth, the director of psychosocial programs at the University of Pennsylvania Cancer Center, in Philadelphia, the study is "the first methodologically sound investigation of the relationship between selected psychosocial factors and survival in advanced malignant disease." At the time the article was written, 75 percent of the patients with inoperable cancers had died, and 26 percent of those who had had cancers removed had had recurrences. Those who survived were "in no way different psychologically from those who died," Cassileth told a conference sponsored by the American Cancer Society in New York City last October. "Something about their own *biology* made them candidates for survival. The point is, their attitude is not what did it."

Jimmie Holland, M.D., the chief of psychiatric services at the Memorial Sloan-Kettering Cancer Center, in New York City, agrees with Cassileth and Angell. "The most common psychological problem I find among the cancer patients I see is a thoroughly understandable mixture of anxiety and depression," Holland says. "Some patients who have heard all about the mind-body connection in cancer blame themselves when they cannot have a positive, cheerful attitude all the time. Patients who get depressed should not be made to feel that they are responsible for getting sicker. Adding guilt to anxiety and depression obviously makes the patient feel worse and is, therefore, self-defeating."

Neither Cassileth nor Holland questions that in some ways the mind influences the body. Adrenaline is produced when someone is frightened; hypnotic suggestion can help to alleviate pain and induce relaxation; and placebos have been known to work—although they don't cure disease, they alleviate symptoms. Both doctors also agree that emotions and attitudes influence the way a person *behaves* in relation to health and illness. "We all know that someone who eats a high-fat diet, smokes three packs of cigarettes a day, and gets no exercise has a much higher chance of becoming seriously ill than someone who lives a healthier life," Holland says. "Someone who is so terrified of being sick that he or she refuses to seek medical help when symptoms appear is also apt to make a potentially dangerous situation worse. This is particularly true of cancer. But that kind of mind-body connection is very different from the belief that a person who is psychologically strong and vital will beat a life-threatening illness, when another person with a less optimistic outlook will not."

The blame-the-victim approach to serious illness is not exactly new. Historically, we have tended to believe that incurable illnesses of mysterious origin were somehow rooted in the personality or activities of the patient. In the Middle Ages, those who suffered from epilepsy or from various forms of mental illness were subjected, if they were lucky, to exorcism to banish evil spirits. Other, not-so-lucky ones were burned as witches.

Author Susan Sontag, who some years ago had surgery for breast cancer, describes the history of myths surrounding tuberculosis and cancer in her book *Illness as Metaphor* (Farrar, Straus & Giroux). In the nineteenth century tuberculosis was thought to be a disease of "excessive feeling," before science discovered that it was caused by a bacillus. Overly passionate persons, frequently artists, got the mysterious illness by "consuming" themselves physically and psychologically—indeed, it was often called "consumption."

In the nineteenth century, the tubercular look and personality became downright fashionable. "For snobs and parvenues and social climbers, TB was one index of being genteel, delicate, sensitive . . .," Sontag writes. " . . . The TB-influenced idea of the body was a new model for aristocratic looks. . . ." Wan, hollow-chested young women and pallid young men vied with one another to capture the look of this incurable, really awful disease. "When I was young," wrote the French Romantic poet Théophile Gautier, "I could not have accepted as a lyrical poet anyone weighing more than ninety-nine pounds."

According to Sontag, cancer has never been romanticized in a similar way. The current mythology suggests that cancer is generated by "a steady repression of feelings. . . . In the earlier, more optimistic form of this fantasy, the repressed feelings were sexual; now, in a notable shift, the repression of *violent* feelings is imagined to cause cancer." Sontag points out that there are actually "cancerphobes," citing as an example Norman Mailer who "recently explained that had he not stabbed his wife . . . he would have gotten cancer and 'been dead in a few years himself.' " Unlike tuberculosis, which was seen as a metaphor for artistic sensitivity, cancer is often used as a metaphor for evil. These metaphors, or course, affect the way we think about people with disease.

Jan van Eys, M.D., Ph.D., the director of the division of pediatrics at the M. D. Anderson Hospital and Tumor Institute, in Houston, helped to write that institution's code of medical ethics. He has found that the mind-healing-the-body myths can be particularly damaging to sick children. "The parents desperately want the child to live, and they have allowed themselves to become convinced that it is in the youngster's power to make himself recover through some method of controlling his own mind," he says. "When the child, in spite of all their urging, does not improve, they often blame themselves, or even worse, they blame the child. A youngster, who is going through the kind of pain and suffering that terminal illness can produce, feels the withdrawal of parents' approval and love. This kind of situation is truly appalling, and every advocate of a direct mind-body connection, or any form of mental healing, should consider what he or she is doing to such an unfortunate family."

Scientists, of course, have known for several decades that some diseases, like asthma and high blood pressure, can be exacerbated by emotions, particularly stress and anxiety, and that neutralizing or changing negative feelings can have a beneficial effect on the course of the illness. Certainly Angell's editorial in the *Journal* is not directed at these practitioners.

Trying to change health-damaging behavior and teaching patients how to eliminate or at least to improve their management of stress is what Joan Borysenko, Ph.D., does at her Mind/Body Clinic at the New England Deaconess Hospital, in Boston. In her book, *Minding the Body, Mending the Mind* (Addison Wesley), she discusses how she helps patients suffering from migraines, allergies, high blood pressure, premenstrual tension, and other stress-related diseases by teaching them meditation and other relaxation techniques. "Recent major studies indicate that approximately 75 percent of visits to the doctor are either for illnesses that will ultimately get better by themselves or for disorders related to anxiety or stress," she writes. "For these conditions, symptoms can be reduced or cured as the body's own natural healing balance is reinstated." Most scientists, including those who in the *Journal* attacked the mind-body connection, would approve of this kind of therapy, especially since Borysenko adds that "for many other chronic or potentially life-threatening disorders, symptoms may be lessened, but the progress of disease will lead inevitably toward death. Death, after all, . . . can be a powerful reminder to live life in a way that maximizes contentment, creativity, and love."

In other words, Borysenko does not assure her patients that positive thinking can cure cancer; at best, it can improve the quality of the patient's life. And she does not blame victims for their suffering.

Neither does Norman Cousins, Ph.D., whose popular book *Anatomy of an Illness as Perceived by the Patient* (Bantam) has been widely misrepresented and misunderstood. In his book, Cousins, formerly the editor of the *Saturday Review* and now an adjunct professor of medical humanities at the UCLA School of Medicine, relates how he used the power of positive emotions, especially laughter, to help himself recover from a disabling and exceedingly painful degenerative disease of the spinal tissue. Since this very popular book was published, however, he has given countless interviews to make it crystal clear that his message had been oversimplified and exaggerated. "I never meant to suggest that laughter is a substitute for competent medical attention," he said in an interview. "Positive attitude and medical science go hand in hand." He does not blame those patients who don't follow his precepts for not getting better or their personalities for having caused the sickness in the first place.

O. Carl Simonton, M.D., a California-based radiation oncologist who now counsels cancer patients, has written a much more disquieting book, *Getting Well Again* (Tarcher), which claims high survival rates for cancer patients practicing his visualization techniques along with medical treatment. Simonton suggests that patients concentrate on imagining, for example, that their white blood cells are fish swimming around in the body, devouring the "greyish cancer cells"—like Pac-Man. He also counsels patients to exercise, and to improve their diet and relationships in order to strengthen their will to live and thus to alter the course of their cancer. It is this book that Van Eys cites most frequently when he talks about parents putting pressure on their seriously ill children to "think themselves well."

In recent years, Simonton, like Cousins, has often said that his ideas may have been overstated by zealous followers. He told an interviewer, "I don't do anyone a service if I engender more depression and guilt. I know it happens, and I'm sorry. I'm glad that I did not know it would happen, or I never would have written the book." He emphasizes that "genuine belief" in his system is vital, and that "real enthusiasm" has to be the motivating factor. What he is describing, of course, is not a new cure to serious disease; it is what most scientists would describe as a placebo effect.

There are others who go much further than Borysenko, Cousins, or Simonton in insisting that patients can cure themselves of any disease by positive thinking and feeling. For instance, Bernie S. Siegel, M.D., a New Haven surgeon—whose book *Love, Medicine & Miracles: Lessons Learned about Self-Healing from a Surgeon's Experience with Exceptional Patients* (Harper & Row) was published in 1986 and has made *The New York Times*'s best-seller list—believes that "there are no incurable diseases, only incurable people." He even cites one patient, William Calderon, "who achieved the first documented recovery from [AIDS]." "By continuing at the job he loved, he refused to give in to the disease," Siegel writes. "Instead, he began meditating and using mental imagery to combat it. He worked to restore strained relationships with his family and achieved peace of mind by forgiving people he felt had hurt him. . . . Two years after the diagnosis, Calderon showed no sign of AIDS." One thing is seriously wrong with this case history, however: Calderon has died of an AIDS-related condition.

Illness is not just a metaphor to Siegel; it's a personality flaw. He quotes Elida Evans, a student of Carl Jung, who wrote in 1926, "Cancer is a symbol, as most illness is, of something going wrong in the patient's life, a warning to him to take another road." Siegel continues, "The typical cancer patient, let's say a man, experienced a lack of closeness to his parents during childhood, a lack of unconditional love that could have assured him of his intrinsic value and ability to overcome challenges. . . . Such a person tends to view himself as stupid, clumsy, weak, and inept at social games or sports, despite real achievements that are often the envy of classmates. At the same time, he may cherish a vision of the 'real me,' who is supremely gifted, destined to benefit the human race with vague but transcendent accomplishments. . . ."

Not only the fact that the patient gets cancer, but the *site* of the cancer in the body is determined by personality and life events, according to Siegel. "Women whose children die young or who have unhappy love relationships are especially vulnerable to breast or cervical diseases," he writes. Testicular cancer in males, however, is not mentioned as a disease that is caused by negative emotions or events; only the primary and secondary sex organs of women seem to be affected by such factors.

According to Siegel, chronic rheumatoid arthritis (a disease of unknown cause for which there is no specific cure) also often originates in a personality disorder: "a *conscious* restriction of one's own achievement." Here, he cites his mother as an example: although frequently a vice president of organizations to which she belonged, she always refused to become president.

Other patients refuse to get well because they "need" their illness to control their families, Siegel claims. Gladys, for example, one of his least favorite cancer patients, refused to get well despite his best efforts. He had offered her a new "miraculous" injection, which, he assured her, would cure her at once. He made an appointment to give her the fictitious miracle drug, which she cancelled. She "needed" that illness, he says, to continue to tyrannize her unfortunate relations. It's possible, of course, that Gladys knew that no miracle drug existed and lost faith in a physician who was clearly trying to dupe her.

There is some preliminary research indicating that some mind states can mini-

mally influence the immune system and the growth of cells. "We are looking at this research with great interest, but the changes are so tiny that they are medically insignificant," says Sloan-Kettering's Holland. "They certainly are not significant enough to influence the course of any disease. We hope to learn more . . . but to date there is simply not enough information on which to base even a workable theory, never mind a course of treatment."

Recently the American Cancer Society summed up what is known about the effects of emotion on cancer: "The American Cancer Society recognizes that a positive mental attitude, psychosocial techniques, and support are important for improving the quality of life for cancer patients. At the present time, available evidence does not support the theory that the use of techniques for reducing stress can change the risk of developing cancer, or duration of survival in humans. The Society recognizes the need for continued research in this area. However, the use of psychosocial interventions that claim to alter tumor growth or spread cannot be recommended at this time."

According to most scientists, including those in the mental-health professions, this statement reflects the extent of our knowledge about the mind-body connection and its relationship to serious disease. Mental and emotional exercises may help the patient feel better and thus improve the quality of life. But no one has proved that anyone with a life-threatening physical illness can get well simply by a change of mind and attitude. Many scientists believe that along that road lies a return to exorcism, anti-medical mumbo-jumbo, magical thinking, and witchcraft.

CHALLENGE QUESTIONS

Is Our State of Mind Responsible for Our State of Health?

1. To what extent are stress and anxiety a part of your life?

2. Do you feel that there are any important differences between changing a mental state to improve the quality of life and changing it to cure an illness?

3. On the basis of these articles, would you expend any special effort to change your attitudes and mental states in order to increase the efficiency of your immune system?

4. If you had a loved one with a serious illness, would you try to persuade him or her to adopt any of the techniques discussed in Switzer's article? If so, which ones and why?

PART 3

Cognitive Processes

The nature and limitations of cognitive processes pose fundamental questions in psychology. Claims of the ability to perceive information beyond the range of known sensory receptors have long been considered a hoax within mainstream psychology. Can we legitimately dismiss the possibility that at least some people may possess the ability to perceive information outside of the usual sensory range?

Can human reasoning be replicated by computers equipped with appropriate programs? If so, some long-cherished notions about uniquely human qualities of thinking must be brought into question.

How we think of what intelligence is depends in part upon the values of our culture. Is intelligence as we view it a fixed trait we are endowed with at conception, or can it actually be increased?

Has Science Discredited ESP?

Can Computers Help Us Understand the Human Mind?

Can Intelligence Be Increased?

ISSUE 7

Has Science Discredited ESP?

YES: C. E. M. Hansel, from *ESP and Parapsychology: A Critical Reevaluation* (Prometheus Books, 1980)

NO: David Loye, from *The Sphinx and the Rainbow* (Bantam Books, 1984)

ISSUE SUMMARY

YES: Psychologist C. E. M. Hansel examines the available research that is used to support the existence of ESP and concludes that all of the studies fail to meet the criteria he establishes for scientific research.
NO: Psychologist David Loye contends that no research of any kind could meet the criteria that Hansel establishes, and he finds that parapsychologists are far ahead of their critics in reliability and objectivity.

All of us, at one time or another, have experienced strange coincidences of events and feelings: premonitions and disasters that actually occur; inexplicable impulses that pay off; feelings of *deja vu*, which is the illusion of remembering events as they are being experienced for the first time, that are hard to put off to mere chance. A popular explanation of such "coincidences" postulates the existence of a sixth sense, an *extra*sensory perception, or ESP. The popularity of this notion and its conflict with many principles of natural science have spawned a great deal of debate and research. Many "parapsychologists" who have devoted much of their lives to this research feel that some experiments conclusively demonstrate the existence of ESP. Other scientists, however, question the scientific rigor of these experiments and thereby the conclusion that ESP exists.

C. E. M. Hansel is considered by some to be parapsychology's most persistent contemporary critic. In his selection, Hansel contends that psychologists generally "do not regard extrasensory perception as an established process." Other people, however, have false impressions about the quantity and quality of the so-called scientific evidence on ESP. Hansel proposes three criteria for evaluating parapsychological research. He then examines some of the stronger ESP research and finds that all the studies fail to meet all three of his criteria. He also questions typical ESP demonstrations. The fact that the particular experimental results of these demonstrations are improbable reveals nothing to Hansel about the existence of ESP.

David Loye, on the other hand, feels that much of Hansel's remarks are a "strange exercise in illogic." Loye contends that Hansel poses "criteria that no research of any kind can ever hope to meet." Loye is specifically interested in one type of ESP, precognition, which he calls *nonlinear forecasting*. He admits that there are "difficulties besetting the entire field of paranormal studies," but he compares these difficulties to the problem a few scientists had in proving the Earth was round. Magellan's methodology in proving that the Earth is round was "unbelievably naive and hopelessly flawed," according to Loye. He concludes that "for all their flaws and foibles, the parapsychologists are light years beyond their critics for sophistication, reliability, and objectivity."

POINT	COUNTERPOINT
• Psychologists do not regard ESP as established.	• Hansel himself states that leading psychologists regard its existence as proved.
• Research on ESP had been very poor.	• Evidence on any "new" phenomena may initially be poor, such as when individuals first tried to prove that the Earth is round.
• No convincing evidence has proven the existence of ESP.	• The existence of ESP has been apparent to many reputable scientists.
• ESP must meet the strict criteria of scientific research.	• Hansel poses criteria that no research of any kind can meet.
• Unbiased researchers have not replicated the findings of ESP researchers.	• Some researchers have discovered findings consistent with ESP but have failed to follow them up.
• The existence of improbable results does not imply the existence of ESP.	• Parapsychologists are sophisticated, reliable, and objective.

YES

C. E. M. Hansel

EXAMINING THE EVIDENCE

Few people have time to examine and test the evidence in parapsychology for themselves. They have to rely on authoritative statements made by investigators and by others who have studied the research. The same is true in any branch of science. A chemist, for example, cannot hope to verify every new claim reported in his field, but he has good reasons for believing that a mistake will be revealed by those specializing in the topic concerned.

How then is an authoritative opinion about the processes postulated by parapsychologists to be obtained? If there were no doubt about the existence of such processes, they would be dealt with as aspects of psychology. However, orthodox psychologists, to judge from what they teach in universities or include in their books, do not regard extrasensory perception as an established process. On the other hand, if a parapsychologist is consulted, he is likely to have no doubts about the existence of ESP.

THE AMOUNT OF EVIDENCE

Experiments testing for the presence of extrasensory perception are fortunately of such a nature that anyone of reasonable intelligence can understand them and even try them out for himself. Many persons are put off at the start, however, because they have a false impression of the amount and type of evidence that has accumulated. For example, Arthur Koestler wrote in the *Observer* of May 7, 1961:

> The card-guessing and dice-throwing experiments repeated over millions of experimental runs with thousands of random experimental subjects—often whole classes of schoolboys who have no idea what the experiment is about; the more and more refined experimental conditions and methods of statistical breakdown; the increasingly elaborate machinery for mechanical card shuffling, dice-throwing, randomizing, recording, and what-have-you, have turned the study of extrasensory perception into an empirical science as sober, down-to-earth and also too often as dreary as teaching rats to run a maze or slicing up generations of flatworms.[1]

Few parapsychologists who know anything about research in their subject would claim that millions of guesses have been made by thousands of subjects under good experimental conditions or that results claiming conclusive evidence for ESP have been reported from many universities.

The experiments differ markedly in complexity: thus an experiment may be relatively simple, involving, say, four persons who meet one afternoon and record 200 trials at guessing card symbols, or it may be highly complicated. Some of the telepathy experiments have, in fact, consisted of a large number of sittings in which the conditions have been changed from one sitting to another. With this latter type of investigation, it becomes particularly necessary to emphasize three principles that should be considered when assessing a study:

1. *Each experiment must be considered on its own merits.* A weakness cannot be excused because it is absent in a second experiment. The first experiment should be ignored and conclusions obtained only from the new experiment.

Professional magicians often rely on the fact that their audience does not practice this kind of assessment. The magician, for example, may demonstrate "thought transference." The essential features of his trick are that a member of the audience takes a card from a pack of playing cards, looks at it, and replaces it. The magician later identifies it. A second member of the audience takes a card. This time, he is allowed to retain it, and the magician again names it. If a member of the audience isolates these essential features of the trick, he may be puzzled as to how it was carried out. He may decide, after the first trick, that the magician is some-

how getting sight of the card after it is replaced in the pack. But, on the second occasion, since the performer does not touch the pack after the card is drawn, this possibility would appear to have been eliminated.

Any professional magician is likely to have many variations of a simple trick of this nature. He may, for example, attempt to force the choice of a card, the identity of which is known to him, on each occasion. If he is successful in doing so, the card need not be replaced in the pack. If he is unsuccessful, he has to ask that it be put back so that he can bring it to the top of the pack by sleight of hand and somehow see its face. Few magicians announce in advance exactly what they are going to do.

2. *An experiment that has any defect such that its result may be due to a cause other than ESP cannot provide conclusive proof of ESP.* In parapsychological research, the process being investigated is both hypothetical and, a priori, extremely unlikely. Any possible known cause of the result is far more likely to be responsible for it than the hypothetical process under consideration.

A possible explanation other than extrasensory perception, provided it involves only well-established processes, should not be rejected on the grounds of its complexity.

For example, in the case of a particular experiment, it may be necessary to decide between two explanations accounting for the scores observed: extrasensory perception, which posits a new process, or a second one that, although complex, is dependent only on known processes. The latter may appear unlikely, but it is *possible*. It must be eliminated before the hypothesis of extrasensory perception can be entertained.

3. *An experiment must be judged on the weakest part of its design.* Inadequacy of control at one point cannot be overcome by extreme control at another.

For example, in the telepathy experiments with George Zirkle as subject, . . . there is a weakness in that reliance must be placed entirely on the accuracy of an experimenter who also acted as agent and who recorded both the symbol she had been thinking about and the guess of the percipient. However stringent the controls of other features of the experiment, they cannot offset this weakness.

THE EFFECTS OF ERROR AND TRICKERY

In addition to the above, no factor that could influence the results of an experiment must be overlooked. If there is the slightest possibility that any or all participants in the experiments did anything to influence the result that is not noted in the experimental report, this possibility must be fully considered.

It is necessary to discuss openly possible trickery or cheating by participants to produce a spurious conclusion. If the result could have arisen through a trick, the experiment must be considered unsatisfactory proof of ESP, whether or not it is finally decided that such a trick was, in fact, used. At this point the concern is with evaluation of the experiment rather than with a decision about whether a particular individual tried to influence the result. As a further step, it may be necessary to establish whether there is any evidence to show that trickery did, in fact, take place.

It may be objected that any experiment can be condemned on the grounds that all of those taking part in it, including the researchers, may be indulging in a trick and that trickery is a well-established process, whereas ESP is not; therefore, no single experiment can be conclusive. This is so. But normally, in science, anyone who suspects an experimental result can repeat the experiment himself and check its conclusions.

Repetition after repetition of an ESP experiment by independent investigators could render the possibility of deception or error extremely unlikely. Thus, if the original result is repeatedly confirmed, the probability of ESP becomes increasingly likely.

Psychical research, in many ways, is like a game, and some of the investigators have emphasized that those taking part in the experiments should treat them as games if they hope to obtain positive results. It may be that conditions required to conduct card-guessing experiments are necessarily somewhat similar to those in which a magician endeavors to demonstrate his powers. The magician has to elaborate the proceedings so that the obvious explanations are ruled out; the psychical researcher, so that normal means of gaining information and of trickery are eliminated. The psychical researcher attempts to remove all loopholes, but the magician has to leave one so that he can perform his trick.

An ESP experiment can be analyzed in much the same way as one tries to discover how the conjurer performs his trick. For example, a girl is sawn in half by a magician. First, she is seen as a complete female figure; later, the legs are seen protruding from one end of a box, the head from the other end. A saw is passed through the region that corresponds with the girl's abdomen. The assumption is that the girl has not, in fact, been sawn in half, since she is intact at the conclusion of the experiment. Thus, no part of the girl was in the space through which the saw passed. Then, either the sawing was an illusion, or she was not in the place through which the saw passed. At a further demonstration, the head and legs protruding from the box are inspected, and the conclusion reached is that they could not be where they are and belong to the same person unless there was a torso in the area through which the saw passed—that is, unless either the head or the legs were dummies. But other observers examine the head and legs and convince us that they are real. Then, the head belongs to the girl, and the legs belong to some other person.

The hypothesis is now formed that two girls are inside the box, so arranged that we see the head of one and the legs of the other and that there is an empty space between them through which the saw can pass. This analysis of the conjuring trick starts with the assumption that what the conjurer claims to do, or appears to have done, is not what he does in reality, since it contradicts too much of what is known about the properties of things.

Thus, in analyzing an experiment that purports to prove ESP, it is wise to adopt initially the assumption that ESP is impossible, just as it is assumed that the conjurer cannot saw the same girl in half twice each evening.

To assume that ESP is impossible is not unreasonable, since there is a great weight of knowledge supporting this point of view, and the main evidence contradicting it is that of the experiment being analyzed. If analysis shows that this assumption is untenable, then the possibility of ESP has to be accepted.

THE STATISTICAL EVALUATION OF AN EXPERIMENT

It will be found that there are enormous odds against the scores produced in many of the experiments under discussion having arisen by chance. Thus, in Soal's experiments with Mrs. Stewart, . . . the odds are quoted as 10^{70} to 1 against chance. If a man bet a penny on a horse at these odds and won, he would have a very difficult task disposing of his fortune. If he gave a million dollars to every man alive—for that matter, if he included every man who has ever lived— he would still have plenty left. After repeating that whole gift a million times every second for a million years, he would not have made the slightest hole in his capital. He would certainly still have a million million times as much money as he had given away.

The great odds against a particular score arising by chance are sometimes quoted as if they indicate that the experiment *proves* the existence of ESP. Thus, in a review of the Soal-Goldney experiment on Basil Shackleton, C.D. Broad, Professor of Philosophy at Cambridge University, came to the conclusion that it provided evidence "which is statistically overwhelming for the occurrence not only of telepathy, but of precognition."[2]

Professor Broad appears to have assumed that the result could have been achieved only if the precipient possessed precognitive telepathy. However, if there is even the smallest possibility of some other explanation, the results of the experiment support that as much as they support the hypothesis of precognition. The probability obtained in the experiment is that of the score having arisen by chance. It tells us nothing about the probability of precognitive telepathy. To provide statistically overwhelming evidence for the occurrence of ESP in experiments of this nature requires satisfaction of two conditions: (1) the scores achieved by the subject must be such as are very unlikely to arise by chance, and (2) the experimental conditions must be such that only ESP could account for them.

The first condition is quite simple to assess. The percipient's score is compared with the one expected to arise by chance, and the frequency with which such a score would be expected to arise in a large number of such experiments if the guesses were made purely at random is calculated. Thus, in the case of the Shackleton experiment, it was found that his score would be expected to arise by chance only once in about 10^{35} such experiments.

The second condition causes the difficulties. For any interpretation as to why the experimental result differs significantly from the chance expectation is dependent on what is known about the conditions under which the experiment was carried out. A low probability that a certain result will occur, as noted in the first condition, reveals nothing about the probability that ESP does or does not exist. This is entirely dependent on the second condition. An example will make this clearer.

A magician performs a thought-reading act in which he correctly identifies 50 cards, each drawn from a pack of 52 and then replaced and shuffled. The odds against his guessing these cards by chance are 52^{50} to 1, and this is even more impressive a result than was achieved by Shackleton. The magician is, however, employing a conjuring trick. In this case, the probability of ESP in the second condition is 0, and the total probability of the result being due to ESP is 0.

The weight attached to an experiment's supposed proof of ESP is entirely dependent on how certain one can be that any alternative explanations of the result are completely eliminated. The subject's score and the probability of its arising by chance serve merely to indicate whether an assessment of the experiment should be made at all.

The second condition is the more difficult to assess. The experimental conditions may be examined most meticulously and no flaw found, but there is no certainty that nothing has been missed. The conclusion that an experiment provides statistically overwhelming evidence for the appearance of ESP is misleading if no allowance is made for the possibility of error in the experimental setup. The incidence of trickery, deception, and error in physical research is such that the probability of their occurrence is certainly far from insignificant. Professor Broad's statement, quoted earlier in this chapter, is based on the assumption that the experiment he is quoting is completely watertight and that there is no possibility of error or trickery.

It could, however, be argued that the probability that ESP exists is insignificantly small and the probability of fraud appreciable. In that case, it could be said that the experiments provide overwhelming evidence for trickery or error. If it can be shown that these conditions could account for the results, a more likely hypothesis has been established.

If, on the other hand, it can be reasonably ascertained that trickery or error have been eliminated through the employment of a completely watertight experimental procedure, then the experiment can provide evidence to support the hypothesis of extrasensory perception. If the result is confirmed by other investigators, ESP eventually will cease to be a hypothesis and will be accepted as fact. If a process really does exist in nature, this fact eventually will silence all objections, since it is as difficult to maintain erroneous criticism as it is to demonstrate the existence of something that is nonexistent. Criticism must be thorough, just as experimental research seeking to establish the facts must be thorough. . . .

CONCLUSION

A Revised Approach

In 1965 there were signs that the arguments put forward to support the work on ESP were changing. In 1961 Rhine and Pratt suggested that the case for ESP does not, after all, depend on conclusive experiments, but on general features that emerge from the whole mass of studies, conclusive or inconclusive; it is as if quantity can make up for quality when the latter has been found lacking. They wrote:

The body of fact in parapsychology is like a many-celled organism. Its strength is that of a growth-relationship, consisting not only of the compounding of one cell with another, but also of the many lawful interrelations that emerge in the growing structure. Going back as Hansel has done, with a one-cell perspective, to fix attention on some incomplete stage of development within a single experimental research is hard to understand in terms of healthy scientific motivation.

But what is the point of presenting conclusive experiments for the consideration of the scientific world if they cannot be criticized? How can an experiment be criticized until it has first been isolated? If experiments are to be considered en masse, will not data be contaminated with results such as those obtained with the Creery sisters, Smith and Blackburn, and others? As soon as criteria are set up by means of which experiments are selected or rejected, it becomes necessary to isolate each experiment to see whether it satisfies those criteria.

Moreover, what precisely are the "lawful interrelations" within the body of fact in parapsychology to which Rhine refers? To date, not a single lawful interrelation appears to have been established. How, for example, does distance affect extrasensory perception? The relationship between scoring rate and distance is completely chaotic, apparently dependent on the investigator, the subject, and the experimental conditions. If it were possible to give a standardized test for ESP to different groups of subjects, systematically varying factors such as age, nationality, intelligence, previous practice, distance, and so on, some lawful interrelations might eventually be expected to reveal themselves. But each of the reported investigations yields a result that has little relationship to any of the others.

Extrasensory perception is not a fact, but a theory put forward to account for high scores obtained during the course of experiments. Parapsychologists have made such observations under a diversity of research conditions from which a number of facts emerge. If these facts can be related to one another by a theory that enables any one to be deducible from knowledge of the others, that theory has some value and plausibility. Predictions might then be made of what will happen in further experiments so that the theory can be tested further. However, a theory that fails to account for a variety of facts and that cannot predict what will happen in further tests is of no value.

If some facts gleaned from the literature on ESP are assembled, they might appear as follows:

1. Subjects, when attempting to guess card symbols, have obtained scores that cannot be attributed to chance.

2. Some of those taking part in ESP experiments have indulged in trickery.

3. Subjects who obtain high scores cannot do so on all occasions.

4. Subjects tend to lose their ability to obtain high scores. This loss often coincides with publication of an experimental result.

5. A successful subject may be unable to obtain high scores when tested by a critical investigator.

6. Some investigators often observe high scores in the subjects they test; others invariably fail to observe such scores.

7. A subject may obtain high scores under one set of experimental conditions and fail to do so under other experimental conditions.

8. No subject has ever demonstrated an ability to obtain consistently high scores when the test procedure is mechanized to the extent that he or she can repeat the exceptional performance when the experimenter is changed.

Assuming that ESP exists, fact 1 is directly applicable. Fact 2 is not relevant to such a hypothesis. Facts 3 and 4 are not predictable but could be said to provide further information about ESP: that is, it appears to be spasmodic and temporary. The remaining facts (5–8) are not predictable, and in the case of any other supposed process investigated by psychologists, would throw doubt on its authenticity. These facts can only be explained by invoking subsidiary characteristics of ESP.

Assuming ESP does not exist, fact 1 is directly applicable to a hypothesis predicting trickery. Fact 2 demonstrates that such a hypothesis is correct in the case of certain experiments. The remaining facts (3–8) are all predictable from what is well-known about trickery.

Lawful relationships can readily be seen among the facts when they are interpreted in accordance with the hypothesis of trickery (or other causes of experimental error). Thus, for example, from fact 7 it might be predicted that those experimental conditions that eliminate the possibility of trickery will also be the ones in which high scores do not arise. This is confirmed by fact 8, and also by examining the experimental conditions under fact 7 in which high scores have, and have not, been observed. Thus, the set of facts given here display lawful interrelationships when interpreted in terms of the hypothesis of trickery, but they are difficult to reconcile with a hypothesis based on the existence of ESP.

A number of other facts could be added to the list to which neither the hypothesis of trickery not that of ESP would be applicable. This is to be expected, since a great deal of research—both in parapsychology and elsewhere—has revealed the manner in which high scores can arise from experimental error.

The conclusions stated here are those reached in 1965. Although the experiments now take a different form they are essentially similar in nature to those of the past. In 1965 I suggested that experiments carried out by the VERITAC team of investigators might be used as a model for further research. This suggestion was misinterpreted, and no further research has been published employing such a model. It requires (1) a team of investigators, (2) a suitable laboratory and apparatus, (3) a systematic experimental procedure, and (4) the possibility that duplicative tests can be conducted under the original experimental conditions. In addition, it is necessary for the investigators to be continually vigilant and on the watch for flaws in the experimental procedure.

If definite conclusions are to be drawn, an essential of such research is that very large samples of individuals be tested. When investigating any human ability it is necessary to obtain some idea of its distribution among the population, and, in the case of an ability peculiar to some people, to find individuals having the ability. The Society for Psychical Research has carried out one such screening test for ESP and found it to be nonexistent in their sample. Other surveys have been made on radio and television shows, from which nothing appears to have emerged, presumably because television producers lose interest when there is nothing sensational to report.

I make the following suggestion to indicate a way to screen large numbers of the public at negligible expense. Booths would be placed in large stores throughout the country, in which members of the public could test their ESP ability for a modest fee and hope to obtain large monetary rewards rather in the manner that they compete on slot machines. In this case, however, rather than gambling they would hope to use ESP to improve their chances of winning. The machines would pay according to the calculated chance odds, retaining a small percentage for running costs—or for a contribution to some worthwhile cause.

The testing machine, rather like a telephone booth, would be on full view to the public with suitable displays and flashing lights to indicate how the occupant was progressing. A large jackpot would take the form of a ticket, and when the winner cashed it in, details of the successful client could be obtained, and a record would be maintained in the machine of each competitor's score over a fixed number of runs (perhaps 10 p per 25 trials). This would enable any successful subjects to be contacted if necessary.

No doubt some large chain store would welcome the opportunity to attract large numbers of the public and to contribute to the cause of scientific enquiry. Good evidence would eventually be obtained of the ESP scoring ability, at least in those members of the public interested enough to compete.

Alternatively, the television producers who seek to attract audiences with sensational programs about the paranormal might do better by arranging mass screening tests in which members of the public could be persuaded to compete. The first ten successful attempts at a concealed target received would entitle the persons involved to appear in the studio and participate in further tests— perhaps matched against celebrities such as Uri Geller or Bernard Levin.

After 100 years of research, not a single individual has been found who can demonstrate ESP to the satisfaction of independent investigators. For this reason alone it is unlikely that ESP exists. But this empirical finding confirms the theoretical viewpoint of psychologists that sensory information is required to provide the causal link between objects and events in the environment and events in the brain that determine perception.

In this research a number of properties of ESP are assumed to have been discovered. Since if ESP is nonexistent these properties are also nonexistent, only utter confusion can exist if the findings from the experiments are retained. The aim of parapsychology should be to produce one individual who can give a reliable and repeatable demonstration of ESP.

In the event such an individual is found, confirmation by independent investigators could easily be arranged. If parapsychologists were to undertake systematic forms of investigation and eliminate all that is not confirmed beyond all doubt, they would have a better chance of revealing any new human abilities that may exist.

NOTES

1. Arthur Koestler, *The Observer* (London) May 7, 1961, p. 23.
2. C. D. Broad, "Discussion: The Experimental Establishment of Telepathic Precognition," *Philosophy*, 19, 74 (1944): 261

NO

David Loye

ON THE EVALUATION
OF THE SO-CALLED PARANORMAL

Though the focus of this book is solely on precognition—or the possibility of what might protectively be called nonlinear forecasting—as this capacity is at the present time (1983) classified as one of a number of so-called paranormal phenomena, its investigation is almost wholly blocked by the difficulties besetting the entire field of paranormal studies. Thus, if we are to see significant progress in gaining more scientific understanding of nonlinear forecasting, the mental blocks against the paranormal must be removed.

Over the years, the debate between the parapsychologists and their critics has become such an involved, tiresome, and professionally wholly unrewarding matter that the overwhelming majority of scientists—having much better things to do with their limited time—have learned to ignore it. Yet many scientists, and perhaps by now a majority, suspect there may be something of importance being trivialized or otherwise hidden by this "backwaters" controversy. All analogies have their problems, but in many ways, the situation is like that confronting the few scientists of that time as the fifteenth gave way to the sixteenth century. At that time, the world was still popularly and generally considered to be a flat object consisting of the known continents of Europe, Africa, and Asia surrounded by water. Legends and rumors born by mariners of something else "out there," and calculations of a peculiar "roundness" by a few heretical astronomers, led scientists to suspect there could be other possibilities. But there was no real urgency for anyone to make up their mind about the matter until Christopher Columbus returned from his voyages in the 1490s with some strange natives and tales of the discovery of the "Indies." Then opinion began to crystalize into three camps: 1) a small minority advocating a belief in a New World and the possibility of a round world; 2) a small minority denying same; and 3) the vast majority of people to whom the matter was still only a peripheral novelty, which might or might not some day become meaningful in their busy lives.

Today we collapse the whole episode into something speedily resolved by Vespucci's discovery of South America as a continent (1499) and Magellan's proof of the earth's roundness by circling it (1521). But around and in between these years only very slowly did there occur a change of mind concerning the nature of this planet Earth, that came about through a series of exchanges with analogues to the "parapsychology debate" in our time.

Today we know that behind the legends and the tales of mariners lay the earlier discoveries of Leif Ericson and other forgotten Norsemen. But in that age, such reports arrived as garbled tall tales composed of impossible treasures and monsters and feats of strength, much like the jumble ranging from UFOs and Bermuda triangles to accounts of telepathy in our day.

Nor was the situation much improved when Columbus and other early explorers arrived with the first "hard data," in our terms. Who was to say that these were really natives from a new land and not some fraudulent Asians, or Africans who had been sneaked aboard? How could there possibly exist ludicrous animals of the type shown in some of the sketches these travelers brought back? (And indeed, we know today many of these sketches purportedly of New World animals were inventions as wild as the unicorn.) And what about the inconsistencies in these traveler's tales, some describing an island, some describing a much, much larger land mass, even this weird claim (Vespucci's) of a new continent? How could one believe any of these accounts when there were discrepancies of so many thousands of miles for sizes and locations?

Even for Magellan's so-called proof that the earth was round, in terms that might be used by today's critic of parapsychology—or of any other purportedly "new" phenomena—the methodology was unbelievably naive and hopelessly flawed. To begin with, the principal investigator didn't even finish the experiment—Magellan was killed only halfway around the earth, in the Philippines. Nor was the experiment thereafter properly conducted by his questionably and poorly credentialed subordinates, as they proceeded to lose all of his ships and most of his men. Nor were the final results of this journey acceptable by even minimum standards, for out of all the loaded ships that set off to circle the purported "globe," only four possibly deranged crewmen lived to reach Spain again—a ridiculously small and unreliable sample upon which to try to base so momentous a conclusion.

This analogy, of course, assumes that there is some degree of "newness" and "roundness" behind the legends and experiments of the paranormal. How valid is this assumption? At present, science has left the matter of an answer to an excluded minority—both the parapsychologists *and* their critics—to try to conduct very demanding experiments, in their spare time, at considerable professional risk, with almost no funding, institutional support, or professional or financial reward. Moreover, at present ninety-five percent of what little time can be given in these circumstances to the investigation of the so-called paranormal is still bogged down in the essentially unproductive question of whether the phenomena are real. For the better part of 100 years now, it has been apparent to reputable scientists, from William James and Sigmund Freud into our day, that such phenomena *do* exist. The critical questions are, Which are "real"? Which are not "real"? And what do they mean? This pursuit must presently receive at best only five percent of available time.

To help reverse this percentage as it affects nonlinear forecasting, I will briefly deal with criticisms by anti-parapsychologists of the precognition experiments. . . .

PRECOGNITION'S CRITICS

Parapsychology's most persistent contemporary critic is British psychologist C.E.M. Hansel of the University of Wales. He begins his most recent book dealing with these matters, *ESP and Parapsychology*, with an absorbing and disarming account of the beginnings of psychical research and present-day attitudes toward the paranormal. Particularly interesting in view of what lies ahead is his citing of the eminent British scientists, including Alfred Russel Wallace—the "Wallace" of Darwin and Wallace—and Sir Oliver Lodge, who have supported and advanced such research. Additionally, he notes that "most of the leading British psychologists . . . who have had anything to say on the matter of extrasensory perception . . . leave no doubt that they regard its existence as proved" (pp. 5, 6).

Can this be *criticism?* One begins to wonder. Then Hansel sets forth the three criteria by which he proposes to evaluate paranormal research and the nature of the game is revealed (p. 20).

1. *"Each experiment must be considered on its own merits"* (p. 20). This sounds reasonable on the surface, but then in the very next line he adds by way of explanation: "A weakness cannot be excused because it is absent in a second experiment." Such a criterion would require that *all* research, no matter how ad-

vanced, must be judged on the basis of its preceding pilot and exploratory studies, which by their very nature are riddled with the holes which the later research is designed to control! Then in the very next line he says: "The first experiment should be ignored and conclusions obtained only from the new experiment." But he has just finished telling us that this "new experiment" will be forever flawed by its predecessor—and now we are supposed to ignore it and go by the new one only?

This strange exercise in illogic sets the tone and reveals the strategy for much that follows. The idea is to pose criteria that no research of any kind can ever hope to meet, and to sap the energy of one's readers and opponents by confusing and obfuscating matters while ostensibly trying to clarify them.

2. *"An experiment that has any defect such that its result may be due to a cause other then ESP cannot provide conclusive proof of ESP"* (p. 20). Again this sounds reasonable, but as most knowledgeable researchers are aware, all phenomena are multivariate—that is, no variable or process produces an effect by itself; in reality, many variables interact to produce all events. We may have, for example, both right brain and left brain at work, and to show that a perception derives from left-brain "rationality" does not thereby rule out that right-brain "intuition" may not also be at work. Strategically, then, this criteria again sets up a "no win" situation which would make it impossible for any kind of research to ever "conclusively" prove anything.

3. *"An experiment must be judged on the weakest part of its design"* (p. 21). As the experienced researcher knows, all experiments—without exception—have flaws and weaknesses. For this reason, all re-

sponsible and knowledgeable evaluation takes strengths as well as weaknesses into account. To judge by so-called weaknesses alone, for example, would have barred recognition of much of the work of two of the giants of modern experimental psychology, Jean Piaget and Kurt Lewin. For as his early critics noted, Piaget's work was based on naive and uncontrolled studies of his own children (!), and Lewin's work was viewed as a methodological nightmare by large numbers of his behaviorist peers.

Having set down such criteria, the rest of Hansel's book becomes a rather meaningless exercise. However, for the sake of completion here, the following precognition studies we report [are] very briefly examined: Soal's studies with Shackleton, the Schmidt work with the strontium 90 random number generator, the Ullman and Krippner dream work, and the Puthoff and Targ remote-viewing experiments. Not unsurprisingly, Hansel finds that all fail to meet all three of his criteria. His explanations for Soal's results are trickery by Soal with the aid of an accomplice. While admitting that the machine procedure that Schmidt used does begin to curb possibilities for fraud and error, he again finds Schmidt suspect on both counts. Curiously, Ullman and Krippner do not come off so badly. While their dream work is woefully flawed, at least Hansel does not accuse them of fraud or trickery. As for Puthoff and Targ, he only repeats the conclusions of critics David Marks and Richard Kamman, which we will next examine.

"After 100 years of research, not a single individual has ever been found who can demonstrate ESP to the satisfaction of independent observers," Hansel concludes. "For this reason alone it is unlikely that ESP exists" (p. 314). Yet if we simply circle back to the beginning of his book, we find his own list of the "eminent British scientists" and "most of the leading British psychologists" who attested—as he himself specifically states— to such an existence!

After such a wearying exercise in elliptical analysis by a psychologist insensitive to the nature of (and I must suspect relatively unpracticed in) research, *The Psychology of the Psychic* by New Zealand psychologists David Marks and Richard Kamman opens like a welcome fresh breeze. For the pair are at least researchers, and rather than merely leisurely chipping away at someone else's hard labor, they undertook the arduous task of both original experiments and attempted replications.

The case I will shortly examine was their attempt to replicate Puthoff and Targ's remote-viewing experiment. First, their specific critique of the four startling cases of apparent precognitive remote viewing by photographer Hella Hammid, reported in Chapter Twelve, should be noted. The alternative explanations they offer are, one: that some form of "cueing" was involved. What is meant by this is unclear and in any case is quickly dropped as "unlikely." Two: that Puthoff and Targ were only reporting four successes out of a longer series of failures. This is to join in Hansel's shopwork tactic of imputing fraud, for Puthoff and Targ specifically identify these experiments as "the first four carried out under this program" (*Mind-Reach*, p. 118). (Moreover, I must note that even had there only been the four successes out of many failures, so striking are the correspondences that the results would still have been impressively beyond an easy explanation of "coincidence.") Three: that all target locations contain so many of the same kinds of visual cues that one can find whatever one is looking for in them. This is to say that most outdoor locations contain trees and roads and other elements in common. The remote viewer draws a picture of what he or she sees, and lo and behold when the spot is visited, out of the hundreds of possible configurations that confront the viewer, invariably something that looks somewhat like what was seen in mind or like the picture that was drawn will be spotted.

"The fact is that any description can be made to match any target," Marks and Kamman blithely claim (p. 40). Yet the history of the psychology of perception—and particularly the Gestalt psychologists to whose work I have extensively referred—has shown that this is *not* the case. While the mind does have the capacity to find what it seeks in its environmental surround, the fact remains that surrounds vary tremendously and *dictate* recognition of this difference.

Apparently sensing the tenuousness of this position, the pair fall back again on the old fraud explanation. This time they specifically accuse Puthoff—though it is unclear whether they claim to know this for a fact or are merely imputing it—of writing the judge's instructions so that they must inevitably pick the appropriate object out of the possibilities when they visit the target site. The swing in the child's park is specifically noted, the imputation being that Puthoff directed the judges to look at the "black triangle-like object" at this locale.

This brings us to their attempt to replicate the Puthoff-Targ experiments. From 1976 through 1978, they report carrying out a total of thirty-five experiments of remote-viewing attempts, with no success. That is, in contrast to the Puthoff-Targ experiments, their judges failed to significantly match the drawings the subjects made of the targets with the actual target sites as later visited by the judges. And it is this failure they report as their chief finding, which Hansel repeats in his book.

However, they report the emergence of an interesting conflict during the study. Both study participants and judges were so displeased with Marks and Kamman's conclusion of failure, *believing themselves that remote viewing had occurred*, that on the final experiment arrangements were made to look deeper into what was happening by having three crews make sound films of the "senders" (who went to the site), the "viewers" (who did the remote viewing), and the judge (who tried to match target sites to drawings).

What they found this time—and actually report in surprising detail in the book—was *precisely what Puthoff and Targ had found*: a striking correspondence between the "viewer's" verbal report of what he saw and the actualities of the randomly chosen target site visited by the "sender." The first target, an A-frame house and steps situated at the foot of a hillside, evoked in the remote viewer "a very open sort of feeling. Something like hills . . . sensation of being high up." He felt "a sense of movement, as though Sally was walking up" (p. 20). Later the sender confirmed that she had indeed walked up the hillside above the roof of the house, and that the view from this height did conform to the feeling expressed by the remote viewer.

The second target was a grave in a local cemetery with a tall and prominent monument and smaller monuments in view, which was apparently on a hilltop, from the picture shown in the book. The reported viewing was of "a fairly enclosed space . . . sort of high . . . I see some kind of monument and some kind of large tall structure . . . a somber feeling" (p. 21). When queried about the "enclosed space," the remote viewer had also reported a sense of no color, only darkness.

The third target was a railroad station, which the sender had described and drawn as a series of geometric patterns and forms, mainly triangles and pyramids, that contained correspondences which even to Marks and Kamman "seemed quite remarkable" (p. 22).

Thereafter, the correspondences between viewing and target grew progressively slighter. Again, the independent judge failed to match the drawings with the targets. But where, as *is evident by their own report*, another investigator would have interpreted this to be a partial *success*, even a partial replication of Puthoff and Targ's work, they do not. Nor do they act further, where another investigator, finding through a change of procedure on the last of thirty-five experiments evidence of what he had set out to find or debunk, would have suspected the thirty-four earlier experiments could also have contained such favoring evidence, calling for reexamination. Rather, in keeping with the pressure upon them to "out-Hansel" Hansel—and blithely disregarding their *own* data—Marks and Kamman reported that "our own extensive experiments have failed to find any evidence of remote-viewing ability" (p. 25).

The reader with sufficient time and motivation is invited to read the works of both the parapsychologists and their critics and reach his or her own conclusions about the investigation of precognition. My own conclusion is that for all their flaws and foibles, the parapsychologists are light years beyond their critics for sophistication, reliability, and objectivity.

CHALLENGE QUESTIONS

Has Science Discredited ESP?

1. Loye contends that Hansel proposes criteria that no research can ever meet. Is this true? Examine the research of some well-established psychological finding and evaluate it in light of Hansel's criteria.

2. Loye and Hansel seem to disagree on the status of ESP research in the minds of modern scientists. What about the views of the instructors in your school? You might consider interviewing them on this issue.

3. Have you had experiences or know anyone who has had experiences of interest to a parapsychologist? Can you think of explanations other than ESP?

4. If ESP does exist, what implications would this have for everyday life, science, technology, and politics?

ISSUE 8

Can Computers Help Us Understand the Human Mind?

YES: Herbert A. Simon, from "Using Cognitive Science to Solve Human Problems," *Science and Public Policy Seminar* (1985)

NO: Ulric Neisser, from "Computers Can't Think," *Creative Computing* (January 1980)

ISSUE SUMMARY

YES: Professor of computer science and psychology Herbert A. Simon contends that computers, like humans, have problem-solving and decision-making abilities and need only to be given general principles in order to solve problems.
NO: Professor of psychology Ulric Neisser argues that the computer's ability to answer questions and store information does not constitute thought in the way it is performed by humans.

America is rushing headlong into an era in which its dependence on computers is as great or greater than its traditional dependence on the automobile and electricity. Computerized cameras decide on proper exposures. Computerized supermarket cashier-stands tabulate and total the descriptions and prices of items bought. And computerized bills and bank statements are addressed to us by computers.

Is the computer merely a machine that follows machine-coded directions or can it be said that it uses an intelligence of its own? The question itself seems to initiate the same concerns as Darwin's concept of evolutionary continuity among species. To some people it appears to be a threat to the uniqueness of humankind. If a computer performs "intelligent" functions by following a program, and if it mimics human intelligent performance, perhaps it is reasonable to consider human intelligence to be like that of a computer. Perhaps our own minds work like a very slow and inefficient computer.

In a seminar entitled "Using Cognitive Science to Solve Human Problems," Herbert A. Simon discusses the role of the computer in scientists' attempts to understand the nature of the mind. In listing some of the uses of the computer, he includes decision-making, problem solving, and the location and correction of spelling and grammatical errors. He claims that human thinking involves the manipulation of symbols and that the computer can be used to test this claim through simulation.

When the computer is spoken of as having intelligence, many people reject this notion, declaring that it only does what it was programmed to do. Simon says this is misunderstood. The computer can figure out on its own what decision rules were used in solving an example that has been worked out. The computer can then store these rules and use them for solving new problems. Like humans, the computer needs to be told general principles but not necessarily each specific step to use for solving each problem.

Ulric Neisser, usually considered to be the father of cognitive psychology, acknowledges that computers answer questions, store information, make decisions, compute, and play an important role in American society. However, he feels that they have not lived up to their promise in intellectual activities, and they do not perform their tasks the same way humans do.

He points out that computers are poor in the use of language. While some programs seem to understand the spoken word in limited domains such as chess-playing, they do not know meanings. They do not change responses to words as contexts change. He says that some game-playing programs can eventually beat their programmers in some instances, but only because they store winning and losing positions in memory. They merely run through a series of steps without intentions or natural responses. They do not use perceptual and simultaneous strategies as humans do.

POINT	COUNTERPOINT
• Computers recognize cues and respond appropriately.	• Computers do not use perceptual strategies.
• Computers can use general principles for solving problems.	• Computers use step-by-step procedures.
• Computers use the same problem-solving strategies humans use.	• Computers use different problem-solving strategies than humans use.

YES

Herbert A. Simon

USING COGNITIVE SCIENCE
TO SOLVE HUMAN PROBLEMS

Today I would like to tell you a little about some of the developments that are currently going on in cognitive science, and point to some of the directions in which they might affect our own lives as human beings individually and collectively. This is obviously much too large a domain to be covered, for I want to leave most of the time for your questions, so I will focus on some specific "for instances."

At Yorktown Heights at the IBM Research Headquarters a couple of days ago I saw an interesting computer program, which illustrates nicely, I believe, the kind of things that I am going to talk about today. It was a computer program which would locate spelling errors in written text. That's old hat now; computers have been doing that for three or four years. It would then correct the spelling, which is even more useful. In addition, it would find most grammatical errors—split infinitives, lack of subject and verb agreement, etc., and give advice about correcting those. This computer program gives a glimpse into the nature of the mind, or at least into the nature of language, which we have always thought of as one of the most essential products of the human mind. This little program, and it is a program of modest size, provides just a slight indication of the sorts of insights we are getting, in cognitive science, into the way the human mind operates when it is using its capabilities to process language.

Most scientific research programs start with exciting problems and the hope that they will lead to answers that might be of some use, but all of you know that it's really the excitement that drives scientists most of the time. There are some scientific problems that are big problems and other problems that are little. Everybody had his own list of big problems. My own list of really big scientific problems goes something like this:

1) *The nature of matter.* That is what the high energy particle physicists are all about. They would really like to know how things behave at the foundations, but the foundations are always a level below where they have been able to dig so far. That's the way science is.

2) *The origins of the universe.* That is what the space program is all about. What is out there? How did it begin? How did it develop?

3) *The nature of life*. That covers the whole range of the biological sciences. How is it that matter can organize itself to exhibit the sort of behavior that living creatures are capable of?

4) *The nature of mind*. How is it that a chamber made out of bone with various kinds of biological structures inside can do the things that we call thinking, problem solving, speaking and so on?

Now, answers in any one of those areas would certainly lead to some possibilities for doing something about everyday practical problems of human beings, not just the problems of understanding ourselves. Deeper understanding of the nature of matter and the origin of the universe underlies the whole practice of engineering and our whole ability to use physical laws to accomplish our human purposes. Likewise, understanding the nature of life leads us to the kinds of knowledge of the human body that provide the basis for advances in medicine.

To what does the understanding of the nature of the mind lead? Presumably it can lead to all kinds of advances in our ability to use the central human resource, the resource that makes us truly human and able to do the things that other creatures in this world cannot do. If we ask what good it can do to understand the mind better, we need to look in the direction of improving management, the processes of learning, the decision making and problem solving that take place in organizations, and perhaps even the decision making and problem solving that take place in Congress. A very large part of the human resources in our society are occupied in learning. We spend the first third or half of our lives learning, and some of us don't quit even then. Learning is a major consumer of this human resource, the brain.

Now, to try to answer scientifically the big exciting questions about matter and the universe, life or mind, science needs techniques. The best problems in the world (i.e., building a gravity shield or a perpetual motion engine) are not good scientific problems unless we have some techniques that tell us what we can do tomorrow, what is the first step toward solving them. A good scientific problem is an important problem combined with some glimmer of an idea about how it can be approached and tackled. So if you are going to study the nature of matter, you are going to need telescopes and space vehicles. If you are going to study biology and the nature of life, you are going to need something like recombinant DNA techniques. Of course, people did biology before they had those, but they answered a different set of questions then. When you are on the frontier, you need powerful techniques.

What about the study of the mind? Beginning about thirty years ago, we began to get a new and powerful tool of research for the study of the mind. It was the now familiar digital computer. Its use in this research rests on a hypothesis that you can accept or not, a hypothesis for which there is a good deal more evidence now than there was thirty years ago. The hypothesis is that the reason the human mind or brain is able to do the things we call "thinking" is because it can perform some very simple operations with symbols. By symbols I simply mean patterns—patterns you can put on the blackboard with chalk, or any kinds of patterns. Biologists will some day tell us how these operations are done inside the brain; we don't know very well yet.

But human thinking is done by simple processes like reading symbols (patterns) as our eyes do, producing symbols as our tongues do and writing symbols as our hands do. We store symbols inside our heads so we can act later, not only storing individual symbols but storing relations among them—big structures of symbols that can represent meanings. We compare symbols and decide when they are alike or when they are different. We can branch if they are different, and do something else if they are alike.

Now all of you who have your own personal computers at home know that these are just the things that computers do. They read symbols. They output symbols on the screen or on the printer. They store symbols in memory. They can relate different symbols and build organized structures in memory (on all of those floppy disks that you have). They can compare symbols. Every computer language has a branch operation, and can compare two symbols and then do one thing if they are different and another if they are alike.

The hypothesis that people have been pursuing in cognitive science research in the last thirty years is that the reason human beings can think is because they are able to carry out with neurons these simple kinds of processes that computers do with tubes or chips. Notice that this isn't quite a biological hypothesis. I am not saying anything about how neurons actually work; I wish I knew. There is still a very large gap between understanding the biology of the human brain and understanding symbolic processes at a level where we can show how they do complicated things like solving problems or producing natural language. It is a little like the physicist's problem. Some physicists study quarks, and others, as well as chemists and biologists, study macromolecules. Now everybody knows that macromolecules are made up of quarks,

but it doesn't help you explain very much how the body works to know about quarks. There are too many levels in between, so you have to build up layers of theory. You build up biochemical theories, chemical theories and physical nuclear theories. Finally several layers down are quarks.

Thus, we are not talking about the biology of the brain. We are talking about the information processes that are supported by that biology. In some happy day in the future, as our research in neuroscience progresses, we will be able to close the gap between those two. We will see not only how a human being thinks in terms of basic memory and input and output processes, we will also eventually learn how that thinking takes place in terms of neurons. That is not what I am going to be able to explain today. I don't know, and as far as I know, nobody does.

Now, I have made a pretty strong claim, a claim that the reason human beings can think is because they can input patterns, output patterns, store patterns and compare patterns. It makes the thinking brain sound like a pretty simple device. How would you test a hypothesis like that? The way in which we have tried to test it is by seeing how closely we can simulate or mimic the processes of human thinking on a digital computer, which demonstrably just uses these simple processes. We know a computer can't do anything else besides the four or five things that I mentioned, and the name of this game is to see whether you can write computer programs that not only do things like use language and solve problems, but do them in a demonstrably human way. . . .

It has commonly been thought that to be a great chess player you have to have unusual visual imagination. Take a chessboard and arrange the pieces on it as in a game between two good players, say maybe twenty-five pieces, after a few of them have been knocked off. Let a chess player look at the board for five to ten seconds, not very long. Then take it away and say, "Reconstruct the board for me. Put those twenty-five pieces back on the board the way they were." The grand master will do that with 95% accuracy—maybe make one mistake occasionally. "Oh," you think, "he must have marvelous visual imagery to remember all of the pieces on the board." You or I (unless there are some grand masters in the audience whom I don't recognize) would be lucky to get six pieces back on the board correctly. Now six turns out to be a very important number. It is very important because in many psychological tasks it turns out that human beings can only hold on to six or seven things at once. I will have to define a little more carefully what a "thing" is. Things are basically familiar patterns—six words or the seven digits in a telephone number....

Now we just make a small change in the experiment: we take the same pieces and put them back on the board at random. We show them to a grand master and to an ordinary player for five or ten seconds, take them away and ask that they be reproduced. What happens? The grand master can put six back on the board correctly, and the ordinary player can put six back on the board correctly. With random boards, there is no difference. The grand master's prowess with positions from real games has nothing to do with ability to do visual imagery. It has a great deal to do with the fact that grand masters have spent an awful lot of time looking at chessboards, and there are lots of familiar friends on any chessboard from well played games—little configurations of pieces that have been seen again and again. I won't test your chess knowledge here, but any chess master who sees a board on which there is a certain pattern called an open file will notice that open file and will even have some ideas about what to do with it. That is all stored in memory. . . .

Today there are computer systems that can operate at an expert level in certain professional fields. In our city of Pittsburgh, we have a program over at the University of Pittsburgh called Caduceus, produced jointly by Jack Meyers, who is a fine internist, and Harry Pople, who is a fine computer scientist. That program diagnoses illnesses in the area of internal medicine, and it diagnoses illness at the level of a good clinician, although it probably isn't as good as Jack Meyers. How does it do it? It does it because that program has well over 10,000 pieces of information and patterns that it can recognize—symptoms that a patient presents to the doctor—that immediately cue an hypothesis. It still doesn't have 50,000 but then Dr. Myers knows a lot of other things besides those diagnostic tricks.

Of course, you don't build an expert system just by having these 50,000 chunks. There has to be a little capability for reasoning about the chunks. Today we know something about how you combine expert knowledge with a little bit, not too much, of reasoning power. You shouldn't romanticize about how much reasoning power the human mind has. There is a small industry burgeoning now of people who write software expert systems for a wide variety of domains. They are not trying to imitate human beings; they are trying to imitate human performance. A lot of the ability to do this today comes out of the research that has been done back and forth between psychology and the part of computer science that we call artificial intelligence. This research has tried to build computer programs that try to understand human performance. . . .

Today we think that is the way in which the skill of solving algebraic equations is stored in the human mind. It is stored in the form of things we call productions— each one of which is a little cue or an ability to recognize a cue whenever it appears, hitched to an ability to remember what to do whenever that cue is seen. Very complicated reasoning skills can be built out of simple structures of that sort and can even be carried one step further. We have today computer programs that can examine a worked-out example and figure out for itself what the rules are that would get it there. I can then store these new rules in its own internal parts and have the capability of doing algebra. So here we have a theory of how human learning takes place—a theory implemented in a computer program. . . .

Finally, you all know the principle that a computer can only do what it is programmed to do. Now that is sometimes misunderstood. Some people understand that to mean that a program only does what you think you programmed it to do. That is demonstrably false, as you all know. Computer programmers spend most of their time debugging programs which don't do what they think they programmed them to do. But more than that, it is often interpreted to mean that a computer can only do things you already know how to do, where you tell the computer step by step exactly how to do it. That is a wrong interpretation of the principle. Of course, a computer has to have a program that tells it step by step what to do. But *step by step* might mean to instruct it to search for answers to some kind of problem and to use some rules of thumb in the conduct of the search. That is the way the medical diagnosis system works, as well as the other expert systems that I described. You don't have to predict an event in advance or program the exact steps it is going to take. What you have to do is to tell the computer what kinds of principles might guide its search. . . .

. . . Several research groups, including one in our shop, have been engaged for a number of years in writing computer programs that are capable of making discoveries in science. A particular slant we took in our project was to say that if the computer program is so smart, then it ought to be able to do the things that Kepler did, or it ought to be able to do the things that Ohm did—or you name your hero. So we have been engaged in giving the program, the main version of which we call BACON in honor of Sir Francis Bacon, the same kinds of data and starting point that Kepler had when he began his search for what we now call "Kepler's Third Law" or that Ohm had when he first decided to find out something about the laws that govern electrical currents. We give it those data, and we ask the computer to find the law. The answer is, it does. As a matter of fact, it finds it so quickly that there is a little embarrassment here. It took Kepler ten years to develop Kepler's Third Law. Now, it is true, he had distractions. His mother was being tried for witchcraft during part of that period, and other things were happening to him. But, nevertheless, he was somehow or another messing around with this problem for a number of years. BACON does it in two minutes.

NO

Ulric Neisser

COMPUTERS CAN'T THINK

Last spring, when we were making plans for a summer seminar on human nature, it seemed natural to include a discussion of the differences between people and computers as well as those between people and animals. We would probably not have found it so natural a decade or two ago, and it's worth wondering why it seems more appropriate today. One of the reasons is surely that modern computers do so many things that people also do. They answer questions; they store information; they make decisions; they compute. Deciding, having memory, and the like are usually regarded as intelligent activities. The study of how they can be carried out in computers has come to be called "artificial intelligence"; a substantial field of study that many people take seriously. In short, one reason for making comparisons between human beings and computers is that computers seem to be intelligent.

Another reason is that computers play such an important role in American society. They send us bills that we must pay every month; they guide rockets that explore other planets; they assist in the control of military ballistic missiles and could probably start the third world war at any moment. Everybody knows that computers do these kinds of things. As a result, we are impressed not only with their intelligence but with their power. That power gives the study of the computer a kind of glamour that is missing when we compare humans and, say, chimpanzees. Chimps may or may not be intelligent, and may or may not use language, but they don't send us bills or go to the moon. They are very much in our control; computers may not be.

A third good reason for the present interest in computers is the boom in science fiction. Many writers have exercised their imaginations to see what might happen if computers became more like people, or had more power. Stanley Kubrick's excellent film "2001" starred a villainous computer named HAL, who talked with the astronauts as a person would. Eventually, HAL attempts to sabotage the expedition and murder them all. (There may be a moral in this. A little elementary cryptography will show that HAL is more than he appears on the surface. Consider the three letters of his name: by going to the next letter of the alphabet in each case you get I-B-M!). Many

From Ulric Neisser, "Computers Can't Think," *Creative Computing* (January 1980). Copyright © 1980 by Ulric Neisser. Reprinted by permission of the author. The author has slightly modified his article for this edition of *Taking Sides: Psychological Issues*.

people believe that HAL is just around the corner. Professors of artificial intelligence told Kubrick that there soon *will* be computers like HAL: computers that you can talk to, that make heavy decisions. To be sure, not all artificial intelligence researchers were equally enthusiastic about "2001." One complained to me that the computer got all the credit in the movie, instead of the programmer. The fact is that a computer is just a piece of hardware; what can make it seem intelligent is a program that somebody wrote. It would be a tremendous achievement to write programs that made a computer do what HAL did, and yet everybody speaks about the computer as if *it* were the bright one.

Scores of science fiction stories, in this same vein, involve computers that are powerful and wonderful. (Perhaps a higher portion of modern sci-fi uses this idea now that the moon and Mars have become less available to fantasy.) One reason for the appeal of these stories is especially worth mentioning. Stories about omniscient and dangerous computers appeal to deep, almost unconscious fears. We are afraid that something is going to go out of control and go wrong, that we are somehow sinful and will bring about our own destruction, that our own creations will destroy us. This fantasy takes the form of zombies and golems and all kinds of creatures as well as of computers, but they are fairly obvious vehicles for it. In addition, it is significant that a computer is something devised by humans, and yet lifelike. Norbert Weiner was very explicit about this: it felt a little like being God to create something so like a person. That possibility again appeals to a deep level of fantasy that we can't easily understand, and therefore makes us anxious.

We are so worried about the possibility that someday a computer won't take orders that there are classical jokes about computers that do. There's a story about a machine developed for Robert McNamara when he was Secretary of Defense during the Vietnam War. This computer was built with the best talent available; all available knowledge was stored in it, and all the best programs were written for it. He was told it could answer any question. Being McNamara, he didn't kid around. As soon as the computer was ready he stepped to the console and typed in, "Will we win the war in Vietnam or will we lose it?" In a flash, the computer typed back "YES." McNamara was outraged: he didn't like to be trifled with. He typed back "Yes *what*?," to which the computer immediately (and properly) replied, "YES SIR."

In evaluating the achievements of computers, two questions should be considered separately. Given any intellectual activity like answering questions or solving problems, the first (artificial intelligence) question is: "Can a properly programmed computer do it, now or ever?" The second (simulation) question is: "Can a properly programmed computer do it the way we do it?" These are two very different issues. (Computers really can compute, for example; they can find the sums of long columns of numbers; they can divide, multiply and subtract. But it's easy to see that they don't do those things as people do them.) The answers to these two questions will depend on what intellectual achievement we are talking about, of course. Nevertheless, I have some fairly strong general opinions about them, at least if we are talking about activities more subtle than simple computation. No, computers do not carry out mental processes as people do; as far as I can see, they will not do so in the future either. With regard to the first question, whether computers can do complex tasks at all, I would say "Rather less than we would have thought." I will try to justify those answers by detailed consideration of two specific domains: language and game-playing.

Can a computer understand language? Let's take a notion of "understanding" and consider it more carefully. Such a question might just mean "Can a computer identify words that are spoken to it?" At a more significant level, however, the question might be interpreted as "Does the computer know what a spoken utterance *means*?" Even the first of these two tasks has proven surprisingly difficult to program. As a child in 1939, I was taken to the New York World's Fair. There I saw a device called the "Vocoder": a machine that could talk. At least, it uttered speech-like sounds. The implication was that technology would soon reach the point where machines could talk fluently, and perhaps also know what was said to them. That was many years ago and it hasn't happened yet. There is still no computer to whom one can talk in the way those astronauts talked to HAL in "2001," no computer that could even identify the words they spoke.

To be sure, there has been some progress in machine recognition of limited vocabularies. As long as you only say digits (e.g., "seven"), some programs are pretty good at recognizing which digit is which. There is also a program at Carnegie-Mellon University with a somewhat larger vocabulary. The program, called HEARSAY, understands spoken chess moves. You can walk up to the microphone at the beginning of the game

and say "Pawn to King four," it will know what move you made. At later stages of the game you can say such things as "Rook takes Rook." This degree of progress was achieved in a very interesting way. HEARSAY understands speech as well as it does because it is a chess-playing program as well as a speech-understanding program. At any point in the game it knows what moves its opponent could legally make, and which of those moves are plausible. Even this rudimentary grasp of the subject matter is a great advantage in understanding speech; it effectively reduces the range of things that might be said. This is an important principle: it means that the two senses of "understand" are not entirely separate. In normal human understanding of a language, knowing what was said and knowing what was meant are intimately related. The reason that computers have failed to fulfill their early promise in speech understanding is that (except in narrow domains like chess) they still don't know what we are talking about.

[Note for this edition from Ulric Neisser: Computer speech recognition has made some progress in the years since this paper was written. Machines can now recognize words from rather large vocabularies, provided they are spoken carefully and in isolation. Nevertheless, none of them comes close to understanding ordinary spoken language.]

That brings me to a second linguistic problem that programmers have tried to solve. In the sixties, the problem was called "machine translation" or "mechanical translation." You can imagine how much the prospect of translating Russian by machine must have appealed to the army and the CIA. They would save a lot of trouble if they could just feed Russian text into a computer and have English text come out. There was a great deal of early optimism about machine translation. Indeed, there was rapid progress at first. It is relatively easy to store the equivalent of a dictionary in a computer, pairing each Russian word with its English equivalent. Then, if you input a Russian text, you can print out the English equivalents of the Russian words. Unfortunately, this does not result in a sensible translation. It is also necessary to know how sentences are put together. "Paul hit Peter" and "Paul was hit by Peter" mean different things. To understand these sentences one must understand how *active* and *passive* work in English. In general, one cannot understand a language unless one has mastered its grammar as well as its vocabulary. A dictionary is not enough.

This insight led to a burst of interest in programming computers with grammar and syntax. Unfortunately, that approach didn't work very well either. Even if you know the general form of a sentence and all the words in it, that may not tell you which *sense* of each word is meant. Consider the sentence above where I said that this approach "didn't work." Obviously I was not claiming that the grammatical approach was on strike, or that it was refusing to do labor! Similarly, you know now that when I say "refusing to do labor" I don't mean anything about having a baby. You make these interpretations automatically, because you know what I'm talking about. You don't stop to consider those alternative meanings even for a moment. But a computer with all the alternative meanings of each word in storage still does not know what you know: that labor pains and labor unions are not likely to come up in a discussion of mechanical translation.

It can't be sure, as you were, that when I said "didn't work" I meant work in the sense of "operate properly." These ambiguities of interpretation don't just occur occasionally. They happen all the time, except where the domain being translated is so limited that only a few things can be said.

We can see now why it is so difficult to program computers to deal with natural language. The process has more levels than we may have suspected. One must understand sentences before one can understand words, but computer programs can't understand sentences because they can't make the right presuppositions. They don't know the background, and they can't appreciate the context in which the discussion is being carried out. When you program computers you must go from the specific to the general, but human beings usually go from the general to the specific. We start out in infancy without knowing much; we find out about our immediate environment and what's important in it before we go beyond it. We acquire a language naturally by hearing it spoken. Could a computer be programmed in this way? Perhaps, but no one has any idea how to set about it.

Let me turn now to a third example of computers' use of language. Here is a portion of a dialogue between a human being and ELIZA, a computer programmed to simulate a non-directive therapist.

H: Men are all alike.
E: In what way?
H: Men are always bugging us about something or other.
E: Can you think of a specific example?
H: My boyfriend made me come here.
E: Your boyfriend made you come here?

H: He says I'm depressed much of the time.

E: I'm sorry to hear that you are depressed.

H: It's true. I am unhappy.

E: Do you think coming here will make you not to be unhappy?

H: Perhaps I could learn to get along with my mother.

E: Tell me more about your family.

The ELIZA program has an interesting history. Joseph Weizenbaum at MIT wrote it as a joke, in the spirit that a conjurer or a parlor magician would do a trick. He was disturbed to find that some people took it seriously. It was clear to him, as it should have been to everyone, that therapists are *people* who try to understand and help other people. ELIZA, however, was a caricature. More exactly, ELIZA was a model of a caricature of a particular kind of treatment: Carl Rogers' non-directive therapy. Rogers argued that therapists should be careful not to force interpretations on their clients. At the same time, he stressed the importance of being genuinely concerned about the client, and showing that interest openly. The purpose of the therapy is to get the client to express and understand some of his own feelings, and then to realize that having and expressing those feelings is not so terrible. The client must feel that his thoughts will be understood, and that somebody can value him as a person despite them. The non-directive technique can work very well, especially in the hands of a skillful therapist.

None of the necessary conditions for therapy is fulfilled by ELIZA. Quite obviously, there is no person present who cares about the patient. More to the point, ELIZA does not have any idea of what is going on; it doesn't know what any of the words mean or what the patient is talking about. It just makes do with a bag of tricks. It can scan through a sentence like "My boyfriend made me come here," transform words like "my" and "mine" and "me" into "you" and "your," and spit out the sentence again in the form of a question. ("Your boyfriend made you come here?") It doesn't know what "my" or "your" means; it has a routine which replaces "mine" with "your" throughout and reprints the sentence. Another part of ELIZA searches for certain words included on a list supplied by the programmer: "depressed," "sad," "unhappy," "blue." When one of these words occurs, ELIZA can print out the sentence "I'm sorry to hear that you are _____," putting the user's word in the blank. In addition, it has a list of stock phrases like "can you think of a specific example?" "Tell me more about your family." ELIZA also has a random generator that ensures it need not always do the same thing. That's all. Tricks such as these are entirely responsible for its "interaction" with users.

ELIZA's responses can lead to interesting misunderstandings. One of them was reported by Dan Bobrow, who used to be associated with the artificial intelligence group at MIT. One Friday evening he had left a message on the console that read, "Type all messages into this teletype and end them with a full stop." On Saturday morning a salesman appeared to sell some kind of computer equipment. The salesman assumed, reasonably enough, that the computer terminal was connected to Bobrow's home (it is customary for AI researchers to have terminals in their homes.) So he began typing away, and the following exchange resulted:

Salesman: Do you think I can use the computer this morning?

Computer: Why do you ask?

S: I might be able to make some additional telecomp sales.

C: Why aren't you sure?

S: My prospective customers have never seen a demonstration of the system.

C: Does this mean very much to you?

S: Of course it does.

C: You seem very positive about that.

S: This is ridiculous.

C: What do you mean this is ridiculous?

S: Is there any reason why I can't use the computer now?

C: Tell me more about your prospective customers.

The salesman had had enough by now, and he typed "Please dial me at 491-8150," which was the number of the telephone by the console. He was so mad that he forgot to end with a full stop, so the computer didn't answer. He sat there for a while, getting neither an answer or a phone call. Finally, he called Bobrow at home on an ordinary phone, woke him out of a sound sleep and said, "Why are you being so snotty to me?" Bobrow replied, "What do you mean, why am I being so snotty to you?"

In 1950, the mathematician Alan Turing proposed a definite test by which we could tell when artificial intelligence had been achieved. He suggested that we put someone at a teletype that communicates both with a person and with a computer. The interrogator can ask any question he likes and take note of the replies; his aim is to determine which is the computer and which is the person. Turing suggested that if the interrogator cannot do this successfully, then the computer has passed the test. I think, though, that ELIZA illustrates the weakness of the test itself. Weizenbaum's program obviously was *not* intelligent, and yet it fooled some of the people who used it. (Of course *you* could easily distinguish

ELIZA now that you know how it works: you could just type in "My XQV PGR TM" and ELIZA would reply "Your XQV PGR TM?") Fooling people is not enough: the test of whether computers think like people is not whether they can fool anyone, but how they think.

The second major area of intellectual activity I will consider is game playing and problem solving. Computers have been fairly successful at it. In 1958, Arthur Samuel wrote a very effective checker-playing program that learned to play better than he did. This was possible because the total number of legal checker positions is smaller than you might think. Samuel's program stored every position it encountered together with the outcome which had resulted from it as the game continues. Its strategy was simply to avoid positions that had lost and bring about positions that had won. Pretty soon it could beat Samuel and everybody else.

Checkers is a difficult game, but it doesn't have the glamour of chess. Chess is the intellectual challenge *par excellence*; many people argue that a computer that could play championship chess would have to be called "intelligent." Now, it is impossible to base a chess program on the principle used in the checker program: there are just too many possible positions. Therefore chess-playing programs work differently. Typically, they examine various possible moves at a given point and their consequences. It is as if the computer said to itself "If I do this, then this position will be reached. Now in this position my opponent might do that or that or that. If he does that, then I could do this or this or this . . ." and so on until an expanding "tree" of possibilities is generated. The nature of chess ensures that the tree is too large to search completely. Some sort of selection is necessary: the program needs some way to "prune" the tree to decide which branches are worth exploring. Typically it uses various strategies based on the programmer's knowledge of chess: it tries not to lose pieces, for example, or tries to capture those of its opponent.

Early programs based on these principles never beat their designers, but they did play chess. They made legal moves. In the late 1950s, when checkers had already been conquered, it seemed that computer chess was on its way to a similar triumph. Herbert Simon predicted that a program would be chess champion of the world by 1967. Time rolled on. The year 1967 came and went, but artificial intelligence buffs were not discouraged. In 1968 several programmers bet £250 each with a Scottish Grandmaster, David Levy, that within ten years some computer program would beat him. He said it wouldn't. In 1978, Levy collected his money. The point of the story is that there has been a recurrent history of strong and confident prophecies about computers and chess; so far, the prophecies have not come true.

In the meantime, the psychological study of chessplaying has made a good deal of progress. We now know quite a bit about what good chess players really do. Most interestingly, we have discovered that they do much less searching of the tree of possibilities than used to be believed. Less than laymen used to believe, anyway: masters may always have known. Capablanca, the former world champion, was once asked by an admirer how many moves he typically examined in a difficult position. He replied, "One, but it is the right one." Capablanca was pretty close to the mark. It turns out that much skill in chess is perceptual rather than calculational. An experienced chess player can glance at the board and see the structure of the position: its strategies and weaknesses, opportunities and dangers. This seeing is quite different from calculation. It is perceptual and simultaneous rather than intellectual and sequential.

You might suppose that this knowledge about how real chess masters play would soon have been incorporated into chessplaying programs. Curiously, just the opposite has happened. There now are programs that play much better chess than those of the 1950s and 1960s; they do not play world championship chess, but they play well and can beat players of master calibre. Some day, one of them will win one of those chess wagers. But this is being achieved at a price: the new programs do not play chess as we do. They have no perceptual abilities, and see no patterns. They succeed because [of] today's very fast computers and today's ingenious programs that can search more possibilities more deeply than before, skimming faster and faster. Although these programs are becoming more successful by external criteria (winning chess games) they function *less* like people than the programs of a decade ago. They are like ELIZA: deceptively similar to a person at first glance, they might pass Turing's test. In fact, however, their "thinking" is not like ours at all.

For a psychologist, the important question is not what computers will be able to do in some other century but how today's programs work, how they are similar to, or different from, people. That question is important because it might shed some light on human nature. Many differences between computers and people are obvious; I would like to conclude by mentioning one that is less often appreciated. People do things (like playing chess) for a variety of reasons. Any chess player knows that you don't always play chess to win. Sometimes you play to keep the game going, or just get interested in a combination that seems elegant. You may even ask your opponent to take back a stupid move so that the game can continue. You might play to be friends with your opponent, or because you hate him. All these things go through the head of a human chess player; none are incorporated in computer programs. It is in the nature of programs to be given arbitrary goals that they pursue "single-mindedly." Their purposes do not arise from their nature and their situation, as ours do. That is why their activities do not incorporate reasonable presuppositions, and don't have any meanings. They merely run through series of steps; they don't intend anything and have no natural responses.

Perhaps the real problem is that computers don't grow up. They don't start small. The human approach to any given problem is based on experience with a whole history of other problems, all the way back to childhood and infancy. That may be why we generally have coherent purposes, why we can almost always step back the necessary number of paces until we understand the context of any problem we encounter in everyday life. Computers can't do this, so they never know what is going on. . . .

I believe that to achieve artificial intelligence we will first have to understand natural intelligence. Then, perhaps, we could figure out how to endow a device with it from the start. (Or, perhaps that would turn out to be impossible.) We are still a long way from that understanding.

So far, the study of "thinking" in computers has contributed relatively little to the enterprise, and that little mostly by contrast. If "thinking" is what people do when they talk, understand language, play chess, and solve problems, then machines can't think.

CHALLENGE QUESTIONS

Can Computers Help Us Understand the Human Mind?

1. Based on your own experiences or on your study of psychology and what you have learned about the human mind, give some examples of aspects of the human mind that computers *cannot* help us understand.

2. If a computer diagnosed and recommended treatment for your most serious medical problems, would you feel comfortable with that? Why or why not?

3. If computers use different strategies than humans, does that mean that computers cannot help us understand the human mind, even though they may beat their programmers at checkers or chess?

4. Should humans try to learn to simulate computer strategies for problem solving?

ISSUE 9

Can Intelligence Be Increased?

YES: Robert J. Sternberg, from "How Can We Teach Intelligence?" *Educational Leadership* (September 1984)

NO: Arthur R. Jensen, from "Compensatory Education and the Theory of Intelligence," *Phi Delta Kappan* (April 1985)

ISSUE SUMMARY

YES: Psychologist Robert J. Sternberg presents his view that intelligence is a changeable and multifaceted characteristic, and he suggests that intelligence can be taught through training programs, three of which he summarizes. **NO:** Psychologist Arthur R. Jensen contends that efforts to increase intelligence have not resulted in any appreciable gains and that programs designed for this purpose had a faulty understanding of the nature of intelligence.

Are we born with all the intelligence we will ever have? To what extent can we ensure that all healthy people will be able to cope with the increasing complexities of our society? As we become increasingly dependent upon our educational systems, these questions assume special importance.

If intelligence is a capacity fixed by the time of birth, then an efficient educational system should not waste the time, space, money, and resources that teach beyond each student's capacity. It might be appropriate for each individual's educational track to be determined in advance through extensive intelligence testing.

The 1960s in America can be characterized in part by the conviction that the educational disadvantages of poverty could be overcome by special "head start" programs early in a child's life. Early outcomes provided some evidence that intelligence could be increased. However, the long-term results were less encouraging. The question of an unchangeable intelligence is still open.

Robert J. Sternberg complains that psychologists' traditional preoccupation with the measurement of intelligence has prevented them from understanding the nature of intelligence. The most serious error, he says, has been the assumption "that intelligence is, for the most part, a fixed and immutable characteristic of the individual." Sternberg alleges that a vested interest in intelligence tests with stable scores has interfered with the view that intelligence is changeable.

Sternberg asserts that his own research findings suggest that intelligence *can* be trained and focuses on the question of *how* it can be trained. He presents his own theory of what intelligence is, then reviews three programs that train aspects of intelligence specified by his theory. Finally, he discusses the variables to be considered by educational administrators in the position of choosing programs for their specific school systems.

Arthur R. Jensen claims, "The plain truth is that compensatory programs have not resulted in any appreciable, durable gains in IQ or scholastic achievement for those youngsters who have taken part in them." He points out that these programs have produced positive gains in care, involvement, and attitudes, but not in intelligence or academic achievement.

Jensen says the specialists responsible for these compensatory programs were wrong in their understanding of what intelligence is and what IQ tests measure. He says their error was in their view of intelligence as "consisting of a general learning ability of almost unlimited plasticity plus the 'knowledge contents' of memory."

POINT	COUNTERPOINT
• Existing intelligence tests are inadequate.	• Existing intelligence tests have high validity.
• Intelligence is plastic.	• Intelligence is fixed.
• Intelligence can be trained.	• Intelligence is not subject to manipulation.

YES

Robert J. Sternberg

HOW CAN WE TEACH INTELLIGENCE?

For most of the century, psychologists studying intelligence have been preoccupied with a single question, "How can we measure intelligence?" In retrospect, this preoccupation has turned out to be a grave mistake for several reasons. First, it has led to neglect of the more important question, "What is intelligence?" If intelligence tests have not improved much over the years—and the evidence suggests that they haven't (Sternberg, 1979, 1980)—one can scarcely be surprised. Better tests of intelligence could arise only from better ideas of what intelligence is; curiously enough, few psychologists have sought better tests through better understanding. Rather, they have sought better tests through small refinements of existing technology, which is limited by the inadequacies of the meager theory underlying it (Sternberg, 1977).

Second, the preoccupation with testing has been based on certain assumptions, at least one of which is seriously in error. This assumption is that intelligence is, for the most part, a fixed and immutable characteristic of the individual. After all, if intelligence is constantly changing, or even potentially changeable, what good could tests be? With scores constantly changing, the usefulness of the tests as measures to rank individuals in a stable way over time would be seriously challenged.

Third, and most important for concerned educators, both the preoccupation with testing and the assumption that intelligence is a fixed entity have led to neglect of an even more productive question, "Can intelligence be trained, and if so, how?" My research findings suggest that intelligence *can* be trained. Thus, the focus of this article is the question of "How?"

Because there is no unanimous agreement among psychologists as to the exact nature of intelligence, my own views are necessarily somewhat idiosyncratic. Nevertheless, they are accepted in large part by many specialists in the field, and especially those who have set their goal to train intelligence rather than merely to measure it (Brown, 1983; de Bono, 1983; Resnick, 1976; Detterman and Sternberg, 1982).

My "componential" theory of intelligence seeks to understand intelligence in terms of the component processes that make up intelligence performance (Sternberg, 1979). I will briefly describe the theory, then review three programs that train aspects of intelligence as specified by the theory. Then I

From Robert J. Sternberg, "How Can We Teach Intelligence?" *Educational Leadership* (September 1984). Copyright © 1984 by the Association for Supervision and Curriculum Development and funded by the National Institute of Education. Reprinted by permission.

will conclude with general remarks and suggestions on the adoption of an intellectual or thinking skills training program.

COMPONENTS OF INTELLIGENCE

The view of intelligence as comprising, in part, a set of processes differs in a fundamental way from the view that led to IQ tests. At the turn of the century, the traditional or psychometric view was (and for some continues to be) that intelligence comprises one or more stable, fixed entities (Cattell, 1971; Guilford, 1967; Vernon, 1971). These entities, called *factors*, were alleged to give rise to the individual differences we observe both in IQ test performance and in students' performances at school. The problem with this view is that it does little to suggest how intelligence can be modified. But if intelligence can be broken down into a set of underlying processes, then it is clear what we can do to improve it: we can intervene at the level of the mental process and teach individuals what processes to use when, how to use them, and how to combine them into workable strategies for task solution.

What exactly are these processes? My research suggests they can be divided into three types (Sternberg, 1984). The first type, *metacomponents*, are the higher order or executive processes that we use to plan what we are going to do, monitor what we are doing, and evaluate what we have done. Deciding on a strategy for solving an arithmetic problem or organizing a term paper are examples of metacomponents at work. The second type of processes are *performance components*. Whereas metacomponents decide what to do, performance components

actually do it. So the actual steps we use in, say, solving an analogy or an arithmetic problem, whether on an IQ test or in everyday life, would be examples of sets of performance components in action. The third type of processes are *knowledge-acquisition components*. Processes of this kind are used in learning new material; for example, in first learning how to solve an analogy or a given type of arithmetic problem.

This may seem very abstract, so let's take a concrete example: an analogy. An analogy provides a particularly apt example because virtually everyone who has ever studied intelligence has found the ability to see and solve analogies to be fundamental to intelligent performance. According to the traditional psychometric view, the ability to solve an analogy would be attributed to a static underlying factor of intelligence. Charles Spearman, a famous psychometrician around the turn of the century, called this factor "g," or general intelligence. Some years later, Louis Thurstone, another psychometrician, called the factor "reasoning." The problem with such labels is that they tell us little either about how analogies are solved, or about how the ability to solve analogous problems can be taught.

In contrast, a process-based approach seeks to identify the mental processes used to solve the analogy or other problem. Consider the processes one might use in solving an analogy such as, "*Washington* is to *one* as *Lincoln* is to (a) five, (b) 15, (c) 20, (d) 50." First, we must decide what processes to use, a decision that is metacomponential in nature. Next we must decide how to sequence these processes so as to form a workable strategy for analogy solution, another metacomponential decision. Then we must use the performance components and strategy we have selected to actually solve the problem. It appears, through experimental data we have collected, that what people do is to *encode*, as they need them, relevant attributes of the terms of the analogy: that Washington was the first President of the United States, that he was a Revolutionary War general, and that his is the portrait that appears on a one-dollar bill. Next they *infer* the relation between the first two terms of the analogy, perhaps in this case recognizing that the basis of the analogy might be either Washington as first president or Washington as the portrait on the one-dollar bill. Then they *map* the relation they have inferred in the first part of the analogy to the second part of the analogy (that is, from the Washington part to the Lincoln part), perhaps recognizing that the topic of the analogy is some property of U.S. presidents. Next people *apply* the relation they inferred in the first part of the analogy, as mapped to the second part of the analogy, to the third term so as to select the best alternative. In this case, "five" is the preferred alternative, because it enables one to carry through the relation of portraits on currency (that is, Lincoln's portrait is on the five-dollar bill just as Washington's is on the one-dollar bill). Although this account is a simplification of my model of reasoning by analogy (Sternberg, 1977), it represents the kind of theorizing that goes into a process-based account of intelligent performance.

Now, how can the metacomponents and performance components of intelligence be taught? How can we make students better at structuring and then solving problems than they would be on their own? I recommend three widely disseminated programs, each of which

has a unique set of strengths and weaknesses.

INSTRUMENTAL ENRICHMENT

The first training program, Reuven Feuerstein's (1980) *Instrumental Enrichment (IE)* program, was originally proposed for use with children showing retarded performance; it has since been recognized by Feuerstein and others to be valuable for children at all levels of the intellectual spectrum. It is based on Feuerstein's theory of intelligence, which emphasizes what I refer to as metacomponential and performance-componential functioning.

Instrumental Enrichment is intended to improve cognitive functioning related to the input, elaboration, and output of information. Feuerstein has compiled a long list of cognitive deficits his program is intended to correct. This list includes:

• Unplanned, impulsive, and unsystematic exploratory behavior. When presented with a number of cues to problem solving that must be scanned, the individual's approach is disorganized, leaving the individual unable to select those cues whose specific attributes make them relevant for a proper solution to the problem at hand.

• Lack of or impaired capacity for considering two sources of information at once, reflected in dealing with data in a piecemeal fashion rather than as a unit of organized facts.

• Inadequacy in experiencing the existence of an actual problem and subsequently in defining it.

• Lack of spontaneous comparative behavior or limitation of its appearance to a restricted field of needs.

• Lack of or impaired strategies for hypothesis testing.

• Lack of orientation toward the need for logical evidence.

• Lack of or impaired planning behavior.

• Episodic grasp of reality. The individual is unable to relate different aspects of his or her experience to one another. Feuerstein seeks to correct these deficits and, at the same time, to increase the student's intrinsic motivation and feeling of personal competence and self-worth.

What are some of the main characteristics of the Feuerstein program? The materials themselves are structured as a series of units, or instruments, each of which emphasizes a particular cognitive function and its relationship to various cognitive deficiencies. Feuerstein defines an instrument as something by means of which something else is effected; hence, performance on the materials is seen as a means to an end, rather than as an end in itself. Emphasis in analyzing *IE* performance is on processes rather than products. A student's errors are viewed as a source of insights into how the student solves problems. *Instrumental Enrichment* does *not* attempt to teach either specific items of information or formal, operational, abstract thinking by means of a well-defined, structured knowlege base. To the contrary, it is as content-free as possible. . . .

What are the strengths and weaknesses of the *IE* program? On the positive side, it (a) can be used for children in a wide age range (from the upper grades of elementary school to early high school) and for children of a wide range of ability levels (from the retarded to the above average) and socioeconomic groups; (b) is well liked by children and appears to be effective in raising their intrinsic motivation and self-esteem; (c) is well

packaged and readily obtainable; and (d) appears effective in raising children's scores on ability tests. Indeed, most of the training exercises contain items similar or identical to those found on intelligence and multiple aptitude tests, so that it should not be totally surprising that intensive practice and training on such items should raise these test scores.

On the more negative side: (a) the program requires extensive teacher training, which must be administered by a designated training authority for the duration of the program; (b) the isolation of the problems from any working knowledge or discipline base (such as social studies or reading, for example) raises questions regarding the transferability of the skills to academic and real-world intellectual tasks, especially over the long term; and (c) despite Feuerstein's aversion to IQ tests, the program trains primarily those abilities that IQ tests tap rather than a broader spectrum of abilities that go beyond intelligence as the tests test it.

To sum up, then, Feuerstein's *Instrumental Enrichment* program is an attractive package in many respects, although with limitations in regard to breadth of skills taught and potential power for generalization. Nevertheless, it is among the best of the available programs that emphasize thinking skill training. Probably it has been the most widely used and field-tested program, both in this country and abroad. As a result, it can be recommended both for members of the majority culture and for members of other cultures and subcultures as well.

PHILOSOPHY FOR CHILDREN

Matthew Lipman's *Philosophy for Children*

program is about as different from *Instrumental Enrichment* as it could be (Lipman, Sharp, and Oscayan, 1980). Yet it seeks to foster many of the same intellectual skills, albeit in a very different manner.

Philosophy for Children consists of a series of texts in which fictional children spend a considerable portion of their time thinking about thinking and about ways in which better thinking can be distinguished from poorer thinking. The keys to learning presented in the program are identification and simulation: through reading the texts and engaging in classroom discussions and exercises that follow the reading, the author's objective is for students to identify with the characters and to join in the kinds of thinking depicted in the program.

Lipman has listed 30 thinking skills that *Philosophy for Children* has intended to foster in children of the upper elementary school, generally grades 5-8. A representative sampling of these skills includes the following:

• *Concept development.* Students clarify their understanding of concepts by applying them to specific cases, learning to identify those cases that are within the boundaries and those that are outside. For example, when considering the concept of friendship, children are asked whether people have to be the same age to be friends, whether two people can be friends and not like each other very much, and whether it is possible for friends ever to lie to one another.

• *Generalizations.* Given a set of facts, students are to note uniformities or regularities and to generalize these regularities from given instances to similar ones. For example, children might be asked to consider generalizations that can be drawn from a set of given facts

such as, "I get sick when I eat raspberries; I get sick when I eat strawberries; I get sick when I eat blackberries."

• *Formulating cause-effect relationships.* Students should discern and construct formulations indicating relationships between causes and effects. For example, students might be given a statement such as "He threw the stone and broke the window," and then be asked whether the statement necessarily implies a cause-effect relationship.

• *Drawing syllogistic inferences.* Students should draw correct conclusions from valid syllogisms and recognize invalid syllogisms when they are presented. For example, they might be given the premises, "All dogs are animals; all collies are dogs," and be asked what valid inference they can draw from these premises.

• *Consistency and contradictions.* Students should recognize internal consistencies and inconsistencies within a given set of statements or other data. For example, they might be asked to ponder whether it is possible to eat animals if one genuinely cares about them.

• *Identifying underlying assumptions.* Students should recognize the often hidden assumptions that underlie statements. For example, they might be given the following sentences: "I love your hair that way, Peg. What beauty parlor did you go to?" and be asked to identify the hidden assumption underlying the question.

• *Grasping part-whole and whole-part connections.* Students should recognize relations between parts and wholes and avoid mistakes in reasoning based on identification of the part with the whole, or vice versa. For example, students might be asked to identify the part-whole fallacy underlying the statement,

"If Mike's face has handsome features, Mike must have a handsome face."

• *Working with analogies.* Students should form and identify analogies. For example, they should be able to solve an analogy such as Germ is to Disease as Candle is to (a) Wax, (b) Wick, (c) White, (d) Light.

The skills trained through the *Philosophy for Children* program are conveyed through a series of stories about children. Consider, for example, the first chapter of *Harry Stottlemeier's Discovery*, the first book in the program series. In this chapter about the consequences of Harry's not paying attention in science class, children are introduced to a wealth of thinking skills. For instance:

• *Problem formulation.* Harry says, "All planets revolve about the sun, but not everything that revolves about the sun is a planet." He realizes that he had been assuming that just because all planets revolve about the sun, everything that revolves about the sun must be a planet.

• *Nonreversibility of logical "all" statements.* Harry says that "a sentence can't be reversed. If you put the last part of a sentence first, it'll no longer be true." For example, he cannot convert "all model airplanes are toys" into "all toys are model airplanes."

• *Reversibility of logical "no" statements.* Lisa, a friend of Harry's, realizes that logical "no" statements can be reversed. "No submarines are kangaroos," for example, can be converted to "No kangaroos are submarines."

• *Application of principles to real-life situations.* Harry intervenes in a discussion between two adults, showing how a principle he had deduced earlier can be applied to disprove one of the adult's argument. . . .

The nature of the *Philosophy for Children* program may be further elucidated by comparing it to Feuerstein's program. The notable similarity between the two programs is that both seek to teach thinking skills, especially what was referred to earlier as executive processes (metacomponents) and nonexecutive processes (performance components). But given the basic similarity of goals, the differences between the programs are striking.

First, whereas Feuerstein's program minimizes the role of knowledge base and customary classroom content, Lipman's program maximizes such involvement. Although the introductory volume, *Harry Stottlemeier's Discovery*, is basically philosophical in tone, the subsequent volumes—*Mark, Pixie, Suki,* and *Lisa*—emphasize infusion of thinking skills into different content areas: the arts, social studies, and science.

Second, whereas the material in Feuerstein's program minimizes the use of written language, the material in Lipman's program is conceptually abstract but is presented through wholly verbal text that deals with highly concrete situations.

Third, although both programs involve class discussion, there is much more emphasis on discussion and interchange in Lipman's program than in Feuerstein's. Similarly, the written exercises are less important in Lipman's program.

Fourth, Feuerstein's program was originally designed for retarded learners, although it has since been extended to children at all points along the continuum of intellectual ability. Lipman's program seems oriented toward children of at least average ability on a scale of national norms. Moreover, the reading in *Philosophy for Children* can be a problem for children much below grade level in reading.

What are the strengths and weaknesses of *Philosophy for Children*? The program has outstanding strengths. First, the stories are exciting and highly motivating to upper elementary school children. Second, it is attractively packaged and easily obtainable. Third, tests of the program have shown it to be effective in raising the level of children's thinking skills. Fourth, the infusion of the thinking skills into content areas should help assure durability and at least some transferability of learning attained through the program. Finally, the thinking skills taught are clearly the right ones to teach for both academic and everyday information processing—no one could possibly complain that the skills are only relevant for IQ tests, although, in fact, the skills are also relevant for performance on such tests. . . .

In summary, although it is limited somewhat by the range of students for whom it is appropriate, no program I am aware of is more likely to teach durable and transferable thinking skills than *Philosophy for Children*.

CHICAGO MASTERY LEARNING READING PROGRAM

Whereas *Instrumental Enrichment* and *Philosophy for Children* emphasize thinking skills (metacomponents and performance components), the *Chicago Mastery Learning Reading Program* emphasizes learning strategies and study skills (knowledge-acquisition [Jones, 1982] components)—a fuzzy but nevertheless useful distinction.

The *Chicago* program, developed by Beau Fly Jones in collaboration with others, equips students with the learning strategies and study skills they need to succeed in school and in their everyday lives. Like *Philosophy for Children*, this program is written for children roughly in grades five through eight. There are four books (tan, purple, silver, and gold), each of which teaches somewhat different skills. The emphasis in all four books, however, is on learning to learn. Within each grade (color) level, there are two kinds of units: comprehension and study skills.

Consider, for example, the purple (Grade 7) sequence. The comprehension program contains units on using sentence context, mood in reading and writing, comprehending complex information, comprehending comparisons, analyzing characters, and distinguishing facts from opinions. The study skills program contains units on parts of a book, graphs and charts, preview-question-read, studying textbook chapters, major and minor ideas, and outlining with parallel structure. The silver (Grade 8) sequence for comprehension contains units of figurative language, word meaning from context, reasoning from facts to complex inferences, analyzing stories and plays, completing a story or a play, signs, and symbols. The sequence for study skills contains units on supporting facts, research aids, notetaking in outline form, summaries and generalizations, comprehending road maps, and understanding forms and directions.

The *Chicago* program is based on the belief that almost all students can learn what only the best students currently learn, if only the more typical or less able students are given appropriate learning opportunities. Mastery learning is described as differing from traditional instruction primarily in the systematic and frequent use of formative and diagnostic testing within each of the instructional units. Instruction is done in groups, with individual assistance and remediation as necessary. Because students typically enter the classroom situation with differing skills and levels of proficiency in the exercise of these skills, instructional units begin with simple, concrete, literal, and familiar material and proceed gradually to the more complex, abstract, inexplicit, and unfamiliar material.

Each instructional unit in the *Chicago* program contains several distinct parts: student activities, optional teaching activities, formative tests, additional activities, enrichment activities, retests, and subject-related applications. Students and teachers are thus provided with a wide variety of materials.

The number and variety of exercises is so great as to rule out the possibility of giving a fair sample of materials in the program. Thus, I can make no claim that the following few examples are representative of the program as a whole:

- *Using sentence context.* In one type of exercise, students read a sentence containing a new word for them to learn. They are assisted in using cues in the sentence to help them determine the word's meaning.
- *Mood in reading and writing.* Students are given a sentence from either expository or fictional text. They are asked to choose which of three words or phrases best describes the mood conveyed by the sentence.
- *Comprehending comparisons.* Students are taught about different kinds of comparisons. They are then given some sample comparisons and asked to elaborate on the meanings, some of which are metaphorical.
- *Facts and opinions.* Students are taught how to distinguish facts from opinions. They are given a passage to read, along with some statements following the passage. Their task is to indicate which statements represent facts and which opinions.

The *Chicago* program is similar to the *Instrumental Enrichment* and *Philosophy for Children* programs in its direct teaching of cognitive skills. The program differs in several key respects, however. First, it resembles typical classroom curriculum more than either of the other two programs. Whereas implementation of either of the others would almost certainly have to follow an explicit policy decision to teach thinking skills as an additional part of the curriculum, the *Chicago* program could very well be implemented as part of an established program, such as the reading curriculum. Second, the program does fit into a specific curriculum area that is common in schools, namely, reading. The Lipman program would fit into a philosophy curriculum, if any school offered such instruction. The Feuerstein program would be unlikely to fit into any existing curricular program, except those explicitly devoted to teaching thinking skills. Third, the *Chicago* program emphasizes learning strategies, whereas the emphasis of the other two programs tends to be on thinking skills. Finally, the *Chicago* program seems most broadly applicable to a wide range of students, including those who are above and below grade level.

Like all programs, the *Chicago* program has both strengths and weaknesses. Its most notable strengths are (1) the wide range of students to whom it can be administered, both in terms of intellectual levels and socio-economic backgrounds; (2) the relatively lesser amount of teacher training required for its implementation; (3) the ease with which the program can be incorporated into existing curricula; and (4) the immediate applicability of the skills to school and other life situations. Students in the program have shown significant pretest to pretest gains in achievement from the program (Jones, 1982).

As for weaknesses, or at least limitations, compared to the *IE* and Lipman's programs, (1) the materials applied are less likely to be intrinsically motivating to students; (2) the skills trained by the *Chicago* program are within a non-limited domain (reading and performing verbal comprehension) than in some other programs; and (3) the program is less clearly based on a psychological theory of cognition.

In conclusion, the *Chicago Mastery Learning Program* offers an attractive means for teaching learning skills, in the context of a reading program. The materials are carefully prepared to be wide ranging and should meet the needs of a wide variety of schools.

CHOOSING THE RIGHT PROGRAM

Do we really need intervention programs for teaching students intellectual skills? The answer is clearly "yes." During the last decade or so we have witnessed an unprecedented decline in the intellectual skills of our school children (Wigdor and Garner, 1982). This is evident, of course, from the decline in scores on tests such as the Scholastic Aptitude Test (SAT); but college professors don't need SAT scores to be apprised of the decline: they can see it in poorer class performance and particularly in the poorer reading and writing of their students. Moreover, thinking skills are needed by more than the college-bound population. Perhaps intellectual skills could be better trained through existing curricula than they are

now. But something in the system is not working, and I view programs such as those described here as exciting new developments for reversing the declines in intellectual performance we have witnessed in recent years.

How does one go about choosing the right program for one's particular school and student needs? I believe that wide-ranging research is needed before selecting any one of several programs for school or districtwide implementation. Which program to select will depend on the grade level, socioeconomic level, and intellectual level of the students; the particular kinds of skills one wishes to teach; the amount of time one can devote to training students; one's philosophy of intellectual skills training (that is, whether training should be infused into or separated from regular curricula); and one's financial resources, among other things. Clearly, the decision of which program to use should be made only after extensive deliberation and outside consultation, preferably with people who have expertise, but not a vested interest, in the implementation of one particular program or another.

The following general guidelines can be applied in selecting a program (see also Sternberg, 1983):

• The program should be based on a psychological theory of the intellectual processes it seeks to train and on an educational theory of the way in which the processes will be taught. A good pair of theories should state what processes are to be trained, how the processes work together in problem solving, and how the processes can be taught so as to achieve durability and transfer of training. Innumerable programs seek to train intelligence, but most of them are worth little or nothing. One can immediately rule out large numbers of the low-value programs by investigating whether they have any theoretical basis. The three programs described here are both strong psychological and educational foundations.

• The program should be socioculturally appropriate. It should be clear from the examples described here that programs differ widely in terms of the student populations to whom they are targeted. The best intentions in such a program may be thwarted if the students cannot relate the program both to their cognitive structures and to the world in which they live.

• The program should provide explicit training both in the mental processes used in task performance (performance components and knowledge-acquisition components) and in self-management strategies for using these components (metacomponents). Many early attempts at process training did not work because investigators assumed that just teaching the processes necessary for task performance would result in improved performance on intellectual tasks. The problem was that students often did not learn when to use the processes or how to implement them in tasks differing even slightly from the ones on which they had been trained. In order to achieve durable and transferable learning, it is essential that students be taught not only how to perform tasks but also when to use the strategies they are taught and how to implement them in new situations.

• The program should be responsive to the motivational as well as the intellectual needs of the students. A program that does not adequately motivate students is bound not to succeed, no matter how excellent the cognitive component may be.

• The program should be sensitive to individual differences. Individuals differ greatly in the knowledge and skills they bring to any educational program. A program that does not take these individual differences into account will almost inevitably fail to engage large numbers of students.

• The program should provide explicit links between the training it provides and functioning in the real world. Psychologists have found that transfer of training does not come easily. One cannot expect to gain transfer unless explicit provisions are made in the program so as to increase its likelihood of occurrence.

• Adoption of the program should take into account demonstrated empirical success in implementations similar to one's own planned implementation. Surprisingly, many programs have no solid data behind them. Others may have data that are relevant only to school or student situations quite different from one's own. A key to success is choosing a program with a demonstrated track record in similar situations.

• The program should have associated with it a well-tested curriculum for teacher training as well as for student training. The best program can fail to realize its potential if teachers are insufficiently or improperly trained.

• Expectations should be appropriate for what the program can accomplish. Teachers and administrators often set themselves up for failure by setting expectations that are inappropriate or too high.

Programs are now available that do an excellent, if incomplete, job of improving children's intellectual skills. The time has come for supplementing the standard curriculum with such programs. We can continue to use intelligence tests, but we will provide more service to children by developing their intelligence than by testing it.

REFERENCES

Brown, A. L. "Knowing When, Where, and How to Remember: A Problem of Metacognition." In *Advances in Instructional Psychology, Vol 1.* Edited by R. Glaser. Hillsdale, N.J.: Erlbaum, 1978.

Brown, J. L. "On Teaching Thinking Skills in the Elementary and Middle Schools." *Phi Delta Kappan* 64 (1983): 709-714.

Cattell, R. B. *Abilities: Their Structure, Growth, and Action.* Boston: Houghton-Mifflin, 1971.

de Bono, E. "The Direct Teaching of Thinking as a Skill." *Phi Delta Kappan* 64 (1983): 703-708.

Detterman, D. K., and Sternberg, R. J., eds. *How and How Much Can Intelligence Be Increased?* Norwood, N.J.: Ablex, 1982.

Feuerstein, R. *Instrumental Enrichment: An Intervention Program for Cognitive Modifiability.* Baltimore: University Park Press, 1980.

Guilford, J. P. *The Nature of Intelligence.* New York: McGraw-Hill, 1967.

Jones, B. F. *Chicago Mastery Learning: Reading.* 2nd ed. Watertown, Mass.: Mastery Education Corporation, 1982.

Lipman, M.; Sharp, A. M.; and Oscanyan, F. S. *Philosophy in the Classroom.* 2nd ed. Philadelphia: Temple University Press, 1980.

Resnick, L. B. *The Nature of Intelligence.* Hillsdale, N.J.: Erlbaum, 1976.

Sternberg, R. J. *Intelligence, Information Processing, and Analogical Reasoning: The Componential Analysis of Human Abilities.* Hillsdale, N.J.: Erlbaum, 1977.

Sternberg, R. J. "The Nature of Mental Abilities." *American Psychologist* 34 (1979): 214-230.

Sternberg, R. J. "The Construct Validity of Aptitude Tests: An Information-Processing Assessment." In *Construct Validity in Psychological Measurement.* Princeton, N.J.: Educational Testing Service, 1980.

Sternberg, R. J. "Criteria for Intellectual Skills Training." *Educational Researcher* 12 (1983): 6-12, 26.

Sternberg, R. J. *Beyond IQ: A Triarchic Theory of Human Intelligence.* New York: Cambridge University Press, 1984.

Vernon, P. E. *The Structure of Human Abilities.* London: Methuen, 1971.

Wigdor, A. K., and Garner, W. R., eds. *Ability Testing: Uses, Consequences, and Controversies* (2 volumes). Washington, D.C.: National Academy Press, 1982.

NO

Arthur R. Jensen

COMPENSATORY EDUCATION
AND THE THEORY OF INTELLIGENCE

The past 20 years have been a period of unparalleled affluence for public education and educational research in the U.S. When the history of this era is written, two features will stand out prominently: racial desegregation of the schools and large-scale experimentation with compensatory education.

The nation focused its educational resources during this period primarily on extending the benefits of education to every segment of the population—especially to those groups that historically have derived the least benefit from the traditional system of schooling. During the past 20 years more young people have gone to school for more years and have obtained more diplomas, per capita, in the U.S. than in any other nation. Fifty percent of U.S. high school graduates in the 1970s went on to college.

These proud facts are one side of the picture. The other side is much less complimentary and should shake any complacency we Americans might feel. The past 20 years, which have brought the most energetic large-scale innovations in the history of U.S. education, have also brought an accelerating decline in Scholastic Aptitude Test scores. And there are other signs of malaise as well. On objective measures of the average level of educational achievement, the U.S. falls below all other industrialized nations, according to the International Association for the Evaluation of Educational Achievement.[1] In fact, average levels of educational achievement lower than that of the U.S. are found only in the industrially under-developed nations of the Third World.

Illiteracy in the U.S. has been grossly underestimated. Until recently, the U.S. Census Bureau routinely estimated the rate of illiteracy as the percentage of Americans with fewer than six years of schooling. The 1980 Census found that only two-tenths of 1% (0.2%) of the U.S. population between the ages of 14 and 24 met this definition of illiteracy—a rate that was the same for both black and white Americans.

Simple tests of actual reading ability reveal a much less rosy picture, however. According to lawyer and psychologist Barbara Lerner, evidence collected by the National Assessment of Educational Progress shows that "the overall rate of illiteracy for cohorts reaching their 18th birthday in the 1970s can safely be estimated to have been at least 20%. . . . [Moreover, the] black-white gap was still dramatic: 41.6% of all black 17-year-olds still enrolled in school in 1975 were functionally illiterate."[2] Lerner goes on to emphasize the broad implications of this finding:

On this basis, it would have seemed reasonable to predict serious shortages of literate workers throughout the 1980s and perhaps beyond, along with high levels of structural unemployment, particularly among younger black workers, and increasing difficulty in meeting economic competition from foreign countries with more literate work forces.[3]

Clearly, those conditions that originally gave rise to the aims and aspirations of compensatory education are as relevant today as they were 20 years ago. Of the many lessons that can be learned from assessments and meta-analyses of the results of 20 years of compensatory education, I intend to dwell in this article on what seems to me to be one of the most important. Because the lesson on which I will dwell is one of the clearest and seemingly least-debatable findings of studies of compensatory education programs of all kinds and because this lesson has important implications for both theory and practice, it is peculiar that this lesson has been soft-pedaled in most published summaries of compensatory education outcomes.

The lesson to which I refer is this: compensatory education has made its least impressive impact on just those variables that it was originally intended (and expected) to improve the most: namely, I.Q. and scholastic achievement. The plain truth is that compensatory programs have not resulted in any appreciable, durable gains in I.Q. or scholastic achievement for those youngsters who have taken part in them. This is an important discovery, and the fact that we do not like this outcome or that it is not what we expected neither diminishes its importance nor justifies downplaying it. Rather, we are challenged to try to understand its theoretical implications for the study of intelligence and its practical implications for the practice of education.

Let us not be distracted from trying to understand the discrepancy between the expected and the actual outcomes of compensatory education programs by the too-easy response of retroactively revising our original expectations. We should gain more from our 20 years of experience than just a list of excuses for the disappointing discrepancy between our expectations and the actual results.

To be sure, Head Start and other compensatory education programs have produced some positive gains. The fact that the bona fide benefits of compensatory education have not been primarily cognitive in nature and not strongly reflected in academic achievement per se should not detract from the social importance of these gains. The positive outcomes of Head Start and similar programs include such things as the improvement of participants' nutrition and of their medical and dental care. The list of positive outcomes also includes greater involvement of parents in their children's schooling, noticeable improvement in the children's attitude toward school and in their self-esteem, fewer behavioral problems among participants, fewer retentions in grade, and a smaller percentage of special education placements.[4]

These socially desirable outcomes have not been accompanied by marked or lasting improvement in either I.Q. or academic performance, however. Even the smaller percentage of special education placements may be attributable to teachers' and administrators' knowledge that certain children have taken part in Head Start or other compensatory education programs, because such children are less apt than nonparticipating peers to be labeled as candidates for special education. Gene Glass and Mary Ellwein offer an insightful observation on this point in their review of As the Twig Is Bent, a book on 11 compensatory education programs and their outcomes, as assessed by the Consortium for Longitudinal Studies. According to Glass and Ellwein:

> [T]hose whose ideas are represented in As the Twig Is Bent see themselves as developmental psychologists molding the inner, lasting core of the individual—one can almost visualize the cortical wiring they imagine being rearranged by ever-earlier intervention. And yet the true lasting effects of a child's preschool experiences may be etched only in the attitudes of the professionals and in the records of the institutions that will husband his or her life after preschool.[5]

Even studies of those compensatory programs that involve the most intensive and prolonged educational experience show the effects of such programs on I.Q. to be relatively modest and subject to "fadeout" within one to three years. The highly publicized "Miracle in Milwaukee" Study by Rick Heber and How-ard Garbert appears to be a case in point. In that study, the researchers gave intensive training designed to enhance cognitive development to children who were deemed at risk for mental retardation because of their family backgrounds. The training lasted from birth until the participants entered school. Unfortunately, no detailed account of the conduct of the Milwaukee Study or of its long-term outcomes has yet appeared in any refereed scientific journal. Because the data are not available for full and proper critical review, I cannot legitimately cite this study with regard to the effects of early intervention on subsequent intelligence and scholastic achievement.

Fortunately, a similar study—the Abecedarian Project,[6] currently under way in North Carolina—is being properly reported in the appropriate journals, and the researchers conducting this study promise the kind of evaluation that Heber and Garber have failed to deliver. From infancy to school age, children in the Abecedarian Project spend six or more hours daily, five days a week, 50 weeks a year, in a cognitive training program. Their I.Q. gains, measured against a matched control group at age 3, look encouraging. However, the possibility exists that the program has merely increased participants' I.Q. scores and not the underlying factor of intelligence that the I.Q. test is intended to measure and upon which its predictive and construct validity depend.[7]

Probably the most scholarly, thorough, and up-to-date examination of the variety of experimental attempts to improve intelligence and other human abilities is How and How Much Can Intelligence Be Increased? edited by Douglas Detterman and Robert Sternberg.[8] In a review of this book, I said:

What this book may bring as something of a surprise to many psychologists who received their education in the 1950s and '60s, in the heyday of what has been termed "naive environmentalism" in American educational psychology, is the evident great difficulty in effecting practically substantial and durable gains in individuals' intelligence. In terms of some conceptions of human intelligence as predominantly a product of cultural learning, this fact should seem surprising. . . . The sum total of the wide-ranging information provided in this book would scarcely contradict the conclusion that, as yet, investigators have not come up with dependable and replicable evidence that they have discovered a psychological method by which they can increase "intelligence" in the sense of Spearman's g.[9]

Thus current claims regarding the plasticity of human intelligence are notably more subdued than were the promises of only 20 years ago. Edward Zigler, one of the founders of and leaders in compensatory education, and his colleague, Winnie Berman, have recently warned that workers in the field "must be on guard never again to make the errors of overpromising and overselling the positive effects of early childhood intervention."[10]

Despite their personal enthusiasm for compensatory education, Zigler and Berman have surveyed the history and developments of this field with critical objectivity. Of the beginning of preschool intervention in the 1960s, they say:

It was widely believed that a program of early environmental enrichment would give lower SES [socioeconomic status] children the boost they needed to perform on a par with their middle SES peers. Intervention was supposed to impart immediate benefits so that class differences would be eliminated by the time of school entry. Furthermore, many expected that the brief preschool experience would be so potent a counteraction to the deficits in poor children's lives that it could prevent further attenuation in age-appropriate performance and a recurrence of the gap between social classes in later grades. . . . What we witnessed in the 1960s was the belief that intelligence quotients can be dramatically increased with minimal effort. . . . Unfortunately, "knowing more" was easily translated into "becoming smarter."[11]

Elsewhere, Zigler describes the thinking in the early days of Head Start, a program that he helped to initiate:

. . . J. McV. Hunt, Benjamin Bloom, and others constructed for us a theoretical view that conceptualized the young child as possessing an almost unlimited degree of plasticity. Joe Hunt continued to assert that the norm of reaction for intelligence was 70 I.Q. points . . . and that relatively short-term intervention efforts could result in I.Q. gains of 49 or 63 points. With such environmental sugarplums dancing in our heads, we actually thought we could compensate for the effects of several years of impoverishment as well as inoculate the child against the future ravages of such impoverishment, all by providing a six- or eight-week summer Head Start experience.[12]

This theoretical view of human intelligence—a view that governed the design and expectations of compensatory education programs in the 1960s—has been put to the test during the past 20 years. And the outcome seems remarkably clear. It turns out that the prevailing views of most psychologists and educators in the 1960s were largely wrong with regard to such questions as, What is the nature of intelligence? What is it that our

I.Q. tests measure primarily? Why is the I.Q. so highly predictive of scholastic performance?

The error lay in believing that the disadvantage with which many poor or culturally different children entered school—and the disadvantage that compensatory education was intended to remedy—was mainly a deficiency in *knowledge*. Implicit in this belief was a view of intelligence as consisting of a general learning ability of almost unlimited plasticity plus the "knowledge contents" of memory, particularly those kinds of knowledge that serve to improve scholastic performance. Holders of this view saw the information content of I.Q. tests as an arbitrary sample of the specific items of knowledge and skill normally acquired by members of the white middle and upper classes.

In this highly behavioristic conception of intelligence, which I have elsewhere termed the *specificity doctrine*,[13] intelligence is erroneously identified with the content of the test items that psychologists have devised for assessing intelligence. These test items cover such things as general information, vocabulary, arithmetic, and the ability to copy certain geometric figures, to make block designs, and to work puzzles. To acquire the knowledge and skills to do these things—or to learn other, similar things that would have positive transfer to performance on I.Q. tests or in coursework—is to become more intelligent, according to this deceptive view of intelligence. As Zigler and Berman have put it, "knowing more" is erroneously translated into "becoming smarter."

Striking findings from two recent lines of research—that on test bias and that on mental chronometry—clearly contradict the view of individual and group differences in intelligence as differences primarily in knowledge.

The research on test bias has shown that the level of difficulty of I.Q. and achievement test items is consistent across all American-born, English-speaking ethnic and social-class groups. Moreover, I.Q. and achievement tests do not differ in their predictive validity for these groups. These findings are highly inconsistent with the hypothesis that cultural differences exist in the knowledge base that these tests sample. Available evidence from studies of test bias makes it extremely implausible that racial and social-class differences can be explained by cultural differences in the knowledge base or by differential opportunity for acquiring the knowledge that existing tests sample.[14] For every American-born social class and racial group, highly diverse test items maintain the same relative standing on indices of item difficulty, regardless of the culture loadings of the items. This phenomenon requires that we find some explanation for group differences on I.Q. and achievement tests other than cultural differences in exposure to the various kind of knowledge sampled by the tests.

We must seek the explanation, I believe, at the most basic level of information processing. In recent years, both the theory and the technology of research on cognitive processes have afforded powerful means for analyzing individual and group differences in abilities. Within the framework of cognitive processes research, the kinds of questions that we can investigate are quite different and more basic than those we can study through traditional psychometric tests and factor analysis. Mental chronometry, or measurement of the time required for various mental events in the course of information processing, permits us to investigate individual differences at the level of elementary cognitive processes—those processes through which individuals attain the complex learning, knowledge, and problem-solving skills that I.Q. tests sample.

Researchers devise the tasks used to measure individual differences in various elementary cognitive processes in such a way as to rule out or greatly minimize individual differences in knowledge. These tasks are so simple, and the error rates on them are so close to zero, that individual differences can be studied only by chronometric techniques. For example, the cognitive tasks that we use in our laboratory are so easy that they typically require less than one second to perform.[15] Yet these very brief response latencies, derived from a number of elementary processing tasks, together can account for some 70% of the variance in scores on untimed standard psychometric tests of intelligence. Very little of the true score variance on such tests can be attributed to the knowledge covered by the tests' content per se.

It is important to understand that the items of standardized psychometric tests are mainly vehicles for reflecting the past and present efficiency of mental processes. That these items usually include some knowledge content is only an incidental and nonessential feature. The fact is that individual differences on these content-laden tests correlate with response latencies on elementary cognitive-processing tasks that have minimal intellectual content. This means that our standard I.Q. tests—and the scholastic achievement tests with which these I.Q. tests are highly correlated—reflect individual differences in the speed and efficiency of basic cognitive processes more than they reflect differences in the information content to which test-takers have been exposed. In fact, we can account for a substantial portion of the variance in I.Q. scores by measuring the evoked electrical potentials of the brain, using an electrode attached to the scalp—a measure that is not only free of any knowledge content but that is not even dependent on any voluntary or overt behavior by the subject.[16]

Thus I suggest that the design of compensatory education and the assessment of its effects should be informed by the recent studies on information processing. The variables that have been measured by researchers in this field to date have correlated not only with I.Q., but with scholastic achievement as well.[17] An important question for future research is, What proportions of the variance in I.Q. and in scholastic achievement are associated with elementary cognitive processes and with meta-processes respectively? A second but equally important question is, What possible effects can various types of compensatory training have on these two levels of cognitive processes?

Elementary cognitive processes include such variables as perceptual speed, stimulus scanning, stimulus encoding, mental rotation or transformation of visual stimuli, short-term memory capacity, efficiency of information retrieval from long-term memory, generalization, discrimination, comparison, transfer, and response execution. *Meta-processes* include those planning and executive functions that select and coordinate the deployment of the elementary cognitive processes to handle specific situations, e.g., strategies for problem recognition, for selecting and combining lower-order cognitive processes, for organizing information, for allocating time and resources, for monitoring one's own performance, and the like.

Meta-processes are thought to be more amenable than elementary processes to improvement through training, but no solid evidence currently exists on this question. And, though much is already known about social-class and racial-group differences in I.Q. and scholastic achievement, psychologists have scarcely begun to try to understand the nature and locus of these differences in terms of the cognitive processes and meta-processes involved.[18] As yet, virtually nothing is known about the effects of compensatory education on the various levels of cognitive processing or about the extent to which the levels of cognitive processing can be influenced by training especially designed for that purpose.

I suspect that a substantial part of the individual variance in I.Q. and scholastic achievement—probably somewhere between 50% and 70%, according to the best evidence on the heritability of I.Q.—is not subject to manipulation by any strictly psychological or educational treatment. The reason for this, I assume, is that the main locus of control of that unyielding source of variance is more biological than psychological or behavioral.

At an even more fundamental level, we might ask why variance in intelligence should be so surprisingly resistant to experimental manipulation. As I have suggested elsewhere,[19] this apparent resistance to manipulation seems less surprising if we view human intelligence as an outcome of biological evolution. Genetic variation is the one absolutely essential ingredient to enable evolution to occur. If intelligence has evolved as a fitness characteristic in the Darwinian sense—that is,

as an instrumentality for the survival of humankind—it is conceivable that the biological basis of intelligence has a built-in stabilizing mechanism, rather like a gyroscope, that safeguards the individual's behavioral capacity for coping with the exigencies of survival. If that were the case, mental development would not be wholly at the mercy of often erratic environmental happenstance. A too-malleable fitness trait would afford an organism too little protection against the vagaries of its environment. Thus, as humanity evolved, processes may also have evolved to buffer intelligence from being pushed too far in one direction or another, whether by adventitiously harmful or by intentionally benevolent environmental forces.

NOTES

1. Barbara Lerner, "Test Scores as Measures of Human Capital," in Raymond B. Cattell, ed., *Intelligence and National Achievement* (Washington, D.C.: Cliveden Press, 1983).

2. Ibid., p. 73.

3. Ibid., p. 74.

4. Consortium for Longitudinal Studies, *As the Twig Is Bent . . . Lasting Effects of Preschool Programs* (Hillsdale, N.J.: Erlbaum, 1983); and Edward Zigler and Jeanette Valentine, *Project Head Start* (New York: Free Press, 1979).

5. Gene V. Glass and Mary C. Ellwein, review of *As the Twig Is Bent . . .*, by the Consortium for Longitudinal Studies, in *Science*, 20 January 1984, p. 274.

6. Craig T. Ramey et al., "The Carolina Abecedarian Project: A Longitudinal and Multidisciplinary Approach to the Prevention of Developmental Retardation," in Theodore D. Tjossem, ed., *Intervention Strategies for High Risk Infants and Young Children* (Baltimore: University Park Press, 1976).

7. Craig T. Ramey and Ron Haskins, "The Modification of Intelligence Through Early Experience," *Intelligence*, January/March 1981, pp. 5-19; and Arthur R. Jensen, "Raising the I.Q.: The Ramey and Haskins Study," *Intelligence*, January/March 1981, pp. 29-40.

8. Douglas K. Detterman and Robert J. Sternberg, eds., *How and How Much Can Intelligence Be Increased?* (Norwood, N.J.: Ablex, 1982).

9. Arthur R. Jensen, "Again, How Much Can We Boost I.Q.?" review of *How and How Much Can Intellignce Be Increased?* edited by Douglas K. Detterman and Robert J. Sternberg, in *Contemporary Psychology*, October 1983, p. 757.

10. Edward Zigler and Winnie Berman, "Discerning the Future of Early Childhood Intervention," *American Psychologist*, August 1983, p. 897.

11. Ibid., pp. 895-96.

12. Quoted in Peter Skerry, "The Charmed Life of Head Start," *Public Interest*, Fall 1983, pp. 18-39.

13. Arthur R. Jensen, "Test Validity: *g* Versus the Specificity Doctrine," *Journal of Biological Structures*, vol. 7, 1984, pp. 93-118.

14. Arthur R. Jensen, *Bias in Mental Testing* (New York: Free Press, 1980); and Cecil R. Reynolds and Robert T. Brown, *Perspectives on Bias in Mental Testing* (New York: Plenum, 1984).

15. Arthur R. Jensen, "Chronometric Analysis of Intelligence," *Journal of Social and Biological Structures*, April 1980, pp. 103-22; idem, "The Chronometry of Intelligence," in Robert J. Sternberg, ed., *Advances in the Psychology of Human Intelligence* (Hillsdale, N.J.: Erlbaum, 1982); and idem, "Reaction Time and Psychometric *g*," in Hans J. Eysenck, ed., *A Model for Intelligence* (Heidelberg: Springer-Verlag, 1982).

16. Donna E. Hendrickson and Alan E. Hendrickson, "The Biological Basis of Individual Differences in Intelligence," *Personality and Individual Differences*, January 1980, pp. 3-34.

17. Jerry S. Carlson and C. Mark Jensen, "Reaction Time, Movement Time, and Intelligence: A Replication and Extension," *Intelligence*, July/September 1982, pp. 265-74.

18. John G. Borkowski and Audrey Krause, "Racial Differences in Intelligence: The Importance of the Executive System," *Intelligence*, October/December 1983, pp. 379-95; Arthur R. Jensen, "Race Differences and Type II Errors: A Comment on Borkowski and Krause," *Intelligence*, in press; and Philip A. Vernon and Arthur R. Jensen, "Individual and Group Differences in Intelligence and Speed of Information Processing," *Personality and Individual Differences*, in press.

19. Jensen, "Again, How Much Can We Boost I.Q.?" p. 758.

CHALLENGE QUESTIONS

Can Intelligence Be Increased?

1. If you had a child about to enter school, and you had the choice between one administered by Jensen and one administered by Sternberg, which school would you choose?

2. If you were a school administrator with concern for efficiently using your resources to make the most of each student's potential, would you give each student an intelligence test to determine which class is most appropriate?

3. If programs for improving the thinking skills of students are successful, has the intelligence of the students been increased?

4. Should it be taken for granted that college students already have mature thinking skills?

5. Should programs with goals similar to those described in Sternberg's article be a part of a college education? If so, should they be separate courses or part of all courses?

D. Steiner/The DPG

PART 4

Human Development

Developmental psychology is concerned with the study of the forces that guide and direct development. The issues in this part present the conflicting opinions experts hold on how best to care for and educate young children and adolescents.

Do Gender Differences Originate from Biological Factors?

Is Day Care Harmful?

Are Children of Divorced Parents at Greater Risk?

Should Adolescents Be Allowed to Make Decisions About Abortion Without Parental Involvement?

ISSUE 10

Do Gender Differences Originate from Biological Factors?

YES: **Steven Goldberg,** from "Reaffirming the Obvious," *Society* (September/October 1986)

NO: **Cynthia Fuchs Epstein,** from "Inevitabilities of Prejudice," *Society* (September/October 1986)

ISSUE SUMMARY

YES: Sociologist Steven Goldberg contends that the biological differences between men and women explain any psychological differences observed in behavior, emotion, or attitude.
NO: Sociologist Cynthia Fuchs Epstein counters Goldberg's claim by citing empirical evidence and recent social developments that she feels indicate the cultural origins of gender differences.

When a group of parents discuss their children, there is usually a general agreement that girls and boys seem to be different. There are, of course, anatomical differences, but these discussions typically focus upon psychological differences—differences in their personalities and behaviors. Many psychologists seem to agree. The more controversial question these days is, "What is responsible for these psychological differences in gender?"

Here, the psychological community seems to split into two basic camps. One camp holds that gender differences translate into behavioral and attitudinal differences. The other camp, however, contends that the differences are more cultural in origin. According to this view, males and females are born with relatively equal potential for most behaviors; they differ primarily in their learning histories. Over time, they have learned from their parents, peers, and teachers what the culture considers to be appropriate masculine and feminine behavior.

These traditional divisions have become further clarified in recent years. Indeed, some language refinements have helped to distinguish between the anatomical and psychological differences of males and females. Increasingly, the term *sex* refers to the biological and physical characteristics that are unique to either the male or female. The term *gender*, on the other hand, has been reserved for the more cultural and psychological aspects of maleness and femaleness. The issue here, therefore, is gender.

Steven Goldberg has long held that sex differences lead to gender differences. He first made this claim in 1973 with his controversial book *The Inevitability of Patriarchy*, and nothing appears to have changed his thinking in the intervening years. If anything, accumulated evidence seems to have further confirmed his initial conclusion: male dominance is inevitable. The reason for this, he claims, is that we cannot escape our biological structures. Differences in the endocrine and central nervous systems result in a greater tendency for males to exhibit dominant behaviors. In Goldberg's framework, the few women who attain leadership positions are anomalies to the natural order to things. These "exceptions" prove nothing.

Cynthia Fuchs Epstein, however, contends that gender differences originate not from the "inevitability of male dominance," as Goldberg claims, but from the "inevitabilities of prejudice." Epstein considers Goldberg's conclusions to be dated in several senses. First, thousands of studies have been conducted since the publication of his book, and the findings of these studies overwhelmingly point to cultural factors as the root of psychological differences in gender. Second, a veritable revolution has occurred in the past 20 years. Women have increasingly exhibited dominant behavior and attained positions of social status. When equal opportunities have been present, the similarities between men and women have far outweighed their differences. The point is, according to Epstein, that such social changes can only be attributed to changes in culture, not in human physiology.

POINT	COUNTERPOINT
• Most cultures associate dominance and attainment with males.	• Advantages of social power stem from chance or historical accident.
• Social science texts have misrepresented ethnographic studies.	• Studies show that men and women display similar personalities and behaviors, given equal opportunities.
• Higher status roles are always associated with men.	• Women have been kept from positions of power through oppression and harassment.
• Male dominance reflects a natural order of things.	• If gender differences were natural, then gender roles would not be coercive.
• Discrimination is the result of an oversimplification of physiological universals.	• Discrimination stems from cultural punishments for those who deviate from social norms.

YES
Steven Goldberg

REAFFIRMING THE OBVIOUS

That anyone doubted it, was astonishing from the start. All experience and observation seemed to attest to the presence of core-deep differences between men and women, differences of temperament and emotion we call masculinity and femininity. All analyses of such differences were, it seemed obvious, empty or incoherent unless they saw the differences as related to substrative differences between men and women, differences that gave masculine and feminine direction to the emotions and behavior of men and women. The question to be answered, it seemed, was how these substrative differences manifest themselves on a social and institutional level—not whether the differences exist.

Yet there it was. A generation of educated people was jettisoning the evidence of both experience and intellect in order to propound a clearly indefensible hypothesis: emotional and behavioral differences between men and women, and the social expectations associated with them, are primarily the result of environmental factors to which physiology is of little relevance. Proponents supported this view with arguments ranging from the confused to the misrepresentative. Individuals who are exceptions were invoked as somehow refuting the possibility of physiological roots of behavior, a maneuver that makes about as much sense as arguing that a six-foot-tall woman somehow demonstrates the social causation of height. Myths about matriarchies were introduced as historical evidence, an approach that would justify a belief in cyclopses. The primary argument supporting this view, an argument accepted even in college textbooks, was the argument that emotional and behavioral differences between men and women were caused primarily by socialization.

The central problem with this approach is that it does not explain anything; it merely begs the question: Why does not one of the thousands of disparate societies on which we have evidence reverse male and female expectations? Why does every society from that of the Pygmy to that of the

Swede associate dominance and attainment with males? To say that males are more aggressive because they have been socialized that way is like saying that men can grow moustaches because boys have been socialized toward that end. There is no outside experimenter for society, setting up whatever rules seem desirable. Possible social values are limited by observation of reality; if male physiology is such that males have a lower threshold for the elicitation of dominance behavior, then social expectations denying this cannot develop.

Ten years ago it was not clear to all that there had never been a society reversing the sexual expectations I discuss. Social science texts, out of ignorance or tendentiousness, misrepresented ethnographic studies and asserted the existence of societies that reversed the sexual expectations. Recourse to the original ethnography on every alleged exception demonstrated beyond the possibility of reasonable dispute that not one of the thousands of societies (past and present) on which we have any sort of evidence lacks any of three institutions: patriarchy, male attainment, and male dominance.

All societies that have ever existed have associated political dominance with males and have been ruled by hierarchies overwhelmingly dominated by men. A society may have a titular queen or a powerful queen when no royal male is available; there were more female heads of state in the first two-thirds of the sixteenth century than the first two-thirds of the twentieth. An occasional woman may gain the highest position in a modern state; the other eighteen ministers in Golda Meir's cabinet, and all other Israeli prime ministers, were male. In every society from the most primitive to the most modern—whatever the yardstick—it is the case that political dominance, in particular, and hierarchical dominance, in general, are overwhelmingly in the hands of men.

Whatever the nonmaternal roles that are given highest status—whichever these are and whatever the reasons they are given high status in any given society—these roles are associated with males. A modern example describes the situation that obtains in every society: if being a medical doctor is given high status (as in the United States), most doctors are male; if being an engineer is given high status and being a doctor relatively low status (as in the Soviet Union), then most engineers are male and most nonhierarchical doctors may be female. There are societies—although modern societies, by their nature, could not be among them—in which women perform objectively far more important economic functions while working harder and longer outside the home than do men. Indeed, save for political and hierarchical leadership, internal and external security, and nurturance of the young, every task is seen as male in some societies and female in others. However, in every society that which is given highest status is associated with men. It is tempting to explain this as a residue of male political dominance, but this view gets things backwards. Male roles do not have high status because they are male; nor do high-status roles have high status because they are male. Many male roles have low status and many low-status roles are male. High-status roles are male because they have (for different reasons in different societies) high status; this high status motivates males to attain the roles—for psychophysiological reasons—more strongly than it does females (statistically speaking). Social expectations conform to limits set by this reality.

The emotions of both males and females of all societies associate dominance with the male in male-female relationships and encounters. The existence of this reality is evidenced by the ethnographies of every society; the observations and statements of the members of every society; the values, songs, and proverbs of every society; and, in our own society, also by feminists who abhor this reality and incorrectly attribute it primarily to social and environmental causes. We might argue that in the family the women of some or all societies have greater power, attributable to either a male abdication or a female psychological acuity that enables women to get around men. But the question relevant to universality is why both the men and women have the emotional expectation of a male dominance that must be gotten around.

The social sciences have discovered precious few nontrivial institutions that are both universal and sufficiently explicable with direct physiological evidence. The three institutions I discuss require explanation and this explanation must be simple. I mention this in anticipation of the inevitable, however wrongheaded, criticism that any physiologically-rooted theory is simplistic, determinist, or reductionist. Were we to attempt to explain variation in the forms of these institutions in physiological terms, an explanation would, in all likelihood, be simplistic. Physiology is in all likelihood irrelevant to differences between, say, American patriarchy and Arabic patriarchy. An explanation sufficient to explain the universal limits within which all variation takes place, if it is to be at all persuasive, requires a single factor common to, and imposing limits on, all societies that have ever existed. Indeed, the very extensiveness of the cross-cultural variation in most institutions emphasizes the need to explain why the institutions we discuss always work in the same direction. No reality is inevitable simply because it is universal, but when an institution is universal we must ask why. If the reason for universality is a physiological factor giving direction to the motivations that make us what we are, then we must entertain the possibility that the institution is an inevitable social resolution of the psychophysiological reality. . . .

Differences between the male and female endocrine/central nervous systems are such that—statistically speaking—males have a greater tendency to exhibit whatever behavior is necessary in any environment to attain dominance in hierarchies and male-female encounters and relationships, and a greater tendency to exhibit whatever behavior is necessary for attainment of nonmaternal status. Using somewhat unrigorous terms, we might say that males are more strongly motivated by the environmental presence of hierarchy, by a member of the other sex, or by status to do what is necessary to attain dominance. It is irrelevant whether we conceptualize this as a lower male threshold for the release of dominance behavior, a greater male drive for dominance, a greater male need for dominance, or a weaker male ego that needs shoring up by attainment of dominance and status. It is the reality of the male-female difference that matters, not the model used to explain the difference that any model must explain. Likewise, it is irrelevant why our species (and those from which we are descended) evolved the psychophysiological differentiation;

all that matters for an explanation of universality is that the differentiation exists. . . .

Physiology does not determine the actual behavior required for dominance and attainment in any given society: that is socially determined. What physiology accounts for is the male's greater willingness to sacrifice the rewards of other motivations—the desire for affection, health, family life, safety, relaxation, vacation and the like—in order to attain dominance and status. This model makes clear why physiology need not be considered in a causal analysis of the behavior of a given individual exception. At the same time physiology is necessary for an analysis of the existence on a societal level of the universal institutions I discuss. Even the effects of virtually pure physiology expect many exceptions (as the six-foot-tall woman demonstrates). Dominance motivation no doubt has other causes—experiential and familial—in addition to the physiological causes and, for the exception, these may counteract the physiological factors.

When we speak of an entire society, the law of large numbers becomes determinative. The statistical, continuous, and quantitative reality of the male's greater dominance tendency becomes concretized on the social level in absolute, discrete, and qualitative terms. The statistical reality of the male's greater aggression becomes in its pure and exaggerated form: "men are aggressive (or dominant); women are passive (or submissive)." This leads to discrimination, often for the woman who is an exception and occasionally for every woman. Discrimination is possible precisely because the statistical reality makes the exception an exception, exposed to the possibility of discrimination. The six-foot-tall girl who wishes she were short lives in a world of boys who are praised for being six feet tall.

As long as societies have hierarchies, differentiated statuses, and intermixing of men and women, they will possess the only environmental cues necessary to elicit greater dominance and attainment behavior from males. In utopian fantasy a society lacking hierarchy, status, and male-female relationships may be possible, but in the real world it is not. In the real world, societies have cultures. These cultures will value some things more than others and—particularly in the modern, bureaucratic society—some positions more than others. If male physiology is such that males are willing to sacrifice more for these things and positions, they will learn what is necessary and do what is necessary—whatever that may be in any given society—for dominance and attainment. There are other necessary conditions: it is not only gender that keeps a black woman from ruling the Republic of South Africa. Nevertheless, within any group possessing the other necessary conditions, dominance will go to those most willing to sacrifice for dominance and status (and social values will lead to such expectations). . . .

The male-female differentiation that I have discussed is the one for which the evidence is by far the most overwhelming. There are other differences that may well be functions of endocrine-central nervous system differentiation. The stereotype that sees logically abstract thinking as "thinking like a man" and psychological perception as "woman's intuition" without question reflect empirical realities; it is only the cause of these realities that is open to question. A score on the SAT mathematics aptitude section that puts a girl in the ninetieth percentile among girls places a boy in only the sixty-eighth percentile among boys; among mathematically-precocious students (thirteen years old), a score of 700 is thirteen times more likely to be attained by a boy than by a girl (with equal numbers of boys and girls with similar mathematical backgrounds taking the test). There also seems to be a linear relationship between the importance of logical abstraction to an area and the percentage of those at the highest levels who are men; there has never been a woman at the highest level of mathematics, chess, or composing music (which is not thought of as a macho enterprise), while there have been many women of genius in literature and the performing arts. . . .

Nothing I have written about patriarchy, male attainment, or male dominance implies (or precludes) males' better performing roles once they attain them. Whether the male tendencies increase performance or retard it is another issue (save for the fact that a position must be attained before it can be performed). Similarly, nothing I have written implies the desirability of any particular social or political program. "Is cannot imply ought," and no scientific analysis of how the world works can entail a subjective decision on which of two programs is preferable. We might accept all that I have written and see this as demonstrating the need for an equal rights law limiting the male physiological advantage for attainment. Or we might see the same evidence as justifying a socialization system that provides clear role models by emphasizing the sex differences I discuss. Science is silent on such a choice.

NO

Cynthia Fuchs Epstein

INEVITABILITIES OF PREJUDICE

Is there any reason to believe that patriarchy is more inevitable than anti-Semitism, child abuse, or any other mode of oppression that has been around for as long as anyone can remember? On the basis of his own experience, Aristotle believed that slavery was inevitable; and although it is still around in some countries, few reasonable people now believe it must be inevitable. Unfortunately, people with credentials for reasonableness, such as a new school of sociobiologists and their popularizers—among them Steven Goldberg—feel comfortable believing that the subordination of women is inevitable, programmed into human nature.

Many forms of oppression seem inevitable because they are so difficult to dislodge. History shows us that. It is easier to maintain oppression than to overthrow it. This is because when a group has a power advantage (which may emerge by chance, or historical accident), even if it is small, it may escalate rapidly if those in power can monopolize not only material resources but the avenues of communication as well. The Nazis did so effectively. Karl Marx cautioned that the owners of production were also the owners of the production of ideas. This means that the values and knowledge of a society usually reflect the views of those who rule, often by convincing those in subordinate statuses that they deserve what they get. The Nazis argued that they belonged to the "master race" and tried to build a science to prove it. They were less subtle than other rulers, but their case is instructive: beware the thesis of any powerful group that claims its power is derived solely from "divine right" or from its genes.

If anything is inevitable, it is change. Change in history is characteristic of human experience and reflects the human capacity to order and reorder it, to understand the processes of its ordering, and to sweep away old superstitions. As Robert K. Merton pointed out in the *American Journal of Sociology* in 1984: "What everyone should know from the history of thought is that what everyone knows turns out not to be so at all."

Some twelve years have passed since Steven Goldberg published his book, *The Inevitability of Patriarchy*, more than a decade which has produced

Published by permission of Transaction Publishers from *Society*, vol. 23, no. 6. Copyright © 1986 by Transaction Publishers.

175

thousands of studies of gender differences and similarities, an extensive reanalysis of the relationship and applicability of primate behavior to human behavior, and debate and analysis of sociobiological interpretation. Goldberg has offered us once again, a view of women's subordination as inevitable simply because it has always existed. The thesis, unchanged from his formulation of a decade ago, is uninformed about the rich body of scholarship that has been published—much of it disproving his assumptions about significant differences in men's and women's emotions, cognitive capacities, and situation in the structure of the social hierarchy. In these intervening years, there have also been changes in the statuses and roles of women in the United States and in other parts of the world—these also invalidate Goldberg's perspective on the constancy and universality of his observations about the subordination of women.

Women in the United States, as elsewhere, have been elected and appointed to positions of power. They have joined the ranks of the prestigious and the powerful in the domains of law and medicine, and are entering specialties and practices to which they were denied admission and discouraged from pursuing only a decade ago. Women are now judges at every level of the judiciary in the United States, as well as prosecutors in the courts engaging in adversarial and assertive behavior, exhibiting what may be termed as "dominant behavior." There is considerable evidence that women perform well, sometimes even better than do men, in examinations that determine admission to all fields in professional and graduate schools, where women constitute from a third to half of all students. Each year sees an increase in the number of women admitted to schools of engineering and science in spite of men's supposed greater social orientation toward careers in these fields.

Women have also become university professors and researchers and have thus been empowered to challenge many biased views about human nature and to fill gaps left by male scholars who have characteristically had little interest or inclination to do research in this field. Therefore, a revised view of what is "natural" or "inevitable" is part of the contemporary intellectual agenda.

Women are also making inroads in blue-collar technical work, heretofore denied them because of restrictions in apprenticeship programs made yet more difficult because of personal harassment. Women have experienced the same exclusionary mechanisms exercised against all minority groups who have had the audacity to compete with white males for the privileged positions guarded by "covenants" instituted by unions and ethnic clusters. According to a 1985 Rand Corporation research study by Linda Waite and Sue Berryman, *Women in Non-Traditional Occupations: Choice and Turnover,* women behave similarly to men in that they exhibit similar work force commitment and turnover rates once involved in nontraditional jobs such as those of the blue-collar crafts or in the army. These researchers emphasize that policies equalizing work conditions for men and women also equalize commitment to the job.

Increasing convergence of gender role behavior is also seen in studies of crime. Girls' crime rates show increasing similarity to that of boys. Girls and boys both commit violent crimes and exhibit increasingly similar criminal histories.

Certainly much of the challenge and change is due to the women's movement and the insistence of women on their rights to equality. Sizable numbers of women in every sphere of society have taken an aggressive role in contesting the domination of men in personal, political, and intellectual life. Given the short period of time in which women have been active on their own behalf and in which they have succeeded in engaging the support of sympathetic men, their strides have been great both with regard to social rank and intellectual accomplishment.

This movement has evolved within the historical context still affected by centuries of oppression that have created and perpetuated the sense that women's inequality is natural. Yet no society, no social group, and especially no ruling group, has ever left gender hierarchy (nor any other form of hierarchy) to nature. It has not been women's incompetence or inability to read a legal brief, to perform brain surgery, to predict a bull market, or to make an intonation to the gods that has kept them from interesting and highly paid jobs. The root of discrimination against women, preventing their access to a variety of fields, has been a rule system replete with severe punishments for those who deviate from "traditional" roles. Access is now achieved through political and social action, and not at all through genetic engineering.

Sociobiologists, on the other hand, argue that the division of labor by sex is a biological rather than a social response. If this were so, sex-role assignments would not have to be coercive. Social groups do not actually depend on instinct or physiology to enforce social arrangements because they cannot reliably do so. Societies assign groups to be responsible

for such social needs as food, shelter, and child care; nowhere do they depend on nature to meet these requirements. The types of work that men and women perform in each society are stipulated by society, allowing few individuals to make choices outside the prescribed range. The assignments are justified on the basis of ideologies claiming that they are just and reflect popular, cultural opinions that the arrangement is good (or that, if not, little can be done about it).

Such ideologies and popular views suppose that a fit exists between the job and worker—a fit that makes sense. This argument relies on the maintenance of gender differences. Division according to sex is reinforced by requirements that men and women dress differently (whether it is to don the veil or a skirt if female; and trousers or a *doti* if male), learn different skills (women's literacy rates are considerably lower than those of males in the Third World; in the Western world males and females still are "encouraged" to choose "sex-appropriate" subjects) and engage in different forms of activity. Violators are punished for infractions. Sometimes a raised eyebrow will keep a woman in line; in the extreme she may even face being stoned to death or burned alive (as in the recent outbreak of deaths over dowries in India).

The literal binding of women's feet or the constraint of their minds by law and social custom is part of the process by which the gender division of human beings perpetuates a two-class system. The hierarchy is kept in place subtly by the insistence that people behave in the way society's opinion molders say they should. Thus, "ideal" roles mask real behavior. If we look at what men and women actually do—or *can* do without the distorting mirror of "ideal" gender roles—there is a fundamental similarity in personalities, behavior, and competence, given equal opportunity and social conditions. This is what the vast array of scholarship in psychology, sociology, and physiology has revealed in the last decade.

The research has been so extensive that it is impossible to summarize it here, although I shall review it in my forthcoming book, *Deceptive Distinctions*. By now, reviewers have reanalyzed thousands of articles on gender differences in every attribution and behavior imaginable. Despite what everyone believes, the similarities far outweigh the differences, even in considering aggression. As for the differences that census takers count —frequencies of women and men in different jobs and leisure activities—these clearly seem to be a result of social rules and habits. . . .

SEX HORMONES

. . . The question relevant to gender in society is the meaning of differences. For Goldberg, there is an unbroken line between "androgen binding sites in the brain, rough and tumble play in infants, and the male domination of state, industry and the nuclear family." E. O. Wilson is more cautious: "we can go against it if we wish, but only at the cost of some efficiency." If the hormone testosterone is supposed to make men aggressive and thus fit for public office, "female" hormones and the cycles attached to them are seen as detrimental to women's participation in public life. Edgar Berman, medical adviser to the late Senator (and Vice President) Hubert Humphrey, warned against women's participation in public affairs because of their "raging hor-

mones." (Berman later published a book, *The Compleat Chauvinist*, in which he provided "biological evidence" for his views that menopausal women might create havoc if they held public office. Chapter titles from his book are: "The Brain That's Tame Lies Mainly in the Dame," "Testosterone, Hormone of Champions," and "Meno: The Pause that Depresses.") More recently, United Nations Ambassador Jeane Kirkpatrick reported that White House critics resisted her advancement into a higher political post because of the "temperament" she exhibited as a woman. No similar attributions of hormonal barriers to decision-making posts have been offered for men, although they have been excused from infidelity that is explained in popular culture by "male menopause," or by the sociobiologists who see it as an evolutionary response of men.

Many sociobiologists of the Wilson school have been committed to a model of inequity as a product of the natural order, arguing that male domination (patriarchy) is the most adaptive form of society, one that has conferred an advantage on individuals who operate according to its precepts. This thesis—put forth by E. O. Wilson, Lionel Tiger, Robin Fox, and Steven Goldberg—maintains that the near universality of male dominance arose because of the long dependence of the human infant and as a result of hunting and gathering, the early modes of obtaining food. Male-based cooperation was expressed through dominance relations. Men guarded the bands and thus ensured survival. There was pressure on men to perfect hunting skills and on women to stay home and mind the children. Each sex would have developed cognitive abilities attached to these activities. A socially imposed hierarchical division of labor between the sexes gradually became genetically fixed. . . .

MAN THE HUNTER; WOMAN THE GATHERER

In recent years, anthropologists have reevaluated the perspective of "man the hunter," which long served as a model of the origins of human society. . . . Using this model, primatologists and anthropologists such as Sherwood Washburn and Irven De Vore in *The Social Life of Early Man* and Desmond Morris in *The Naked Ape* had reasoned that hunting, a male activity, was a creative turning point in human evolution—that it required intelligence to plan and to stalk game, and to make hunting and other tools. It also required social bonding of men, the use of language to cooperate in the hunt, and then the distribution of meat and the development of tools for hunting and cutting the meat. According to Washburn and Lancaster in Lee and De Vore's *Man the Hunter,* "In a very real sense our intellect, interests, emotions and basic social life—all are evolutionary products of the success of the hunting adaptation." . . . The question is, what merit is there to the model and the explanations derived from it?

Among others, Frances Dahlbert in *Woman the Gatherer* suggests the account can only be considered a "just-so story" in the light of new scholarship. Beginning in the 1960s, research on primates, on hunter-gatherer societies, and archaeological and fossil records made this story obsolete. For example, the paleoanthropological myth of man the hunter was deflated when the "killer ape" of Robert Ardrey's *The Hunting Hypothesis,* the presumed australopithecine forebear of humans, turned out to be predominantly vegetarian. . . . A greater challenge to the man the hunter model came from Sally Linton in Sue Ellen Jacobs's *Women in Cross-Cultural Perspective.* Linton attacked the validity of theories of evolution that excluded or diminished women's contributions to human culture and society. She noted that women contribute the bulk of the diet in contemporary hunting and gathering societies, that small-game hunting practiced by both sexes preceded large-game hunting practiced by men, and that females as well as males probably devised tools for their hunting and gathering and some sort of carrying sling or net to carry babies. According to this view, the collaboration and cooperation of women was probably as important to the development of culture as that of men. . . .

People persist in wanting to view the world in terms of sex differences. They insist that individuals conform to ideal roles and turn away from their real roles, common interests, and goals, and from their mutual fate. These people disregard the obvious truth that most things that most people do most of the time can be performed equally well by either sex. The persistence of the view, as well as the persistence of physical and symbolic sex segregation, is created and maintained for a purpose, which is to maintain the privileges of men who predictably resist claims to the contrary. I suspect that the debates will continue and may do so as long as one group derives advantage from suppressing another. But evidence is mounting that supports equality between the sexes and which no truly reasonable people can continue to deny.

CHALLENGE QUESTIONS

Do Gender Differences Originate from Biological Factors?

1. Do you think that the fact that Goldberg is a male and Epstein is a female has anything to do with their respective positions on this issue? Does a consideration of gender in this regard discount what each author has to say? Why or why not?

2. Take a position on this issue yourself and support it with related studies, either from the articles or from your own research.

3. Both Goldberg and Epstein claim that the research supports their positions. Explain how this is possible.

4. How can Goldberg claim that physiology influences the general tendencies of a culture, but not the specific behavior of an individual?

ISSUE 11

Is Day Care Harmful?

YES: Burton L. White, from "Should You Stay Home With Your Baby?" *Young Children* (1981)

NO: Joanne Curry O'Connell, from "Children of Working Mothers: What the Research Tells Us," *Young Children* (1983)

ISSUE SUMMARY

YES: Burton L. White, educator and researcher, contends that the absence of a primary caretaker during a child's first few years produces serious emotional and psychological debilitation.

NO: Joanne Curry O'Connell, a professor of educational psychology, asserts that child development investigators have found no consistent adverse effects of out-of-home child day care.

In 1952 a report by John Bowlby, *Maternal Care and Mental Health*, was published by the World Health Organization in Geneva. It described how babies reared in various foundling homes and orphanages around the world, despite excellent medical care in some institutions, had an alarmingly high death rate within their first year. Many of the surviving babies were physically and mentally retarded and remarkably unresponsive to other people. This report and similar literature spawned many laboratory experiments with animals that indicated the importance of environment during early development.

These studies were of great interest to parents and anyone else concerned with child care. They began to have exceptional significance in the 1970s as women, many of them mothers, entered the work force in accelerating numbers. Mothers who left their children to go to work were concerned about what would happen to the emotional bonds usually taken for granted between mother and child. Researchers began to study how children of working mothers behaved with their parents and with their peers in a variety of situations.

Burton L. White points out that throughout nature, warm-blooded newborns are cared for by their parents during their early developmental stages. The bond between human family members involves a delight in observing a child develop that is rarely matched outside of the family. Parents encourage curiosity and take pride in an infant's achievements in a way that no temporary caregiver could ever duplicate.

White recommends that the government should resist providing full-time substitute baby care for everybody who wants it, or encouraging it by making it necessary for both parents to be employed outside of the home. He feels that a baby gets only one chance to make his or her first human attachment and to begin to understand the world. These opportunities, according to White, are too precious to leave to anyone outside the immediate family.

Joanne Curry O'Connell discusses popular attitudes toward working mothers. She declares that "it is incumbent upon professionals in early childhood education to review the *facts*, and form an educated opinion on the effects of daycare." She then asks a series of relevant questions and examines the related research.

O'Connell introduces a series of child development variables and touches upon the way researchers study them. She then relates a succession of investigations that provide answers to questions commonly asked by concerned parents. She concludes that researchers have discovered no consistent detrimental effects of day care.

POINT

- Studies show impaired development when deficient care is given during a child's early years.

- Parents show a special kind of attention that generates legitimate pride of achievement within the child.

- Family members are most likely to satisfy and encourage an infant's curiosity.

- Studies have focused on what harm is being done rather than on what is best for young children.

COUNTERPOINT

- Early studies on infant development did not focus on the variables pertinent to day care.

- Children reared in day-care centers do at least as well in school as children reared completely at home.

- Day-care children show the same behavior in strange situations as home-reared children.

- With regard to the variables most relevant to parental concerns, no consistent differences have been found between day care and full-time home rearing.

YES

Burton L. White

SHOULD YOU STAY HOME
WITH YOUR BABY?

For a long time, it has been traditional for women to assume the primary responsibility for raising their own children, especially during the first years of the child's life. Today, more than ever before, that tradition is being challenged. Today, more infants and toddlers are spending the majority of their waking hours in the care of someone other than a member of the immediate family. As one who has specialized in the study of the development of children for more than twenty years, I am very disturbed by this situation. I'm worried most about the effects on children, but I'm also worried about the pressure being put on women who don't want to join in the trend. I'm also saddened by the thought that many adults stand to miss some of life's sweetest pleasures.

I do not pretend to be expert in all aspects of family life. Rather, I present myself as someone with knowledge of the educational needs of young children. The focus of my message, then, will be the impact on the development of the child of various forms of childrearing. I am writing not only because I feel qualified to do so, but also because, in spite of the many privately expressed concerns, only a few of my colleagues (Fraiberg, 1977; Glickman & Springer, 1978) have spoken out on this topic.

I'd like to state the heart of my position at the outset. Given the current incomplete state of knowledge about children's needs and substitute care, I firmly believe that most children will get off to a better start in life when they spend the majority of their waking hours being cared for by their parents and other family members rather than in any form of substitute care.

REASONS FOR MY CONCERN

The Needs of Infants and Toddlers
In the eyes of most students of human development, the first three years of life are extremely important and like no other. While experts may differ on

many points, there are many areas of agreement. Clearly, what most of us (including parents) worry about most is the emotional development of babies. Few would debate the almost mystical significance of the mother-infant bond. Research from many fields, including psychiatry, child psychology, and studies of other animal species, has confirmed our intuitive respect for the mother-infant bond beyond any doubt. Research has also pointed to the first two years of life as the particular time in life when that bond forms (Scott, 1963; Bowlby, 1958). For obvious reasons, we have not performed experiments with babies to see how far one can deviate from ordinary childrearing practices before that bond is harmfully affected. We have, however, information gained from a few unusual kinds of circumstances. We have information about major deviations from the usual and we have information on lesser deviations from the normal.

During this century, a large number of studies have been performed involving physically normal babies reared in institutions (Bowlby, 1951; Yarrow, 1961). In most such instances, no single adult has had the primary responsibility for a baby. These studies have almost always indicated that the absence of a primary caretaker during a child's first few years produces serious emotional and psychological debilitation. Observing an unattached toddler is a chilling experience for most adults.

Not many people would advocate such institutional childrearing. What about lesser deviations from the usual? Several forms of part-time substitute childrearing of infants and toddlers have existed long enough for us to learn something from them. There is the phenomenon of the British nanny. There is also the expe-rience of the Israeli kibbutz. These and related practices have shown clearly that having an adult other than a baby's mother or father or grandparents assume the primary caretaking role need not lead to any obvious harmful consequences. Indeed, such substitute child care has undoubtedly been in widespread use throughout the world for a long time. Just what the consequences of such practices are is simply not known because no substantial research has (to my knowledge) ever been done on the topic. It is worth pointing out that the selection of substitute caretakers, both in the British system and in the kibbutzim, is done with great care. The caliber of the treatment the baby receives in most such situations appears to be quite good.

Another major source of information about the mother-infant bond and its presumed importance is studies of other animal species (Scott, 1963). Throughout nature the general rule seems to be that nonprecocious, warm-blooded newborns are cared for by their parents during their early developmental stages. Couple this apparent fact of nature with the predominant tendency in diverse human societies for babies to be reared by their mothers, and you have a very imposing argument against full-time substitute care.

Though widespread and longstanding custom is not always correct or beneficial, most people are unwilling to behave in a contrary manner if the stakes are high. Since the stakes here appear to involve a new child's lifelong emotional health, there has been much resistance to any initiatives that would prevent infants from being with their mothers most, if not all, of the time. So, when the U.S. government offered support to low-income families with babies during the

1930s, the first goal was to make it possible for the women in such families to remain the primary caretakers of their children, rather than be obliged to enter the work force. The Aid to Families with Dependent Children program typifies the judgment of policy makers in family services in many Western countries. Setting aside the question of the success or failure of the program, few people disagree with that goal.

Another basis for my objection to the practice of full-time substitute care for infants and toddlers is what I have learned through my research in human development. I've specialized in the study of successful childrearing (White et al., 1973, 1978, 1979). I've had the privilege of being able to compare the everyday experiences of many children getting off to a fine start in life with those not so fortunate. Of particular relevance to this issue is my judgment that, all things being equal, a baby's parents are more likely to meet her most important developmental needs than other people. That kind of statement could be little more than wishful thinking. My experience has convinced me that it is indeed much more.

My favorite example involves one of the many inevitable achievements of all healthy infants, the first steps. The first unaided walking usually takes place when the child is about eleven months old. When a baby is being raised at home, especially if he's a first baby, both parents and all other close family members look forward to the event. There is anticipation and, perhaps, even some mild anxiety. When the time comes, the impact on close family members is powerful and enormously pleasant. The parents of such a child ordinarily become excited to a degree that can be somewhat boring to their friends. The parents' response to the baby is to envelop him in praise and excitement. This is one of a large number of unique pleasures babies can bring to their parents. It is the sheer joy and enthusiasm of such events that impress me the most. Such intensely rewarding experiences seem to me to be important both for the child and his parents. For the parents, these experiences reinforce the commitment to the child and to family life. For the child, they help solidify the sense of personal security and worth. One of the defining characteristics of good early development pinpointed by our research is a sure sense of pride in achievement. Experiences such as the one just described are the basis for that fundamental attribute. Between seven and eleven months of life, as part of the process of mastering the body, most babies learn to sit up, crawl, stand up, climb, walk while supported, and, finally, to walk alone. Each of these achievements is both attainable by all normal infants and, at the same time, an opportunity for parents to make a big fuss over the baby. In doing so, they help generate legitimate pride within the child.

I believe that process is one of several which underlie good development and where parents have a natural advantage over other adults. While first-rate, loving childcare workers will usually enjoy and applaud a baby's achievements, they simply cannot match the enthusiasm and excitement expressed by most parents. After all, when you've seen 200 babies take their first step, your reaction to the 201st cannot reflect the excitement typically present in the response of the baby's parents.

This is one way in which parents have an edge. Another has to do with the satisfaction and encouragement of an infant's curiosity. Once a baby learns to crawl (at about seven months of age), she becomes capable of exploring a much expanded world. Over the next year-and-a-half, a major part of her curriculum consists of close examinations of small objects and their motions, wonder at the way simple mechanisms work, and the study of people and other spectacles. To get the most out of these experiences, nothing seems better than if an infant has ready access to an older person who is especially interested in her and is anxious to serve as a personal consultant. No one fits that definition quite so well as a baby's parents or grandparents.

These are some of the ways to describe the natural advantages parents and other close family members have in raising babies. What about the abilities of substitute caretakers?

Substitute caretakers come in many shapes. They can be well-trained, experienced child development specialists with master's degrees in early education. (If so, the cost of their services is very high.) They can be high school graduates with special training in child development. They can be aunts, cousins, or even older siblings. They may care for a baby or group of babies in an infant's home, in their home, in a nonprofit center, or in a profit-oriented center. It is clear that the variety of substitute care conditions is large. What about the quality of care the baby receives? As you might expect, that varies widely too. It varies from warm and knowledgeable to indifferent and unskilled. How much it varies and what the impact is on babies is not yet known. The practice of full-time substitute care for children younger than three years of age is too new for much research to have been done. The few studies that have

been done produced reassuring results (Belsky and Steinberg, 1978). At least in the case of well-financed and well-managed nonprofit programs, no substantial negative impact has been seen. Unfortunately, the programs studied represent only a minority of those operating across the country. As you might imagine, it is a lot easier to do research in a university-affiliated nonprofit center than in some of the many other kinds of programs currently available.

Even though first reports show no obvious harm being done to infants in high quality programs, I am not about to endorse such practices for all families. The reason is that I'm not only concerned with obvious harmful effects, but with what is likely to be very good for infants and toddlers as well. None of the few evaluations performed to date has addressed the question of what is very good for young children. Their focus has naturally been on the more pressing concern about whether any harm is being done, particularly in regard to a child's emotional health. Put simply, after more than twenty years of research on how children develop well, I would not think of putting a child of my own into any substitute care program on a full-time basis, especially a center-based program. If I don't believe full-time substitute care during the first years of life would be in my own child's best interest, how can I recommend it to other parents? The answer is, I can't, except under extraordinary circumstances.

SITUATIONS WHERE SUBSTITUTE CARE MAKES SENSE

There are three kinds of situations where I think substitute child care not only makes sense but is, in fact, a necessity.

When a Family Cannot Raise Its Own Children

In certain family situations, alcoholism, drug abuse, or some other debilitating condition afflicts parents to such a degree that childrearing is a casualty. The conclusion social workers have come to is that, in many such families, the situation is so bad that the only hope for the children is to remove them from the family and place them in foster care.

There are about three million babies born in the United States each year. Not all the parents are happy, intelligent, in love, and thrilled with their child. Many babies are born to mothers who are less than eighteen years old and already have two or three other children. In some of these situations the prospect for the new baby is grim, and full-time substitute care, if it's of good quality, may very well make good sense. In fact, there are some good government-sponsored programs geared to these circumstances.

When a Family Just Does Not Want the Job

At times, for any number of reasons, parents don't want the time-consuming, occasionally stressful job of raising a baby. In such situations, I believe some substitute arrangement is likely to be preferable.

On a Part-time Basis

I'm a strong advocate of substitute childcare, *on a part-time basis, for all families who would like it*. In our research, I've met parents for whom the concept of substitute care is almost unthinkable. They were having such a good time with their babies, especially during the baby's first year, that they almost dreaded any separation. Now, I'm not talking about perverted or bizarre men and women. They were just people extraordinarily happy about being parents. I would be reluctant to urge such people to use substitute care, although by the child's second year I believe it would probably be good for both baby and parents. For most families, however, part-time care is both desired and desirable.

There are several reasons why *part-time* substitute care might be a good idea.

1. Economics: Part-time substitute care can free up the time of either or both parents to hold outside employment.

2. Personal development: Part-time substitute care can give parents the time to pursue education and avocations.

3. Enjoyment: Part-time substitute care can give parents time simply to have fun off duty.

4. Psychological relief: While this benefit generally comes with the previous advantages, it is very important in its own right. Babies are precious and vulnerable. For years, young women have been bearing a continuous responsibility for the well-being of children. To most people, this situation seems to be perfectly normal and unworthy of comment. If you observe women with their infants regularly in their homes, as we have done, you can't help but be impressed with the stress that can be generated, particularly if there are two or more young children in the family. One of the most popular features of an early education project I helped initiate was the offer of three hours of no-strings-attached baby-sitting each week. Its purpose was to allow the mother to take a break from the constant responsibility of her children. By combining this service with the provision of a lounge where parents could talk to each other or to child development professionals, we helped overcome a sense of isolation and stress which many at-home mothers feel.

FATHERS AND GRANDPARENTS MAKE GOOD "MOTHERS" TOO

No study anywhere has indicated that mothers are the only people capable of raising young babies. We have observed many fathers and grandparents who seem perfectly suited to the task, and are willing or eager to share the job. Furthermore, it has always seemed unfair to me that fathers and grandparents usually have such limited opportunities to share the many exciting and memorable everyday events in babies' lives. To the extent fathers and grandparents assume more of the chores, they will be rewarded by more of the pleasures. These people comprise an enormous underused resource.

RECOMMENDATIONS

For Government
During the last five years or so, tremendous pressure has been put on government at all levels to provide more substitute child care for everyone, including families with babies younger than three years of age. These are my suggestions.

1. Where families (regardless of income level) are unable or unwilling to care for their own infants and toddlers, provide high quality full-time substitute care or foster homes.

2. Resist the cries for free full-time substitute care for babies for all who want it. Good quality care costs more than $3,500 per year per child and, therefore, the cost of such a broad program is prohibitive anyway.

3. In support programs for young parents, provide the option for either or both parents to be the primary caretaker during their child's first three years. Do not deliberately or inadvertently encourage full-time substitute care for families that do not want it by making out-of-the-home employment mandatory.

For Families
Parents should consider sharing the childrearing function. They might also consider using part-time (up to four hours a day) substitute care, if necessary, as an important resource in meeting their needs for income or self-expression. (Remember, in most cases, substitute child care has been sought to meet the needs of *the parents not the babies*.) High quality, part-time substitute care can make the difference between an oppressive childrearing situation and a very rewarding one. It can be the means by which a young woman can continue a career or pursue personal interests, without penalty to her child. In general, if you can find and afford high quality substitute care, I encourage you to use it. But sparingly.

Unless you have a very good reason, I also urge you not to delegate the primary childrearing task to anyone else during your child's first years of life. Nothing a young mother or father does out of the home is more important or rewarding than raising a baby. Furthermore, it's a one-time opportunity. Babies form their first human attachment only once. Babies begin to learn language only once. Babies begin to get to know the world only once. The outcomes of these processes play a major role in shaping the future of each new child.

If You Have No Choice, or If I Have Not Convinced You
My suggestions about the types of substitute care are presented here in order of descending preference.

• Individual care in your own home: A warm, intelligent, and experienced person caring for your child in your own home.

• Individual care in someone else's home: A warm, intelligent, and experienced person caring for your child in that person's home.

• Family daycare: The same kind of person caring for no more than three children in her or his own home.

• Nonprofit center-based care: A carefully selected center where the ratio of children to staff is no more than four to one, and where the total number of children in each room is preferably fewer than ten. There should be at least one person with some formal training in early childhood development among the supervisory staff.

• Profit-oriented center-based care: A *very* carefully selected center which meets all the aforementioned requirements.

SUMMARY

If you are the parent of a baby or if you soon will be, I urge you to give serious consideration to the points raised in this analysis. Of course, if you feel you have no option but full-time substitute care for your baby, so be it. For those fortunate enough to have a choice, it is my judgment that the majority of a baby's waking hours should be spent with her parents or grandparents. For most families, I believe that such an arrangement is the surest way to see to it that a baby gets the best beginning in life. Furthermore, when childrearing is shared, it can become one of life's sweetest and most rewarding experiences.

REFERENCES

Belsky, J., & Steinberg, L. D. "The Effects of Day Care: A Critical Review." *Child Development* 49, no. 4 (1978): 929–49.

Bowlby, J. "The Nature of the Child's Tie to His Mother." *International Journal of Psychoanalysis* 39 (1958): 350–73.

Bowlby, J. *Maternal Care and Mental Health*, Monograph no. 2. Geneva: World Health Organization, 1951.

Fraiberg, S. *Every Child's Birthright: In Defense of Mothering*. New York: Basic Books, 1977.

Glickman, B. M., & Springer, N. B. *Who Cares for Baby? Choices in Child Care*. New York: Schocken Books, 1978.

Scott, J. P. "The Process of Primary Socialization in Canine and Human Infants." *Monographs of the Society for Research in Child Development* 28, no. 1 (1963): 1–47.

White, B. L., Kaban, B., Attanucci, J., & Shapiro, B. *Experience and Environment: Major Influences on the Development of the Young Child*. Vol. 2. Englewood Cliffs, N.J.: Prentice-Hall, 1978.

White, B. L., Watts, J. C., Barnett, I., Kaban, B. T., Marmor, J. R., & Shapiro, B. B. *Experience and Environment: Major Influences on the Development of the Young Child*. Vol. 1. Englewood Cliffs, N.J.: Prentice-Hall, 1973.

White, B. L. with B. Kaban & J. Attanucci. *The Origins of Human Competence: The Final Report of the Harvard Preschool Project*. Lexington, Mass.: Lexington Books, 1979.

Yarrow, L. J. "Maternal Deprivation: Toward an Empirical and Conceptual Reevaluation." *Psychological Bulletin* 58 (1961): 459–90.

NO

Joanne Curry O'Connell

CHILDREN OF WORKING MOTHERS: WHAT THE RESEARCH TELLS US

Labor statistics . . . provide evidence of the increasing number of mothers who are choosing to work outside the home. The factors influencing this decision are well known and range from the need for additional family income to the need for personal self-fulfillment. The impact of this decision on the family unit, the parents, and the child, however, is not yet fully understood. In fact, the complexity of investigating this issue has eluded even the best researchers.

What is available to early educators in the professional literature developed over the past decade is the attempt to systematically assess the impact of daycare placement on the growth and development of the young child. I would like to review this research as a counterargument to Burton White's position. White advocated that women, with few exceptions, should not work outside the home while their children are young.

This counterviewpoint was undertaken for several reasons. First, White's formulation of a question requiring a yes or no response oversimplified the issue and ignored factors critical to the decision that may be tied to external forces, such as single parent families, economic needs, and so on. Secondly, White's argument was primarily based on institutional research and animal studies of the past (such as Bowlby, 1951, and Yarrow, 1961). Belsky & Steinberg (1978) in their review of the daycare issue noted that negative attitudes toward working mothers are perpetuated by those who rely on research conducted in the 1950s with institutionalized children raised in isolated, unstimulating environments. These studies have led some to make statements about the "obvious harmful effects" of daycare programs (White, 1981, p. 14), while at the same time they neglect a wealth of investigations conducted more recently. Additionally, Etaugh (1980), in a review of feature articles in the popular press on daycare versus homecare, documented a predominantly negative attitude toward today's working mothers. This is, indeed, an emotionally charged issue for the American public for several reasons, and it is incumbent upon

From Joanne Curry O'Connell, "Children of Working Mothers: What the Research Tells Us," *Young Children*, vol. 38, no. 2 (1983). Copyright © 1983 by the National Association for the Education of Young Children. Reprinted by permission.

professionals in early childhood education to review the *facts*, and form an educated opinion on the effects of daycare.

This review will summarize research related to four popular questions often posed when discussing the effects of daycare on young children's development:

1. How does daycare affect mother/child emotional attachment?
2. How does daycare affect intellectual growth and development?
3. Does daycare help children learn to get along with their peers?
4. What is the effect of maternal attitude toward childcare settings on the child's development?

This information can also assist mothers in making their decisions related to "staying at home with your baby."

HOW DOES DAYCARE AFFECT MOTHER/CHILD EMOTIONAL ATTACHMENT?

This question is addressed first because professionals and parents alike have focused much of the daycare versus homecare issue on whether or not daycare disrupts the maternal/child bond. To provide a cogent answer to this question, it is necessary to describe the nature of the investigations and the procedure for assessing maternal attachment and emotional bonding. Most investigations have relied heavily on the Ainsworth and Wittig (1969) strange situation experiment. This procedure assesses the child's proximity-seeking and attention-seeking behavior when separated and reunited with the mother in the presence of a stranger (Heist, 1981). The level of anxiety induced in the child by these strange situations is also noted. This empirical paradigm assumes that the quality of the mother/child relationship can be measured by the approach-avoidance response of the child to her or his mother and to the stranger (Belsky & Steinberg, 1978). Other investigators have employed observational techniques in a similar setting to measure behaviors such as crying, smiling, giving, and touching the mother during interaction sessions. The studies using the above-mentioned procedures have generally contrasted groups of children reared exclusively at home to groups of children receiving daily substitute care. The children studied also represent a cross-section of the preschool years, from six months to five years.

Out of ten studies investigating the effects of substitute care on the maternal/child bond, eight reported no significant difference between the home-reared group and the out-of-home group across the variables studied (Doyle, 1975; Caldwell et al., 1970; Cochran, 1977; Hock, 1980; Kagan, Kearsley, & Zelazo, 1977; Moskowitz, Schwarz, & Corsini, 1977; Portnoy & Simmons, 1978; Rubenstein, 1979). In fact, the conclusions drawn by these investigators can best be characterized by Cochran's (1977) summary, in which he stated that the similarities in behavior between the groups far outweighed any observed differences. The mother/child attachment was not found to be weakened or abnormal in the children attending daycare.

The two studies reporting negative findings in terms of the group of children receiving substitute care were Blehar (1974) and Vaughn, Gove, and Egeland (1980). Blehar's study has since been refuted by several investigators who have unsuccessfully attempted to replicate her results. They failed to find that daycare children cried more and interacted less with their mothers than did home-reared children (Moskowitz, Schwarz, & Corsini, 1977; Portnoy & Simmons, 1978). The more recent study (Vaughn, Gove, & Egeland, 1980) looked at a group of infants who were being cared for primarily in an alternate caregiver home. These infants, placed in substitute care prior to their first birthday, exhibited a significantly greater amount of anxious-avoidant behavior than infants remaining at home with their mothers. Although it is difficult to account for these differences without an attempt at replication, the results are not in agreement with the bulk of the research.

An important feature of the eight studies reporting no difference in maternal attachment behaviors is the fact that the age of entry into substitute care situations varied from two months to four years. Thus, even children entering substitute care during infancy were not adversely affected. In fact, one author (Blehar, 1974) has suggested that infants receiving substitute care early in life may not experience the anxiety that separation might produce in older children. Rubenstein (1979) suggests that infants use self-comforting behaviors, and that peers can effectively reduce the effects of separation. One investigation (Portnoy & Simmons, 1979) systematically studied the effects of age of entry into substitute care and found no differences between the groups.

Caretaker Versus Maternal Attachment
In addition to the assessment of mother/child attachment by studying the child's reaction to a stranger, several investigations have been concerned with the effects the substitute caregiver has on the child's preference for the mother versus the caregiver (Cummings, 1980; Farran & Ramey, 1977; Kagan, Kearsley, & Zelazo,

1977; Ricciuti, 1974). A variation of the attachment paradigm was used in which both the primary caregiver and mother are present in the room and a stressful situation was produced by introducing a stranger to the setting. When children were placed in a conflict situation, they consistently showed an overwhelming preference for their mothers. Although the children were placed daily in a secure environment with a substitute caregiver, the naturally occurring bond between mother and child was not disrupted nor relinquished to the caregiver.

HOW DOES DAYCARE AFFECT INTELLECTUAL GROWTH AND DEVELOPMENT?

The early intervention projects of the last decade and a half offer convincing evidence that preschool children from low-income homes can benefit greatly from an enriched daycare environment (Golden et al., 1978; Heber et al., 1972; Ramey & Smith, 1976). Probably the most exciting recent research is provided in several longitudinal, follow-up studies which have evaluated the high-school status of children receiving early intervention during the preschool years (Fredericks, Moore, & Baldwin, 1979; Lazar et al., 1977; Palmer, 1977; Schweinhart & Weikart, 1980). These investigators found that fewer daycare children were placed in special education classes and fewer were retained in later grades. The daycare children had significantly higher expectations and occupational aspirations than children from control groups. These follow-up studies can lay to rest the fears that the intellectual gains which the daycare children exhibited over the control children during the preschool years would not be maintained as they entered public schools.

Indeed, the follow-up investigations provide evidence that high-risk children from daycare enrichment programs are more likely to succeed in our society as they reach adulthood.

One must still ask, however, what happens to the low-risk child—the child from the middle- and upper-middle-income homes? Belsky and Steinberg (1978) reported eight studies that found no difference between low-risk daycare-reared children and matched home-reared children on measures of intellectual development.

Differences in Provider Behavior

Although few investigations have systematically compared daycare settings to family group homes, the recent national Day Care Home Study (Davison & Ellis, 1980; Fosburg, 1981; Singer et al., 1980; Stallings & Porter, 1980) provides information on differences within family group home settings by conducting direct behavioral observations of provider behavior. In a recent summary of the study, Stevens (1982) reported that the regulatory status of the homes was related to provider behavior. In the study, family daycare homes were classified as (1) sponsored—requiring affiliation with an external administrative agency; (2) regulated—requiring state licensure or registration; or (3) unregulated—no external control or scrutiny. The providers from sponsored homes spent significantly more time interacting directly with the children than providers of regulated homes, who interacted more with children than providers from unregulated homes. Stevens also notes that "training in early childhood education was strongly associated with more positive and stimulating behaviors" (p. 62). If adult/child interactions are deemed important to growth and development, par-

ticularly in the early years, then settings in which the provider spends more time in interaction with children may facilitate children's intellectual and other areas of development.

DOES DAYCARE HELP CHILDREN LEARN TO GET ALONG WITH THEIR PEERS?

The first two questions posed in this review tend to address the concepts about daycare raised by professionals and the popular press. However, when Bronfenbrenner (1970) surveyed a group of Massachusetts parents regarding the most important outcome of substitute care for their child, the majority response could be summarized as: "Help my child get along with others." The issues surrounding this question can be viewed in two ways: (1) daycare promotes peer relationships and behaviors for getting along with others, or (2) group care promotes aggression and negative behaviors directed toward peers.

Belsky and Steinberg (1978) reviewed four studies related to the issue of peer relationships among daycare children (Cornelius & Denney, 1975; Doyle, 1975; Kagan, Kearsley, & Zelazo, 1977; Ricciuti, 1974). Heist (1981) reviewed an additional seven studies (Howes, 1979; Finkelstein et al. 1978; Johnson, 1979; Macrae & Herbert-Jackson, 1976; McCutcheon & Calhoun, 1976; Rubenstein, 1979; Schwarz, Strickland, & Krolick, 1974). One of the findings consistently reported across studies is the lack of aggression and negative behaviors in center and family daycare settings. Although instances of aggression may occur, they are infrequent and the exception rather than the rule. Heist (1981) has speculated that the degree to which the setting is restrictive may be more important than the type of daycare—highly restrictive homes could result in excessive acting-out behaviors.

Most investigations of the effect of substitute care on social development and peer interactions were based on direct observation. Only two studies used a rating device by which caretaker judgment determined the measure of peer social skills (Macrae & Herbert-Jackson, 1976; Schwarz, Strickland, & Krolick, 1974). Most studies observed the children's behaviors in a small group setting outside the daycare environment (Cornelius & Denney, 1975; Doyle, 1975; Kagan, Kearsley, & Zelazo, 1977). Often, home-reared children were matched with daycare children and observed as pairs (Johnson, 1979; Rubenstein, 1979).

The behaviors that were studied and identified as representative of peer social interactions ranged from frequency counts of behaviors (such as the number of visual regards for peers, joint toy usage, smiling, and hitting); to the proportion of time spent in joint interaction and type of play activity (solitary or cooperative). Although each of the studies may have reported significant differences between the groups on one or two isolated variables, they tended to be balanced in terms of those reporting more favorable social behaviors in daycare children (Rubenstein, 1979; Johnson, 1979; Kagan, Kearsley, & Zelazo, 1977; Ricciuti, 1978) and those reporting more acceptable social skills in home-reared children (Doyle, 1975; Howes, 1979; Schwarz, Strickland, & Krolick, 1974). Finkelstein (1982) recently reported, however, that although no significant problems were found in the social development of their daycare children studied, significant differences in aggressiveness and hostility were found between daycare children and a peer control group upon entry into kindergarten. No reasons were

provided for this discrepancy. In reviewing the literature related to daycare issues, the lack of difference between daycare and home-reared children in their behaviors, including social behaviors, is particularly striking. At the very least, no consistent, adverse effects were noted by any investigator, and, in fact, some reported that children in daycare were more skilled socially.

Finkelstein et al. (1978) observed the development of a group of daycare infants at 9, 10, 11, and 12 months of age. They reported that social behaviors in young children were more a function of age and development than of the type of childcare setting. Johnson (1979) reached a similar conclusion, and additionally suggested that social behaviors may be related more to the numbers of peers available to a child than to the setting within which the social interactions occur. It is unclear from current research whether or not mere placement in a group setting will result in a significant change in social abilities. As noted above, for normally developing children, maturation may provide the key ingredient. However, it is incumbent upon daycare providers to be sensitive to their role in facilitating social development. Rather than intervening only when trouble arises, it may be necessary to actively facilitate cooperative play and verbal exchange through modeling and reinforcement. Learning may then occur that will facilitate the maturation process.

WHAT IS THE EFFECT OF MATERNAL ATTITUDE TOWARD CHILDCARE SETTINGS ON THE CHILD'S DEVELOPMENT?

One study (Farel, 1980) approached the issue of the effects of daycare on kindergarten children's development from the perspective of the mother. Farel's study is unique in two ways: first, it assessed the effect of maternal attitude toward her work status on the child's development; and second, it employed a variety of child outcome measures. A questionnaire administered to 212 mothers of kindergarten children was designed to elicit information related to identifying mothers' attitudes about the needs of young children, such as (1) whether or not working makes a better or poorer mother, (2) whether or not mothers with preschoolers should work, (3) whether or not children have a negative attitude toward working mothers, and (4) the importance of intrinsic motivation to work for personal satisfaction. Child outcome measures included a classroom adjustment measure (task orientation, persistence, concentration, creativity and curiosity, intelligence, and consideration for others), as well as school achievement data.

Farel concluded that there was no evidence from her data that a mother's working per se interferes with the development of her child. There was no significant relationship between a child's successful school adjustment and whether or not the mother was employed outside the home. Children of mothers whose attitudes toward work and work behavior were congruent (wanted to work and was working, or did not want to work and was not working) scored significantly higher on several measures of adjustment and competence than children of mothers whose behavior and attitudes were not congruent (working and did not want to, or not working and wanted to).

Farel's study contributes a more comprehensive picture because, by looking at maternal attitude, we consider one of the many complex variables that may influence children's development, regardless of where they spend their day.

SUMMARY

A review of research evidence leads to this conclusion: *no consistent adverse effect of out-of-home child daycare has been found by over a dozen child development investigators.* Although professionals in child development are influenced by our own experiences, values, and beliefs, we must also be knowledgeable about the research evidence when we assist parents in making such important decisions. This approach to formulating an opinion is indeed part of what differentiates the professional early childhood educator from the general public. It is our professional responsibility to keep up with the current research, to contribute to the developing knowledge base in our field, and to broaden our understanding about these and other controversial issues.

It is true that much more research needs to be conducted before we have a more complete picture of all the factors involved regarding the influence of daycare, and what components comprise quality care. Several of the major reviews of daycare research cited in this report discuss the current research limitations and future needs. The four critical questions here are still in need of further vigorous investigation. Mothers are choosing to work in increasing numbers, so our professional efforts should be aimed at answering these and other questions, such as

1. What are the critical differences in substitute care that facilitate or inhibit child growth and development?

2. What is the effect of the high turnover rate in substitute care arrangements

on the child's adjustment and emotional security?

3. What is the father's influence on the child's success in out-of-home care settings (attitude, sharing of responsibilities, flexibility in assisting with sick children, etc.)?

There are many other pressing questions that can be formulated. We must shift both professional and parent concerns away from the limited question, "Should you stay home with your baby?" to more critical and realistic issues related to the quality of young children's care and the family's impact on the child's development.

REFERENCES

Ainsworth, M. D., & Wittig, B. A. "Attachment and Exploratory Behavior of One-Year-Olds in a Strange Situation." In *Determinants of Infant Behavior*, Vol. 4, ed. B. M. Foss. New York: Barnes & Noble, 1969.

Belsky, J., & Steinberg, L. D. "The Effects of Day Care: A Critical Review." *Child Development* 49 (1978): 929–49.

Blehar, M. "Anxious Attachment and Defensive Reactions Associated with Day Care." *Child Development* 45 (1974): 683–92.

Bowlby, J. *Maternal Care and Mental Health.* Monograph no. 2. Geneva, Switz.: World Health Organization, 1951.

Bronfenbrenner, U. *Two Worlds of Childhood: U.S. and U.S.S.R.* New York: Sage, 1970.

Caldwell, B. M., Wright, C. M., Honig, A. S., & Tannenbaum, J. "Infant Care and Attachment." *American Journal of Orthopsychiatry* 40 (1970): 397–412.

Cochran, M. "A Comparison of Group Day and Family Child-Rearing Patterns in Sweden." *Child Development* 48 (1977): 702–07.

Cornelius, S., & Denney, N. "Dependency in Day Care and Home Care Children." *Developmental Psychology* 11 (1975): 575–82.

Cummings, E. M. "Caregiver Stability and Day Care." *Developmental Psychology* 16 (1980): 31–37.

Davison, J. L., & Ellis, W. W. *Family Day Care in the United States: Parent Component. Final Report of the National Day Care Home Study. Vol. 4.* Washington, D.C.: U.S. Department of Health and Human Services, Administration for Children, Youth and Families, 1980. (DHHS Publication No.[OHDS] 81–30299)

Doyle, A. "Infant Development in Day Care." *Developmental Psychology* 11 (1975): 655–56.

Etaugh, C. "Effects of Nonmaternal Care on Children: Research Evidence and Popular Views." *American Psychologist* 35 (1980): 309–19.

Farel, A. "Effects of Preferred Maternal Roles, Maternal Employment, and Sociodemographic Status on School Adjustment and Competence." *Child Development* 51 (1980): 1179–86.

Farran, D., & Ramey, C. T. "Infant Day Care and Attachment Behaviors Toward Mothers and Teachers." *Child Development* 48 (1977): 1112–16.

Finkelstein, N. W. "Aggression: Is It Stimulated by Day Care?" *Young Children* 37, no. 6 (September 1982): 3–9.

Finkelstein, N. W., Dent, C., Gallagher, K., & Ramey, C. T. "Social Behavior of Infants and Toddlers in a Day-Care Environment." *Developmental Psychology* 14 (1978): 257–62.

Fosburg, S. *Family Day Care in the United States: Summary of Findings. Final Report of the National Day Care Home Study. Vol. 1.* Washington, D. C.: U.S. Department of Health and Human Services, Administration for Children, Youth and Families, 1981. (DHHS Publication No. [OHDS] 80–30282)

Fredericks, H. D., Moore, M. G., & Baldwin, V. L. *The Long-Range Effects of Early Childhood Education on a TMR Population.* Paper presented at the Alice Hayden Symposium, Seattle, Washington, 1979.

Golden, M., Rosenbluth, L., Grossi, M., Policare, H., Freeman, H., & Brownlee, E. *The New York City Infant Day Care Study.* New York: Medical and Health Research Association of New York City, 1978.

Heber, R., Garber, H., Harrington, D., Hoffman, C., & Falender, C. *Rehabilitation of Families at Risk for Mental Retardation.* Madison: Rehabilitation Research and Training Center in Mental Retardation, University of Wisconsin, 1972.

Heist, M. "The Effects of Day Care: A Literature Review. *Resources in Education* 16 (1981): 120. (ERIC Document Reproduction Service No. 197 812)

Hock, E. "Working and Nonworking Mothers and Their Infants: A Comparative Study of Maternal Caregiving Characteristics and Infants' Social Behavior." *Merrill-Palmer Quarterly* 46 (1980): 79–101.

Howes, C. "Toddler Social Competence in Family and Center Day-Care." *Dissertation Abstracts International* 39, no. 12 (1979): 6097-B. (University Microfilms, No. 7912147, 196)

Johnson, R. L. "Social Behavior of Three-Year-Old Children in Day Care and Home Settings." *Child Study Journal* 9 (1979): 109–22.

Kagan, J. "Emergent Themes in Human Development." *American Scientist* 64 (1976): 186–96.

Kagan, J., Kearsley, R., & Zelazo, P. "The Effects of Infant Day Care on Psychological Development." *Evaluation Quarterly* 1, no. 1 (1977): 109–42.

Lazar, I., Hubbell, R., Murray, H., Rosche, M., & Royce, J. *Preliminary Findings of the Developmental Continuity Longitudinal Study.* Presented at the Office of Child Development Conference, "Parents, Children, and Continuity," El Paso, Texas, 1977.

Macrae, J. W., & Herbert-Jackson, E. "Are Behavioral Effects of Infant Day Care Programs Specific?" *Developmental Psychology* 12 (1976): 269–70.

McCutcheon, B., & Calhoun, K. "Social and Emotional Adjustment of Infants and Toddlers to a Day Care Setting." *American Journal of Orthopsychiatry* 46 (1976): 104–08.

Moskowitz, D. G., Schwarz, J. C., & Corsini, D. A. "Initiating Day Care at Three Years of Age: Effects on Attachment." *Child Development* 48 (1977): 1271–76.

Palmer, F. "The Effects of Early Childhood Educational Intervention on School Performance." Paper presented at the President's Commission on Mental Health, 1977.

Portnoy, F. C., & Simmons, C. H. "Day Care and Attachment." *Child Development* 49 (1978): 239–42.

Ramey, C. T., & Smith, B. "Assessing the Intellectual Consequences of Early Intervention with High-Risk Infants." *American Journal of Mental Deficiency* 81 (1976): 318–24.

Ricciuti, H. N. "Fear and the Development of Social Attachments in the First Year of Life." In *The Origins of Human Behavior. Vol. 2. The Origins of Fear*, ed. M. Lewis and L. A. Rosenblum. New York: Wiley, 1974.

Ricciuti, H. N. "Effects of Infant Day Care Experience on Behavior and Development: Research and Implications for Social Policy." *Resources in Education* 13, no. 11 (1978): 149, (ERIC Document Reproduction Service No. 156 340)

Rubenstein, J. "Caregiving and Infant Behavior in Day Care and in Homes." *Developmental Psychology* 15, no. 1 (1979): 1–24.

Schwarz, J. C. "Reconciling Women's Changing Status with Children's Enduring Needs." *Educational Horizons* 59, no. 1 (Fall 1980): 15–21.

Schwarz, J. C., Strickland, R. G., & Krolick, G. "Infant Day Care: Behavioral Effects at Preschool Age." *Developmental Psychology* 10 (1974): 502–06.

Schweinhart, L. J., & Weikart, D. P. "Young Children Grow Up: The Effects of the Perry Preschool Program on Youths Through Age 15." *Monographs of the High/Scope Educational Research Foundation* 7 (1980).

Singer, J. D., Fosburg, S., Goodson, B. D., & Smith, J. M. *Family Day Care in the United States: Research Report. Final Report of the National Day Care Home Study. Vol. 2.* Washington, D.C.: U.S. Department of Health and Human Services, Administration for Children, Youth and Families, 1980. (DHHS Publication No. [OHDS] 80–30283)

Stallings, J., & Porter, A. *Family Day Care in the United States: Observation Component. Final Report of the National Day Care Home Study. Vol. 3.* Washington, D.C.: U.S. Department of Health and Human Services, Administration for Children, Youth and Families, 1980. (DHHS Publication No. [OHDS] 80–30284)

Stevens, J. H., Jr. "Research in Review. The National Day Care Home Study: Family Day Care in the United States." *Young Children* 37, no. 4 (May 1982): 59–66.

Vaughn, B. E., Gove, F. L., & Egeland, B. "The Relationship Between Out-of-Home Care and the Quality of Infant-Mother Attachment in an Economically Disadvantaged Population." *Child Development* 51, no. 4 (1980): 1203–14.

White, B. L. "Viewpoint. Should You Stay Home with Your Baby?" *Young Children* 37, no. 1 (November 1981): 11–17.

Women's Bureau, "Number of Mothers in the Labor Force Continues to Rise." *Working Mothers and Their Children.* Washington, D.C.: U.S. Department of Labor, 1977. Doc. no. 77–16479.

Yarrow, M. R. "Maternal Deprivation: Toward an Empirical and Conceptual Re-evaluation." *Psychological Bulletin* 58 (1961): 459–90.

CHALLENGE QUESTIONS

Is Day Care Harmful?

Assume that you and your spouse are just now planning to have children and that you would both like to pursue careers important to you.

1. What have the authors in this issue contributed to your planning?

2. Are you satisfied with the data provided by the researchers? What additional questions would you like to have researchers consider?

3. Assuming that you have planned to leave your children in a day-care center and that you could choose from among several, what care characteristics would you look for? Why?

4. If you were a researcher, how would you try to find answers for the questions O'Connell poses at the end of her article?

ISSUE 12

Are Children of Divorced Parents at Greater Risk?

YES: Judith S. Wallerstein, from "Children of Divorce: The Dilemma of a Decade," In Elam W. Nunnally, Catherine S. Chilman, and Fred M. Cox, eds., *Troubled Relationships* (Sage Publications, 1988)

NO: David H. Demo and Alan C. Acock, from "The Impact of Divorce on Children," *Journal of Marriage and the Family* (August 1988)

ISSUE SUMMARY

YES: Clinician and researcher Judith S. Wallerstein contends that children of divorced parents are at greater risk than children of intact families for mental and physical problems.
NO: Sociologists David H. Demo and Alan C. Acock question the idea that intact, two-parent families are always best for children, and they argue instead that any negative effects of divorce are short-lived and often include many positive changes.

Over half of all marriages now end in divorce. What effect do these divorces have upon the young children involved? Many people assume that the changes involved in divorce would naturally lead to some emotional problems, with potentially permanent ramifications. Hidden in this view, however, is the assumption that the traditional, two-parent family is the most appropriate environment in which to raise children. Indeed, most research on children of divorce has been based on this assumption.

Several developmental psychologists have recently begun to question this assumption. They suggest that nontraditional families—single-parent families, for example—can also produce happy, emotionally stable children. This could mean that divorce is not always negative. In fact, the effects of living in a highly conflictual environment—such as the environment of a couple contemplating divorce—could be more damaging than the actual act of divorce itself. In this sense, the level of family conflict would have more to do with a child's adjustment than the number of parents he or she has.

Judith S. Wallerstein, while acknowledging certain limitations on the relevant research, contends that children of divorce are at great risk of developing problems. She argues that increased attention to education, treatment, and prevention programs is needed for this special population of children. She identifies three broad stages in the divorcing process along with the effects each stage has on the children. Wallerstein also chronicles changes in the parent-child relationship during the divorce process. These include a diminished capacity of adults to parent their children, a decline in emotional sensitivity and support for the children, decreased pleasure in the parent-child relationship, and less interaction with the children. All of these changes, she concludes, have a negative impact on the development of the children. She asserts that for most children, divorce is "the most stressful period of their lives."

David H. Demo and Alan C. Acock, on the other hand, argue that "it is simplistic and inaccurate to think of divorce as having uniform consequences for children." They contend that most current research is based upon Freudian or social learning concepts that emphasize that both parents are necessary for a child to develop normally. Demo and Acock, however, question the necessity of the traditional two-parent family. They cite evidence showing that parental separation is actually beneficial for children when the alternative is continued familial conflict. Other studies reveal that factors such as maternal employment and social support are more important than the actual divorce in determining how successfully a child develops following a family breakup. Unfortunately, most studies do not distinguish between the effects of family structure (one- versus two-parent families, for example) and the effects of divorce. Studies that make this distinction are required before any final conclusions can be drawn about the effects of divorce on children.

POINT	COUNTERPOINT
• Children of divorce are at greater risk of developing problems than are children in traditional, two-parent families.	• Nontraditional families can also produce healthy, emotionally stable children.
• Children experience parental separation and its aftermath as the most stressful period of their lives.	• Children who experienced divorce indicated that it was preferable to living in conflict.
• There are significant, negative changes in the parent-child relationship during the divorce process.	• There are positive outcomes of divorce, such as greater assumption of responsibility and internal locus of control.
• A child's age and developmental stage appear to be the most important factors affecting his or her response to divorce.	• These factors are not as important as family characteristics in understanding the effects of divorce.

YES

Judith S. Wallerstein

CHILDREN OF DIVORCE: THE DILEMMA OF A DECADE

It is now estimated that 45% of all children born in 1983 will experience their parents' divorce, 35% will experience a remarriage, and 20% will experience a second divorce (A. J. Norton, Assistant Chief, Population Bureau, United States Bureau of the Census, personal communication, 1983). . . .

Although the incidence of divorce has increased across all age groups, the most dramatic rise has occurred among young adults (Norton, 1980). As a result, children in divorcing families are younger than in previous years and include more preschool children. . . .

Although many children weather the stress of marital discord and family breakup without psychopathological sequelae, a significant number falter along the way. Children of divorce are significantly overrepresented in outpatient psychiatric, family agency, and private practice populations compared with children in the general population (Gardner, 1976; Kalter, 1977; Tessman, 1977; Tooley, 1976). The best predictors of mental health referrals for school-aged children are parental divorce or parental loss as a result of death (Felner, Stolberg, & Cowen, 1975). A national survey of adolescents whose parents had separated and divorced by the time the children were seven years old found that 30% of these children had received psychiatric or psychological therapy by the time they reached adolescence compared with 10% of adolescents in intact families (Zill, 1983).

A longitudinal study in northern California followed 131 children who were age 3 to 18 at the decisive separation. At the 5-year mark, the investigators found that more than one-third were suffering with moderate to severe depression (Wallerstein & Kelly, 1980a). These findings are especially striking because the children were drawn from a nonclinical population and were accepted into the study only if they had never been identified before the divorce as needing psychological treatment and only if they were performing at age-appropriate levels in school. Therefore, the deterioration observed in these children's adjustment occurred largely following the family breakup. . . .

Divorce is a long, drawn-out process of radically changing family relationships that has several stages, beginning with the marital rupture and its immediate aftermath, continuing over several years of disequilibrium, and finally coming to rest with the stabilization of a new postdivorce or remarried family unit. A complex chain of changes, many of them unanticipated and unforeseeable, are set into motion by the marital rupture and are likely to occupy a significant portion of the child or adolescent's growing years. As the author and her colleague have reported elsewhere, women in the California Children of Divorce study required three to three-and-one-half years following the decisive separation before they achieved a sense of order and predictability in their lives (Wallerstein & Kelly, 1980a). This figure probably underestimates the actual time trajectory of the child's experience of divorce. A prospective study reported that parent–child relationships began to deteriorate many years prior to the divorce decision and that the adjustment of many children in these families began to fail long before the decisive separation (Morrison, 1982). This view of the divorcing process as long lasting accords with the perspective of a group of young people who reported at a 10-year follow-up that their entire childhood or adolescence had been dominated by the family crisis and its extended aftermath (Wallerstein, 1978).

Stages in the Process

The three broad, successive stages in the divorcing process, while they overlap, are nevertheless clinically distinguishable. *The acute phase* is precipitated by the decisive separation and the decision to divorce. This stage is often marked by steeply escalating conflict between the adults, physical violence, severe distress, depression accompanied by suicidal ideation, and a range of behaviors reflecting a spilling of aggressive and sexual impulses. The adults frequently react with severe ego regression and not unusually behave at odds with their more customary demeanor. Sharp disagreement in the wish to end the marriage is very common, and the narcissistic injury to the person who feels rejected sets the stage for rage, sexual jealousy, and depression. Children are generally not shielded from this parental conflict or distress. Confronted by a marked discrepancy in images of their parents, children do not have the assurance that the bizarre or depressed behaviors and moods will subside. As a result, they are likely to be terrified by the very figures they usually rely on for nurturance and protection.

As the acute phase comes to a close, usually within the first 2 years of the divorce decision, the marital partners gradually disengage from each other and pick up the new tasks of reestablishing their separate lives. *The transitional phase* is characterized by ventures into new, more committed relationships; new work, school, and friendship groups; and sometimes new settings, new lifestyles, and new geographical locations. This phase is marked by alternating success and failure, encouragement and discouragement, and it may also last for several years. Children observe and participate in the many changes of this period. They share the trials and errors and the fluctuations in mood. For several years life may be unstable, and home may be unsettled.

Finally, *the postdivorce phase* ensues with the establishment of a fairly stable single-parent or remarried household. Eventually three out of four divorced women and four out of five divorced men reenter wedlock (Cherlin, 1981). Unfortunately, though, remarriage does not bring immediate tranquility into the lives of the family members. The early years of the remarriage are often encumbered by ghostly presences from the earlier failed marriages and by the actual presences of children and visiting parents from the prior marriage or marriages. Several studies suggest widespread upset among children and adolescents following remarriage (Crohn, Brown, Walker, & Beir, 1981; Goldstein, 1974; Kalter, 1977). A large-scale investigation that is still in process reports long-lasting friction around visitation (Jacobson, 1983).

Changes in Parent–Child Relationships
Parents experience a diminished capacity to parent their children during the acute phase of the divorcing process and often during the transitional phase as well (Wallerstein & Kelly, 1980a). This phenomenon is widespread and can be considered an expectable, divorce-specific change in parent–child relationships. At its simplest level this diminished parenting capacity appears in the household disorder that prevails in the aftermath of divorce, in the rising tempers of custodial parent and child, in reduced competence and a greater sense of helplessness in the custodial parent, and in lower expectations of the child for appropriate social behavior (Hetherington, Cox, & Cox, 1978; 1982). Diminished parenting also entails a sharp decline in emotional sensitivity and support for the child; decreased pleasure in the parent–child relationship; decreased attentiveness to the child's needs and wishes; less talk, play, and interaction with the child; and a steep escalation in inappropriate expression of anger. One not uncommon component of the parent–child relationship

coincident with the marital breakup is the adult's conscious or unconscious wish to abandon the child and thus to erase the unhappy marriage in its entirety. Child neglect can be a serious hazard.

In counterpoint to the temporary emotional withdrawal from the child, the parent may develop a dependent, sometimes passionate, attachment to the child or adolescent, beginning with the breakup and lasting throughout the lonely postseparation years (Wallerstein, 1985). Parents are likely to lean on the child and turn to the child for help, placing the child in a wide range of roles such as confidante, advisor, mentor, sibling, parent, caretaker, lover, concubine, extended conscience or ego control, ally within the marital conflict, or pivotal supportive presence in staving off depression or even suicide. This expectation that children should not only take much greater responsibility for themselves but also should provide psychological and social support for the distressed parent is sufficiently widespread to be considered a divorce-specific response along with that of diminished parenting. Such relationships frequently develop with an only child or with a very young, even a preschool, child. Not accidentally, issues of custody and visitation often arise with regard to the younger children. While such disputes, of course, reflect the generally unresolved anger of the marriage and the divorce, they may also reflect the intense emotional need of one or both parents for the young child's constant presence (Wallerstein, 1985).

Parents may also lean more appropriately on the older child or adolescent. Many youngsters become proud helpers, confidantes, and allies in facing the difficult postdivorce period (Weiss, 1979b). Other youngsters draw away from close involvement out of their fears of engulf- ment, and they move precipitously out of the family orbit, sometimes before they are developmentally ready. . . .

CHILDREN'S REACTIONS TO DIVORCE

Initial Responses

Children and adolescents experience sep- aration and its aftermath as the most stressful period of their lives. The family rupture evokes an acute sense of shock, intense anxiety, and profound sorrow. Many children are relatively content and even well-parented in families where one or both parents are unhappy. Few young- sters experience any relief with the di- vorce decision, and those who do are usually older and have witnessed physi- cal violence or open conflict between their parents. The child's early responses are governed neither by an understand- ing of issues leading to the divorce nor by the fact that divorce has a high inci- dence in the community. To the child, divorce signifies the collapse of the struc- ture that provides support and protec- tion. The child reacts as to the cutting of his or her lifeline.

The initial suffering of children and adolescents in response to a marital sep- aration is compounded by realistic fears and fantasies about catastrophes that the divorce will bring in its wake. Children suffer with a pervasive sense of vul- nerability because they feel that the pro- tective and nurturant function of the family has given way. They grieve over the loss of the noncustodial parent, over the loss of the intact family, and often over the multiple losses of neighborhood, friends, and school. Children also worry about their distressed parents. They are concerned about who will take care of the parent who has left and whether the custodial parent will be able to manage alone. They experience intense anger to- ward one or both parents whom they hold responsible for disrupting the fam- ily. Some of their anger is reactive and defends them against their own feelings of powerlessness, their concern about being lost in the shuffle, and their fear that their needs will be disregarded as the parents give priority to their own wishes and needs. Some children, espe- cially young children, suffer with guilt over fantasied misdeeds that they feel may have contributed to the family quar- rels and led to the divorce. Others feel that it is their responsibility to mend the broken marriage (Wallerstein & Kelly, 1980a).

The responses of the child also must be considered within the social context of the divorce and in particular within the loneliness and social isolation that so many children experience. Children face the tensions and sorrows of divorce with little help from anybody else. Fewer than 10% of the children in the California Children of Divorce study had any help at the time of the crisis from adults out- side the family although many people, including neighbors, pediatricians, min- isters, rabbis, and family friends, knew the family and the children (Wallerstein & Kelly, 1980a). Thus, another striking feature of divorce as a childhood stress is that it occurs in the absence of or falling away of customary support.

Developmental factors are critical to the responses of children and adoles- cents at the time of the marital rupture. Despite significant individual differences in the child, in the family, and in par- ent–child relations, the child's age and developmental stage appear to be the most important factors governing the initial response. The child's dominant needs, his or her capacity to perceive and understand family events, the central psychological preoccupation and conflict, the available repertoire of defense and coping strategies, and the dominant patterning of relationships and expectations all reflect the child's age and developmental stage.

A major finding in divorce research has been the common patterns of response within different age groups (Wallerstein & Kelly, 1980a). The age groups that share significant commonalities in perceptions, responses, underlying fantasies, and behaviors are the preschool ages 3 to 5, early school age or early latency ages 5½ to 8, later school age or latency ages 8 to 11, and, finally, adolescent ages 12 to 18 (Kelly & Wallerstein, 1976; Wallerstein, 1977; Wallerstein & Kelly, 1974; 1975; 1980a). These responses, falling as they do into age-related groupings, may reflect children's responses to acute stress generally, not only their responses to marital rupture.

Observations about preschool children derived from longitudinal studies in two widely different regions, namely, Virginia and northern California, are remarkably similar in their findings (Hetherington, 1979; Hetherington et al., 1978; 1982; Wallerstein & Kelly, 1975, 1980a). Preschool children are likely to show regression following one parent's departure from the household, and the regression usually occurs in the most recent developmental achievement of the child. Intensified fears are frequent and are evoked by routine separations from the custodial parent during the day and at bedtime. Sleep disturbances are also frequent, with preoccupying fantasies of many of the little children being fear of abandon-

ment by both parents. Yearning for the departed parent is intense. Young children are likely to become irritable and demanding and to behave aggressively with parents, with younger siblings, and with peers.

Children in the 5- to 8-year-old group are likely to show open grieving and are preoccupied with feelings of concern and longing for the departed parent. Many share the terrifying fantasy of replacement. "Will my daddy get a new dog, a new mommy, a new little boy?" were the comments of several boys in this age group. Little girls wove elaborate Madame Butterfly fantasies, asserting that the departed father would some day return to them, that he loved them "the best." Many of the children in this age group could not believe that the divorce would endure. About half suffered a precipitous decline in their school work (Kelly & Wallerstein, 1979).

In the 9- to 12-year-old group the central response often seems to be intense anger at one or both parents for causing the divorce. In addition, these children suffer with grief over the loss of the intact family and with anxiety, loneliness, and the humiliating sense of their own powerlessness. Youngsters in this age group often see one parent as the "good" parent and the other as "bad," and they appear especially vulnerable to the blandishments of one or the other parent to engage in marital battles. Children in later latency also have a high potential for assuming a helpful and empathic role in the care of a needy parent. School performances and peer relationships suffered a decline in approximately one-half of these children (Wallerstein & Kelly, 1974).

Adolescents are very vulnerable to their parents' divorce. The precipitation of acute depression, accompanied by suicidal preoccupation and acting out, is frequent enough to be alarming. Anger can be intense. Several instances have been reported of direct violent attacks on custodial parents by young adolescents who had not previously shown such behavior (Springer & Wallerstein, 1983). Preoccupied with issues of morality, adolescents may judge the parents' conduct during the marriage and the divorce, and they may identify with one parent and do battle against the other. Many become anxious about their own future entry into adulthood, concerned that they may experience marital failure like their parents (Wallerstein & Kelly, 1974). By way of contrast, however, researchers have also called attention to the adolescent's impressive capacity to grow in maturity and independence as they respond to the family crisis and the parents' need for help (Weiss, 1979a). . . .

Long-Range Outcomes

The child's initial response to divorce should be distinguished from his or her long-range development and psychological adjustment. No single theme appears among all of those children who enhance, consolidate, or continue their good development after the divorce crisis has finally ended. Nor is there a single theme that appears among all of those who deteriorate either moderately or markedly. Instead, the author and her colleague (Wallerstein & Kelly, 1980a) have found a set of complex configurations in which the relevant components appear to include (a) the extent to which the parent has been able to resolve and put aside conflict and anger and to make use of the relief from conflict provided by the divorce (Emery, 1982; Jacobson, 1978 a, b, c); (b) the course of the custodial parent's

handling of the child and the resumption or improvement of parenting within the home (Hess & Camara, 1979); (c) the extent to which the child does not feel rejected by the noncustodial or visiting parent and the extent to which this relationship has continued regularly and kept pace with the child's growth; (d) the extent to which the divorce has helped to attenuate or dilute a psychopathological parent–child relationship; (e) the range of personality assets and deficits that the child brought to the divorce, including both the child's history in the predivorce family and his or her capacities in the present, particularly intelligence, the capacity for fantasy, social maturity, and the ability to turn to peers and adults; (f) the availability to the child of a supportive human network (Tessman, 1977); (g) the absence in the child of continued anger and depression; and (h) the sex and age of the child. . . .

FUTURE DIRECTIONS

Despite the accumulating reports of the difficulties that many children in divorced families experience, society has on the whole been reluctant to regard children of divorce as a special group at risk. Notwithstanding the magnitude of the population affected and the widespread implications for public policy and law, community attention has been very limited; research has been poorly supported; and appropriate social, psychological, economic, or preventive measures have hardly begun to develop. Recently the alarm has been sounded in the national press about the tragically unprotected and foreshortened childhoods of children of divorce and their subsequent difficulties in reaching maturity (Winn,

1983). Perhaps this reflects a long-over-due awakening of community concern.

The agenda for research on marital breakdown, separation, divorce, and re-marriage and the roads that families travel between each of these way stations [are] long and [have] been cited repeatedly in this [article]. The knowledge that we have acquired is considerable but the knowledge that we still lack is critical. More knowledge is essential in order to provide responsible advice to parents; to consult effectively with the wide range of other professionals whose daily work brings them in contact with these families; to design and mount education, treatment, or prevention programs; and to provide guidelines for informed social policy.

AUTHOR'S NOTE: The Center for the Family in Transition, of which the author is the Executive Director, is supported by a grant from the San Francisco Foundation. The Zellerback Family Fund supported the author's research in the California Children of Divorce Project, one of the sources for this [article]. A slightly different version of this paper has been published in *Psychiatry Update: The American Psychiatric Association Annual Review, Vol. III.* L. Grinspoon (Ed.), pp. 144–158, 1984.

REFERENCES

Cherlin, A. J. (1981). *Marriage, divorce, remarriage.* Cambridge, MA: Harvard University Press.

Crohn, H., Brown, H., Walker, L., & Beir, J. (1981). Understanding and treating the child in the remarried family. In I. R. Stuart & L. E. Abt (Eds.), *Children of separation and divorce: Management and treatment.* New York: Van Nostrand Reinhold.

Emery, R. E. (1982). Interparental conflict and children of discord and divorce. *Psychological Bulletin, 92,* 310–330.

Felner, R. D., Stolberg, A. L., & Cowen, E. L. (1975). Crisis events and school mental health

referral patterns of young children. *Journal of Consulting and Clinical Psychology, 43,* 303–310.

Gardner, R. A. (1976). *Psychotherapy and children of divorce.* New York: Jason Aronson.

Goldstein, H. S. (1974). Reconstructed families: The second marriage and its children. *Psychiatric Quarterly, 48,* 433–440.

Hess, R. D., & Camara, K. A. (1979). Post-divorce relationships as mediating factors in the consequences of divorce for children. *Journal of Social Issues, 35,* 79–96.

Hetherington, E. (1979). Divorce: A child's perspective. *American Psychology, 34,* 79–96.

Hetherington, E., Cox, M., & Cox, R. (1978). The aftermath of divorce. In H. Stevens & M. Mathews (Eds.), *Mother–child relations.* Washington, DC: National Association for the Education of Young Children.

Hetherington, E. M., Cox, M., & Cox, R. (1982). Effects of divorce on parents and children. In M. E. Lamb (Ed.), *Nontraditional families: Parenting and child development.* Hillsdale, NJ: Lawrence Erlbaum Associates.

Jacobson, D. (1978a). The impact of marital separation/divorce on children: I. Parent–child separation and child adjustment. *Journal of Divorce, 1,* 341–360.

Jacobson, D. (1978b). The impact of marital separation/divorce on children: II. Interparent hostility and child adjustment. *Journal of Divorce, 2,* 3–20.

Jacobson, D. (1978c). The impact of marital separation/divorce on children: III. Parent–child communication and child adjustment, and regression analysis of findings from overall study. *Journal of Divorce, 2,* 175–194.

Jacobson, D. S. (1983). *Conflict, visiting and child adjustment in the stepfamily: A linked family system.* Paper presented at annual meeting of the American Orthopsychiatric Association, Boston.

Kalter, N. (1977). Children of divorce in an outpatient psychiatric population. *American Journal of Orthopsychiatry, 47,* 40–51.

Kelly, J. B., & Wallerstein, J. S. (1976). The effects of parental divorce: Experiences of the child in early latency. *American Journal of Orthopsychiatry, 46,* 20–32.

Kelly, J. B., & Wallerstein, J. S. (1979). The divorced child in the school. *National Principal, 59,* 51–58.

Morrison, A. L. (1982). *A prospective study of divorce: Its relation to children's development and parental functioning.* Unpublished dissertation, University of California at Berkeley.

Norton, A. J. (1980). The influence of divorce on traditional life cycle measures. *Journal of Marriage and the Family, 42,* 63–69.

Springer, C., & Wallerstein, J. S. (1983). Young adolescents' responses to their parents' divorces. In L. A. Kurdek (Ed.), *Children and divorce*. San Francisco: Jossey-Bass.

Tessman, L. H. (1977). *Children of parting parents*. New York: Jason Aronson.

Tooley, K. (1976). Antisocial behavior and social alienation post divorce: The "man of the house" and his mother. *American Journal of Orthopsychiatry, 46*, 33–42.

Wallerstein, J. S. (1977). Responses of the preschool child to divorce: Those who cope. In M. F. McMillan & S. Henao (Eds.), *Child psychiatry: Treatment and research*. New York: Brunner/Mazel.

Wallerstein, J. S. (1978). Children of divorce: Preliminary report of a ten-year follow-up. In J. Anthony & C. Chilland (Eds.), *The child in his family* (Vol. 5). New York: Wiley.

Wallerstein, J. S. (1985). Parent–child relationships following divorce. In E. J. Anthony & G. Pollock (Eds.), *Parental influences in health and disease* (pp. 317–348). Boston: Little, Brown.

Wallerstein, J. S., & Kelly, J. B. (1974). The effects of parental divorce: The adolescent experience. In J. Anthony & C. Koupernik (Eds.), *The child in his family: Children at psychiatric risk* (Vol. 3). New York: Wiley.

Wallerstein, J. S., & Kelly, J. B. (1975). The effects of parental divorce: The experiences of the preschool child. *American Journal of Orthopsychiatry, 46*, 256–269.

Wallerstein, J. S., & Kelly, J. B. (1980a). *Surviving the breakup: How children and parents cope with divorce*. New York: Basic Books.

Weiss, R. S. (1979a). *Going it alone: The family life and social situation of the single parent*. New York: Basic Books.

Weiss, R. S. (1979b). Growing up a little faster. *Journal of Social Issues, 35*, 97–111.

Winn, M. (8 May 1983). The loss of childhood. *The New York Times Magazine*.

Zill, N. (22 March 1983). *Divorce, marital conflict, and children's mental health: Research findings and policy recommendations*. Testimony before Subcommittee on Family and Human Services, United States Senate Subcommittee on Labor and Human Resources.

NO

David H. Demo and
Alan C. Acock

THE IMPACT OF DIVORCE ON CHILDREN

With the acceleration of the divorce rate from the mid-1960s to the early 1980s, the number of nontraditional families (such as single-parent families and reconstituted families) have increased relative to intact, first-time nuclear families. This article reviews empirical evidence addressing the relationship between divorce, family composition, and children's well-being. Although not entirely consistent, the pattern of empirical findings suggests that children's emotional adjustment, gender-role orientation, and antisocial behavior are affected by family structure, whereas other dimensions of well-being are unaffected. But the review indicates that these findings should be interpreted with caution because of the methodological deficiencies of many of the studies on which these findings are based. Several variables, including the level of family conflict, may be central variables mediating the effect of family structure on children.

The purpose of this article is to review and assess recent empirical evidence on the impact of divorce on children, concentrating on studies of nonclinical populations published in the last decade. We also direct attention to a number of important theoretical and methodological considerations in the study of family structure and youthful well-being. We begin by briefly describing some of the theoretical propositions and assumptions that guide research in this area.

THEORETICAL UNDERPINNINGS

Consistent with the Freudian assumption that a two-parent group constitutes the minimal unit for appropriate sex-typed identification, anthropologists, sociologists, and social psychologists have long maintained the necessity of such a group for normal child development. Representative of structural-functional theorizing, Parsons and Bales argued that one of the basic functions of the family is to serve as a stable, organically integrated "factory" in which human personalities are formed.

From David H. Demo and Alan C. Acock, "The Impact of Divorce on Children," *Journal of Marriage and the Family*, vol. 50, no. 3 (August 1988). Copyright © 1988 by the National Council on Family Relations, 3989 Central Avenue, NE, Suite #550, Minneapolis, MN 55421. Reprinted by permission. Notes and references omitted.

Similarly, social learning theory emphasizes the importance of role models, focusing on parents as the initial and primary reinforcers of child behavior (Bandura and Walters, 1963). Much of the research adopting this perspective centers on parent-child similarities, analyzing the transmission of response patterns and the inhibitory or disinhibitory effect of parental models. The presence of the same-sex parent is assumed to be crucial in order for the child to learn appropriate sex-typed behavior. This assumption is shared by developmental and symbolic interactionist theories, various cognitive approaches to socialization, and confluence theory, as well as anthropological theories.

It logically follows that departures from the nuclear family norm are problematic for the child's development, especially for adolescents, inasmuch as this represents a crucial stage in the developmental process. Accordingly, a large body of research literature deals with father absence, the effects of institutionalization, and a host of "deficiencies" in maturation, such as those having to do with cognitive development, achievement, moral learning, and conformity. This focus has pointed to the crucial importance of both parents' presence but also has suggested that certain causes for parental absence may accentuate any negative effects. . . .

Divorce and Family Structure

In examining [the] research, . . . it is important to distinguish between studies investigating the effects of family structure and those investigating the effects of divorce. Most studies compare intact units and single-parent families, guided by the assumption that the latter family structure is precipitated by divorce. Of course, this is not always the case. Single-parent families consist of those with parents who have never married, those formed by the permanent separation of parents, and those precipitated by the death of a parent. Simple comparisons between one-and two-parent families are also suspect in that *two*-parent families are not monolithic. First-time or non-divorced units differ from divorced, remarried units in which stepparents are involved. In addition, little recognition has been given to the fact that families of different types may exhibit varying levels of instability or conflict, a potentially confounding variable in establishing the effects of family structure. In short, most investigations of the linkage between family structure and youthful well-being have failed to recognize the complexity of present-day families. . . .

Bearing in mind these conceptual distinctions, we now move to a systematic review of recent evidence on the impact of divorce on children and adolescents.

EXISTING RESEARCH

A substantial amount of research has examined the effects of family structure on children's social and psychological well-being. Many studies document negative consequences for children whose parents divorce and for those living in single-parent families. But most studies have been concerned with limited dimensions of a quite complex problem. Specifically, the research to date has typically (a) examined the effects of divorce or father absence on children, ignoring the effects on adolescents; (b) examined only selected dimensions of children's well-being; (c) compared intact units and single-parent families but not recognized important variations (e.g., levels of marital instability and conflict) within these structures; and (d) relied on cross-sectional designs to assess developmental processes.

Social and psychological well-being includes aspects of personal adjustment, self-concept, interpersonal relationships, antisocial behavior, and cognitive functioning. . . .

Personal Adjustment

Personal adjustment is operationalized in various ways by different investigators but includes such variables as self-control, leadership, responsibility, independence, achievement orientation, aggressiveness, and gender-role orientation. . . .

On the basis of her review of research conducted between 1970 and 1980, Cashion (1984: 483) concludes: "The evidence is overwhelming that after the initial trauma of divorce, the children are as emotionally well-adjusted in these [female-headed] families as in two-parent families." Investigations of long-term effects (Acock and Kiecolt, 1988; Kulka and Weingarten, 1979) suggest that, when socioeconomic status is controlled, adolescents who have experienced a parental divorce or separation have only slightly lower levels of adult adjustment. . . .

While their findings are not definitive, Kinard and Reinherz speculate that either "the effects of parental divorce on children diminish over time; or that the impact of marital disruption is less severe for preschool-age children than for school-age children" (1986: 291). Children's age at the time of disruption may also mediate the impact of these events on other dimensions of their well-being (e.g., self-esteem or gender-role orientation) and thus will be discussed in greater detail below. . . . But two variables that critically affect children's adjustment to divorce are marital discord and children's gender.

Marital discord. . . . [E]xtensive data on children who had experienced their parents' divorce indicated that, although learning of the divorce and adjusting to the loss of the noncustodial parent were painful, children indicated that these adjustments were preferable to living in conflict. Many studies report that children's adjustment to divorce is facilitated under conditions of low parental conflict—both prior to *and* subsequent to the divorce (Guidubaldi, Cleminshaw, Perry, Nastasi, and Lightel, 1986; Jacobson, 1978; Lowenstein and Koopman, 1978; Porter and O'Leary, 1980; Raschke and Raschke, 1979; Rosen, 1979).

Children's gender. Children's gender may be especially important in mediating the effects of family disruption, as most of the evidence suggests that adjustment problems are more severe and last for longer periods of time among boys (Hess and Camara, 1979; Hetherington, 1979; Hetherington, Cox, and Cox, 1978, 1979, 1982; Wallerstein, 1984; Wallerstein and Kelly, 1980b). Guidubaldi and Perry (1985) found, controlling for social class, that boys in divorced families manifested significantly more maladaptive symptoms and behavior problems than boys in intact families. Girls differed only on the dimension of locus of control; girls in divorced households scored significantly higher than their counterparts in intact households. . . .

While custodial mothers provide girls with same-sex role models, most boys have to adjust to living without same-sex parents. In examining boys and girls living in intact families and in different custodial arrangements, Santrock and Warshak (1979) found that few effects could be attributed to family structure per se, but that children living with opposite-sex parents (mother-custody boys and father-custody girls) were not as well adjusted on measures of competent social behavior. . . .

Along related lines, a number of researchers have examined gender-role orientation and, specifically, the relation of father absence to boys' personality development. Most of the evidence indicates that boys without adult male role models demonstrate more feminine behavior (Biller, 1976; Herzog and Sudia, 1973; Lamb, 1977a), except in lower-class families (Biller, 1981b). A variety of studies have shown that fathers influence children's gender role development to be more traditional because, compared to mothers, they more routinely differentiate between masculine and feminine behaviors and encourage greater conformity to conventional gender roles (Biller, 1981a; Biller and Davids, 1973; Bronfenbrenner, 1961; Heilbrun, 1965; Lamb, 1977b; Noller, 1978). . . . But it should be reiterated that these effects have been attributed to father absence and thus would be expected to occur among boys in all female-headed families, not simply those that have experienced divorce. . . .

[M]ost of the research on boys' adjustment fails to consider the quality or quantity of father-child contact or the availability of alternative male role models (e.g., foster father, grandfather, big brother, other male relatives, coach, friend, etc.), which makes it difficult to assess the impact of changing family structure on boys' behavior. There are also limitations imposed by conceptualizing and measuring masculinity-femininity as a bipolar construct (Bem, 1974; Constantinople, 1973; Worell, 1978), and there is evidence that boys and girls in father-absent families are better described as androgynous (Kurdek and Siesky, 1980a).

Positive outcomes of divorce. . . . [T]he tendency of children in single-parent families to display more androgynous behavior may be interpreted as a beneficial effect. Because of father absence, children in female-headed families are not pressured as strongly as their counterparts in two-parent families to conform to traditional gender roles. These children frequently assume a variety of domestic responsibilities to compensate for the absent parent (Weiss, 1979), thereby broadening their skills and competencies and their definitions of gender-appropriate behavior. Divorced parents also must broaden their behavioral patterns to meet increased parenting responsibilities, thereby providing more androgynous role models. Kurdek and Siesky (1980a: 250) give the illustration that custodial mothers often "find themselves needing to acquire and demonstrate a greater degree of dominance, assertiveness, and independence while custodial fathers may find themselves in situations eliciting high degrees of warmth, nurturance, and tenderness."

Aside from becoming more androgynous, adolescents living in single-parent families are characterized by greater maturity, feelings of efficacy, and an internal locus of control (Guidubaldi and Perry, 1985; Kalter, Alpern, Spence, and Plunkett, 1984; Wallerstein and Kelly, 1974; Weiss, 1979). For adolescent girls this maturity stems partly from the status and responsibilities they acquire in peer and confidant relationships with custodial mothers. . . .

There is evidence (Kurdek et al., 1981) that children and adolescents with an internal locus of control and a high level of interpersonal reasoning adjust more easily to their parents' divorce and that children's divorce adjustment is related to their more global personal adjustment.

Self-Concept . . .

Marital discord. . . . [F]amily structure is unrelated to children's self-esteem (Feldman and Feldman, 1975; Kinard and Reinherz, 1984; Parish, 1981; Parish, Dostal, and Parish, 1981), but parental discord is negatively related (Amato, 1986; Berg and Kelly, 1979; Cooper, Holman, and Braithwaite, 1983; Long, 1986; Raschke and Raschke, 1979; Slater and Haber, 1984). Because this conclusion is based on diverse samples of boys and girls of different ages in different living arrangements, the failure to obtain effects of family structure suggests either that family composition really does not matter for children's self-concept or that family structure alone is an insufficient index of familial relations. Further, these studies suggest that divorce per se does not adversely affect children's self-concept. Cashion's (1984) review of the literature indicates that children living in single-parent families suffer no losses to self-esteem, except in situations where the child's family situation is stigmatized (Rosenberg, 1979). . . .

Cognitive Functioning

. . . Many . . . studies find that family conflict and disruption are associated with inhibited cognitive functioning (Blanchard and Biller, 1971; Feldman and Feldman, 1975; Hess and Camara, 1979; Kinard and Reinherz, 1986; Kurdek, 1981; Radin, 1981). . . . In this section we summarize the differential effects of family disruption on academic performance by gender and social class and offer some insights as to the mechanisms by which these effects occur.

Children's gender. Some studies suggest that negative effects of family disruption on academic performance are stronger for boys than for girls (Chapman, 1977; Werner and Smith, 1982), but most of the evidence suggests similar effects by gender (Hess and Camara, 1979; Kinard and Reinherz, 1986; Shinn, 1978). While females traditionally outscore males on standardized tests of verbal skills and males outperform females on mathematical skills, males who have experienced family disruption generally score higher on verbal aptitude (Radin, 1981). Thus, the absence of a father may result in a "feminine" orientation toward education (Fowler and Richards, 1978; Herzog and Sudia, 1973). But an important and unresolved question is whether this pattern results from boys acquiring greater verbal skills in mother-headed families or from deficiencies in mathematical skills attributable to father absence. The latter explanation is supported by evidence showing that father-absent girls are disadvantaged in mathematics (Radin, 1981).

Children's race. . . . [M]ost studies show academic achievement among black children to be unaffected by family structure (Hunt and Hunt, 1975, 1977; Shinn, 1978; Solomon, Hirsch, Scheinfeld, and Jackson, 1972). Svanum, Bringle, and McLaughlin (1982) found, controlling for social class, that there are no significant effects of father absence on cognitive performance for white or black children. Again, these investigations focus on family composition and demonstrate that the effects of family structure on academic performance do not vary as much by race as by social class, but race differences in the impact of divorce remain largely unexplored. . . .

Family socioeconomic status. . . . When social class is controlled, children in female-headed families fare no worse than children from two-parent families on measures of intelligence (Bachman, 1970; Kopf, 1970), academic achievement (Shinn, 1978; Svanum et al., 1982), and educational attainment (Bachman, O'Malley, and Johnston, 1978). . . . In order to disentangle the intricate effects of family structure and SES [socioeconomic status] on children's cognitive performance, family researchers need to examine the socioeconomic history of intact families and those in which disruption occurs, to examine the economic resources available to children at various stages of cognitive development, and to assess changes in economic resources and family relationships that accompany marital disruption.

Family processes. . . . First, family disruption alters daily routines and work schedules and imposes additional demands on adults and children living in single-parent families (Amato, 1987; Furstenberg and Nord, 1985; Hetherington et al., 1983; Weiss, 1979). Most adolescents must assume extra domestic and child care responsibilities, and financial conditions require some to work part-time. These burdens result in greater absenteeism, tardiness, and truancy among children in single-parent households (Hetherington et al., 1983). Second, children in recently disrupted families are prone to experience emotional and behavioral problems such as aggression, distractibility, dependency, anxiety, and withdrawal (Hess and Camara, 1979; Kinard and Reinherz, 1984), factors that may help to explain problems in school conduct and the propensity of teachers to label and stereotype children from broken families (Hess and Camara, 1979; Hetherington et al., 1979, 1983). Third, emotional problems may interfere with study patterns, while demanding schedules reduce the time available for single parents to help with homework. . . .

Interpersonal Relationships . . .

Peer relations. Studies of preschool children (Hetherington et al., 1979) and preadolescents (Santrock, 1975; Wyman, Cowen, Hightower, and Pedro-Carroll, 1985) suggest that children in disrupted families are less sociable: they have fewer close friends, spend less time with friends, and participate in fewer shared activities. Stolberg and Anker (1983) observe that children in families disrupted by divorce exhibit psychopathology in interpersonal relations, often behaving in unusual and inappropriate ways. Other studies suggest that the effects are temporary. Kinard and Reinherz (1984) found no differences in peer relations among children in intact and disrupted families, but those in recently disrupted families displayed greater hostility. Kurdek et al. (1981) conducted a two-year follow-up of children whose parents had divorced and showed that relationships with peers improved after the divorce and that personal adjustment was facilitated by opportunities to discuss experiences with peers, some of whom had similar experiences. . . .

Dating patterns. Hetherington (1972) reported that adolescent girls whose fathers were absent prior to age 5 had difficulties in heterosexual relations, but Hainline and Feig's (1978) analyses of female college students indicated that early and later father-absent women could not be distinguished on measures of romanticism and heterosexual attitudes.

An examination of dating and sexual behavior among female college students found that women with divorced parents began dating slightly later than those in intact families, but women in both groups were socially active (Kalter, Riemer, Brickman, and Chen, 1985). Booth, Brinkerhoff, and White (1984) reported that, compared to college students with intact families, those whose parents were divorced or permanently separated exhibited higher levels of dating activity, and this activity increased further if parental or parent-child conflict persisted during and after the divorce. . . . Regarding adolescent sexual behavior, the findings consistently demonstrate that males and females not living with both biological parents initiate coitus earlier than their counterparts in intact families (Hogan and Kitagawa, 1985; Newcomer and Udry, 1987). But Newcomer and Udry propose that, because parental marital status is also associated with a broad range of deviant behaviors, these effects may stem from general loss of parental control rather than simply loss of control over sexual behavior. Studies of antisocial behavior support this interpretation.

Antisocial Behavior

Many studies over the years have linked juvenile delinquency, deviancy, and antisocial behavior to children living in broken homes (Bandura and Walters, 1959; Glueck and Glueck, 1962; Hoffman, 1971; McCord, McCord, and Thurber, 1962; Santrock, 1975; Stolberg and Anker, 1983; Tooley, 1976; Tuckman and Regan, 1966). Unfortunately, these studies either relied on clinical samples or failed to control for social class and other factors related to delinquency. However, . . . a number of studies involving large representative samples and controlling for social class provide similar findings (Dornbusch, Carlsmith, Bushwall, Ritter, Leiderman, Hastorf, and Gross, 1985; Kalter et al., 1985; Peterson and Zill, 1986; Rickel and Langner, 1985). Kalter et al. (1985) studied 522 teenage girls and found that girls in divorced families committed more delinquent acts (e.g., drug use, larceny, skipping school) than their counterparts

in intact families. Dornbusch et al. (1985) examined a representative national sample of male and female youth aged 12–17 and found that adolescents in mother-only households were more likely than their counterparts in intact families to engage in deviant acts, partly because of their tendency to make decisions independent of parental input. The presence of an additional adult (a grandparent, an uncle, a lover, a friend) in mother-only households increased control over adolescent behavior and lowered rates of deviant behavior, which suggests that "there are functional equivalents of two-parent families—nontraditional groupings that can do the job of parenting" (1985: 340). . . .

A tentative conclusion based on the evidence reviewed here is that antisocial behavior is less likely to occur in families where two adults are present, whether as biological parents, stepparents, or some combination of biological parents and other adults. Short-term increases in antisocial behavior may occur during periods of disruption, however, as children adjust to restructured relationships and parents struggle to maintain consistency in disciplining (Rickel and Langner, 1985). . . . Peterson and Zill (1986) demonstrated that, when social class was controlled, behavior problems were as likely to occur among adolescents living in intact families characterized by persistent conflict as among those living in disrupted families. . . . Peterson and Zill found that "poor parent-child relationships lead to more negative child behavior, yet maintaining good relationships with parents can go some way in reducing the effects of conflict and disruption" (1986: 306). Hess and Camara's (1979) analyses of a much smaller sample yielded a similar conclusion: aggressive behavior in children was unrelated to family type but was more common in situations characterized by infrequent or low-quality parent-child interaction and parental discord. . . .

CONCLUSIONS

There is reason to question the validity of the family composition hypothesis. Theoretically, it has been assumed that the nuclear family is the norm and, by implication, that any departure from it is deviant and therefore deleterious to those involved. Even if this were the case, no theoretical perspective recognizes that these effects may be short-lived or otherwise mitigated by compensatory mechanisms and alternative role models. In the absence of a parent, it is possible that developmental needs are met by other actors.

It is simplistic and inaccurate to think of divorce as having uniform consequences for children. The consequences of divorce vary along different dimensions of well-being, characteristics of children (e.g., pre-divorce adjustment, age at the time of disruption) and characteristics of families (e.g., socioeconomic history, pre- and post-divorce level of conflict, parent-child relationships, and maternal employment). Most of the evidence reviewed here suggests that some sociodemographic characteristics of children, such as race and gender, are not as important as characteristics of families in mediating the effects of divorce. Many studies report boys to be at a greater disadvantage, but these differences usually disappear when other relevant variables are controlled. At present, there are too few methodologically adequate studies comparing white and black children to conclude that one group is more damaged by family disruption than the other.

Characteristics of families, on the other hand, are critical to youthful well-being. Family conflict contributes to many problems in social development, emotional stability, and cognitive skills (Edwards, 1987; Kurdek, 1981), and these effects continue long after the divorce is finalized. Slater and Haber (1984) report that ongoing high levels of conflict, whether in intact or divorced homes, produce lower self-esteem, increased anxiety, and a loss of self-control. Conflict also reduces the child's attraction to the parents (White, Brinkerhoff, and Booth, 1985). Rosen (1979) concludes that parental separation is more beneficial for children than continued conflict. . . . Such conflict and hostility may account for adolescent adjustment problems whether the family in question goes through divorce or remains intact (Hoffman, 1971). The level of conflict is thus an important dimension of family interaction that can precipitate changes in family structure and affect children's well-being.

Maternal employment is another variable mediating the consequences of divorce for children. Divorced women often find the dual responsibilities of provider and parent to be stressful (Bronfenbrenner, 1976). But studies indicate that women who work prior to the divorce do not find continued employment problematic (Kinard and Reinherz, 1984); the problem occurs for women who enter the labor force after the divorce and who view the loss of time with their children as another detriment to the children that is caused by the divorce (Kinard and Reinherz, 1984). As a practical matter, the alternative to employment for single-parent mothers is likely to be poverty or, at best, economic dependency. The effects of maternal employment on children's well-being need to be compared to the effects of nonemployment and consequent poverty.

Other bases of social support for single-parent mothers and their children must also be examined. The presence of strong social networks may ease the parents' and, presumably, the child's adjustment after a divorce (Milardo, 1987; Savage et al., 1978). However, women who are poor, have many children, and must work long hours are likely to have limited social networks and few friends. Typically, the single mother and her children are also isolated from her ex-husband's family (An-

spach, 1976). By reuniting with her family of origin, the mother may be isolated from her community and new social experiences for herself and her children (McLanahan, Wedemeyer, and Adelberg, 1981). Kinship ties are usually strained, as both biological parents and parents-in-law are more critical of the divorce than friends are (Spanier and Thompson, 1984). Little has been done to relate these considerations about kinship relations and social networks of divorced women to the well-being of children and adolescents. We believe that these social relations are important, but empirical verification is needed.

CHALLENGE QUESTIONS

Are Children of Divorced Parents at Greater Risk?

1. How should parents help their children adjust to divorce? What types of educational and treatment programs should be established to support children of divorce?

2. Which do you feel is more damaging to children, divorce or continuing to live in a conflictual environment? Give reasons (and possibly research) to support your stance.

3. What do you feel is the most significant factor affecting children's adjustment following divorce? Why? How would this affect treatment strategies for children?

4. Demo and Acock list several positive outcomes of divorce. Why do you think these occur, and can you think of other possible positive outcomes?

ISSUE 13

Should Adolescents Be Allowed to Make Decisions About Abortion Without Parental Involvement?

YES: APA Interdivisional Committee on Adolescent Abortion, from "Adolescent Abortion: Psychological and Legal Issues," *American Psychologist* (January 1987)

NO: Everett L. Worthington, Jr., David B. Larson, Malvin W. Brubaker, Cheryl Colecchi, James T. Berry, and David Morrow, from "The Benefits of Legislation Requiring Parental Involvement Prior to Adolescent Abortion," *American Psychologist* (December 1989)

ISSUE SUMMARY

YES: A committee of psychologists affiliated with the American Psychological Association (APA) argues that empirical research shows that adolescents are competent enough to make their own decisions concerning abortion.
NO: Psychologist Everett L. Worthington, Jr., et al. summarize research that they feel evidences the benefits of adolescents involving the family in decisions such as abortion.

The issue of abortion is one of the most emotional issues of our time. Unfortunately, important aspects of the issue sometimes get lost in this emotionality. One such aspect concerns the psychological costs of pregnancy and abortion. Along with the medical and moral problems associated with abortion, women must also undergo psychological stresses. What anxieties does a pregnant woman endure when she is attempting to decide whether or not she should abort her baby? Do women who abort their babies experience greater psychological and emotional problems than those who carry their babies to term?

These questions take on added importance when we consider the over 1 million *adolescents* who sustain unwanted pregnancies yearly. About 40 percent terminate their pregnancies through induced abortions. Does the young age and inexperience of these women make them more vulnerable to the stresses of this situation? Are these adolescents less able than adults to make sound decisions about abortion?

If the answer is "yes" to these questions, many people would argue that the adolescent's parents should be involved in the decision to abort. One problem is that many adolescents do not want the involvement of their parents, because they fear that their parents will force their will upon them, or that their own stress will increase with parental involvement. Should these adolescents be allowed to make their own decisions regarding their own abortions?

The members of the APA committee note that the laws (in some states) that require parental involvement assume that adolescents are less likely than adults to make sound decisions. They contend, however, that the best available evidence either does not support or contradicts this assumption. Moreover, there is no evidence to indicate that adolescents are more vulnerable than adults to psychological harm as a result of abortion.

Everett L. Worthington, Jr., et al. feel that the committee members' focus upon individual liberty led them to overlook relevant research. Some of this research points to the many differences between adolescents and adults in regard to decision-making, as well as the importance of multiple perspectives in making sound judgments. This research actually argues *for* parental involvement. Even if this involvement is forced, it is better to have the family included than to have the adolescent bear the stresses of abortion in relative isolation.

POINT	COUNTERPOINT
• Adolescents are as able as adults to reason and make decisions about abortion.	• Adolescents and adults differ greatly in their abilities and experiences in making sound decisions.
• It is the ethical responsibility of psychologists to preserve the privacy of their clients.	• It is the ethical responsibility of psychologists to include responsible adults in important decisions regarding their children.
• Adolescents may know that parental involvement will actually heighten the stresses entailed in making such decisions.	• Research suggests that adolescents underestimate the support they will receive from their parents.
• Because of confidentiality and privacy, adolescents should have the right to make their own decisions.	• Psychological research and theory show that the soundest judgments are made when multiple perspectives are sought.
• Involving parents may result in parent-adolescent alienation, thus making the situation worse.	• Parent-adolescent alienation is usually greater when the parents have not been involved.

YES

APA Interdivisional Committee on
Adolescent Abortion

ADOLESCENT ABORTION:
PSYCHOLOGICAL AND LEGAL ISSUES

ABSTRACT: Findings from empirical research differ greatly from the Supreme Court's assumptions about psychosocial factors in adolescent abortion. Psychological research does not support age-graded policies about abortion. Psychologists should be careful to preserve adolescent clients' privacy in counseling about pregnancy-related decisions. Government should encourage counseling services for pregnant adolescents and research on psychological aspects of their decisions.

Few issues in our society are as emotion laden as the question of the circumstances under which abortion should be legally available. The issue is especially charged in regard to adolescents, because it raises the profound dilemmas of the proper ordering of the interests of the adolescent, her family, and the state. The question is no less basic than whether adolescents are to be considered true persons entitled to respect for privacy in personal decisions.

Beyond the general public interest in issues related to adolescent abortion, psychologists have special interest in the problem for several reasons. First, although the Supreme Court has recognized the application of the right to privacy for minors in abortion decisions, the Court has also made clear that states may regulate minors' access to abortions in ways that would be unconstitutional if applied to adult women (see Melton & Pliner, 1986, for a review). It has based the latter conclusion on assumptions that minors are especially vulnerable to deleterious psychological effects of abortions and that pregnant minors are substantially less able than adult pregnant women to make a reasonable decision about whether to terminate a pregnancy. Psychologists can assist courts and legislatures in evaluating the validity of these and related assumptions so as to determine whether there is any compelling basis for age-based regulation of women's access to abortion. Similarly, psychologists can evaluate legal procedures to ensure that they

From APA Interdivisional Committee on Adolescent Abortion, "Adolescent Abortion: Psychological and Legal Issues," American Psychologist, vol. 42, no. 1 (January 1987). Copyright © 1987 by the American Psychological Association. Reprinted by permission.

enhance support for pregnant adolescents and that they do not themselves add undue stress or create other unintended negative effects.

Second, as clinicians or counselors in schools, mental health centers, and health care settings, psychologists are often involved in assisting adolescent clients or other health professionals in decisions about abortion. Few situations raise as many complex ethical and legal issues for psychologists (see Scott, 1986, for a review). Analogously, there are special ethical and legal problems for psychologists who seek to provide the scientific basis for practice through study of pregnant adolescents' decisions or the effects of their decisions.

Third, and most generally, as scientists and professionals committed to the promotion of human welfare (American Psychological Association [APA], 1981, Preamble), psychologists are dedicated to ensuring that adolescents and families faced with difficult decisions have access to services that will assist them in understanding the alternatives and dealing with their consequences. Psychologists are ethically bound to respect individual privacy and to protect the civil rights of their clients (APA, 1981, Principle 3c).

WHAT DO WE KNOW?

In both absolute and relative terms, abortion is common among adolescents (see Russo, 1986, for a review). About 40% of the 1.1 million pregnancies in females under age 20 annually are terminated by induced abortions. Nearly one third of all abortions are performed on females under age 20. Among younger adolescents (under age 15), almost half of the abortions occur among minority youth. Thus, beyond the moral and social issues involved in abortion generally, the sheer frequency of adolescent abortion, especially among disadvantaged groups, marks it as a social phenomenon worthy of careful policy analysis.

Quality of Decision Making

The Supreme Court has assumed that adolescents are less likely than adults to make sound decisions when they are faced with an unintended pregnancy. There are few studies directly focused on abortion decision making by adolescents. However, the available evidence on health care decision making generally suggests that adolescents are as able to conceptualize and reason about treatment alternatives as adults are (see, for reviews, Grisso & Vierling, 1978; Melton, 1981; Melton, 1984, pp. 463-466; Melton, Koocher, & Saks, 1983; Weithorn, 1982; see also Weithorn & Campbell, 1982). The developmental differences that occur in decisions about abortion appear to be related largely to differences in adolescents' and adults' social situations, not their psychological maturity. Thus, adolescents are more likely to perceive their decision as externally determined (Lewis, 1980), and parents frequently *are* involved in helping to make the decision (Clary, 1982; Rosen, 1980). Adolescents are also more likely to delay their decision (Bracken & Kasl, 1975; Russo, 1986), probably because of a variety of social factors: fear of familial consequences; lack of experience in contacting professionals; lack of money to pay professional fees; concern about confidentiality.

Several states have enacted statutory requirements for notification of parents before a minor obtains an abortion, and the Supreme Court has upheld the constitutionality of such requirements, at least when applied to immature, unemancipated minors. Parental notice requirements would serve a compelling state interest, however, only if they resulted in a more reasoned decision by the minor. Although the effects of the notice statutes have yet to be evaluated directly, there is reason to believe that they will frequently not have such a positive effect. First, studies of family planning clinics have shown that confidentiality is an important factor for adolescents considering whether to use their services (Torres, Forrest, & Eisman, 1980; Zabin & Clark, 1983). Lack of confidentiality may increase the tendency already observed among pregnant teenagers, particularly younger teenagers, to delay in seeking professional help. Second, there is considerable evidence that parent-daughter communication about sexuality often leaves much to be desired (Fox & Inazu, 1980; Furstenberg, 1971; Rothenberg, 1980). There is little reason to believe that the quality of communication would be greatly improved with a daughter's announcement that she believes that she may be pregnant, even when the law requires parental consultation. Third, although parental involvement is often desirable—perhaps more frequently than adolescents estimate (cf. Furstenberg, 1976)—it is also clear that there are circumstances in which parental consultation is likely to result in neither more reasoned decision making nor diminished risk of psychological harm. That is, when parents support their daughter's decision—whether to abort or to carry to term—and permit their daughter to make her own decision with their assistance, the probability of a positive outcome is increased (Adler & Dolcini, 1986). However, when these conditions are absent, parental involvement may exacerbate stress.

Psychological Effects

The Supreme Court has assumed that adolescents are especially vulnerable to serious psychological harm as a result of having an abortion and that these risks are substantially greater than the psychological risks that arise in the decisions required when a minor carries a fetus to full term. There is no research evidence to support these assumptions (see Adler & Dolcini, 1986, for a review). Although adolescents' reactions to abortions may be somewhat more negative on the average than adults', the magnitude of the age differences is small (see, e.g., Bracken, Hachamovitch, & Grossman, 1974). Moreover, when negative reactions occur, they are almost always mild and transitory. Indeed, the most common reaction to abortion among both minors and adults is one of relief (Olson, 1980; Osofsky, Osofsky, & Rajan, 1973). The slightly more negative average response of adolescents is probably related largely to their tendency to delay; the medical procedures involved in abortion late in gestation tend to be more stressful. If increased governmental regulation of adolescent abortion in fact results in even greater delay, legal procedures ostensibly designed to protect pregnant adolescents may in fact increase the probability of undue distress.

It is noteworthy that the medical morbidity and mortality rates arising from full-term adolescent pregnancy are much greater than those arising from adolescent abortion, especially in the first trimester (Cates, 1981). Although the data on psychological effects of adoption are limited, the available research indicates that the psychological risks entailed in adolescents' completion of their pregnancies—whether they keep their babies or relinquish them for adoption—are substantially greater than the psychological risks of adolescent abortion (Adler & Dolcini, 1986).

Social Effects

That abortion is typically a relatively benign alternative for pregnant adolescents is unsurprising when one considers the social consequences of becoming a teenage parent (see, for reviews, Marecek, 1986; Scott, 1984). Adolescent mothers frequently find their education interrupted, their occupational aspirations stunted, their income diminished, and their marriage (when it occurs), strained. There is often financial and emotional strain for the mother's family of origin, and adolescent fathers often also experience emotional strain and disruptions of education and occupation. Moreover, the children of adolescent mothers are at risk for developmental problems, and they may be more likely to have problems of psychosocial adjustment. In cross-national research, particularly deleterious developmental effects have been observed in children resulting from pregnancies in which an abortion was sought and denied (David & Matejcek, 1981). However, care must be taken in generalizing from these studies involving European populations to the American experience.

WHAT SHOULD PSYCHOLOGISTS DO?

As the preceding review of the state of knowledge about adolescent abortion indicates, legal policy has often been grounded on assumptions that do not withstand empirical scrutiny or for which no empirical evidence exists. Whatever the wisdom of existing law, however, psychologists must, of course, assist their adolescent clients within that legal context. This context is often ambiguous and complex and the underlying moral issues are themselves difficult. Counseling adolescents about abortion decisions (or conducting related research) thus requires extraordinary attention to ethical concerns (see Scott, 1986, for a review).

Respect for personal autonomy and privacy demands support for freedom of choice in decisions of great personal significance, such as abortion. This general principle is consonant not only with psychologists' Ethical Principles (APA, 1981); it is also consistent with existing legal doctrine, which has been based on concern about the limits of adolescents' rational decision making. Within such an ethical and legal framework, psychologists who counsel adolescents about abortion decisions have the following two principal tasks: (a) to assist adolescents in weighing the alternatives (e.g., abortion; completing the pregnancy and relinquishing the baby for adoption; completing the pregnancy and keeping the baby), and (b) to provide emotional support for adolescents so that they can make sound personal decision under relatively unstressful conditions and that they will not suffer untoward psychological sequelae of the decision itself.

In order to assist adolescents in decision making psychologists must, of course, be willing to explore the alternatives. Psychologists whose moral scruples prevent such open discussion should so inform their clients and provide referrals to other counselors, as needed. In order to be of assistance, psychologists must know the alternatives; accordingly, they should be able to explain the legal procedures in their jurisdiction for minors' obtaining abortions with or without parental consent and for placing a child for adoption.

In some jurisdictions, psychologists may be unable to guarantee confidentiality to minors who seek counseling about abortion. These constraints should be made clear to clients when they initiate counseling. When legal strictures are unclear (e.g., whether counseling by school psychologists is confidential; whether state-imposed parental notice requirements may be applied to mature minors and, if not, how "maturity" is to be assessed), legal advice should be sought (e.g., an attorney general's opinion). Psychologists should advocate laws that will safeguard their clients' privacy.

In jurisdictions in which judicial permission is required for an adolescent to receive an abortion without parental consent, psychologists may be asked to determine whether the client is "mature" and whether an abortion would be in her best interest. These are legal and moral determinations about which psychologists and other health professionals have no special expertise (cf. Bonnie & Slobogin, 1980; Morse, 1978). Thus, although psychologists may be able to provide information that will be helpful to the court in making its decision, they should resist offering ultimate-issue opinions (i.e., opinions about whether the legal standards for "maturity" and "best interest" have been met).

There are still sizable gaps in what is known about alternatives for policy on adolescent abortion. For example, there have been few evaluations of the effects of the various limitations that states have imposed on minors' access to abortion (but see Cartoof & Klerman, 1986; Donovan, 1983; Mnookin, 1985; Pliner & Yates, 1986). The literature on the psychology of pregnant adolescents' decisions is also still quite limited. Psychologists can and should conduct the research needed to answer these questions, because they are crucial both to policy formulation and the development of counseling techniques. However, it must be acknowledged that there are special ethical and practical problems in conducting such research. Can a minor who is able to consent to an abortion independently also consent to research about abortion? Federal regulations permit minors to consent to research independently and privately in such a circumstance, but state laws may provide no specific imprimatur for an exception to the usual rule that minors are per se incompetent to consent to research. In view both of the private nature of the decision involved and the societal interest in increasing knowledge about adolescent abortion, states clearly should permit minors to consent independently to research about abortion if they are able to demonstrate an understanding of the risks and benefits of the research. However, in view of the emotional loading of the topic and the usual legal presumption that adolescents are incompetent to consent, psychologists conducting research on adolescent abortion should pay special attention to the ethical issues in their research. In addition to the usual review by institutional review boards, researchers might consider establishment of an independent advisory group to safeguard the welfare of participants.

WHAT SHOULD POLICYMAKERS DO?

Although the policy chosen is likely to have significant psychological consequences, the questions of whether family privacy is superior to individual privacy and when abortion is to be permitted are issues of morality and law, and are not subject to empirical psychological study. However, insofar as the legal calculus is based on psychological assumptions, policymakers should stimulate and attend to relevant psychological research. In that regard, there is little evidence to support age-graded policies about abortion; research supports neither the contention that adolescents are especially unlikely to make reasoned decisions about abortion nor the assumption that adolescents are vulnerable to serious psychological harm as a result of abortion.

Consideration should be given to abolishing mature minor standards in determination of whether minors are able to obtain an abortion without parental notification or consent. It is hard to imagine a minor too immature to make the decision but mature enough to rear a child. In any case, no research has been conducted to determine whether "maturity" can be reliably and validly assessed. In the absence of clear legal standards, it is very probable that such assessments are often erroneous. In view of the time consumed in performing such assessments and their questionable validity, it is unclear whether a mature minor standard can be effectively implemented even if it makes sense in the abstract.

Finally, government should encourage the development of counseling services for pregnant adolescents and their families. As the Supreme Court has recognized, these services should be provided by professionals with special training in counseling. Competent counseling is likely to enhance the quality of adolescents' decision making and to minimize emotional strain. Support for research is also essential if counselors are to be able to respond optimally to pregnant adolescents' needs for information and emo-

tional support. The policy of the current Administration to provide few, if any grants, for abortion-related research and counseling services is apt ironically to hamper efforts to facilitate careful and relatively unstressful decisions by pregnant adolescents.

REFERENCES

Adler, N. E., & Dolcini, P. (1986). Psychological issues in abortion for adolescents. In G. B. Melton (Ed.), *Adolescent abortion: Psychological and legal issues* (pp. 74–95). Lincoln: University of Nebraska Press.

American Psychological Association. (1981). Ethical principles of psychologists. *American Psychologist, 36,* 633–638.

Bonnie, R. J., & Slobogin, C. (1980). The role of mental health professionals in the criminal process: The case for informed speculation. *Virginia Law Review, 66,* 427–522.

Bracken, M., Hachamovitch, M., & Grossman, A. (1974). The decision to abort and psychological sequelae. *Journal of Nervous and Mental Disorders, 15,* 155–161.

Bracken, M. & Kasl, S. (1975). Delay in seeking induced abortion: A review and theoretical analysis. *American Journal of Obstetrics and Gynecology, 121,* 1008–1019.

Cartoof, V. G., & Klerman, L. V. (1986). Parental consent for abortion: Impact of the Massachusetts law. *American Journal of Public Health, 76,* 397–400.

Cates, W., Jr. (1981). Abortions for teenagers. In J. E. Hodgson (Ed.), *Abortion and sterilization: Medical and social aspects* (pp. 139–154). London: Academic Press.

Clary, F. (1982). Minor women obtaining abortions: A study of parental notification in a metropolitan area. *American Journal of Public Health, 72,* 283–285.

David, H. P., & Matejcek, Z. (1981). Children born to women denied abortion: An update. *Family Planning Perspectives, 13,* 32–34.

Donovan, P. (1983). Judging teenagers: How minors fare when they seek court-authorized abortions. *Family Planning Perspectives, 15,* 259–267.

Fox, G. L., & Inazu, J. J. (1980). Mother-daughter communication about sex. *Family Relations, 29,* 347–352.

Furstenberg, F. F., Jr. (1971). Birth control experience among pregnant adolescents: The process of unplanned parenthood. *Social Problems, 19,* 192–203.

Furstenberg, F. F., Jr. (1976). The social consequences of teenage parenthood. *Family Planning Perspectives, 8,* 148–164.

Grisso, T., & Vierling, L. (1978). Minors' consent to treatment: A developmental perspective. *Professional Psychology, 9,* 412–427.

Lewis, C. (1980). A comparison of minors' and adults' pregnancy decisions. *American Journal of Orthopsychiatry, 50,* 446–453.

Marecek, J. (1986). Consequences of adolescent childbearing and abortion. In G. B. Melton (Ed.), *Adolescent abortion: Psychological and legal issues* (pp. 96–115). Lincoln: University of Nebraska Press.

Melton, G. B. (1981). Children's participation in treatment planning: Psychological and legal issues. *Professional Psychology, 12,* 647–654.

Melton, G. B. (1984). Developmental psychology and the law: The state of the art. *Journal of Family Law, 22,* 445–482.

Melton, G. B. (Ed.). (1986). *Adolescent abortion: Psychological and legal issues.* Lincoln: University of Nebraska Press.

Melton, G. B., Koocher, G. P., & Saks, M. J. (Eds.). (1983). *Children's competence to consent.* New York: Plenum.

Melton, G. B., & Pliner, A. J. (1986). Adolescent abortion: A psycholegal analysis. In G. B. Melton (Ed.), *Adolescent abortion: Psychological and legal issues* (pp. 1–39). Lincoln: University of Nebraska Press.

Mnookin, R. H. (1985). *Bellotti v. Baird:* A hard case. In R. H. Mnookin (Ed.), *In the interest of children: Advocacy, law, reform, and public policy* (pp. 149–264). New York: W. H. Freeman.

Morse, S. J. (1978). Crazy behavior, morals and science: An analysis of mental health law. *Southern California Law Review, 51,* 527–654.

Olson, L. (1980). Social and psychological correlates of pregnancy resolution among adolescent women: A review. *American Journal of Orthopsychiatry, 42,* 48–60.

Osofsky, J. D., Osofsky, H. J., & Rajan, R. (1973). Psychological effects of abortion: With emphasis upon immediate reactions and followup. In H. J. Osofsky & J. D. Osofsky (Eds.), *The abortion experience: Psychological and medical impact* (pp. 188–205). Hagerstown, MD: Harper & Row.

Pliner, A. J., & Yates, S. M. (1986, August). *The Massachusetts judicial consent hearing: A rubberstamp proceeding?* Paper presented at the meeting of the American Psychological Association, Washington, DC.

Rosen, R. H. (1980). Adolescent pregnancy decision-making: Are parents important? *Adolescence, 15,* 43–54.

Rothenberg, P. B. (1980). Communication about sex and birth control between mothers and their adolescent children. *Population and Environment, 3,* 35–50.

Russo, N. F. (1986). Adolescent abortion: The epidemiological context. In G. B. Melton (Ed.), *Adolescent abortion: Psychological and legal issues* (pp. 40–73). Lincoln: University of Nebraska Press.

Scott, E. S. (1984). Adolescents' reproductive rights: Abortion, contraception, and sterilization. In N. D. Reppucci, L. A. Weithorn, E. P. Mulvey, & J. Monahan (Eds.), *Children, mental health, and the law* (pp. 125–150). Beverly Hills, CA: Sage.

Scott, E. S. (1986). Legal and ethical issues in counseling pregnant adolescents. In G. B. Melton (Ed.), *Adolescent abortion: Psychological and legal issues* (pp. 116–137). Lincoln: University of Nebraska Press.

Torres, A., Forrest, J. D., & Eisman, S. (1980). Telling parents: Clinic policies and adolescents' use of family planning and abortion services. *Family Planning Perspectives, 12,* 284–292.

Weithorn, L. A. (1982). Developmental factors and competence to make informed treatment decisions. In G. B. Melton (Ed.), *Legal reforms affecting child and youth services* (pp. 85–100). New York: Haworth.

Weithorn, L. A., & Campbell, S. B. (1982). The competency of children and adolescents to make informed treatment decisions. *Child Development, 53,* 1589–1599.

Zabin, L. S., & Clark, S. D., Jr. (1983). Institutional factors affecting teenagers' choice and reasons for delay in attending a family planning clinic. *Family Planning Perspectives, 15,* 25–29.

NO

Everett L. Worthington, Jr.,
David B. Larson, Malvin W. Brubaker,
Cheryl Colecchi, James T. Berry,
and David Morrow

THE BENEFITS OF LEGISLATION REQUIRING PARENTAL INVOLVEMENT PRIOR TO ADOLESCENT ABORTION

Since *Roe v. Wade* (1973), a majority of the states have enacted legislation calling for mandatory parental involvement in some form prior to a minor's securing an abortion. Due to procedural difficulties with the statutes, though, more than half of them have been enjoined by courts and are not currently in effect.

In this comment, we summarize evidence on adolescent pregnancy that supports the position that mandatory parental involvement legislation is beneficial for the adolescent, her family, and her family unity. We do not discuss the potential costs to the adolescents, such as restrictions on the adolescent's liberty, potential coercion by some parents, possible noncompliance with laws, delays by adolescents who seek abortion because they fear their parents' reactions, costs of travel to another state to obtain a legal abortion, or the psychological consequences to the adolescent and parents (whether the consequences are positive or negative) of impersonal legal notification of the pregnancy. The costs, but not the benefits, of mandatory parental notification have been discussed in some detail in five recent articles in the *American Psychologist* (Interdivisional Committee on Adolescent Abortion, 1987; Lewis, 1987; Marecek, 1987; Melton, 1987; Melton & Russo, 1987). For a more balanced picture of the issues, the reader should refer to both this comment and the previous articles.

The number of adolescents to whom the following discussion applies is limited. Over half of the adolescents already involve their parents in decision making about abortion (Lewis, 1987; Rosen, 1980). The pivotal question, then, is whether adolescents who ordinarily abort without or before consulting parents will be helped or harmed by requiring parental involvement.

Perhaps the fundamental disagreement undergirding the issue of mandated parental involvement in adolescent pregnancy decision making is between individual liberty and communal responsibility. Opponents of parental involvement legislation tend to focus on adolescents and their liberties. Other social units are considered less important than the adolescent's presumed rights. Although research is generally treated fairly, the underlying assumption that individual liberty is the penultimate relevant value shapes the choice of research examined and results in a limited examination of the issue—the case against parental involvement.

In the present comment, we affirm an adolescent's decision about her pregnancy but also assume that other individuals, such as parents, have a responsibility and right to contribute to those decisions. With adolescent pregnancy considered in individual and familial contexts, data besides those considered by the Interdivisional Committee become relevant for evaluation. As a consequence, we argue that most pregnant adolescents and their families benefit from mandatory parental involvement in decisions regarding abortion versus bearing to term.

BENEFITS FOR THE ADOLESCENT

Initial Assumptions
Opponents of legislation mandating parental involvement in abortion decisions by adolescent minors might argue that adolescents can predict whether their parents will or will not be supportive and then decide when to involve their parents. Research does not support this argument.

Recent research and pre-*Roe v. Wade* (1973) studies (in which adolescents did not have access to legal abortion) suggest that pregnant adolescents tend to underestimate their parents' support (Clary, 1982; Furstenberg, 1976; Marecek, 1987). Thus, adolescents often do not tell their parents they are pregnant. When parents are informed of their daughter's pregnancy, they usually become angry. After brief turmoil, from two thirds to four fifths of parents have been found to be supportive (for reviews, see Baptiste, 1986; Bolton, 1980; Rue, 1985)—if given the chance. Support by parents may include assistance with decision making and emotional support.

Adolescents Can Gain Assistance With Decision Making
Opponents of parental involvement legislation argue that adolescents are generally as competent as adults to make decisions regarding the continuation of termination of their pregnancy (see Melton, 1987). However, despite claims to the contrary by the American Psychological Association (1987) and Lewis (1987), clinical studies of actual decision making in pregnancy generally show clear differences in decision making between adolescents and adults. In fact, there is substantial evidence from both clinical and laboratory studies that adolescents differ across the adolescent years and differ from adults in the ways they actually make decisions.

1. Younger adolescents consult different people for advice than do older adolescents and adults (Ashton, 1979; Clary, 1982; Lewis, 1980; Rosen, 1980; Torres, Forrest, & Eisman, 1980).

2. Adolescents and adults differ in their abilities to view situations from the perspective of others. For example, 52 two-parent families with an adolescent between 13 and 16 took a moral decision-

making test three times—once themselves and once each as if they were the other two members in the family (Whitbeck & Mullis, 1987). Adults were better able to take the perspective of others than were adolescents.

3. Adolescents at varying ages between 15 and adulthood consider different factors in their pregnancy decisions (Hatcher, 1976) and in their consideration about their potential for child rearing (Leibowitz, Eisen, & Chow, 1984; Lewis, 1980).

4. In decision-making instances, adolescents consider future solutions and goals less often than do adults (Verstraeten, 1980).

5. Adolescents differ from adults in their consideration of future consequences in some dilemmas. For example, Eisen, Zellman, Leibowitz, Chow, and Evans (1983) concluded that many teens did not have the ability to reason abstractly or foresee future consequences in many sexual decisions (cf. Lewis, 1987).

These 6 differences in decision making across adolescence and between adolescents and adults suggest that adolescents and adults differ in the quality of their decision making. The theory of Janis and Mann (1977), a well-respected theory of decision making, suggests that effective decision-making processes are more important than decisional outcomes in determining "good" decision making. To that end, good decision making involves (a) seeking multiple perspectives, (b) understanding multiple perspectives, (c) considering potential costs and benefits about all reasonable alternatives (not just the first alternatives that are considered), (d) identifying future solutions and goals, (e) considering consequences of outcomes and (f) avoiding long delays or procrastination in making decisions. Fur-

thermore, good decision making is not prematurely foreclosed through hasty, impulsive decision making. By the criteria set forth by Janis and Mann, these 6 points of evidence support the belief that older adolescents and adults engage in "better" decision making than do younger adolescents.

Given that adult parents are better decision makers than their adolescent daughters, we believe that legislation requiring parental involvement with adolescents helps the adolescent, especially the early adolescent, make better decisions about how to resolve her pregnancy. First, notifying parents involves them in the decision making. Generally, parents have more experience making decisions under emotional strain and will presumably be more likely to consider carefully a variety of options than will the adolescent. Second, parents supply other points of view for the adolescent to consider in her decision, which will broaden the adolescent's understanding of the ramifications of her decision. Third, parents can correct misapprehensions that their daughter might have and challenge erroneous beliefs (Marecek, 1987). Fourth, the adolescent must take at least 24 hours to consider the decision to abort. This brief delay mitigates the demand-laden situation in which an adolescent finds she is pregnant while at a clinic where there is the potential to have an abortion. Cobliner (1974) suggested that pregnant adolescents are particularly vulnerable to immediate situational cues in making pregnancy resolution decisions.

Sometimes concern is expressed that the parents whom the adolescent would not have consulted without parental involvement legislation will intervene and either decide the fate of the pregnancy for the adolescent or pressure the adolescent to decide as they want her to. This happens in a small minority of instances and when it does, it can cause psychological problems regardless of what decision is made (Adler & Dolcini, 1986). However, whomever the adolescent tells about her pregnancy will communicate their opinions to the girl, who will inevitably feel pressure. In fact, the girl will feel pressure to consider her parents' views whether or not she consults them (Lewis, 1980). Even counselors, who usually try to avoid influencing the outcome of the adolescent's decision will often be perceived as exerting pressure (Marecek, 1987).

In summary, we believe that the available evidence suggests that most adolescents facing pregnancy-related decisions can be assisted by their adult parents—even when parental involvement is mandated against the initial wishes of the adolescent.

Adolescents Can Gain Support

An adolescent who is afraid to consult her parents prior to an abortion and who is empowered by legislation to the extent that she need not consult them probably will not consult them. Ultimately, she must either keep her pregnancy and abortion secret from her parents, which can cause guilt and anxiety that her parents might somehow discover the secret, or tell her parents that not only did she become pregnant but also that she made an important life decision without notifying them. We propose that the potential for parent-adolescent alienation is usually greater from not informing parents than from informing them, which harkens back to our presuppositions concerning the importance of communal responsibility.

Adolescents who seek abortion without parental involvement include those whose parents would not support them and those whose parents would support them (see Adler & Dolcini, 1986; Ashton, 1979; Torres et al., 1980).

Most adolescents who truly lack parental support will experience distress whether or not parents are informed of an impending abortion (Adler, 1981; Bolton, 1980; Melton, 1987; Rue, 1985; Shusterman, 1976). If they have an abortion without involving their parents (because there is no parental involvement law), then they are likely to have trouble coping with abortion (Adler, 1981; Adler & Dolcini, 1986). If they must (by law) notify their parents and their parents do not support them, they likely will have difficulty bearing the child to term.

On the other hand, other adolescents seek abortion without prior parental involvement but the parents would have ultimately supported the adolescent's decision to abort (Ashton, 1979; Torres et al., 1980). Without parental involvement legislation, girls who opt for abortions out of a mistaken perception of their parents' reactions deprive themselves of their parents' support during their crisis—their most powerful and permanent social support.

Failure to consider the social supportive role of families is also relevant to some of the arguments advanced by Judge Alsop in *Hodgson v. Minnesota* (1986). Judge Alsop heard testimony from judges, who claimed that the girls who petitioned for judicial bypass of parental notification (a) were generally mature, (b) were approved almost perfunctorily, and (c) were apprehensive about their court apperance. The weakness in Judge Alsop's "research design" is his failure to recognize the importance of including matched control groups. He did not interview families of girls who would have aborted without parental notification but according to this statute notified their parents and subsequently found their parents to be supportive. He also interviewed clinic counselors who testified about cases in which parental notification "disrupted and harmed families" (p. 37). Again, the clinic counselor cannot know whether the adolescent and her family would be more or less traumatized by an abortion without parental notification.

BENEFITS FOR THE ADOLESCENT'S PARENTS

Parents of pregnant adolescents will be primarily responsible for any medical or psychological expenses that result from or follow an abortion. Abortion is an operation that frequently may have both short-term and long-term sequelae (Adler, 1981; Bolton, 1980; Tishler, McKenry, & Morgan, 1981). It is contestable whether the effects of abortion or child bearing are more serious (for reviews, see Huckeba & Mueller, 1987; Rue, 1985; Shusterman, 1976). Whether abortion is chosen or not, parents who are notified at least can prepare for possible consequences of adolescents' decisions.

Because parents are held legally responsible for the health of their children, most states require that parents of unemancipated adolescent minors give written permission for medical personnel to dispense medication or administer even routine medical care. Certainly, most mental health therapists who work with adolescents vigorously seek to at least notify, and usually actively consult or involve, adolescents' parents prior to therapy. It is ironic that many states do not require that physicians inform parents prior to an adolescent's abortion. This is usually justified by the assumption that the girl has a right to make her own decision about her own body. Yet, when an adolescent has a fever or headache at school, the school nurse cannot dispense aspirin without the parent's approval. Physical and mental health decisions involve consequences to both unemancipated adolescents and their parents. Although adverse reactions might be rare, parents are nonetheless responsible for consequences to their daughter.

Parents might derive other benefits from being informed prior to their adolescent daughter's abortion, although research has not tested these potential benefits. First, informed parents can support each other as well as their daughter. Second, the communication between parents and daughter might be enhanced. (It might also be destructive.) Third, informed parents may experience a greater sense of input than uninformed parents.

BENEFITS FOR FAMILY UNITY

A number of researchers argue that out-of-wedlock pregnancy contributes to increased family estrangement unless the family is involved (for reviews, see Baptiste, 1986; Rue, 1985). For example, Baptiste (1986) listed six reasons for family involvement with adolescent pregnancies:

1. *The family's need to deal with its pervasive sense of failure precipitated by the pregnancy.*

2. *Family members' need to clarify their different views about the pregnancy and the unborn baby.*

3. *The need for the adolescent and her parents to resolve any conflict existing prior to the pregnancy, especially those resulting from the pregnancy situation.*

4. *The importance of maintaining and/or improving communication in a crisis situation for the adolescent and her family.*

5. *Parents' need to maintain their relationship while they "parent" their daughter through the crisis of pregnancy.*

6. *Parents' and adolescents' need to resolve developmental independency–dependency issues. (pp. 168–169, emphasis in the original)*

A substantial number of adolescents use sexual behavior (and often pregnancy) as a means of power in rebellion against their parents (Group for the Advancement of Psychiatry, 1986). When the adolescent uses her sexual power by becoming pregnant, she sets up or increases conflict in her family. The pregnant adolescent who then aborts without consulting her parents compounds the power struggle. The problem is further exacerbated if the pregnancy and abortion later become known as a *fait accompli*. Mandatory parental involvement legislation provides an opportunity for families to resolve their conflicts, thus possibly avoiding repeat pregnancies and abortions (Henshaw, Binkin, & Smith, 1985).

Opponents of legislation mandating parental involvement often assume that mandatory parental involvement will exacerbate already dysfunctional family dynamics. Yet, if adolescents run afoul of the legal system through juvenile delinquency or other acting out, the adolescent's family is mandatorily involved with little hesitation, usually with the assumption that the crisis will *help* a troubled family deal with its dysfunctional dynamics or at least reduce the likelihood of a recurrence.

SUMMARY

Adolescent pregnancy, whether it terminates in abortion or childbirth, is stressful for adolescents and their families. When mandatory parental involvement legislation is in effect, there will be tragic cases just as when such legislation is not operative. We believe the weight of evidence, though, favors such legislation.

CHALLENGE QUESTIONS

Should Adolescents Be Allowed to Make Decisions About Abortion Without Parental Involvement?

1. How might stages of cognitive development (such as those forwarded by Jean Piaget) enter into the issue of a young woman's ability to make sound decisions?

2. Hypothetically, you are a clinical psychologist with an adolescent as a client. In your most recent session she reveals to you that she is pregnant, does not want the baby, but is afraid to tell her parents. Describe how you would work with and advise her.

3. Worthington, Jr., et al. contend that the APA committee members made certain assumptions that "shaped" the research they decided to examine. How could these assumptions affect the research they reviewed as well as the conclusions they drew?

4. How did the assumptions of Worthington, Jr., et al. differ from the assumptions of the APA committee? How might this have affected their research reviews and final conclusions?

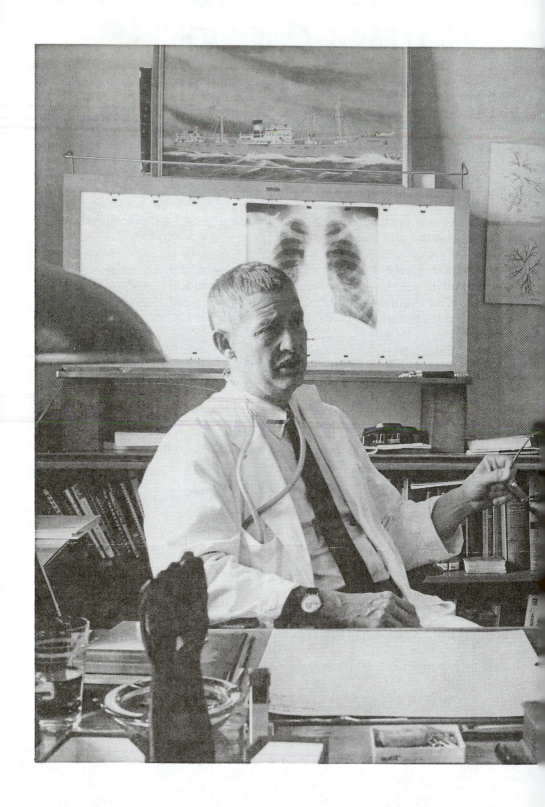

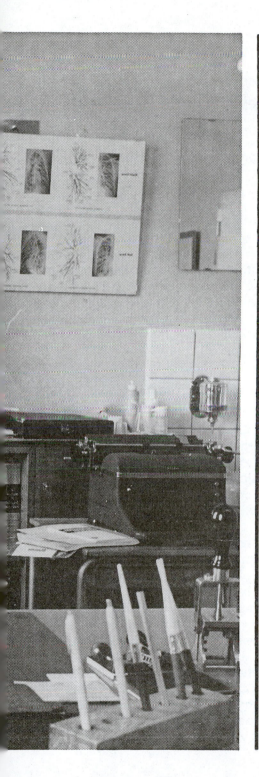

PART 5

Mental Health and Psychotherapy

What is the difference between normal mental health and disorder? In the case of suicidal persons, should psychotherapists be responsible for preventing such individuals from killing themselves? Or should suicide be considered a moral act, not necessarily that of a mentally ill person?

We usually think of diagnosis as an important prerequisite to treatment. But when we apply it to behavior we run the risk of prejudicing the way we think about that behavior. How great is that risk for competent treatment?

Religion is a large part of many people's lives, both mentally healthy and disordered. Are theistic values, however, appropriate for a clinician's use in the treatment of patients?

The use of electroconvulsive therapy in treating severely depressed persons, primarily, has been attacked as a dangerous and damaging procedure. Is this assertion correct, or is electroconvulsive therapy a safe and effective, though misunderstood, treatment?

Should Psychotherapists Allow Suicide?

Do Diagnostic Labels Hinder the Effective Treatment of Persons with Mental Disorders?

Should Psychotherapy Include Religious Values?

Is Electroconvulsive Therapy Safe?

ISSUE 14

Should Psychotherapists Allow Suicide?

YES: Thomas Szasz, from "The Case Against Suicide Prevention," *American Psychologist* (July 1986)

NO: George A. Clum, from "Abandon the Suicidal? A Reply to Szasz," *American Psychologist* (September 1987)

ISSUE SUMMARY

YES: Psychiatrist and psychoanalyst Thomas Szasz considers the patients of psychotherapists to be moral agents who are able to decide for themselves whether or not suicide is a viable option.

NO: Psychologist and suicide researcher George A. Clum views suicidal behavior as temporary and impulsive, and he argues that suicidal patients need external restraint to reduce the danger.

Suicidal behavior has been viewed throughout history as either irrational or sinful. People have long been thought to have the right to live but not the right to die. Some people, however, feel that suicide is a "victimless crime," which has no direct effect on anyone other than the person committing the act. Although others may suffer emotionally when someone they love commits suicide, the act itself does not violate their rights. From this perspective, suicide itself may be considered a human right, and any attempt to prevent suicide violates this right.

Currently, mental health practitioners are considered responsible for the people under their care who might commit suicide. Such practitioners are charged with keeping such people alive, regardless of the cost or circumstances. The problem is that preventing suicide sometimes requires restraint—even involuntary hospitalization. Some feel that involuntary hospitalization is justified when its purpose is to protect an individual from self-harm. others feel it takes away the individual's rights and responsibility for his or her own actions.

Thomas Szasz agrees with the latter. He argues that persons who are suicidal are responsible for their own behavior and that suicide prevention forces mental health practitioners into conflicting and contradictory roles. By assuming control over persons who wish to kill themselves, mental health professionals patronize their patients. They also promise them more than they can deliver. Szasz contends that it is virtually impossible to prevent the suicide of a determined person, and forcibly imposed interventions to prevent suicide deprive the patient of liberty and dignity. The use of coercion, therefore, is both impractical and immoral. Szasz, however, does not hold that we must accept suicide as a morally legitimate option. He simply asks that we refrain from empowering agents of the state to coercively prevent it.

George A. Clum, on the other hand, argues that the issue of legal responsibility is irrelevant to the question of treatment. He considers suicidal persons to be less responsible for their actions. Responsibility in general is diminished, he contends, when depression, hopelessness, and stress have limited conscious choices. Suicidal persons who seek treatment must be ambivalent about their suicidal impulses or they would have already committed suicide. Furthermore, suicidal behavior is often temporary and warrants temporary restraint. Treatment may reduce the danger of suicide, but failure to take action will not. Clum concludes that the potential for saving lives is worth the risk of coercive prevention.

POINT	COUNTERPOINT
• Rejecting suicide prevention as a professional responsibility would protect the mental health practitioner from having to take on conflicting roles.	• Serious-minded practitioners acknowledge and struggle with the conflicts surrounding suicide.
• Failure to prevent suicide is one of the leading reasons for successful malpractice suits against psychotherapists.	• Legal suits concerning suicide are few, and they are successful only after failure to take action against suicide.
• Most professionals mistakenly assume that suicidal persons are irrational and therefore not responsible for their actions.	• Certain circumstances diminish a person's responsibility, and others must then take charge.
• It is virtually impossible to prevent a determined individual from committing suicide.	• There are no data to indicate that persons bent on committing suicide *cannot* be prevented from doing so.
• Interventions that prevent suicide deprive the patient of liberty and dignity.	• The number of lives that are saved by suicide prevention is worth the risk of coercive action.

YES

Thomas Szasz

THE CASE AGAINST SUICIDE
PREVENTION

ABSTRACT: "Common sense" now tells us that suicide is a mental health problem, that mental health practitioners and institutions have a professional duty to try to prevent it, and that it is a legitimate function of the state to empower such professionals and institutions (especially psychiatrists and psychiatric institutions) to impose coercive interventions on persons "diagnosed" as posing a "suicidal risk." Hence, when an individual—formally identified as a "patient" or "client"—commits suicide while in the care of mental health clinicians or clinics, the latter may be sued for and found guilty of professional negligence for failing to prevent suicide. The author challenges this perspective and presents a different view of suicide as an act of a moral agent for which that agent himself or herself is ultimately responsible. Eschewing suicide prevention and rejecting it as a professional responsibility would not only protect the mental health clinician from being forced into internally conflicting and contradictory roles and the client of mental health services from coercion in the name of suicide prevention, but would also protect our nation from a mental health policy that needlessly undermines the ethic of self-responsibility.

Failure to prevent suicide is now one of the leading reasons for successful malpractice suits against mental health professionals and institutions. . . . Although psychiatrists and psychiatric hospitals now bear the brunt of such litigation, all mental health practitioners run the risk of being accused of professional negligence for failing to prevent a client's or patient's suicide. As I shall show, this situation is an inexorable consequence of the way suicide is now viewed by mental health professionals, lawyers, judges, and other educated persons.

SUICIDE: FROM SIN TO SICKNESS

Insofar as suicide is perceived as immoral or undesirable, it is inevitable that people will hold someone or something responsible for it. In the history

From Thomas Szasz, "The Case Against Suicide Prevention," *American Psychologist*, vol. 41, no. 7 (July 1986). Copyright © 1986 by the American Psychological Association. Reprinted by permission.

of Western civilization, the end of the Enlightenment—roughly the year 1800—marks a dramatic change in the perception of suicide. Before that time, suicide was considered to be both a sin and a crime for which the actor was responsible; since then, suicide has increasingly been regarded as a manifestation of madness for which the actor is not responsible (Fedden, 1938; Sprott, 1961). . . .

Because the history of suicide is not germane to our present concerns, suffice it here to note that the definition of suicide as self-murder originates from a specifically Judeo-Christian cosmology in which God is viewed as both "giving" and "taking" each human being's life: Hence, taking one's own life is a most grievous offense against God. The modern "scientific" view of suicide represents a secularized version of the same belief concerning the impermissibility of the act. "We are now . . . in agreement," declared Stanley Yolles in 1967, then the director of the National Institute of Mental Health, "that this [suicide] is a public health matter and that the state should combat the disease of suicide" (pp. 16–17). The idea that anyone who kills himself or herself is crazy reinforces the negative valuation of the act, exonerates the suicide from wrongdoing, and excuses the survivors from punishing the deed.

The dominant image of suicide today—as a mental abnormality or illness (or as a symptom of such a condition)—explains why mental health professionals, philosophers, and ethicists, as well as laypersons, are all so skittish about suicide that it is virtually impossible to engage in a reasoned examination of this subject. If suicide is "bad" because it injures society, then why is it not a crime (as it used to be) and punished accordingly by the state? If suicide is "bad" because it in-jures the soul or spirit of the "victim," then why is it not a sin (as it used to be) and punished accordingly by the church? (Individuals who die by suicide are no longer denied a Christian burial.) Finally, if suicide is "bad" because it injures both the suicide and others, like a disease (as people now seem to believe), then why is it not treated as such? Other potentially life-threatening diseases are treated by professionals who claim competence to treat such conditions and are formally accorded the privilege of doing so. Instead of seriously pondering such questions, people now prefer to explain away the problem of suicide by claiming to view it "scientifically," creating an image of it that combines the features not only of sin, sickness, and crime, but also irrationality, incompetence, and insanity. The result is a stubborn unwillingness to view suicide as we view other morally freighted acts—like abortion or divorce—as good or bad, desirable or undesirable, depending on the circumstances in which they occur and the criteria by which they are judged.

PROFESSIONAL LIABILITY FOR SUICIDE

If clients suffer harm that they attribute to their relationship with a professional, it does not automatically follow that the professional is guilty of negligence ("malpractice"). To successfully prosecute a suit for professional negligence, the plaintiff must show that the professional had a specific duty to perform (typically, because he or she voluntarily assumed said duty); that this duty was performed negligently or not at all; that the plaintiff suffered injuries as a result; and that the injury is directly attributable to the malperformance or nonperformance of the professional's duty (Warren, 1978, Vol. 2C, pp. 729–752).[1]

The main reason mental health professionals and mental institutions are found liable for a patient's or client's suicide is because they assume the duty (responsibility) of preventing suicide. It is important to emphasize that, in our free society, people can (as a rule) choose to seek or not seek professional help and that professionals can (as a rule) choose to assume or not assume a particular duty. For example, a Catholic gynecologist, who wishes to obey the strictures of his or her faith, is free to refuse to perform an abortion; a neurosurgeon, burdened by astronomical malpractice insurance premiums, is free to refuse to perform surgery (and to limit his or her practice to neurology); and a mental health professional is free, if he or she so chooses, to refrain from assuming the duty of trying to prevent a patient's or client's suicide. It must, of course, be clear and explicit what duties one assumes or does not assume. . . . [M]ental health professionals and institutions could not be successfully sued for failing to prevent suicide if they explicitly eschewed assuming the duty of suicide prevention as a professional service. In short, as long as mental health professionals insist on imposing their services on unwilling recipients by claiming that the clients or patients are "dangerous to themselves," they should not be surprised that when clients or patients commit suicide (or otherwise injure themselves while under professional care), the clients or their families insist on holding the mental health professionals responsible for failing to fulfill their promises, and courts find them guilty of professional negligence. The fact that suicide prevention—with or without the cooperation of patients or clients—is one of the duties and services now specifically attributed to, accepted by, and expected from mental health professionals and institutions constitutes the context for my following remarks.

If troubled individuals confide their "suicidal ideation" to a priest, the priest is not expected to intervene coercively to prevent their suicide. Neither is the lawyer who, especially if engaged in matrimonial disputes, often hears clients say such things as, "If my wife (or husband) leaves me, I will kill myself" or "If my child is taken from me, I will kill myself." Mental health professionals, however, are expected to prevent suicide: If they are psychiatrists, they have the duty to commit the "patient"; if they are psychologists, social workers, nurse practitioners, or lay therapists—who are not (or not yet) licensed, or even required, by the state to commit—then they are expected to make an appropriate referral to a physician (who may or may not be a psychiatrist) to forcibly prevent the patient's suicide. Although mental health professionals sometimes complain about the burden this duty entails, in the main they clearly enjoy the power and prestige that go along with it. After all, if psychiatrists did not want to engage in coercive suicide prevention, they could say so and could refuse to participate in such work. Similarly, if psychologists viewed coercive suicide prevention negatively, they too could say so, instead of seeking (as many do) the professional privilege and legal authority to involuntarily confine persons deemed to be dangerous to themselves.

I should like to add that, strictly speaking, I am opposed only to coercive methods of preventing, or trying to prevent, suicide. It would be hypocritical, however, to deny that in practice suicide prevention rests on the actual or potential use of force to restrain the would-be suicide: The term *prevention* itself, especially when coupled with *suicide*, implies coercion. Preventive medical measures, exemplified by vaccinating children against contagious diseases, are typically (although not necessarily) backed by the force of the law. Psychological counseling in connection with conflicts about pregnancy or marriage are thus properly called abortion and divorce *counseling*. It would be wrong—indeed, it would be absurd—to refer to such counseling as abortion or divorce prevention. . . .

Mental health professionals bear an especially heavy burden with respect to the moral and social dilemmas posed by suicide; hence, they must be especially thoughtful and forthright in coming down on one side or the other on the issue of (coercive) suicide prevention. Mental health professionals could do this together, combining their forces in a united front, or separately as differing factions, each clearly identified to the public by the professional duties they assume and decline. Psychiatrists, psychologists, social workers, family therapists, nurse practitioners, clinical sociologists—everyone who identifies himself or herself as a "therapist" or member of a "helping profession"—could thus choose to embrace coercive suicide prevention, as psychiatrists (qua physicians) typically do, or eschew such coercion, as the clergy (qua priests or ministers) typically do. Opting for either course would be defensible and moral. Tying to go both ways and claiming to serve the "best interests" of both the individual and society, despite the dilemma that suicide poses, is impossible to achieve and immoral to attempt.

ON PREVENTING SUICIDE

Why do we now give mental health professionals (especially psychiatrists) and judges special privileges and powers to intervene vis-à-vis suicidal persons? The reason is that in the modern "scientifically enlightened" view, the person who threatens to commit suicide or actually does so is considered to be irrational or mentally ill (Szasz, 1971). However, there is neither philosophical nor empirical support for viewing suicide as different, in principle, from other acts, such as getting married.

The phrase "suicide prevention" is itself a misleading slogan characteristic of our therapeutic age. Insofar as suicide is a physical possibility, there can be no suicide prevention; insofar as suicide is a fundamental right, there ought to be no such thing. If one person is to prevent another person from killing himself or herself, the former clearly cannot, and should not be expected to, accomplish that task unless he or she can exercise complete control over the suicidal person. But it is either impossible to do this, or would require reducing the so-called patient to a social state beneath that of a slave. The slave is compelled only to labor against his or her will, whereas the suicidal person would thus be compelled to live against his or her will. Such a life is not the life of a person or human being, but only that of a human organism or "living human thing."

This does not mean that individuals troubled by suicidal ideas or impulses should not be able to secure the assistance they seek, provided they can find others willing to render such assistance. It only means that expressions of so-called suicidal behavior—in any of their now-familiar psychopathological forms or shapes, such as "suicidal ideation," "suicidal impulse," "suicide attempt," and so forth—would no longer qualify as a justification for coercing the subject. Were such a policy adopted, people would have to make do with noncoercive methods of preventing suicide, just as they must now make do with noncoercive methods of preventing other forms of "self-harming" actions—such as warnings from the Surgeon General on packages of cigarettes or diet soda.

No one can deny that policies aimed at preventing suicide by means of legal and psychiatric coercion imply a paternalistic attitude toward the "client" or "patient" and require giving certain privileges and powers to a special class of "protectors" vis-à-vis a special class of "victims." Clearly, all such "solutions" to human or social problems are purchased at the cost of creating the classic problem of "Who shall guard the guardians?" The demonstrable harms generated by the mistakes and misuses of the powers of mental health professionals and judges (delegated to them on the grounds that they are "protecting" suicidal persons from themselves) must be balanced against the alleged or ostensible benefits generated by coercive policies of suicide prevention. Inasmuch as we have no generally agreed upon criteria for adjudicating controversies concerning such a trade-off, our acceptance or rejection of coercive suicide prevention is perhaps best viewed as a manifestation of our moral and political (existential, religious) beliefs in certain ideas and their practical implications—such as free will and personal responsibility on the one hand and "mental illness" and therapeutic paternalism on the other hand. . . .

ASSIGNING AND ASSUMING RESPONSIBILITY FOR SUICIDE

We are ready now to consider the question of the mental health professional's responsibility for the suicide of a client or patient. However, before examining the specific question of the mental health professional's responsibility for the so-called suicidal patient, let us clarify what we mean, more generally, when we speak of one person's responsibility for a client or patient. We use the term *responsible* to describe a person's accountability for the conduct or welfare of others or himself or herself. For example, parents are responsible for their children (especially when the children are young), whereas competent adults are responsible for themselves.

The idea of responsibility is intertwined with two other concepts: liberty and control. Liberty and responsibility are, in fact, two sides of the same coin. Ordinarily, we assume that adults are moral agents endowed with free will; that is, they choose their behavior from among a range of options, large or small. We also assume that they are responsible for their actions; that is, they are praised or blamed, rewarded or punished, depending on whether their conduct is judged to be good or bad.

Where there is no freedom, there is no responsibility: We do not hold infants responsible for their behavior; duress is a complete excuse in the criminal law; and so forth. And where there is no control, there can be no responsibility: A person cannot be held responsible for something he or she does not control. Asserting that "X is responsible for Y" (for Y's welfare, health, not committing suicide, and so on) is tantamount to asserting that X can, and indeed must, have enough control over Y to bring about the desired condition of Y. This is why persons who want to assume control over others typically claim to be responsible for them (called "paternalism") and why persons who want to reject responsibility for their own conduct typically claim to have no control over their actions (called "mental illness").

These principles are recognized in countless contractual arrangements, as, for example, when a bank trustee is empowered to manage someone else's money or an anesthesiologist to put someone else to sleep. Such experts undertake to exercise a specific responsibility, for the proper discharge of which they are granted control over specific objects or functions (money, respiration, and so forth). In every such situation, the controllers become responsible for what they control, and only for what they control. It follows, then, that anyone who assumes the task of preventing another person from committing suicide must assume the most far-reaching control over that person's capacity to act. Because, in fact, it is virtually impossible to prevent the suicide of a person determined on killing himself or herself, and because forcibly imposed interventions to prevent suicide deprive the patient of liberty and dignity, the use of psychiatric coercion to prevent suicide is at once impractical and immoral. It should, of course, be noted that because children have neither the rights nor responsibilities of adults, and because, unlike adults, children are typically treated coercively by the medical system (as well as in other situations), we must always clearly distinguish between policies aimed at children and policies aimed at adults. The principle of coercive paternalism obliterates this basic distinction. In this discussion, I shall be concerned only with *adult* suicidal persons and moreover only with those subjected to *involuntary* interventions. (Interventions by mental health professionals provided noncoercively for voluntary clients or patients pose no special conceptual or moral problems.)

SUICIDE AND THE MENTAL HEALTH PROFESSIONAL

What, then, *is* the mental health professional's responsibility insofar as he or she deals with (counsels, ministers to, treats) suicidal clients or patients? What *should be* the clinician's responsibility in that situation? These are different questions, requiring different answers. To the first question, I would answer that the clinician's responsibility for his or her patient's suicide is whatever the law and social custom say it is. To the second I would answer that the clinician's responsibility vis-à-vis the suicidal patient should be the same as any other physician's or psychologist's vis-à-vis his or her competent adult patient or client. If the patient or client wants or is willing to accept help for "being suicidal," the mental health professional has a moral obligation—and, depending on the circumstances, perhaps also a legal obligation—to provide some sort of help for that person. However, if the patient or client does not want such help and actively rejects it, then the mental health professional's duty ought to be to leave him or her alone (or, perhaps, to try to persuade him or her to accept help). . . .

THE RIGHT TO SUICIDE

In a free society a person is not only presumed to be innocent until proven guilty but also sane until proven insane.[2]

This presumption has far-reaching implications, especially insofar as a person's right to his or her own body is concerned. . . .

[W]hen it comes to suicide we deny the moral complexity; namely, that although life is precious, disease, disability, and dishonor may render a person's life not worth living and thus may make suicide a blessing for himself or herself as well as for others and society. Nevertheless, we, in the West, impose coercive measures on every would-be suicide (even the hopelessly sick and very aged), as if suicide were never desirable enough to justify it. . . .

I do not mean that killing oneself is always good or praiseworthy; I mean only that the power of the state should not be legitimately invoked or deployed to prohibit or prevent persons from killing themselves.[3]

This distinction between the illegal and the immoral is, in fact, deeply ingrained in Anglo-American law. Some acts are thus regarded not only as crimes but also as violations of widely shared moral values. For example, the unprovoked killing of another person is a *malum in se*, a wrong in itself. Other acts are regarded as crimes because they violate existing laws without being immoral, for example, exceeding the speed limit by 10 miles per hour on the open road or harboring an illegal alien. Such an act is *malum prohibitum*, a wrong because it is prohibited. Finally, there are acts that only some people may consider wrongs, for example, the use of artificial methods of birth control or eating pork. In a secular society, such acts are not illegal but are of course, against the precepts of one or another religion. . . .

Thus, treating suicide as a right does not mean that we must accept committing suicide as a morally legitimate option; it means only that we must abstain from empowering agents of the state to coercively prevent it. Mental health professionals could then treat suicide as they treat, say, abortion—in other words, as an act they may approve or disapprove in general and may choose to counsel for or against in any particular case.

SUICIDE OR DEATH CONTROL?

The effort to seriously ponder the issue of suicide probes some of our most passionately held, but not universally shared, beliefs about ending our own lives. Is such an act like homicide and accordingly properly called "suicide"? Or is it more like birth control and accordingly better termed "death control"? The behavior of countless successful and prominent persons shows us unmistakably that most Americans view suicide ambivalently, as a dreaded enemy as well as a trusted friend.

The belief that it is the legitimate function of the state to coerce persons because they might kill themselves is a characteristically modern, quasi-therapeutic idea, catering at once to our craving for dependency and omnipotence. The result is an intricate web of interventions and institutions that have themselves become powerful engines of hypocrisy and seemingly indispensable mechanisms for satisfying human needs now buried in hidden agendas.

It has taken a long time to get mental health professionals deeply enmeshed in the suicide business, and it will take a long time to get them out of it. In the meantime, mental health professionals and their clients and patients are doomed to wander aimlessly in the existential-legal labyrinth generated by treating suicide as if it constituted a mental health problem. However, if we refuse to play a part in the drama of coercive suicide prevention, then we shall be sorely tempted to conclude that mental health professionals and their partners in suicide richly deserve each other and the torment each is so ready and eager to inflict on the other.

REFERENCES

Bean, E. (1985, May 1). Cigarettes and cancer: Lawyers in U.S. gird to battle tobacco firms on liability. *The Wall Street Journal*, p. 1.

Black, H. C. (1968). *Black's law dictionary.* St. Paul, MN: West.

Blackstone, W. (1962). *Commentaries on the laws of England: Of public wrongs.* Boston: Beacon Press. (Original work published 1755–1765).

Fedden, H. R. (1938). *Suicide: A social and historical study.* London: Peter Davies.

Margolick, D. (1985, March 15). Antismoking is encouraging suits against the tobacco industry. *The New York Times*, p. 15.

Sprott, S. E. (1961). *The English debate on suicide: From Donne to Hume.* Lasalle, IL: Open Court.

Szasz, T. S. (1971). The ethics of suicide. *The Antioch Review, 31,* 7–17.

Warren, O. L. (1978). *Negligence in New York courts.* New York: Matthew Bender.

Yolles, S. F. (1967). The tragedy of suicide in the United States. In L. Yochelson (Ed.), *Symposium on suicide* (pp. 15–26). Washington, DC: George Washington University.

NOTES

1. *Black's Law Dictionary* states that, "As a technical term of the law, 'duty' signifies . . . that which is due from another person; that which a person owes to another. An obligation to do a thing" (Black, 1968, p. 595). How does a person or party incur such an obligation? In one or both of two ways: *explicitly,* by contracting for it, as airline companies do, for example, when they promise, in exchange for a sum of money, to transport a passenger from place A to place B; and *implicitly,* by promising to do so without causing injuries to the passengers during the flight.

2. This fundamental principle is now being eroded, due in no small part to the ideology of mental illness and the activities of mental health professionals. The far-advanced state of this erosion is exemplified by the fact that competent (sane), adult Americans now claim that they are not responsible for smoking cigarettes, that mental health professionals eagerly support this claim with "expert" opinions and testimony, and that judges legitimize this claim by allowing smokers to sue tobacco companies for causing "tobacco addiction" (Bean, 1985; Margolick, 1985). The belief that we can have liberty without responsibility is, of course, an illusion people are often unwilling to relinquish until it is too late to do so.

3. Asserting that X is a right does not mean that doing X is (always or sometimes or ever) good or praiseworthy; it means only that the power of the state cannot be legitimately invoked or deployed to prevent or prohibit doing X. For example, treating freedom of religion as a right does not compel us to accept abortion as a morally legitimate act; it compels us only to abstain from using the power of the state to impose that judgment on those who fail to impose it on themselves.

NO

George A. Clum

ABANDON THE SUICIDAL?
A REPLY TO SZASZ

Szasz's article on suicide prevention (July 1986) essentially does a disservice to serious-minded practitioners struggling with legitimate issues of how best to deal with suicidal behavior. Hiding behind the twin shields of liberty and responsibility, Szasz contended that the suicidal person has the right to commit suicide and that health professionals attack the dignity of the individual by implementing coercive treatment methods and, in the process, open themselves up for lawsuits by claiming to do something they cannot—prevent suicide. I will argue that the issue of litigation is irrelevant to the question of treatment, that responsibility is often diminished during periods of suicidal behavior, and that suicidal behavior is often temporary, and as such warrants temporary restraint at times. I will further argue that treatment may reduce the danger of suicide, but that inaction most certainly will not.

THE DANGER OF SUICIDE

Szasz would have us believe that mental health practitioners who respond coercively to suicide behavior (in this case, coercion presumably means temporary hospitalization) court legal action by co-opting the individual's responsibility for his or her own life. A simple analysis of the facts contradicts this allegation on several counts. A recent summary of the history of legal action against psychologists reveals 100 suits per year over the last 10 years, only a portion of which were settled against psychologists. Further, suits based on suicide claims account for only 11% of the total number of suits (Turkington, 1986). At most, suits following suicide average no more than 11 per year. Finally, common sense tells us that successful suits follow, not decisive action taken to prevent suicide, but the failure to take action. The issue of legal suits, moreover, panders to the fears now rampant among health providers. In addition to the preponderance of data that suggest that only a very small percentage of individuals with suicidal behavior actually

From George A. Clum, "Abandon the Suicidal? A Reply to Szasz," *American Psychologist*, vol. 42, no. 9 (September 1987). Copyright © 1987 by the American Psychological Association. Reprinted by permission.

commit suicide, the number of suits relative to the number of successful suicides is very low.

What, then, is the consequence of adopting a policy of nonintervention? Judging from the number of suicides, the numbers of attempters and ideators are high indeed. The consequence of adopting a policy of nonintervention is tantamount, therefore, to eschewing responsibility for treatment for a large number of individuals. Szasz was correct when he implied that there are no data to indicate that persons bent on committing suicide can be dissuaded. He did not tell us that there are also no data to indicate they cannot. In the absence of such data, clinical wisdom and prudence dictate a conservative course in order to reduce the chance of professional negligence and to increase the chance of effective intervention. Szasz did not attack treatment per se, however, only coercive treatment. The basis for this argument is his contention that suicide is an act of a responsible person.

THE ISSUE OF RESPONSIBILITY

Szasz implied that suicide, except in the rarest instance, is the product of a free and responsible choice. He acknowledged possible exceptions to this, though he was ultimately unclear as to whether he would restrain a delirious or acutely psychotic person who believed he or she could fly or stop speeding trains with his or her body. Because no stand is taken on this issue, let me presume that Szasz would adopt an interventionist stance in some rare instances. He hinted at this possibility by acknowledging the importance of an anesthesiologist's taking coercive action for the patient's welfare when the patient is emerging from anesthesia.

Clearly, even for Szasz, there are times when it is necessary for responsible people to assume responsibility. The question then is not whether but when and how. Individuals presenting with suicidal behavior have not decided to take their lives—otherwise they would have done it. They are presenting with the possibility of taking their lives. They are, in a word, ambivalent. This ambivalence may be validated or inferred from their actions. Under such circumstances, individuals' responsibility for their own actions is diminished, not necessarily in the legal sense but rather in the sense that their conscious choices have been narrowed to a very few. The degree to which responsibility is diminished varies depending on such things as stress levels, severity of anxiety or depression, and the perceived alternative courses of action. To suggest, as Szasz did, that responsibility is a black-and-white affair is overly legalistic and insensitive to psychological data bearing on responsibility.

What do we mean by responsibility, and when is a person able to act freely, and thus responsibly? In the case of suicide, there is, of course, always a choice— to attempt suicide or not. As the number of alternatives increases, he or she can be said to have more freedom and, therefore, more responsibility. Conversely, as alternatives decrease, freedom and responsibility diminish. If alternatives to suicide are diminished in suicidal persons, their responsibility with regard to choosing suicide can be considered to be diminished.

The ability to perceive alternative problem-solving strategies is directly related to a person's affective state. It is axiomatic that high levels of anxiety diminish complex problem-solving ability. Depression states have likewise been shown within the learned helplessness model to result in diminished problem-solving ability. Hopelessness, a correlate of depression, can, a fortiori, be considered to reduce the number of perceived options. Hopelessness, in fact, can be defined as an inability to perceive any positive outcome for one's actions.

If it could be shown that periods of acute suicidal behavior are accompanied by high levels of affective discharge in the form of depression and hopelessness, there would be indirect evidence that suicidal behavior is accompanied by decreased responsibility. If, in addition, actual deficits in problem-solving ability could be shown to accompany suicidal behaviors, we would have direct evidence of diminished responsibility during these episodes. Finally, if it could be shown that these episodes are stress related and therefore likely transient, and that they were responsive to treatment, we would have some basis for intervening, even coercively, on a time-limited basis.

SUICIDE AS PROBLEM SOLVING

The belief that suicide as a behavior is untreatable is based on an inaccurate premise, that is, that suicide is the problem to be resolved. Suicide is not the problem but the solution to the problem. Like all solutions, it is reasonable in some instances and unreasonable in others. It is unreasonable, for example, when it is disproportionate to the problem being solved. A clear example of this is provided when an adolescent, having failed a course, believes suicide is a preferable solution to the problem of facing disgruntled parents, particularly if the disgruntlement is imaginary or overblown.

Evidence for suicide as a failure in problem solving has come recently from my and my students' work (Patsiokas, Clum, & Luscomb, 1979; Schotte & Clum, 1982, 1987). Specifically, these studies demonstrate that, relative to depressed but nonsuicidal college students, and relative to psychiatrically hospitalized and nonsuicidal patients, suicide ideators and attempters are more cognitively rigid and are unable to generate as many alternative solutions to both generic and idiosyncratic problems. Considered in this way, suicide becomes the product of a problem that may or may not prove solvable by other means. If it is solvable by other means, temporary coercive strategies may buy time until alternative solutions can be explored. Such temporary emergency actions are frequently taken when negative consequences exist for either action or inaction.

SUICIDE AS A TRANSIENT PHENOMENON

Further evidence for the transient quality of suicidal behavior comes from data linking it to stressful events, time limited in nature, as well as hopelessness and depression. A variety of studies have shown a strong link between life events, particularly losses and exits, and both suicide ideation and suicide attempts. Specifically, suicide attempters report four times as many negative life events in the six months preceding their attempts as do normal individuals and one and one half times the number reported by depressives (Paykel, Prusoff, & Myers, 1975). Such life events also are higher in hospitalized individuals on suicide precautions as compared with other hospitalized psychiatric patients. Both depression (Schotte & Clum, 1982) and hopelessness (Beck, Steer, Kovacs, & Garrison, 1985; Schotte & Clum, 1987) have been found to differentiate suicide ideators and attempters from comparable psychiatric groups who are not suicidal. The life changes that precede suicidal behavior are typically acute in nature, and thus their effects can be expected to dissipate with the passing of time. Further, the affective disturbance that accompanies suicidal behavior has been shown to be amenable to treatment (Patsiokas & Clum, 1985), as has the suicidal behavior itself (Liberman & Eckman, 1981). Thus, there exists a growing body of literature that indicates that suicide is accompanied by large increases in depression and hopelessness that temporarily diminish individual responsibility. In a number of individuals, high levels of acute stress appear to precipitate these affective states.

RESPONSE TO TREATMENT

Suicidal behavior is serious business and should be treated as such. It is often a last-gasp effort to deal with life's difficulties. I have argued elsewhere (Clum, Patsiokas, & Luscomb, 1979) that crisis intervention approaches are inadequate to this task, precisely because such approaches take suicidal behavior out of context and do not deal with the problems that form the basis for such behavior. Few studies exist that have specifically targeted suicidal behavior, but those that do exist are promising. The two published controlled studies (Liberman & Eckman, 1981; Patsiokas & Clum, 1985) have demonstrated that correlates of suicidal behavior, such as hopelessness and deficient problem-solving behavior, and suicidal behavior itself can be reduced by

appropriate treatment strategies. In both of these treatment studies the comparison groups were receiving treatment of some other type that was also effective in reducing both suicidal behavior and its correlates. Such data begin to suggest that suicidal individuals might indeed be dissuaded when viable alternatives for dealing with life's problems are incorporated into their repertoire.

OVERVIEW

Szasz's remarks on suicide are persuasive but alarmingly shortsighted. Szasz overestimated the legal threat facing professionals who have the courage to assume responsibility for suicidal persons. Compared with the large numbers of suicidal ideators, threateners, and attempters who come to the attention of mental health professionals, the number who commit suicide and whose cases end up in litigation is minuscule. We could be adopting an extremely restrictive policy for very small increases in security if Szasz's recommendations were to be implemented.

The other side of the issue, namely, the mental health professional's temporary assumption of responsibility for the suicidal individual's welfare, is a subtler and more sensitive issue. I have argued that responsibility is a function of perceived alternatives. I have also argued that during the acutely suicidal state, responsibility is decreased through a rapid increase in hopelessness and depression preceded by high levels of stress. It is specifically because such states are temporary that coercive action may be warranted. The fact that treatment programs for suicidal individuals may work to reduce these affective states and increase the perceived alternatives is further justification for such action. Admittedly, such a stance increases the chances that unnecessary or inappropriate coercive action may be taken. The potential gains, however, in terms of lives that have been restored to a less precarious existence, seem worth the risks.

REFERENCES

Beck, A., Steer, R., Kovacs, M., & Garrison, B. (1985). Hopelessness and eventual suicide: A 10-year prospective study of patients hospitalized with suicidal ideation. *American Journal of Psychiatry, 142,* 559–563.

Clum, G. A., Patsiokas, A. T., & Luscomb, R. L. (1979). Empirically based comprehensive treatment program for parasuicide. *Journal of Consulting and Clinical Psychology, 47,* 937–945.

Liberman, R. P., & Eckman, T. (1981). Behavior therapy vs. insight-oriented therapy for repeated suicide attempters. *Archives of General Psychiatry, 38,* 1126–1130.

Patsiokas, A., & Clum, G. A. (1985). Effects of psychotherapeutic strategies in the treatment of suicide attempters. *Psychotherapy: Theory, Research and Practice, 22,* 281–290.

Patsiokas, A., Clum, G. A., & Luscomb, R. (1979). Cognitive characteristics of suicide attempters. *Journal of Consulting and Clinical Psychology, 47,* 478–484.

Paykel, E., Prusoff, B., & Myers, J. (1975). Suicide attempts and recent life events. *Archives of General Psychiatry, 32,* 327–333.

Schotte, D., & Clum, G. A. (1982). Suicide ideation in a college population: A test of a model. *Journal of Consulting and Clinical Psychology, 50,* 690–696.

Schotte, D., & Clum, G. A. (1987). Problem-solving skills in suicidal psychiatric patients. *Journal of Consulting and Clinical Psychology, 55,* 49–54.

Szasz, T. (1986). The case against suicide prevention. *American Psychologist, 41,* 806–812.

Turkington, C. (1986, November). Suit data show no need to panic. *APA Monitor,* p. 9.

CHALLENGE QUESTIONS

Should Psychotherapists Allow Suicide?

1. Do you believe people who are suicidal are not responsible for their actions? Are there exceptions to your position?

2. Should mental health professionals assume responsibility for suicide prevention? Why or why not?

3. Do you believe a person who is determined to commit suicide can be realistically prevented? If not, how can mental health professionals fulfill their assumed role in suicide prevention?

4. Do suicidal persons have mixed feelings about their wishes to die? Why do suicidal people leave suicide notes or tell others of their intentions?

5. If your only options were a debilitating and terminal illness on the one hand and a suicide on the other, which would you choose? How would your choice affect those closest to you?

ISSUE 15

Do Diagnostic Labels Hinder the Effective Treatment of Persons With Mental Disorders?

YES: D. L. Rosenhan, from "On Being Sane in Insane Places," *Science* (January 19, 1973)

NO: Robert L. Spitzer, from "On Pseudoscience in Science, Logic in Remission and Psychiatric Diagnosis: A Critique of 'On Being Sane in Insane Places,' " *Journal of Abnormal Psychology* (1975)

ISSUE SUMMARY

YES: Psychologist D. L. Rosenhan describes an experiment that, he contends, demonstrates that once a patient is labeled as schizophrenic, his behavior is seen as such by mental health workers regardless of the true state of the patient's mental health.

NO: Psychiatrist Robert L. Spitzer argues that diagnostic labels are necessary and valuable, and that Rosenhan's experiment has many flaws.

Traditionally, the first step in treating a disorder is to diagnose it. When a disorder is diagnosed, presumably the most effective treatment can then be applied. But diagnosis often involves classifying the person and attaching a label. Could such a label do more harm than good?

How would you think and behave if you were introduced to someone described as a high school dropout? A heroin addict? A schizophrenic? What would you think and how would you behave if, having recently taken a series of personality tests, you were told by an expert that you were schizophrenic?

Some people believe that diagnostic labels may actually serve as self-fulfilling prophecies. Labels seem to have a way of putting blinders on the way a problem is seen. Those who are labeled may behave differently toward others or develop self-concepts consistent with the diagnosis—and thereby exaggerate, or even create anew, behavior considered to be "abnormal."

In his article, D. L. Rosenhan asks the question, "If sanity and insanity exist, how shall we know them?" He then describes an experiment that he conducted to help answer this question. Rosenhan interprets the results of his investigation as demonstrating that "the normal are not detectably sane' by a mental hospital staff because "having once been labeled schizophrenic, there is nothing the pseudopatient can do to overcome this tag." He believes that mental institutions impose a specific environment in which the meaning of even normal behaviors can be looked on as abnormal. If this is so, Rosenhan wonders, "How many people are sane . . . but not recognized as such in our psychiatric institutions?"

Robert L. Spitzer criticizes Rosenhan's experiment on many grounds and, in fact, contends that "a correct interpretation of his own [Rosenhan's] data contradicts his conclusions." Rosenhan's data, Spitzer contends, show that in "a psychiatric hospital, psychiatrists are remarkably able to distinguish the 'sane' from the 'insane.' " Although Spitzer recognizes some of the dangers of diagnostic classification, he believes Rosenhan has not presented fairly the purpose and necessity of diagnoses. The misuse of diagnoses, he maintains, "is not a sufficient reason to abandon their use because they have been shown to be of value when properly used." They "enable mental health professionals to communicate with each other . . . , comprehend the pathological processes involved . . . , and control psychiatric disorders," says Rosenhan.

POINT	COUNTERPOINT
• Psychiatric diagnoses are in the minds of the observers and do not reflect the behavior of the patients.	• A diagnosis based on real or false symptoms *is* based on a patient's behavior.
• A diagnosis can become a self-fulfilling prophecy for the doctor or the patient.	• Competent diagnoses derive from a necessary classification of the symptoms of disorder.
• In the setting of a mental institution, almost any behavior could be considered abnormal.	• Mental patients *do* eventually get discharged when they continue to show no symptoms of behavior pathology.
• Diagnostic labels serve no useful purpose, especially in view of the harm they do.	• Diagnoses enable psychiatrists to communicate, comprehend, and control the disorder.

YES
D. L. Rosenhan

ON BEING SANE IN INSANE PLACES

If sanity and insanity exist, how shall we know them?

The question is neither capricious nor itself insane. However much we may be personally convinced that we can tell the normal from the abnormal, the evidence is simply not compelling. It is commonplace, for example, to read about murder trials wherein eminent psychiatrists for the defense are contradicted by equally eminent psychiatrists for the prosecution on the matter of the defendant's sanity. More generally, there are a great deal of conflicting data on the reliability, utility, and meaning of such terms as "sanity," "insanity," "mental illness," and "schizophrenia." Finally, as early as 1934, Benedict suggested that normality and abnormality are not universal. What is viewed as normal in one culture may be seen as quite aberrant in another. Thus, notions of normality and abnormality may not be quite as accurate as people believe they are.

To raise questions regarding normality and abnormality is in no way to question the fact that some behaviors are deviant or odd. Murder is deviant. So, too, are hallucinations. Nor does raising such questions deny the existence of the personal anguish that is often associated with "mental illness." Anxiety and depression exist. Psychological suffering exists. But normality and abnormality, sanity and insanity, and the diagnoses that flow from them may be less substantive than many believe them to be.

At its heart, the question of whether the sane can be distinguished from the insane (and whether degrees of insanity can be distinguished from each other) is a simple matter: do the salient characteristics that lead to diagnoses reside in the patients themselves or in the environments and contexts in which observers find them? From Bleuler, through Kretchmer, through the formulators of the recently revised *Diagnostic and Statistical Manual* of the American Psychiatric Association, the belief has been strong that patients present symptoms, that those symptoms can be categorized, and, implicitly, that the sane are distinguishable from the insane. More recently, however, this belief has been questioned. Based in part on theoretical and anthro-

From D. L. Rosenhan, "On Being Sane in Insane Places," *Science*, vol. 179 (January 13, 1973). Copyright © 1973 by the American Association for the Advancement of Science. Reprinted by permission.

pological considerations, but also on philosophical, legal, and therapeutic ones, the view has grown that psychological categorization of mental illness is useless at best and downright harmful, misleading, and pejorative at worst. Psychiatric diagnoses, in this view, are in the minds of the observers and are not valid summaries of characteristics displayed by the observed.

Gains can be made in deciding which of these is more nearly accurate by getting normal people (that is, people who do not have, and have never suffered, symptoms of serious psychiatric disorders) admitted to psychiatric hospitals and then determining whether they were discovered to be sane and, if so, how. If the sanity of such pseudopatients were always detected, there would be prima facie evidence that a sane individual can be distinguished from the insane context in which he is found. Normality (and presumably abnormality) is distinct enough that it can be recognized wherever it occurs, for it is carried within the person. If, on the other hand, the sanity of the pseudopatients were never discovered, serious difficulties would arise for those who support traditional modes of psychiatric diagnosis. Given that the hospital staff was not incompetent, that the pseudopatient had been behaving as sanely as he had been outside of the hospital, and that it had never been previously suggested that he belonged in a psychiatric hospital, such an unlikely outcome would support the view that psychiatric diagnosis betrays little about the patient but much about the environment in which an observer finds him.

This article describes such an experiment. Eight sane people gained secret admission to 12 different hospitals. Their diagnostic experiences constitute the data of the first part of this article; the remainder is devoted to a description of their experiences in psychiatric institutions. Too few psychiatrists and psychologists, even those who have worked in such hospitals, know what the experience is like. They rarely talk about it with former patients, perhaps because they distrust information coming from the previously insane. Those who have worked in psychiatric hospitals are likely to have adapted so thoroughly to the settings that they are insensitive to the impact of the experience. And while there have been occasional reports of researchers who submitted themselves to psychiatric hospitalization, these researchers have commonly remained in the hospitals for short periods of time, often with the knowledge of the hospital staff. It is difficult to know the extent to which they were treated like patients or like research colleagues. Nevertheless, their reports about the inside of the psychiatric hospital have been valuable. This article extends those efforts.

PSEUDOPATIENTS AND THEIR SETTINGS

The eight pseudopatients were a varied group. One was a psychology graduate student in his 20s. The remaining seven were older and "established." Among them were three psychologists, a pediatrician, a psychiatrist, a painter, and a housewife. Three pseudopatients were women, five were men. All of them employed pseudonyms, lest their alleged diagnoses embarrass them later. Those who were in mental health professions alleged another occupation in order to avoid the special attentions that might be accorded by staff, as a matter of courtesy or caution, to ailing colleagues. With the exception of myself (I was the first pseudopatient and my presence was known to the hospital administrator and chief psychologist and, so far as I can tell, to them alone), the presence of pseudopatients and the nature of the research program was not known to the hospital staffs.

The settings were similarly varied. In order to generalize the findings, admission into a variety of hospitals was sought. The 12 hospitals in the sample are located in five different states on the East and West coasts. Some were old and shabby, some were quite new. Some were research-oriented, others not. Some had good staff-patient ratios, others were quite understaffed. Only one was a strictly private hospital. All the others were supported by state or federal funds or, in one instance, by university funds.

After calling the hospital for an appointment, the pseudopatient arrived at the admissions office complaining that he had been hearing voices. Asked what the voices said, he replied that they were often unclear, but as far as he could tell they said "empty," "hollow," and "thud." The voices were unfamiliar and were of the same sex as the pseudopatient. The choice of these symptoms was occasioned by their apparent similarity to existential symptoms. Such symptoms were alleged to arise from painful concerns about the perceived meaninglessness of one's life. It is as if the hallucinating person were saying, "My life is empty and hollow." The choice of these symptoms was also determined by the *absence* of a single report of existential psychoses in the literature.

Beyond alleging the symptoms and falsifying name, vocation, and employment, no further alterations of person, history, or circumstances were made. The significant events of the pseudopatient's life history were presented as they had actually occurred. Relationships with parents and siblings, with spouse and children, with people at work and in school, consistent with the aforementioned exceptions, were described as they were or had been. Frustrations and upsets were described along with joys and satisfactions. These facts are important to remember. If anything, they strongly biased the subsequent results in favor of detecting sanity, since none of their histories or current behaviors were seriously pathological in any way.

Immediately upon admission to the psychiatric ward, the pseudopatient ceased simulating *any* symptoms of abnormality. In some cases, there was a brief period of mild nervousness and anxiety, since none of the pseudopatients really believed that they would be admitted so easily. Indeed their shared fear was that they would be immediately exposed as frauds and greatly embarrassed. Moreover, many of them had never visited a psychiatric ward; even those who had, nevertheless had some genuine fears about what might happen to them. Their nervousness, then, was quite appropriate to the novelty of the hospital setting, and it abated rapidly.

Apart from that short-lived nervousness, the pseudopatient behaved on the ward as he "normally" behaved. The pseudopatient spoke to patients and staff as he might ordinarily. Because there is uncommonly little to do on a psychiatric ward, he attempted to engage others in conversation. When asked by staff how he was feeling, he indicated that he was fine, that he no longer experienced symptoms. He responded to instructions from attendants, to calls for medication (which was not swallowed), and to dining-hall instructions. Beyond such activities as were available to him on the admissions ward, he spent his time writing down his observations about the ward, its patients, and the staff. Initially these notes were written "secretly," but as it soon became clear that no one much cared, they were subsequently written on standard tablets of paper in such public places as the dayroom. No secret was made of these activities.

The pseudopatient, very much as a true psychiatric patient, entered a hospital with no foreknowledge of when he would be discharged. Each was told that he would have to get out by his own devices, essentially by convincing the staff that he was sane. The psychological stresses associated with hospitalization were considerable, and all but one of the pseudopatients desired to be discharged almost immediately after being admitted. They were, therefore, motivated not only to behave sanely, but to be paragons of cooperation. That their behavior was in no way disruptive is confirmed by nursing reports, which have been obtained on most of the patients. These reports uniformly indicate that the patients were "friendly," "cooperative," and "exhibited no abnormal indications."

THE NORMAL
ARE NOT DETECTABLY SANE

Despite their public "show" of sanity, the pseudopatients were never detected. Admitted, except in one case, with a diagnosis of schizophrenia each was discharged with a diagnosis of schizophrenia "in remission." The label "in remission" should in no way be dismissed as a formality, for at no time during any hospitalization had any question been raised about any pseudopatient's simulation. Nor are there any indications in the hospital records that the pseudopatient's status was suspect. Rather, the evidence is strong that, once labeled schizophrenic, the pseudopatient was stuck with that label. If the pseudopatient was to be discharged, he must naturally be "in remission"; but he was not sane, nor, in the institution's view, had he ever been sane.

The uniform failure to recognize sanity cannot be attributed to the quality of the hospitals, for, although there were considerable variations among them, several are considered excellent. Nor can it be alleged that there was simply not enough time to observe the pseudopatients. Length of hospitalization ranged from 7 to 52 days, with an average of 19 days. The pseudopatients were not, in fact, carefully observed, but this failure clearly speaks more to traditions within psychiatric hospitals than to lack of opportunity.

Finally, it cannot be said that the failure to recognize the pseudopatients' sanity was due to the fact that they were not behaving sanely. While there was clearly some tension present in all of them, their daily visitors could detect no serious behavioral consequences—nor, indeed, could other patients. It was quite common for the patients to "detect" the pseudopatients' sanity. During the first three hospitalizations, when accurate counts were kept, 35 of a total of 118 patients on the admissions ward voiced their suspicions, some vigorously. "You're not crazy. You're a journalist, or a professor [referring to the continual note-taking]. You're checking up on the hospital." While most of the patients were reassured by the pseudopatient's insistence that he had been sick before he came in but was fine now, some continued to believe that the pseudopatient was sane throughout his hospitalization. The fact that the patients often recognized normality when staff did not raises important questions.

Failure to detect sanity during the course of hospitalization may be due to the fact that physicians operate with a strong bias toward what statisticians call the type 2 error. This is to say that physicians are more inclined to call a healthy person sick (a false positive, type 2) than a sick person healthy (a false negative, type 1). The reasons for this are not hard to find: it is clearly more dangerous to mis-diagnose illness than health. Better to err on the side of caution, to suspect illness even among the healthy.

But what holds for medicine does not hold equally well for psychiatry. Medical illnesses, while unfortunate, are not commonly pejorative. Psychiatric diagnoses, on the contrary, carry with them personal, legal, and social stigmas. It was therefore important to see whether the tendency toward diagnosing the sane insane could be reversed. The following experiment was arranged at a research and teaching hospital whose staff had heard these findings but doubted that such an error could occur in their hospital. The staff was informed that at some time during the following 3 months, one or more pseudopatients would attempt to be admitted into the psychiatric hospital. Each staff member was asked to rate each patient who presented himself at admissions or on the ward according to the likelihood that the patient was a pseudopatient. A 10-point scale was used, with a 1 and 2 reflecting high confidence that the patient was a pseudopatient.

Judgments were obtained on 193 patients who were admitted for psychiatric treatment. All staff who had had sustained contact with or primary responsibility for the patient—attendants, nurses, psychiatrists, physicians, and psychologists— were asked to make judgments. Forty-one patients were alleged, with high confidence, to be pseudopatients by at least one member of the staff. Twenty-three were considered suspect by at least one psychiatrist. Nineteen were suspected by one psychiatrist *and* one other staff member. Actually, no genuine pseudopatient (at least from my group) presented himself during this period.

The experiment is instructive. It indicates that the tendency to designate sane people as insane can be reversed when the stakes (in this case, prestige and diagnostic acumen) are high. But what can be said of the 19 people who were suspected of being "sane" by one psychiatrist and another staff member? Were these people truly "sane," or was it rather the case that in the course of avoiding the type 2 error the staff tended to make more errors of the first sort— calling the crazy "sane"? There is no way of knowing. But one thing is certain: any diagnostic process that lends itself so readily to massive errors of this sort cannot be a very reliable one.

THE STICKINESS OF PSYCHODIAGNOSTIC LABELS

Beyond the tendency to call the healthy sick—a tendency that accounts better for diagnostic behavior on admission than it does for such behavior after a lengthy period of exposure—the data speak to the massive role of labeling in psychiatric assessment. Having once been labeled schizophrenic, there is nothing the pseudopatient can do to overcome this tag. The tag profoundly colors others' perceptions of him and his behavior.

From one viewpoint, these data are hardly surprising, for it has long been known that elements are given meaning by the context in which they occur. Gestalt psychology made this point vigorously, and Asch demonstrated that there are "central" personality traits (such as "warm" versus "cold") which are so powerful that they markedly color the meaning of other information in forming an impression of a given personality.

"Insane," "schizophrenic," "manic-depressive," and "crazy" are probably among the most powerful of such central traits. Once a person is designated abnormal, all of his other behaviors and characteristics are colored by that label. Indeed, that label is so powerful that may of the pseudopatients' normal behaviors were overlooked entirely or profoundly misinterpreted. Some examples may clarify this issue.

Earlier I indicated that there were no changes in the pseudopatient's personal history and current status beyond those of name, employment, and, where necessary, vocation. Otherwise, a veridical description of personal history and circumstances was offered. Those circumstances were not psychotic. How were they made consonant with the diagnosis of psychosis? Or were those diagnoses modified in such a way as to bring them into accord with the circumstances of the pseudopatient's life, as described by him?

As far as I can determine, diagnoses were in no way affected by the relative health of the circumstances of a pseudopatient's life. Rather, the reverse occurred: the perception of his circumstances was shaped entirely by the diagnosis. A clear example of such translation is found in the case of a pseudopatient who had had a close relationship with his mother but was rather remote from his father during his early childhood. During adolescence and beyond, however, his father became a close friend, while his relationship with his mother cooled. His present relationship with his wife was characteristically close and warm. Apart from occasional angry exchanges, friction was minimal. The children had rarely been spanked. Surely there is nothing especially pathological about such a history. Indeed, many readers may see a similar pattern in their own experiences, with no markedly deleterious consequences. Observe, however, how such a history was translated in the psycho-pathological context, this from the case summary prepared after the patient was discharged:

This white 39-year-old male . . . manifests a long history of considerable ambivalence in close relationships, which begins in early childhood. A warm relationship with his mother cools during his adolescence. A distant relationship to his father is described as becoming very intense. Affective stability is absent. His attempts to control emotionality with his wife and children are punctuated by angry outbursts and, in the case of the children, spankings. And while he says that he has several friends, one senses considerable ambivalence embedded in these relationships also....

The facts of the case were unintentionally distorted by the staff to achieve consistency with a popular theory of the dynamics of a schizophrenic reaction. Nothing of an ambivalent nature had been described in relations with parents, spouse, or friends. To the extent that ambivalence could be inferred, it was probably not greater than is found in all human relationships. It is true the pseudopatient's relationships with his parents changed over time, but in the ordinary context that would hardly be remarkable—indeed, it might very well be expected. Clearly, the meaning ascribed to his verbalizations (that is, ambivalence, affective instability) was determined by the diagnosis: schizophrenia. An entirely different meaning would have been ascribed if it were known that the man was normal.

All pseudopatients took extensive notes publicly. Under ordinary circumstances, such behavior would have raised questions in the minds of observers, as, in fact, it did among patients. Indeed, it seemed so certain that the notes would elicit suspicion that elaborate precautions were taken to remove them from the ward each day. But the precautions proved needless. The closest any staff member came to questioning these notes occurred when one pseudopatient asked his physician what kind of medication he was receiving and began to write down the response. "You needn't write it," he was told gently. "If you have trouble remembering, just ask me again."

If no questions were asked of the pseudopatients, how was their writing interpreted? Nursing records for three patients indicate that the writing was seen as an aspect of their pathological behavior. "Patient engages in writing behavior" was the daily nursing comment on one of the pseudopatients who was never questioned about his writing. Given that the patient is in the hospital, he must be psychologically disturbed. And given that he is disturbed, continuous writing must be a behavioral manifestation of that disturbance, perhaps a subset of the compulsive behaviors that are sometimes correlated with schizophrenia.

One tacit characteristic of psychiatric diagnosis is that it locates the sources of aberration within the individual and only rarely within the complex of stimuli that surrounds him. Consequently, be-

haviors that are stimulated by the environment are commonly misattributed to the patient's disorder. For example, one kindly nurse found a pseudopatient pacing the long hospital corridors. "Nervous, Mr. X?" she asked. "No, bored," he said.

The notes kept by pseudopatients are full of patient behaviors that were misinterpreted by well-intentioned staff. Often enough, a patient would go "berserk" because he had, wittingly or unwittingly, been mistreated by, say, an attendant. A nurse coming upon the scene would rarely inquire even cursorily into the environmental stimuli of the patient's behavior. Rather, she assumed that his upset derived from his pathology, not from his present interactions with other staff members. Occasionally, the staff might assume that the patient's family (especially when they had recently visited) or other patients had stimulated the outburst. But never were the staff found to assume that one of themselves or the structure of the hospital had anything to do with a patient's behavior. One psychiatrist pointed to a group of patients who were sitting outside the cafeteria entrance half an hour before lunchtime. To a group of young residents he indicated that such behavior was characteristic of the oral-acquisitive nature of the syndrome. It seemed not to occur to him that there were very few things to anticipate in a psychiatric hospital besides eating.

A psychiatric label has a life and an influence of its own. Once the impression has been formed that the patient is schizophrenic, the expectation is that he will continue to be schizophrenic. When a sufficient amount of time has passed, during which the patient has done nothing bizarre, he is considered to be in remission and available for discharge. But the label endures beyond discharge, with the unconfirmed expectation that he will behave as a schizophrenic again. Such labels, conferred by mental health professionals, are as influential on the patient as they are on his relatives and friends, and it should not surprise anyone that the diagnosis acts on all of them as a self-fulfilling prophecy. Eventually, the patient himself accepts the diagnosis, with all of its surplus meanings and expectations, and behaves accordingly.

The inferences to be made from these matters are quite simple. Much as Zigler and Phillips have demonstrated that there is enormous overlap in the symptoms presented by patients who have been variously diagnosed, so there is enormous overlap in the behaviors of the sane and the insane. The sane are not "sane" all of the time. We lose our tempers "for no good reason." We are occasionally depressed or anxious, again for no good reason. And we may find it difficult to get along with one or another person—again for no reason that we can specify. Similarly, the insane are not always insane. Indeed, it was the impression of the pseudopatients while living with them that they were sane for long periods of time—that the bizarre behaviors upon which their diagnoses were allegedly predicated constituted only a small fraction of their total behavior. If it makes no sense to label ourselves permanently depressed on the basis of an occasional depression, then it takes better evidence than is presently available to label all patients insane or schizophrenic on the basis of bizarre behaviors or cognitions. It seems more useful, as Mischel has pointed out, to limit our discussions to *behaviors*, the stimuli that provoke them, and their correlates.

It is not known why powerful impressions of personality traits, such as "crazy" or "insane," arise. Conceivably, when the origins of and stimuli that give rise to a behavior are remote or unknown, or when the behavior strikes us as immutable, trait labels regarding the *behaver* arise. When, on the other hand, the origins and stimuli are known and available, discourse is limited to the behavior itself. Thus, I may hallucinate because I am sleeping, or I may hallucinate because I have ingested a peculiar drug. These are termed sleep-induced hallucinations, or dreams, and drug-induced hallucinations, respectively. But when the stimuli to my hallucinations are unknown, that is called craziness, or schizophrenia — as if that inference were somehow as illuminating as the others.

THE EXPERIENCE OF PSYCHIATRIC HOSPITALIZATION

The term "mental illness" is of recent origin. It was coined by people who were humane in their inclinations and who wanted very much to raise the station of (and the public's sympathies toward) the psychologically disturbed from that of witches and "crazies" to one that was akin to the physically ill. And they were at least partially successful, for the treatment of the mental ill *has* improved considerably over the years. But while treatment has improved, it is doubtful that people really regard the mentally ill in the same way that they view the physically ill. A broken leg is something one recovers from, but mental illness allegedly endures forever. A broken leg does not threaten the observer, but a crazy schizophrenic? There is by now a host of evidence that attitudes toward the mentally ill are characterized by fear, hostility, aloofness, suspicion, and dread. The mentally ill are society's lepers.

That such attitudes infect the general population is perhaps not surprising, only upsetting. But that they affect the professionals—attendants, nurses, physicians, psychologists, and social workers—who treat and deal with the mentally ill is more disconcerting, both because such attitudes are self-evidently pernicious and because they are unwitting. Most mental health professionals would insist that they are sympathetic toward the mentally ill, that they are neither avoidant nor hostile. But it is more likely that an exquisite ambivalence characterizes their relations with psychiatric patients, such that their avowed impulses are only part of their entire attitude. Negative attitudes are there too and can easily be detected. Such attitudes should not surprise us. They are the natural offspring of the labels patients wear and the places in which they are found.

Consider the structure of the typical psychiatric hospital. Staff and patients are strictly segregated. Staff have their own living space, including their dining facilities, bathrooms and assembly places. The glassed quarters that contain the professional staff, which the pseudopatients came to call "the cage," sit out on every dayroom. The staff emerge primarily for caretaking purposes—to give medication, to conduct a therapy or group meeting, to instruct or reprimand a patient. Otherwise, staff keep to themselves, almost as if the disorder that afflicts their charges is somehow catching.

So much is patient-staff segregation the rule that, for four public hospitals in which an attempt was made to measure the degree to which staff and patients mingle, it was necessary to use "time out of the staff cage" as the operational measure. While it was not the case that all time spent out of the cage was spent mingling with patients (attendants, for example, would occasionally emerge to watch television in the dayroom), it was the only way in which one could gather reliable data on time for measuring.

The average amount of time spent by attendants outside of the cage was 11.3 percent (range, 3 to 52 percent). This figure does not represent only time spent mingling with patients, but also includes time spent on such chores as folding laundry, supervising patients while they shave, directing ward clean-up, and sending patients to off-ward activities. It was the relatively rare attendant who spent time talking with patients or playing games with them. It proved impossible to obtain a "percent mingling time" for nurses, since the amount of time they spent out of the cage was too brief. Rather, we counted instances of emergence from the cage. On the average, daytime nurses emerged from the cage 11.5 times per shift, including instances when they left the ward entirely (range, 4 to 39 times). Late afternoon and night nurses were even less available, emerging on the average 9.4 times per shift (range, 4 to 41 times). Data on early morning nurses, who arrived usually after midnight and departed at 8 a.m., are not available because patients were asleep during most of this period.

Physicians, especially psychiatrists, were even less available. They were rarely seen on the wards. Quite commonly, they would be seen only when they arrived and departed, with the remaining time being spent in their offices or in the cage. On the average, physicians emerged on the ward 6.7 times per day (range 1 to 17 times). It proved difficult to make an accurate estimate in this regard, since physicians often maintained hours that allowed them to come and go at different times.

The hierarchical organization of the psychiatric hospital has been commented on before, but the latent meaning of that kind of organization is worth noting again. Those with the most power have least to do with patients, and those with the least power are most involved with them. Recall, however, that the acquisition of role-appropriate behaviors occurs mainly through the observation of others, with the most powerful having the most influence. Consequently, it is understandable that attendants not only spend more time with patients than do any other members of the staff—that is required by their station in the hierarchy—but also, insofar as they learn from their superiors' behavior, spend as little time with patients as they can. Attendants are seen mainly in the cage, which is where the models, the action, and the power are.

I turn now to a different set of studies, these dealing with staff response to patient-initiated contact. It has long been known that the amount of time a person spends with you can be an index of your significance to him. If he initiates and maintains eye contact, there is reason to believe that he is considering your requests and needs. If he pauses to chat or actually stops and talks, there is added reason to infer that he is individuating you. In four hospitals, the pseudopatient approached the staff member with a request which took the following form: "Pardon me, Mr. [or Dr. or Mrs.] X, could you tell me when I will be eligible for grounds privileges?" (or " . . . when I will be presented at the staff meeting?" or " . . . when I am likely to be discharged?"). While the content of the question varied according to the appropriateness of the target and the pseudopatient's (apparent) current needs, the form was always a courteous and relevant request for information. Care was taken never to approach a particular member of the staff more than once a day, lest the staff member become suspicious or irritated. In examining these data, remember that the behavior of the pseudopatients was neither bizarre nor disruptive. One could indeed engage in good conversation with them.

The data for these experiments are shown in Table 1, separately for physicians (column 1) and for nurses and attendants (column 2). Minor differences between these four institutions were overwhelmed by the degree to which staff avoided continuing contacts that patients had initiated. By far, their most common response consisted of either a brief response to the question offered while they were "on the move" and with head averted, or no response at all.

The encounter frequently took the following bizarre form: (pseudopatient) "Pardon me, Dr. X. Could you tell me when I am eligible for grounds privileges?" (physician) "Good morning Dave. How are you today?" (moves off without waiting for a response).

It is instructive to compare these data with data recently obtained at Stanford University. It has been alleged that large and eminent universities are characterized by faculty who are so busy that they have no time for students. For this comparison, a young lady approached individual faculty members who seemed to be walking purposefully to some meeting or teaching engagement and asked them the following questions.

1) "Pardon me, could you direct me to Encina Hall?" (at the medical school: " . . . to the Clinical Research Center?").

2) "Do you know where Fish Annex is?" (there is no Fish Annex at Stanford).

3) "Do you teach here?"

4) "How does one apply for admission to the college?" (at the medical school: " . . . to the medical school?").

5) "Is it difficult to get in?"

6) "Is there financial aid?"

Without exception, as can be seen in Table 1 (column 3), all of the questions were answered. No matter how rushed they were, all respondents not only maintained eye contact, but stopped to talk. Indeed, many of the respondents went out of their way to direct or take the questioner to the office she was seeking, to try to locate "Fish Annex," or to discuss with her the possibilities of being admitted to the university.

Similar data, also shown in Table 1 (columns 4, 5, and 6), were obtained in the hospital. Here too, the young lady came prepared with six questions. After the first question, however, she remarked to 18 of her respondents (column 4), "I'm looking for a psychiatrist," and to 15 others (column 5), "I'm looking for an internist." Ten other respondents received no inserted comment (column 6). The general degree of cooperative responses is considerably higher for these university groups than it was for pseudopatients in psychiatric hospitals. Even so, differences are apparent with the medical school setting. Once having indicated that she was looking for a psychiatrist, the degree of cooperation elicited was less than when she sought an internist.

POWERLESSNESS AND DEPERSONALIZATION

Eye contact and verbal contact reflect concern and individuation: their absence, avoidance and depersonalization. The data I have presented do not do justice to the rich daily encounters that grew up around matters of depersonal-

Table 1

Self-initiated contact by pseudopatients with psychiatrists and nurses and attendants, compared with other groups.

| Contact | Psychiatric hospitals | | University campus (nonmedical) | University medical center | | |
| | | | | Physicians | | |
	(1) Psychiatrists	(2) Nurses and attendants	(3) Faculty	(4) "Looking for a psychiatrist"	(5) "Looking for an internist"	(6) No additional comment
Responses						
Moves on, head averted (°)	71	88	0	0	0	0
Makes eye contact (°)	23	10	0	11	0	0
Pauses and chats (°)	2	2	0	11	0	10
Stops and talks (°)	4	0.5	100	78	100	90
Mean number of questions answered (out of 6)	*	*	6	3.8	4.8	4.5
Respondents (No.)	13	47	14	18	15	10
Attempts (No.)	185	1283	14	18	15	10
*Not applicable						

ization and avoidance. I have records of patients who were beaten by staff for the sin of initiating verbal contact. During my own experience, for example, one patient was beaten in the presence of other patients for having approached an attendant and told him, "I like you." Occasionally, punishment meted out to patients for misdemeanors seemed so excessive that it could not be justified by the most radical interpretations of psychiatric canon. Nevertheless, they appeared to go unquestioned. Tempers were often short. A patient who had not heard a call for medication would be roundly excoriated, and the morning attendants would often wake patients with, "Come on, you m---- f----s, out of bed!"

Neither anecdotal nor "hard" data can convey the overwhelming sense of powerlessness which invades the individual as he is continually exposed to the depersonalization of the psychiatric hospital. It hardly matters *which* psychiatric hospital—the excellent public ones and the very plush private hospital were better than the rural and shabby ones in this regard, but again, the features that psychiatric hospitals had in common overwhelmed by far their apparent differences.

Powerlessness was evident everywhere. The patient is deprived of many of his legal rights by dint of his psychiatric commitment. He is shorn of credibility by virtue of his psychiatric label. His freedom of movement is restricted. He cannot initiate contact with the staff, but may only respond to such overtures as they make. Personal privacy is minimal. Patient quarters and possessions can be entered and examined by any staff member, for whatever reason. His personal history and anguish are available to any staff member (often including the "grey lady" and "candy striper" volunteer) who chooses to read his folder, regardless of their therapeutic relationship to him. His personal hygiene and waste evacuation are often monitored. The water closets may have no doors.

At times, the depersonalization reached such proportions that pseudopatients had the sense that they were invisible, or at least unworthy of account. Upon being admitted, I and other pseudopatients took the initial physical examination in a semipublic room, where staff members went about their own business as if we were not there.

On the ward, attendants delivered verbal and occasionally serious physical abuse to patients in the presence of other observing patients, some of whom (the pseudopatients) were writing it all down. Abusive behavior, on the other hand, terminated quite abruptly when other staff members were known to be coming. Staff are credible witnesses. Patients are not.

A nurse unbuttoned her uniform to adjust her brassiere in the presence of an entire ward of viewing men. One did not have the sense that she was being seductive. Rather, she didn't notice us. A group of staff persons might point to a patient in the dayroom and discuss him animatedly, as if he were not there.

One illuminating instance of depersonalization and invisibility occurred with regard to medications. All told, the pseudopatients were administered nearly 2100 pills, including Elavil, Stelazine, Compazine, and Thorazine, to name but a few. (That such a variety of medications should have been administered to patients presenting identical symptoms is itself worthy of note.) Only two were swallowed. The rest were either pocketed or deposited in the toilet. The pseudopatients were not alone in this. Although I have no precise records on how many patients rejected their medications, the pseudopatients frequently found the medications of other patients in the toilet before they deposited their own. As long as they were cooperative, their behavior and the pseudopatients' own in this matter, as in other important matters, went unnoticed throughout.

Reactions to such depersonalization among pseudopatients were intense. Although they had come to the hospital as participant observers and were fully aware that they did not "belong," they nevertheless found themselves caught up in and fighting the process of depersonalization. Some examples: a graduate student in psychology asked his wife to bring his textbooks to the hospital so he could "catch up on his homework"—this despite the elaborate precautions taken to conceal his professional association. The same student, who had trained for quite some time to get into the hospital, and who had looked forward to the experience, "remembered" some drag races that he had wanted to see on the weekend and insisted that he be discharged by that time. Another pseudopatient attempted a romance with a nurse. Subsequently, he informed the staff that he was applying for admission to graduate school in psychology and was very likely to be admitted, since a graduate professor was one of his regular hospital visitors. The same person began to engage in psychotherapy with other patients—all of this as a way of becoming a person in an impersonal environment.

THE SOURCES OF
DEPERSONALIZATION

What are the origins of depersonalization? I have already mentioned two. First,

are attitudes held by all of us toward the mentally ill—including those who treat them—attitudes characterized by fear, distrust, and horrible expectations on the other. Our ambivalence leads us, in this instance as in others, to avoidance.

Second, and not entirely separate, the hierarchical structure of the psychiatric hospital facilitates depersonalization. Those who are at the top have least to do with patients, and their behavior inspires the rest of the staff. Average daily contact with psychiatrists, psychologists, residents, and physicians combined ranged from 3.9 to 25.1 minutes, with an overall mean of 6.8 (six pseudopatients over a total of 129 days of hospitalization). Included in this average are time spent in the admissions interview, ward meetings in the presence of a senior staff member, group and individual psychotherapy contacts, case presentation conferences, and discharge meetings. Clearly, patients do not spend much time in interpersonal contact with doctoral staff. And doctoral staff serve as models for nurses and attendants.

There are probably other sources. Psychiatric installations are presently in serious financial straits. Staff shortages are pervasive, staff time at a premium. Something has to give, and that something is patient contact. Yet, while financial stresses are realities, too much can be made of them. I have the impression that the psychological forces that result in depersonalization are much stronger than the fiscal ones and that the addition of more staff would not correspondingly improve patient care in this regard. The incidence of staff meetings and the enormous amount of record-keeping on patients, for example, have not been as substantially reduced as has patient contact. Priorities exist, even during hard times. Patient contact is not a significant priority in the traditional psychiatric hospital, and fiscal pressures do not account for this. Avoidance and depersonalization may.

Heavy reliance upon psychotropic medication tacitly contributes to depersonalization by convincing staff that treatment is indeed being conducted and that further patient contact may not be necessary. Even here, however, caution needs to be exercised in understanding the role of psychotropic drugs. If patients were powerful rather than powerless, if they were viewed as interesting individuals rather than diagnostic entities, if they were socially significant rather than social lepers, if their anguish truly and wholly compelled our sympathies and concerns, would we not *seek* contact with them, despite the availability of medications? Perhaps for the pleasure of it all?

THE CONSEQUENCES OF LABELING AND DEPERSONALIZATION

Whenever the ratio of what is known to what needs to be known approaches zero, we tend to invent "knowledge" and assume that we understand more than we actually do. We seem unable to acknowledge that we simply don't know. The needs for diagnosis and remediation of behavioral and emotional problems are enormous. But rather than acknowledge that we are just embarking on understanding, we continue to label patients "schizophrenic," "manic-depressive," and "insane," as if in those words we had captured the essence of understanding. The facts of the matter are that we have known for a long time that diagnoses are often not useful or reliable, but we have nevertheless continued to use them. We

now know that we cannot distinguish insanity from sanity. It is depressing to consider how that information will be used.

Not merely depressing, but frightening. How many people, one wonders, are sane but not recognized as such in our psychiatric institutions? How many have been needlessly stripped of their privileges of citizenship, from the right to vote and drive to that of handling their own accounts? How many have feigned insanity in order to avoid the criminal consequences of their behavior, and, conversely, how many would rather stand trial than live interminably in a psychiatric hospital—but are wrongly thought to be mentally ill? How many have been stigmatized by well-intentioned, but nevertheless erroneous, diagnoses? On the last point, recall again that a "type 2 error" in psychiatric diagnosis does not have the same consequences it does in medical diagnosis. A diagnosis of cancer that has been found to be in error is cause for celebration. But psychiatric diagnoses are rarely found to be in error. The label sticks, a mark of inadequacy forever.

Finally, how many patients might be "sane" outside the psychiatric hospital but seem insane in it—not because craziness resides in them, as it were, but because they are responding to a bizarre setting, one that may be unique to institutions which harbor nether people? Goffman calls the process of socialization to such institutions "mortification"—an apt metaphor that includes the processes of depersonalization that have been described here. And while it is impossible to know whether the pseudopatients' responses to these processes are characteristic of all inmates—they were after all, not real patients—it is difficult to believe that these processes of socialization to a psychiatric hospital provide useful attitudes or habits of response for living in the "real world."

SUMMARY AND CONCLUSIONS

It is clear that we cannot distinguish the sane from the insane in psychiatric hospitals. The hospital itself imposes a special environment in which the meanings of behavior can easily be misunderstood. The consequences to patients hospitalized in such an environment—the powerlessness, depersonalization, segregation, mortification, and self-labeling—seem undoubtedly countertherapeutic.

I do not, even now, understand this problem well enough to perceive solutions. But two matters seem to have some promise. The first concerns the proliferation of community mental health facilities, of crisis intervention centers, of the human potential movement, and of behavior therapies that, for all of their own problems, tend to avoid psychiatric labels, to focus on specific problems and behaviors, and to retain the individual in a relatively nonpejorative environment. Clearly, to the extent that we refrain from sending the distressed to insane places, our impressions of them are less likely to be distorted. (The risk of distorted perceptions, it seems to me, is always present, since we are much more sensitive to an individual's behaviors and verbalizations than we are to the subtle contextual stimuli that often promote them. At issue here is a matter of magnitude. And, as I have shown, the magnitude of distortion is exceedingly high in the extreme context that is a psychiatric hospital).

The second matter that might prove promising speaks to the need to increase the sensitivity of mental health workers and researchers to the Catch-22 position of psychiatric patients. Simply reading materials in this area will be of help to some such workers and researchers. For others, directly experiencing the impact of psychiatric hospitalization will be of enormous use. Clearly, further research into the social psychology of such total institutions will both facilitate treatment and deepen understanding.

I and the other pseudopatients in the psychiatric setting had distinctly negative reactions. We do not pretend to describe the subjective experiences of true patients. Theirs may be different from ours, particularly with the passage of time and the necessary process of adaptation to one's environment. But we can and do speak to the relatively more objective indices of treatment within the hospital. It could be a mistake, and a very unfortunate one, to consider that what happened to us derived from malice or stupidity on the part of the staff. Quite the contrary, our overwhelming impression of them was of people who really cared, who were committed and who were uncommonly intelligent. Where they failed, as they sometimes did painfully, it would be more accurate to attribute those failures to the environment in which they too, found themselves than to personal callousness. Their perceptions and behavior were controlled by the situation, rather than being motivated by a malicious disposition. In a more benign environment, one that was less attached to global diagnosis, their behaviors and judgments might have been more benign and effective.

NO

Robert L. Spitzer

ON PSEUDOSCIENCE IN SCIENCE, LOGIC IN REMISSION AND PSYCHIATRIC DIAGNOSIS

Some foods taste delicious but leave a bad aftertaste. So it is with Rosenhan's study, "On Being Sane in Insane Places" (Rosenhan, 1973a), which, by virtue of the prestige and wide distribution of *Science*, the journal in which it appeared, provoked a furor in the scientific community. That the *Journal of Abnormal Psychology*, at this late date, chooses to explore the study's strengths and weaknesses is a testament not only to the importance of the issues that the study purports to deal with but to the impact that the study has had in the mental health community.

Rosenhan apparently believes that psychiatric diagnosis is of no value. There is nothing wrong with his designing a study the results of which might dramatically support this view. However, "On Being Sane in Insane Places" is pseudoscience presented as science. Just as his pseudopatients were diagnosed at discharge as "schizophrenia, in remission," so a careful examination of this study's methods, results, and conclusions leads me to a diagnosis of "logic, in remission."

Let us summarize the study's central question, the methods used, the results reported, and Rosenhan's conclusions. Rosenhan (1973a) states the basic issue simply: "Do the salient characteristics that lead to diagnoses reside in the patients themselves or in the environments and contexts in which observers find them?" Rosenhan proposed that by getting normal people who had never had symptoms of serious psychiatric disorders admitted to psychiatric hospitals "and then determining whether they were discovered to be sane" was an adequate method of studying this question. Therefore, eight "sane" people, pseudopatients, gained secret admission to 12 different hospitals with a single complaint of hearing voices. Upon admission to the psychiatric ward, the pseudopatients ceased simulating any symptoms of abnormality.

From Robert L. Spitzer, "On Pseudoscience in Science, Logic in Remission and Psychiatric Diagnosis: A Critique of 'On Being Sane in Insane Places,' " *Journal of Abnormal Psychology*, vol. 84 (1975). Copyright © 1975 by the American Psychological Association. Reprinted by permission.

The diagnostic results were that 11 of the 12 diagnoses on admission were schizophrenia and 1 was manic-depressive psychosis. At discharge, all of the patients were given the same diagnosis, but were qualified as "in remission."[1] Despite their "show of sanity" the pseudopatients were never detected by any of the professional staff, nor were any questions raised about their authenticity during the entire hospitalization. Rosenhan (1973a) concluded: "It is clear that we cannot distinguish the sane from the insane in psychiatric hospitals" (p. 257). According to him, what is needed is the avoidance of "global diagnosis," as exemplified by such diagnoses as schizophrenia or manic-depressive psychosis, and attention should be directed instead to "behaviors, the stimuli that provoke them, and their correlates."

THE CENTRAL QUESTION

One hardly knows where to begin. Let us first acknowledge the potential importance of the study's central research question. Surely, if psychiatric diagnoses are, to quote Rosenhan, "only in the minds of the observers," and do not reflect any characteristics inherent in the patient, then they obviously can be of no use in helping patients. However, the study immediately becomes confused when Rosenhan suggests that this research question can be answered by studying whether or not the "sanity" of pseudopatients in a mental hospital can be discovered. Rosenhan, a professor of law and psychology, knows that the terms "sane" and "insane" are legal, not psychiatric, concepts. He knows that no psychiatrist makes a diagnosis of "sanity" or "insanity" and that the true meaning of these terms, which varies from state to state, involves the inability to appreciate right from wrong—an issue that is totally irrelevant to this study.

DETECTING THE SANITY OF A PSEUDOPATIENT

However, if we are forced to use the terms "insane" (to mean roughly showing signs of serious mental disturbance) and "sane" (the absence of such signs), then clearly there are three possible meanings to the concept of "detecting the sanity" of a pseudopatient who feigns mental illness on entry to a hospital, but then acts "normal" throughout his hospital stay. The first is the recognition, when he is first seen, that the pseudopatient is feigning insanity as he attempts to gain admission to the hospital. This would be detecting sanity in a sane person simulating insanity. The second would be the recognition, after having observed him acting normally during his hospitalization, that the pseudopatient was initially feigning insanity. This would be detecting that the currently sane never was insane. Finally, the third possible meaning would be the recognition, during hospitalization, that the pseudopatient, though initially appearing to be "insane," was no longer showing signs of psychiatric disturbance.

These elementary distinctions of "detecting sanity in the insane" are crucial to properly interpreting the results of the study. The reader is misled by Rosenhan's implication that the first two meanings of detecting the sanity of the pseudopatient to be a fraud, are at all relevant to the central research question. Furthermore, he obscures the true results of his study—because they fail to support his conclusion—when the third meaning of detecting sanity is considered, that is, a recognition that after their admission as "insane," the pseudopatients were not psychiatrically disturbed while in the hospital.

Let us examine these three possible meanings of detecting the sanity of the pseudopatient, their logical relation to the central question of the study, and the actual results obtained and the validity of Rosenhan's conclusions.

THE PATIENT
IS NO LONGER "INSANE"

We begin with the third meaning of detecting sanity. It is obvious that if the psychiatrists judged the pseudopatients as seriously disturbed while they acted "normal" in the hospital, this would be strong evidence that their assessments were being influenced by the context in which they were making their examination rather than the actual behavior of the patient, which is the central research question. (I suspect that many readers will agree with Hunter who, in a letter to *Science* (Hunter, 1973), pointed out that, "The pseudopatients did *not* behave normally in the hospital. Had their behavior been normal, they would have walked to the nurses' station and said, 'Look, I am a normal person who tried to see if I could get into the hospital by behaving in a crazy way or saying crazy things. It worked and I was admitted to the hospital, but now I would like to be discharged from the hospital' " [p. 361].)

What were the results? According to Rosenhan, all the patients were diagnosed at discharge as "in remission."[2] The meaning of "in remission" is clear: It means without signs of illness. Thus, all of the psychiatrists apparently recognized that all of the pseudopatients were, to use Rosenhan's term, "sane." How-

ever, lest the reader appreciate the significance of these findings, Rosenhan (1973a) quickly gives a completely incorrect interpretation: "If the pseudopatient was to be discharged, he must naturally be 'in remission'; but he was not sane, nor, in the institution's view, had he ever been sane" (p. 252). Rosenhan's implication is clear: The patient was diagnosed "in remission" not because the psychiatrist correctly assessed the patient's hospital behavior but only because the patient had to be discharged. Is this interpretation warranted?

I am sure that most readers who are not familiar with the details of psychiatric diagnostic practice assume, from Rosenhan's account, that it is common for schizophrenic patients to be diagnosed "in remission" when discharged from a hospital. As a matter of fact, it is extremely unusual. The reason is that a schizophrenic is rarely completely asymptomatic at discharge. Rosenhan does not report any data concerning the discharge diagnoses of the real schizophrenic patients in the 12 hospitals used in his study. However, I can report on the frequency of a discharge diagnosis of schizophrenia "in remission" at my hospital, the New York State Psychiatric Institute, a research, teaching, and community hospital where diagnoses are made in a routine fashion, undoubtedly no different from the 12 hospitals of Rosenhan's study. I examined the official book that the record room uses to record the discharge diagnoses and their statistical codes for all patients. Of the over 300 patients discharged in the last year with a diagnosis of schizophrenia, not one was diagnosed "in remission." It is only possible to code a diagnosis of "in remission" by adding a fifth digit (5) to the 4-digit code number for the subtype of schizophrenia (e.g., paranoid schizophrenia is coded as 295.3, but paranoid schizophrenia "in remission" is coded as 295.35). I therefore realized that a psychiatrist might intend to make a discharge diagnosis of "in remission" but fail to use the fifth digit, so that the official recording of the diagnosis would not reflect his full assessment. I therefore had research assistants read the discharge summaries of the last 100 patients whose discharge diagnosis was schizophrenia to see how often the term "in remission," "recovered," "no longer ill," or "asymptomatic" was used, even if not recorded by use of the fifth digit in the code number. The result was that only one patient, who was diagnosed paranoid schizophrenia, was described in the summary as being "in remission" at discharge. The fifth digit code was not used.

To substantiate my view that the practice at my hospital of rarely giving a discharge diagnosis of schizophrenia "in remission" is not unique, I had a research assistant call the record room librarians of 12 psychiatric hospitals, chosen catch as catch can.[3] They were told that we were interested in knowing their estimate of how often, at their hospital, schizophrenics were discharged "in remission" (or "no longer ill" or "asymptomatic"). The calls revealed that 11 of the 12 hospitals indicated that the term was either never used or, at most, used for only a handful of patients in a year. The remaining hospital, a private hospital, estimated that the terms were used in roughly 7 percent of the discharge diagnoses.

This leaves us with the conclusion that, because 11 of the 12 pseudopatients were discharged as "schizophrenia in remission," a discharge diagnosis that is rarely given to real schizophrenics, the diagnoses given to the pseudopatients

were a function of the patients' behaviors and not of the setting (psychiatric hospital) in which the diagnoses were made. In fact, we must marvel that 11 psychiatrists all acted so rationally as to use at discharge the category of "in remission" or its equivalent, a category that is rarely used with real schizophrenic patients.

It is not only in his discharge diagnosis that the psychiatrist had an opportunity to assess the patient's true condition incorrectly. In the admission mental status examination, during a progress note or in his discharge note the psychiatrist could have described any of the pseudopatients as "still psychotic," "probably still hallucinating but denies it now," "loose associations," or "inappropriate affect." Because Rosenhan had access to all of this material, his failure to report such judgments of continuing serious psychopathology strongly suggests that they were never made.

All pseudopatients took extensive notes publicly to obtain data on staff and patient behavior. Rosenhan claims that the nursing records indicate that "the writing was seen as an aspect of their pathological behavior." The only datum presented to support this claim is that the daily nursing comment on one of the pseudopatients was, "Patient engaged in writing behavior." Because nursing notes frequently and intentionally comment on nonpathological activities that patients engage in so that other staff members have some knowledge of how the patient spends his time, this particular nursing note in no way supports Rosenhan's thesis. Once again, the failure of Rosenhan to provide data regarding instances where normal hospital behavior was categorized as pathological is remarkable. The closest that Rosenhan comes to providing such data is his report of an instance where a kindly nurse asked if a pseudopatient, who was pacing the long hospital corridors because of boredom, was "nervous." It was, after all, a question and not a final judgment.

Let us now examine the relation between the other two meanings of detecting sanity in the pseudopatients: the recognition that the pseudopatient was a fraud, either when he sought admission to the hospital or during this hospital stay, and the central research question.

DETECTING "SANITY" BEFORE ADMISSION

Whether or not psychiatrists are able to detect individuals who feign psychiatric symptoms is an interesting question but clearly of no relevance to the issue of whether or not the salient characteristics that lead to diagnoses reside in the patient's behavior or in the minds of the observers. After all, a psychiatrist who believes in a pseudopatient who feigns a symptom *is* responding to the pseudopatient's behavior. And Rosenhan does not blame the psychiatrist for believing the pseudopatient's fake symptom of hallucinations. He blames him for the diagnosis of schizophrenia. Rosenhan (1973b) states:

> The issue is not that the psychiatrist believed him. Neither is it whether the pseudopatient should have been admitted to the psychiatric hospital in the first place. . . . The issue is the diagnostic leap that was made between the single presenting symptom, hallucinations, and the diagnosis schizophrenia (or in one case, manic-depressive psychosis). Had the pseudopatients been diagnosed "hallucinating," there would have been no further need to examine the diagnosis issue. The diagnosis of hallucinations implies only that: no

more. The presence of hallucinations does not itself define the presence of "schizophrenia." And schizophrenia may or may not include hallucinations. (p. 366)

Unfortunately, as judged by many of the letters to *Science* commenting on the study (Letters to the editor, 1973), many readers, including psychiatrists, accepted Rosenhan's thesis that it was irrational for the psychiatrists to have made an initial diagnosis of schizophrenia as *the most likely condition* on the basis of a single symptom. In my judgment, these readers were wrong. Their acceptance of Rosenhan's thesis was aided by the content of the pseudopatients' auditory hallucinations, which were voices that said "empty," "hollow," and "thud." According to Rosenhan (1973a), these symptoms were chosen because of "their apparent similarity to existential symptoms [and] the *absence* of a single report of existential psychoses in the literature" (p. 251). The implication is that if the content of specific symptoms has never been reported in the literature, then a psychiatrist should somehow know that the symptom is fake. Why then, according to Rosenhan, should the psychiatrist have made a diagnosis of hallucinating? This is absurd. Recently I saw a patient who kept hearing a voice that said, "It's O.K. It's O.K." I know of no such report in the literature. So what? I agree with Rosenhan that there has never been a report of an "existential psychosis." However, the diagnoses made were schizophrenia and manic-depressive psychosis, not existential psychosis.

DIFFERENTIAL DIAGNOSIS OF AUDITORY HALLUCINATIONS

Rosenhan is entitled to believe that psychiatric diagnoses are of no use and therefore should not have been given to the pseudopatients. However, it makes no sense for him to claim that within a diagnostic framework it was irrational to consider schizophrenia seriously as the most likely condition without his presenting a consideration of the differential diagnosis. Let me briefly give what I think is a reasonable differential diagnosis, based on the presenting picture of the pseudopatient when he applied for admission to the hospital.

Rosenhan says that "beyond alleging the symptoms and falsifying name, vocation, and employment, no further alterations of person, history, or circumstances were made" (p. 251). However, clearly the clinical picture includes not only the symptom (auditory hallucinations) but also the desire to enter a psychiatric hospital, from which it is reasonable to conclude that the symptom is a source of significant distress. (How often did the admitting psychiatrist suggest what would seem to be reasonable care: outpatient treatment? Did the pseudopatient have to add other complaints to justify inpatient treatment?) This, plus the knowledge that the auditory hallucinations are of 3 weeks duration,[4] establishes the hallucinations as significant symptoms of psychopathology as distinguished from so-called "pseudohallucinations" (hallucinations while falling asleep or awakening from sleep, or intense imagination with the voice heard from inside of the head).

Auditory hallucinations can occur in several kinds of mental disorders. The absence of a history of alcohol, drug abuse, or some other toxin, the absence of any signs of physical illness (such as high fever), and the absence of evidence of distractibility, impairment in concen-

tration, memory or orientation, and a negative neurological examination all make an organic psychosis extremely unlikely. The absence of a recent precipitating stress rules out a transient situational disturbance of psychotic intensity or (to use a nonofficial category) hysterical psychosis. The absence of a profound disturbance in mood rules out an effective psychosis (we are not given the mental status findings for the patient who was diagnosed manic-depressive psychosis).

What about simulating mental illness? Psychiatrists know that occasionally an individual who has something to gain from being admitted to a psychiatric hospital will exaggerate or even feign psychiatric symptoms. This is a genuine diagnostic problem that psychiatrists and other physicians occasionally confront and is called "malingering." However, with the pseudopatients there was no reason to believe that any of them had anything to gain from being admitted into a psychiatric hospital except relief from their alleged complaint, and therefore no reason to suspect that the illness was feigned. Dear Reader: There is only one remaining diagnosis for the presenting symptom of hallucinations under these conditions in the classification of mental disorders used in this country, and that is schizophrenia.

Admittedly, there is a hitch to a definitive diagnosis of schizophrenia: Almost invariably there are other signs of the disorder present, such as poor premorbid adjustment, affective blunting, delusions, or signs of thought disorder. I would hope that if I had been one of the 12 psychiatrists presented with such a patient, I would have been struck by the lack of other signs of the disorder, but I am rather sure that having no reason to doubt the authenticity of the patients' claim of auditory hallucinations, I also would have been fooled into noting schizophrenia as the most likely diagnosis.

What does Rosenhan really mean when he objects to the diagnosis of schizophrenia because it was based on a "single symptom"? Does he believe that there are real patients with the single symptom of auditory hallucinations who are misdiagnosed as schizophrenic when they actually have some other condition? If so, what is the nature of that condition? Is Rosenhan's point that the psychiatrist should have used "diagnosis deferred," a category that is available but rarely used? I would have no argument with this conclusion. Furthermore, if he had presented data from real patients indicating how often patients are erroneously diagnosed on the basis of inadequate information and what the consequences were, it would have been a real contribution.

Until now, I have assumed that the pseudopatients presented only one symptom of psychiatric disorder. Actually, we know very little about how the pseudopatients presented themselves. What did the pseudopatients say in the study reported in *Science*, when asked as they must have been, what effect the hallucinations were having on their lives and why they were seeking admission into a hospital? The reader would be much more confident that a single presenting symptom was involved if Rosenhan had made available for each pseudopatient the actual admission work-up from the hospital record.

DETECTING SANITY
AFTER ADMISSION

Let us now examine the last meaning of detecting sanity in the pseudopatients,

namely, the psychiatrist's recognition, *after observing him act normally during* his hospitalization, that the pseudopatient was initially feigning insanity and its relation to the central research question. If a diagnostic condition, by definition, is always chronic and never remits, it would be irrational not to question the original diagnosis if a patient were later found to be asymptomatic. As applied to this study, if the concept of schizophrenia did not admit the possibility of recovery, then failure to question the original diagnosis when the pseudopatients were no longer overtly ill would be relevant to the central research question. It would be an example of the psychiatrist allowing the context of the hospital environment to influence his diagnostic behavior. But neither any psychiatric textbook nor the American Psychiatric Association's *Diagnostic and Statistical Manual of Mental Disorders* (American Psychiatric Association, 1968) suggests that mental illnesses endure forever. Oddly enough, it is Rosenhan (1973a) who, without any reference to the psychiatric literature, says: "A broken leg is something one recovers from, but mental illness allegedly endures forever" (p. 254). Who, other than Rosenhan, alleges it?

As Rosenhan should know, although some American psychiatrists restrict the label of schizophrenia to mean chronic or process schizophrenia, most American psychiatrists include an acute subtype. Thus, the *Diagnostic and Statistical Manual*, in describing the subtype, acute schizophrenic episode, states that "in many cases the patient recovers within weeks."

A similar straw man is created when Rosenhan (1973a) says,

The insane are not always insane . . . the bizarre behaviors upon which their (the pseudopatients) behaviors were allegedly predicated constituted only a small fraction of their total behavior. If it makes no sense to label ourselves permanently depressed on the basis of an occasional depression, then it takes better evidence than is presently available to label all patients insane or schizophrenic on the basis of behaviors or cognitions. (p. 254)

Who ever said that the behaviors that indicate schizophrenia or any other diagnostic category comprise the total of a patient's behavior? A diagnosis of schizophrenia does not mean that all of the patient's behavior is schizophrenic anymore than a diagnosis of carcinoma of the liver means that all of the patient's body is diseased.

Does Rosenhan at least score a point by demonstrating that, although the professional staff never considered the possibility that the pseudopatient was a fraud, this possibility was often considered by other patients? Perhaps, but I am not so sure. Let us not forget that all of the pseudopatients "took extensive notes publicly." Obviously this was highly unusual patient behavior and Rosenhan's quote from a suspicious patient suggests the importance it had in focusing the other patients' attention on the pseudopatients: "You're not crazy. You're a journalist or a professor (referring to the continual note-taking). You're checking up on the hospital." (Rosenhan, 1973a, p. 252)

Rosenhan presents ample evidence, which I find no reason to dispute, that the professional staff spent little time actually with the pseudopatients. The note-taking may easily have been overlooked, and therefore they developed no

suspicion that the pseudopatients had simulated illness to gain entry into the hospital. Because there were no pseudopatients who did not engage in such unusual behaviors, the reader cannot assess the significance of the patients' suspicions of fraud when the professional staff did not. I would predict, however, that a pseudopatient in a ward of patients with mixed diagnostic conditions would have no difficulty in masquerading convincingly as a true patient to both staff and patients if he did nothing unusual to draw attention to himself.

Rosenhan presents one way in which the diagnosis affected the psychiatrist's perception of the patient's circumstances: Historical facts of the case were often distorted by the staff to achieve consistency with psychodynamic theories. Here, for the first time, I believe Rosenhan has hit the mark. What he described happens all the time and often makes attendance at clinical case conferences extremely painful, especially for those with a logical mind and a research orientation. Although his observation is correct, it would seem to be more a consequence of individuals attempting to rearrange facts to comply with an unproven etiological theory than a consequence of diagnostic labeling. One could as easily imagine a similar process occurring when a weakminded, behaviorally-oriented clinician attempts to rewrite the patient's history to account for "hallucinations reinforced by attention paid to patient by family members when patient complains of hearing voices." Such is the human condition.

One final finding requires comment. In order to determine whether "the tendency toward diagnosing the sane insane could be reversed," the staff of a research and teaching hospital was informed that at some time during the following three months, one or more pseudopatients would attempt to be admitted. No such attempt was actually made. Yet approximately 10 percent of the 193 real patients were suspected by two or more staff members (we are not told how many made judgments) to be pseudopatients. Rosenhan (1973a) concluded: "Any diagnostic process that lends itself so readily to massive errors of this sort cannot be a very reliable one" (p. 179). My conclusion is that this experimental design practically assures only one outcome.

ELEMENTARY PRINCIPLES OF RELIABILITY OF CLASSIFICATION

Some very important principles that are relevant to the design of Rosenhan's study are taught in elementary psychology courses and should not be forgotten. One of them is that a measurement or classification procedure is not reliable or unreliable in itself but only in its application to a specific population. There are serious problems in the reliability of psychiatric diagnosis as it is applied to the population to which psychiatric diagnoses are ordinarily given. However, I fail to see, and Rosenhan does not even attempt to show, how the reliability of psychiatric diagnoses applied to a population of pseudopatients (or one including the threat of pseudopatients). The two populations are just not the same. Kety (1974) has expressed it dramatically:

> If I were to drink a quart of blood and, concealing what I had done, come to the emergency room of any hospital vomiting blood, the behavior of the staff would be quite predictable. If they labeled and treated me as having a bleeding peptic ulcer, I doubt that I could argue convincingly that medical

science does not know how to diagnose that condition. (p. 959)

(I have no doubt that if the condition known as pseudopatient ever assumed epidemic proportions among admittants to psychiatric hospitals, psychiatrists would in time become adept at identifying them, though at what risk to real patients, I do not know.)

ATTITUDES TOWARD THE INSANE

I shall not dwell on the latter part of Rosenhan's study, which deals with the experience of psychiatric hospitalization. Because some of the hospitals participated in residency training programs and were research oriented, I find it hard to believe that conditions were quite as bad as depicted, but they may well be. I have always believed that psychiatrists should spend more time on psychiatric wards to appreciate how mind dulling the experience must be for patients. However, Rosenhan does not stop at documenting the horrors of life on a psychiatric ward. He asserts, without a shred of evidence from his study, that "negative attitudes [toward psychiatric patients] are the natural offspring of the labels patients wear and the places in which they are found." This is nonsense. In recent years large numbers of chronic psychiatric patients, many of them chronic schizophrenics and geriatric patients with organic brain syndromes, have been discharged from state hospitals and placed in communities that have no facilities to deal with them. The affected communities are up in arms not primarily because they are mental patients labeled with psychiatric diagnoses (because the majority are not recognized as ex-patients) but because the behavior of some of them is sometimes incomprehensible, deviant, strange, and annoying.

There are at least two psychiatric diagnoses that are defined by the presence of single behaviors, much as Rosenhan would prefer a diagnosis of hallucinations to a diagnosis of schizophrenia. They are alcoholism and drug abuse. Does society have negative attitudes toward these individuals because of the diagnostic label attached to them by psychiatrists or because of their behavior?

THE USES OF DIAGNOSIS

Rosenhan believes that the pseudopatients should have been diagnosed as having hallucinations of unknown origin. It is not clear what he thinks the diagnosis should have been if the pseudopatients had been sufficiently trained to talk, at times, incoherently, and had complained of difficulty in thinking clearly, lack of emotion, and that their thoughts were being broadcast so that strangers knew what they were thinking. Is Rosenhan perhaps suggesting multiple diagnoses of (a) hallucinations, (b) difficulty thinking clearly, (c) lack of emotion, and (d) incoherent speech . . . all of unknown origin?

It is no secret that we lack a full understanding of such conditions as schizophrenia and manic-depressive illness, but are we quite as ignorant as Rosenhan would have us believe? Do we not know, for example, that hallucinations of voices accusing the patient of sin are associated with depressed affect, diurnal mood variation, loss of appetite, and insomnia? What about hallucinations of God's voice issuing commandments, associated with

euphoric affect, psychomotor excitement, and accelerated and disconnected speech? Is this not also an entirely different condition?

There is a purpose to psychiatric diagnosis (Spitzer & Wilson, 1975). It is to enable mental health professionals to (a) communicate with each other about the subject matter of their concern, (b) comprehend the pathological processes involved in psychiatric illness, and (c) control psychiatric disorders. Control consists of the ability to predict outcome, prevent the disorder from developing, and treat it once it has developed. Any serious discussion of the validity of psychiatric diagnosis, or suggestions for alternative systems of classifying psychological disturbance, must address itself to these purposes of psychiatric diagnosis.

In terms of its ability to accomplish these purposes, I would say that psychiatric diagnosis is moderately effective as a shorthand way of communicating the presence of constellations of signs and symptoms that tend to cluster together, is woefully inadequate in helping us understand the pathological processes of psychiatric disorders, but does offer considerable help in the control of many mental disorders. Control is possible because psychiatric diagnosis often yields information of value in predicting the likely course of illness (e.g., an early recovery, chronicity, or recurrent episodes) and because for many mental disorders it is useful in suggesting the best available treatment.

Let us return to the three different clinical conditions that I described, each of which had auditory hallucinations as one of its manifestations. The reader will have no difficulty in identifying the three hypothetical conditions as schizophrenia, psychotic depression, and mania. Anyone familiar with the literature on psychiatric treatment will know that there are numerous well-controlled studies (Klein & Davis, 1969) indicating the superiority of the major tranquilizers for the treatment of schizophrenia, of electroconvulsive therapy for the treatment of psychotic depression and, more recently, of lithium carbonate for the treatment of mania. Furthermore, there is convincing evidence that these three conditions, each of which is often accompanied by hallucinations, are influenced by separate genetic factors. As Kety (1974) said, "If schizophrenia is a myth, it is a myth with a strong genetic component."

Should psychiatric diagnosis be abandoned for a purely descriptive system that focuses on simple phenotypic behaviors before it has been demonstrated that such an approach is more useful as a guide to successful treatment or for understanding the role of genetic factors? I think not. (I have a vision. Traditional psychiatric diagnosis has long been forgotten. At a conference on behavioral classification, a keen research investigator proposes that the category "hallucinations of unknown etiology" be subdivided into three different groups based on associated symptomatology. The first group is characterized by depressed affect, diurnal mood variation, and so on, the second group by euphoric mood, psychomotor excitement. . . .)

If psychiatric diagnosis is not quite as bad as Rosenhan would have us believe, that does not mean that it is all that good. What is the reliability of psychiatric diagnosis prior to 1972 (Spitzer & Fleiss, 1974) revealed that "reliability is only satisfactory for three categories: mental deficiencies, organic brain syndrome, and alcoholism. The level of reliability is no better than fair for psychosis and schizo-

phrenia, and is poor for the remaining categories." So be it. But where did Rosenhan get the idea that psychiatry is the only medical specialty that is plagued by inaccurate diagnosis? Studies have shown serious unreliability in the diagnosis of pulmonary disorders (Fletcher, 1952), in the interpretation of electrocardiograms (Davis, 1958), in the interpretation of X-rays (Cochrane & Garland, 1952; Yerushalmy, 1947), and in the certification of causes of death (Markush, Schaaf, & Siegel, 1967). A review of diagnostic unreliability in other branches of physical medicine is given by Garland (1960) and the problem of the vagueness of medical criteria for diagnosis is thoroughly discussed by Feinstein (1967). The poor reliability of medical diagnosis, even when assisted by objective laboratory tests, does not mean that medical diagnosis is of no value. So it is with psychiatric diagnosis.

Recognition of the serious problems of the reliability of psychiatric diagnosis has resulted in a new approach to psychiatric diagnosis—the use of specific inclusion and exclusion criteria, as contrasted with the usually vague and ill-defined general descriptions found in the psychiatric literature and in the standard psychiatric glossary of the American Psychiatric Association. This approach was started by the St. Louis group associated with the Department of Psychiatry of Washington University (Feighner, Robins, Guze, Woodruff, Winokur, & Munoz, 1972) and has been further developed by Spitzer, Endicott, and Robins (1974) as a set of criteria for a selected group of functional psychiatric disorders, called the Research Diagnostic Criteria (RDC). The Display shows the specific criteria for a diagnosis of schizophrenia from the latest version of the RDC.[5]

DIAGNOSTIC CRITERIA FOR SCHIZOPHRENIA FROM THE RESEARCH DIAGNOSTIC CRITERIA

1. At least two of the following are required for definite diagnosis and one for probable diagnosis:
   a. Thought broadcasting, insertion, or withdrawal (as defined in the RDC).
   b. Delusions of control, other bizarre delusions, or multiple delusions (as defined in the RDC), of any duration as long as definitely present.
   c. Delusions other than persecutory or jealousy, lasting at least 1 week.
   d. Delusions of any type if accompanied by hallucinations of any type for at least 1 week.
   e. Auditory hallucinations in which either a voice keeps up a running commentary on the patient's behaviors or thoughts as they occur, or two or more voices converse with each other (of any duration as long as definitely present).
   f. Nonaffective verbal hallucinations spoken to the subject (as defined in this manual).
   g. Hallucinations of any type throughout the day for several days or intermittently for at least 1 month.
   h. Definite instances of formal thought disorder (as defined in the RDC).
   i. Obvious catatonic motor behavior (as defined in the RDC).

2. A period of illness lasting at least 2 weeks.

3. At no time during the active period of illness being considered did the patient meet the criteria for either probable or definite manic or depressive syndrome (Criteria 1 and 2 under Major Depressive or Manic Disorders) to such a degree that it was a prominent part of the illness.

Reliability studies using the RDC with case record material (from which all cues as to diagnosis and treatment were removed), as well as with live patients, indicate high reliability for all of the major categories and reliability coefficients generally higher than have ever been reported (Spitzer, Endicott, Robins, Kuriansky, & Garland, in press). It is therefore clear that the reliability of psychiatric diagnosis can be greatly increased by the use of specific criteria. (The interjudge reliability [chance corrected agreement, K] for the diagnosis of schizophrenia using an earlier version of RDC criteria with 68 newly admitted psychiatric inpatients at the New York State Psychiatric Institute was .88, which is a thoroughly respectable level of reliability). It is very likely that the next edition of the American Psychiatric Association's *Diagnostic and Statistical Manual* will contain similar specific criteria.

There are other problems with current psychiatric diagnosis. The recent controversy over whether or not homosexuality per se should be considered a mental disorder highlighted the lack of agreement within the psychiatric profession as to the definition of a mental disorder. A definition has been proposed by Spitzer (Spitzer & Wilson, 1975), but it is not at all clear whether a consensus will develop supporting it.

There are serious problems of validity. Many of the traditional diagnostic categories, such as some of the subtypes of schizophrenia and of major affective illness, and several of the personality disorders, have not been demonstrated to be distinct entities or to be useful for prognosis or treatment assignment. In addition, despite considerable evidence supporting the distinctness of such conditions as schizophrenia and manic-depressive illness, the boundaries separating these conditions from other conditions are certainly not clear. Finally, the categories of the traditional psychiatric nomenclature are of least value when applied to the large numbers of outpatients who are not seriously ill. It is for these patients that a more behaviorally or problem-oriented approach might be particularly useful.

I have not dealt at all with the myriad ways in which psychiatric diagnostic labels can be, and are, misused to hurt patients rather than to help them. This is a problem requiring serious research which, unfortunately, Rosenhan's study does not help illuminate. However, whatever the solutions to that problem the misuse of psychiatric diagnostic labels is not a sufficient reason to abandon their use because they have been shown to be of value when properly used.

In conclusion, there are serious problems with psychiatric diagnosis, as there are with other medical diagnoses. Recent developments indicate that the reliability of psychiatric diagnosis can be considerably improved. However, *even with the poor reliability of current psychiatric diagnosis, it is not so poor that it cannot be an aid in the treatment of the seriously disturbed psychiatric patient.* Rosenhan's study, "On Being Sane in Insane Places," proves that pseudopatients are not detected by psychiatrists as having simulated signs of mental illness. This rather remarkable finding is not relevant to the real problems of the reliability and validity of psychiatric diagnosis and only serves to obscure them. A correct interpretation of his own data contradicts his conclusions. In the setting of a psychiatric hospital, psychiatrists are remarkably able to distinguish the "sane" from the "insane."

NOTES

1. The original article only mentions that the 11 schizophrenics were diagnosed "in remission." Personal communication from D. L. Rosenhan indicates that this also applied to the single pseudopatient diagnosed as manic-depressive psychosis.

2. In personal communication D. L. Rosenhan said that "in remission" referred to a use of that term or one of its equivalents, such as recovered or no longer ill.

3. Rosenhan has not identified the hospitals used in this study because of his concern with issues of confidentiality and the potential for ad hominem attack. However, this does make it impossible for anyone at those hospitals to corroborate or challenge his account of how the pseudopatients acted and how they were perceived. The 12 hospitals used in my mini-study were: Long Island Jewish-Hillside Medical Center, New York; Massachusetts General Hospital, Massachusetts; St. Elizabeth's Hospital, Washington, D.C.; McLean Hospital, Massachusetts; UCLA, Neuropsychiatric Institute, California; Meyer-Manhattan Hospital (Manhattan State), New York; Vermont State Hospital, Vermont; Medical College of Virginia, Virginia; Emory University Hospital, Georgia; High Point Hospital, New York; Hudson River State Hospital, New York, and New York Hospital-Cornell Medical Center, Westchester Division, New York.

4. This was not in the article but was mentioned to me in personal communication by D. L. Rosenhan.

5. For what it is worth, the pseudopatient would have been diagnosed as "probable" schizophrenia using these criteria because of 1(f). In personal communication, Rosenhan said that when the pseudopatients were asked how frequently the hallucinations occurred, they said "I don't know." Therefore, Criterion 1(g) is not met.

REFERENCES

American Psychiatric Association. *Diagnostic and statistical manual of mental disorders* (2nd ed.). Washington, D.C.: American Psychiatric Association, 1968.

Cochrane, A. L., & Garland, L. H. Observer error in interpretation of chest films: International Investigation. *Lancet,* 1952, 2, 505–509.

Davies, L. G. Observer variation in reports on electrocardiograms. *British Heart Journal,* 1958, 20, 153–161.

Feighner, J. P., and Robins, E., Guze, S. B., Woodruff, R. A., Winokur, G., & Munoz, R. Diagnostic criteria for use in psychiatric research. *Archives of General Psychiatry*, 1972, 26, 57–63.

Feinstein, A. *Clinical judgment*. Baltimore, Md.: Williams & Wilkins, 1967.

Fletcher, C. M. Clinical diagnosis of pulmonary emphysema—an experimental study. *Proceedings of the Royal Society of Medicine*, 1952, 45, 577–584.

Garland, L. H. The problem of observer error. *Bulletin of the New York Academy of Medicine*, 1960, 36, 570–584.

Hunter, F. M. Letters to the editor. *Science*, 1973, 180, 361.

Kety, S. S. From rationalization to reason. *American Journal of Psychiatry*, 1974, 131, 957–963.

Klein, D., & Davis, J. *Diagnosis and drug treatment of psychiatric disorders*. Baltimore, Md.: Williams & Wilkins, 1969.

Letters to the editor. *Science*, 1973, 180, 356–365.

Markush, R. E., Schaaf, W. E., & Siegel, D. G. The influence of the death certifier on the results of epidemiologic studies. *Journal of the National Medical Association*, 1967, 59, 105–113.

Rosenhan, D. L. On being sane in insane places. *Science*, 1973, 179, 250–258. (a)

Rosenhan, D. L. Reply to letters to the editor. *Science*, 1973, 180, 365–369. (b)

Spitzer, R. L., Endicott, J., & Robins, E. *Research diagnostic criteria*. New York: Biometrics Research, New York State Department of Mental Hygiene, 1974.

Spitzer, R. L., Endicott, J., Robins, E., Kuriansky, J., & Garland, B. Preliminary report of the reliability of research diagnostic criteria applied to psychiatric case records. In A. Sudilofsky, B. Beer, & S. Gershon (Eds.), *Prediction in psychopharmacology*, New York: Raven Press, in press.

Spitzer, R. L. & Fleiss, J. L. A reanalysis of the reliability of psychiatric diagnosis. *British Journal of Psychiatry*, 1974. 125, 341–347.

Spitzer, R. L., & Wilson, P. T. Nosology and the official psychiatric nomenclature. In A. Freedman & H. Kaplan (Eds.), *Comprehensive textbook of psychiatry*. New York: Williams & Wilkins, 1975.

Yerushalmy, J. Statistical problems in assessing methods of medical diagnosis with special reference to X-ray techniques. *Public Health Reports*, 1947, 62, 1432–1449.

CHALLENGE QUESTIONS

Do Diagnostic Labels Hinder the Effective Treatment of Persons With Mental Disorders?

1. Would society be better off if there were no names (such as "normal" or "abnormal") for broad categories of behavior?

2. Who would you consider best qualified to judge a person's mental health: a parent, a judge, or a doctor? Why?

3. If a person at any time displays symptoms of a mental disorder, even fraudulently, is it helpful to consider that the same symptoms of disorder may appear again?

4. Is there any danger in teaching the diagnostic categories of mental behavior to beginning students of psychology?

ISSUE 16

Should Psychotherapy Include Religious Values?

YES: Allen E. Bergin, from "Psychotherapy and Religious Values," *Journal of Consulting and Clinical Psychology* (vol. 48, no. 1, 1980)

NO: Albert Ellis, from "Psychotherapy and Atheistic Values: A Response to A. E. Bergin's 'Psychotherapy and Religious Values,' " *Journal of Consulting and Clinical Psychology* (vol. 48, no. 5, 1980)

ISSUE SUMMARY

YES: Clinical psychologist and researcher Allen E. Bergin advocates injecting theistic religious values into the psychotherapeutic context.
NO: Albert Ellis, president of the Institute for Rational-Emotive Therapy, feels that extreme religiosity leads to emotional disturbance, and he advances values that are based upon a humanistic-atheistic system of beliefs.

Many people think of psychotherapy as a value-free enterprise. The therapist is viewed either as a disinterested problem-solver or a facilitator of the patient's own values. The problem with this concept is that it underestimates the complexity and humanness of the therapeutic endeavor.

Values of all sorts are indeed part of the therapeutic process. Psychotherapists establish standards for good or right living, and they occupy a position in our culture not unlike that of ministers or priests. One danger with this situation, of course, it that the psychotherapist could, knowingly or unknowingly, become the purveyor of unethical or subversive values. It is therefore vital that psychologists have some awareness of their values and that the consumers of therapy understand what values are being purveyed.

In a move intended to realize these goals, Allen E. Bergin attempts to reveal the main value systems of mainstream psychotherapists. He finds two broad classes of value frameworks, neither of which is religious in nature. In fact, both value systems clash with religious values in important ways. Bergin asks whether psychotherapists really wish to exclude Judeo-Christian values from their psychotherapies. His own answer as a therapist is a resounding "no." He proposes a spiritual and theistic alternative, which he believes would be a positive addition to the therapeutic endeavor. According to Bergin, this value system would better match those of the patients and still allow for scientific testing to determine its helpfulness in therapy.

Albert Ellis begins his article by agreeing with Bergin on the pervasiveness of values in psychotherapy. Ellis objects, however, to Bergin's characterization of the prominent value systems of psychotherapy. Ellis subscribes to a value system that Bergin does not discuss, but it is, according to Ellis, the value system of the majority of psychotherapists—"probabilistic atheism." He openly questions just how helpful religious values would be in therapy. In his view, the absolutistic thinking and devout beliefs of many religious people are signs of an underlying emotional disturbance. Moreover, Ellis feels that Bergin needs to acknowledge that "therapeutic solutions" are often "quite unreligious" in nature.

POINT	COUNTERPOINT
• There are currently two broad classes of values among psychotherapists.	• These two classes misrepresent or overlook a third class.
• A missing assumption in most therapeutic value systems is that God exists.	• People should be able to live their lives with the assumption that there is no God.
• Important knowledge can be attained through faith and spiritual insight.	• Knowledge can only be obtained through self-effort and the efforts of others.
• More religious values could possibly help many patients.	• Encouraging more religiosity could result in greater emotional disturbance.
• Therapists' values are often not in harmony with those of their patients.	• If patient values stem from devout religious values, then therapists should not hold such values.

YES
Allen E. Bergin

PSYCHOTHERAPY AND RELIGIOUS VALUES

The importance of values, particularly religious ones, has recently become a more salient issue in psychology. The pendulum is swinging away from the naturalism, agnosticism, and humanism that have dominated the field for most of this century. . . .

These shifting conceptual orientations are especially manifest in the field of psychotherapy, in which the value of therapy and the values that pervade its processes have become topics of scrutiny by both professionals (Lowe, 1976; Smith, Glass, & Miller, in press; Szasz, 1978) and the public (Gross, 1978).

In what follows, these issues are analyzed, as they pertain to spiritual values, in terms of six theses.

Thesis 1: Values are an inevitable and pervasive part of psychotherapy. As an applied field, psychotherapy is directed toward practical goals that are selected in value terms. It is even necessary when establishing criteria for measuring therapeutic change to decide, on a value basis, what changes are desirable. This necessarily requires a philosophy of human nature that guides the selection of measurements and the setting of priorities regarding change. Strupp, Hadley, and Gomes-Schwartz (1977) argued that there are at least three possibly divergent value systems at play in such decisions—those of the client, the clinician, and the community at large. They stated that though there is no consensus regarding conceptions of mental health, a judgment must always be made in relation to some implicit or explicit standard, which presupposes a definition of what is better or worse. They asked that we consider the following:

> If, following psychotherapy, a patient manifests increased self-assertion coupled with abrasiveness, is this good or a poor therapy outcome? . . . If . . . a patient obtains a divorce, is this to be regarded as a desirable or an undesirable change? A patient may turn from homosexuality to heterosexuality or he may become more accepting of either; an ambitious, striving person may abandon

previously valued goals and become more placid (e.g., in primal therapy). How are such changes to be evaluated? (Strupp et al., 1977, pp. 92–93)

Equally important is the fact that

in increasing number, patients enter psychotherapy not for the cure of traditional "symptoms" but (at least ostensibly) for the purpose of finding meaning in their lives, for actualizing themselves, or for maximizing their potential. (Strupp et al., 1977, p. 93)

Consequently, "every aspect of psychotherapy presupposes some implicit moral doctrine" (London, 1964, p. 6). Lowe's (1976) treatise on value orientations in counseling and psychotherapy reveals with painstaking clarity the philosophical choices on which the widely divergent approaches to intervention hinge. He argued cogently that everything from behavioral technology to community consultation is intricately interwoven with secularized moral systems, and he supported London's (1964) thesis that psychotherapists constitute a secular priesthood that purports to establish standards of good living.

Techniques are thus a means for mediating the value influence intended by the therapist. It is inevitable that the therapist be such a moral agent. The danger is in ignoring the reality that we do this, for then patient, therapist, and community neither agree on goals nor efficiently work toward them. A correlated danger is that therapists, as secular moralists, may promote changes not valued by the client or the community, and in this sense, if there is not some consensus and openness about what is being done, the therapists may be unethical or subversive.

The impossibility of a value-free therapy is demonstrated by certain data. I allude to just one of many illustrations that might be cited. Carl Rogers personally values the freedom of the individual and attempts to promote the free expression of each client. However, two independent studies done a decade apart (Murray, 1956; Truax, 1966) showed that Carl Rogers systematically rewarded and punished expressions that he liked and did not like in the verbal behavior of clients. His values significantly regulated the structure and content of therapeutic sessions as well as their outcomes (cf. Bergin, 1971). If a person who intends to be nondirective cannot be, then it is likely that the rest of us cannot either.

Similarly, when we do research with so-called objective criteria, we select them in terms of subjective value judgments, which is one reason we have so much difficulty in agreeing on the results of psychotherapy outcome studies. If neither practitioners nor researchers can be nondirective, then they must accept certain realities about the influence they have. A value-free approach is impossible.

Thesis 2: Not only do theories, techniques, and criteria reveal pervasive value judgments, but outcome data comparing the effects of diverse techniques show that nontechnical, value-laden factors pervade professional change processes. Comparative studies reveal few differences across techniques, thus suggesting that nontechnical or personal variables account for much of the change. Smith et al. (in press), in analyzing 475 outcome studies, were able to attribute only a small percentage of outcome variance to technique factors. Among these 475 studies were many that included supposedly technical behavior therapy procedures. The lack of technique differences thrusts value questions upon us because change appears to be a function of common human interactions, including personal and belief factors—the so-called nonspecific or common ingredients that cut across therapies and that may be the core of therapeutic change (Bergin & Lambert, 1978; Frank, 1961, 1973).

Thesis 3: Two broad classes of values are dominant in the mental health professions. Both exclude religious values, and both establish goals for change that frequently clash with theistic systems of belief. The first of these can be called clinical pragmatism. Clinical pragmatism is espoused particularly by psychiatrists, nurses, behavior therapists, and public agencies. It consists of straightforward implementation of the values of the dominant social system. In other words, the clinical operation functions within the system. It does not ordinarily question the system, but tries to make the system work. It is centered, then, on diminishing pathologies or disturbances, as defined by the clinician as an agent of the culture. This means adherence to such objectives as reducing anxiety, relieving depression, resolving guilt, suppressing deviation, controlling bizarreness, smoothing conflict, diluting obsessiveness, and so forth. The medical origins of this system are clear. It is pathology oriented. Health is defined as the absence of pathology. Pathology is that which disturbs the person or those in the environment. The clinician then forms an alliance with the person and society to eliminate the disturbing behavior.

The second major value system can be called humanistic idealism. It is espoused particularly by clinicians with interests in philosophy and social reform such as Erich Fromm, Carl Rogers, Rollo May and various group and community interventionists. Vaughan's (1971) study of this approach identified quantifiable themes that define the goals of positive change within this frame of reference.

They are flexibility and self-exploration; independence; active goal orientation with self-actualization as a core goal; human dignity and self-worth; interpersonal involvement; truth and honesty; happiness; and a frame of orientation or philosophy by which one guides one's life. This is different from clinical pragmatism in that it appeals to idealists, reformers, creative persons, and sophisticated clients who have significant ego strength. It is less practical, less conforming, and harder to measure than clinical pathology themes because it addresses more directly broad issues such as what is good and how life should be lived. It embraces a social value agenda and is often critical of traditional systems of religious values that influence child rearing, social standards, and ultimately, criteria of positive therapeutic change. Its influence is more prevalent in private therapy, universities, and independent clinical centers or research institutes, and among theologians and clinicians who espouse spiritual humanism (Fromm, 1950).

Though clinical pragmatism and humanistic idealism have appropriate places as guiding structures for clinical intervention and though I personally endorse much of their content, they are not sufficient to cover the spectrum of values pertinent to human beings and the frameworks within which they function. Noticeably absent are theistically based values.

Pragmatic and humanistic views manifest a relative indifference to God, the relationship of human beings to God, and the possibility that spiritual factors influence behavior. A survey of the leading reference sources in the clinical field reveals little literature on such subjects, except for naturalistic accounts. An examination of 30 introductory psychology texts turned up no references to the possible reality of spiritual factors. Most did not have the words *God* or *religion* in their indexes.

Psychological writers have a tendency to censor or taboo in a casual and sometimes arrogant way something that is sensitive and precious to most human beings (Campbell, 1975).

As Robert Hogan, new section editor of the *Journal of Personality and Social Psychology*, stated in a recent *APA Monitor* interview,

> Religion is the most important social force in the history of man. . . . But in psychology, anyone who gets involved in or tries to talk in an analytic, careful way about religion is immediately branded a meathead; a mystic; an intuitive, touchy-feely sort of moron. (Hogan, 1979, p. 4)

Clinical pragmatism and humanistic idealism thus exclude what is one of the largest sub-ideologies, namely, religious or theistic approaches espoused by people who believe in God and try to guide their behavior in terms of their perception of his will.

Other alternatives are thus needed. Just as psychotherapy has been enhanced by the adoption of multiple techniques, so also in the values realm, our frameworks can be improved by the use of additional perspectives.

The alternative I wish to put forward is a spiritual one. It might be called theistic realism. I propose to show that this alternative is necessary for ethical and effective help among religious people, who constitute 30% to 90% of the U.S. population (more than 90% expressed belief, while about 30% expressed strong conviction about their belief; American Institute of Public Opinion, 1978). I also argue

that the values on which this alternative is based are important ingredients in reforming and rejuvenating our society. Pragmatic and humanistic values alone, although they have substantial virtues, are often part of the problem of our deteriorating society.

What are the alternative values? The first and most important axiom is that God exists, that human beings are the creations of God, and that there are unseen spiritual processes by which the link between God and humanity is maintained. As stated in the Book of Job (32:8),

> There is a spirit in man and the inspiration of the Almighty giveth them understanding.

This approach, beginning with faith in God, assumes that spiritual conviction gives values an added power to influence life. . . .

[I]t is possible to draw contrasts between theistic and clinical humanistic values as they pertain to personality and change. These are my own constructions based on clinical and religious experience and are not intended to support organized religion in general. History demonstrates that religions and religious values can be destructive, just as psychotherapy can be if not properly practiced. I therefore am not endorsing all religion. I am simply extracting from religious traditions prominent themes I hypothesize may be positive additions to clinical thinking. These are depicted in Table 1 alongside the contrasting views.

It should be noted that the theistic values do not come ex nihilo [from nothing], but are consistent with a substantial psychological literature concerning responsibility (Glasser, 1965; Menninger, 1973), moral agency (Rychlak, 1979), guilt

Table 1

Theistic Versus Clinical and Humanistic Values

Theistic	Clinical-Humanistic
God is supreme. Humility, acceptance of (divine) authority, and obedience (to the will of God) are virtues.	Humans are supreme. The self is aggrandized. Autonomy and rejection of external authority are virtues.
Personal identity is eternal and derived from the divine. Relationship with God defines self-worth.	Identity is ephemeral and mortal. Relationships with others define self-worth.
Self-control in terms of absolute values. Strict morality. Universal ethics.	Self-expression in terms of relative values. Flexible morality. Situation ethics.
Love, affection, and self-transcendence are primary. Service and self-sacrifice are central to personal growth.	Personal needs and self-actualization are primary. Self-satisfaction is central to personal growth.
Committed to marriage, fidelity, and loyalty. Emphasis on procreation and family life as integrative factors.	Open marriage or no marriage. Emphasis on self-gratification or recreational sex without long-term responsibilities.
Personal responsibility for own harmful actions and changes in them. Acceptance of guilt, suffering, and contrition as keys to change. Restitution for harmful effects.	Others are responsible for our problems and changes. Minimizing guilt and relieving suffering before experiencing its meaning. Apology for harmful effects.
Forgiveness of others who cause distress (including parents) completes the therapeutic restoration of self.	Acceptance and expression of accusatory feelings are sufficient.
Knowledge by faith and self-effort. Meaning and purpose derived from spiritual insight. Intellectual knowledge inseparable from the emotional and spiritual. Ecology of knowledge.	Knowledge by self-effort alone. Meaning and purpose derived from reason and intellect. Intellectual knowledge for itself. Isolation of the mind from the rest of life.

(Mowrer, 1961, 1967), and self-transcendence (Frankl, Note 1).

The comparisons outlined in the table highlight differences for the sake of making the point. It is taken for granted, however, that there are also domains of significant agreement, such as many of the humanistic values outlined by Vaughan (1971) that are fundamental to personal growth. Fromm's brilliant essays on love (1956) and independence (1947), for example, illustrate value themes that must be given prominence in any comprehensive system. The point of difference is their relative position or emphasis in the values hierarchy. Mutual

commitment to fundamental human rights is also assumed, for example, to those rights pertaining to life, liberty, and the pursuit of happiness specified in the Declaration of Independence. Both theistic and atheistic totalitarianism deprive people of the basic freedoms necessary to fully implement any of the value systems outlined here; therefore, clinical humanists, pragmatists, and theists all reject coercion and value freedom of choice. This basic common premise is a uniting thesis. Without it, theories of mental health would have little meaning.

Substantial harmony can thus be achieved among the views outlined, but there is a tendency for clinical pragmatism and humanistic idealism to exclude the theistic position. On the other hand, religionists have tended to be unempirical and need to adopt the value of rigorous empiricism advocated by humanists and pragmatists. My view then would be to posit what each tradition can learn from the other rather than to create an artificial battle in which one side purports to win and the other to lose. Thus, the religion-based hypotheses stated later in Thesis 6 are an open invitation to think about and test these ideas.

Thesis 4: There is a significant contrast between the values of mental health professionals and those of a large proportion of clients. Whether or not one agrees with the values I have described above, one must admit that they are commonplace. Therapists therefore need to take into account possible discrepancies between their values and those of the average client. Four studies document this point. Lilienfeld (1966) found at the Metropolitan Hospital in New York City large discrepancies between the values of the mental health staff members and their clients, who were largely of Puerto Rican, Catholic background. With respect to topics like sex, aggression, and authority, the differences were dramatic. For example, in reply to one statement, "Some sex before marriage is good," all 19 mental health professionals agreed but only half the patients agreed. Vaughan (1971), in his study of various samples of patients, students, and professionals in the Philadelphia area, found discrepancies similar to those Lilienfeld obtained. Henry, Sims, and Spray (1971), in their study of several thousand psychotherapists in New York, Chicago, and Los Angeles, found the values of therapists to be religiously liberal relative to those of the population at large. Ragan, Malony, and Beit-Hallahmi (Note 2) reported that of a random sample of psychologists from the American Psychological Association, 50% believed in God. This is about 40% lower than the population at large, though higher than one would expect on the basis of the impression created in the literature and at convention presentations. This study also indicated that 10% of the psychologists held positions in their various congregations, which also indicates more involvement than is predictable from the public statements of psychologists. Nevertheless, the main findings show that the beliefs of mental health professionals are not very harmonious with those of the subcultures with which they deal, especially as they pertain to definitions of moral behavior and the relevance of moral behavior to societal integration, familial functioning, prevention of pathology, and development of the self.

Thesis 5: In light of the foregoing, it would be honest and ethical to acknowledge that we are implementing our own value systems via our professional work and to be more explicit about what we believe while also respecting the value systems of others. If values are pervasive, if our values tend to be on the whole discrepant from those of the community or the client population, it would be ethical to publicize where we stand. Then people would have a better choice of what they want to get into, and we would avoid deception.

Hans Strupp and I (Bergin & Strupp, 1972) had an interesting conversation with Carl Rogers on this subject in La Jolla a few years ago, in which Carl said,

Yes, it is true, psychotherapy is subversive. I don't really mean it to be, but some people get involved with me who don't know what they are getting into. Therapy theories and techniques promote a new model of man contrary to that which has been traditionally acceptable. (Paraphrase cited in Bergin & Strupp, 1972, pp. 318–319)

Sometimes, as professionals, we follow the leaders of our profession or our graduate professors in assuming that what we are doing is professional without recognizing that we are purveying under the guise of professionalism and science our own personal value systems (Smith, 1961), whether the system be psychodynamic, behavioral, humanistic, cognitive, or whatever.

During my graduate and postdoctoral training, I had the fortunate experience of working with several leaders in psychology, such as Albert Bandura, Carl Rogers, and Robert Sears. (Later, I had opportunities for substantial discussions with Joseph Wolpe, B. F. Skinner, and many others.) These were good experiences with great men for whom I continue to have deep respect and warmth; but I gradually found our views on values issues to be quite different. I had expected their work to be "objective" science, but it became clear that these leaders' research, theories, and techniques were implicit expressions of humanistic and naturalistic belief systems that dominated both psychology and American universities generally. Since their professional work was an expression of such views, I felt constrained from full expression of my values by their assumptions or faiths and the prevailing, sometimes coercive, ideologies of secular universities.

Like others, I too have not always overtly harmonized my values and professional work. By now exercising the right to integrate religious themes into mainstream clinical theory, research, and practice, I hope to achieve this. By being explicit about what I value and how it articulates with a professional role, I hope to avoid unknowingly drawing clients or students into my system. I hope that, together, many of us will succeed in demonstrating how this can be healthy and fruitful.

If we are unable to face our own values openly, it means we are unable to face ourselves, which violates a primary principle of professional conduct in our field. Since we expect our clients to examine their perceptions and value constructs, we ought to do likewise. The result will be improved capacity to understand and help people, because self-deceptions and role playing will decrease and personal congruence will increase.

Thesis 6: It is our obligation as professionals to translate what we perceive and value intuitively into something that can be openly tested and evaluated. I do not expect anyone to accept my values simply because I have asserted them. I only ask that we accept the notion that our values arise out of a personal milieu of experience and private intuition or inspiration. Since they are personal and subjective and are shaped by the culture with which we are most familiar, they should influence professional work only to the extent that we can openly justify them. As a general standard, I would advocate that we (a) examine our values within our idiosyncratic personal milieus; (b) acknowledge that our value commitments are subjective; (c) be clear; (d) be open; (e) state the values in a professional context without fear, as hypotheses for testing and common consideration by the pluralistic groups with which we work; and (f) subject them to test, criticism, and verification. . . .

CONCLUSION

Although numerous points of practical contact can be made between religious and other value approaches, it is my view that the religious ones offer a distinctive challenge to our theories, inquiries, and clinical methods. This challenge has not fully been understood or dealt with.

Religion is at the fringe of clinical psychology when it should be at the center. Value questions pervade the field, but discussion of them is dominated by viewpoints that are alien to the religious subcultures of most of the people whose behavior we try to explain and influence. Basic conflicts between value systems of clinical professionals, clients, and the public are dealt with unsystematically or not at all. Too often, we opt for the comforting role of experts applying technologies and obscure our role as moral agents, yet our code of ethics declares that we should show a "sensible regard for the social codes and moral expectations of the community" (American Psychological Association, 1972, p. 2).

I realize that there are difficulties in applying the notion of a particular spiritual value perspective in a pluralistic and secular society. I think it should be done on the basis of some evidence that supports doing it as opposed to the basis of the current format, which is to implement one's values without the benefit of either a public declaration or an effort to gather data on the consequences of doing so.

It is my hope that the theses I have proposed will be contemplated with deliberation and not emotional dismissal. They have been presented in sincerity, with passion tempered by reason, and with a hope that our profession will become more comprehensive and effective in its capacity to help all of the human family.

REFERENCE NOTES

1. Frankl, V. Honors seminar lecture, Brigham Young University, November 3, 1978.
2. Ragan, C. P., Malony, H. N., & Beit-Hallahmi, B. *Psychologists and religion: Professional factors related to personal religiosity.* Paper presented at the meeting of the American Psychological Association, Washington, D.C., September 1976.

REFERENCES

American Institute of Public Opinion. Religion in America, 1977–78. *Gallup opinion index*, Report No. 145, Princeton, N.J.: Author, 1978.

American Psychological Association. *Ethical standards of psychologists.* Washington, D.C.: Author, 1972.

Bergin, A. E. Carl Rogers' contribution to a fully functioning psychology. In A. R. Mahrer & L. Pearson (Eds.), *Creative developments in psychotherapy* (Vol. 1). Cleveland, Ohio: Case Western Reserve University Press, 1971.

Bergin, A. E., & Lambert, M. J. The evaluation of therapeutic outcomes. In S. L. Garfield & A. E. Bergin (Eds.), *Handbook of psychotherapy and behavior change* (2nd ed.). New York: Wiley, 1978.

Bergin, A. E., & Strupp, H. H. *Changing frontiers in the science of psychotherapy.* Chicago: Aldine, 1972.

Campbell, D. T. On the conflicts between biological and social evolution and between psychology and moral tradition. *American Psychologist*, 1975, 30, 1103–1120.

Frank, J. D. *Persuasion and healing.* Baltimore, Md.: Johns Hopkins University Press, 1961.

Frank, J. D. *Persuasion and healing* (2nd ed.). Baltimore, Md.: Johns Hopkins University Press, 1973.

Fromm, E. *Man for himself.* New York: Rinehart, 1947.

Fromm, E. *Psychoanalysis and religion.* New Haven, Conn.: Yale University Press, 1950.

Fromm, E. *The art of loving.* New York: Harper & Row, 1956.

Glasser, W. *Reality therapy.* New York: Harper & Row, 1965.

Gross, M. L. *The psychological society.* New York: Random House, 1978.

Henry, W. E., Sims, J. H., & Spray, S. L. *The fifth profession: Becoming a psychotherapist.* San Francisco: Jossey-Bass, 1971.

Hogan, R. Interview. *APA Monitor*, April 1979, pp. 4–5.

Lilienfeld, D. M. The relationship between mental health information and moral values of lower class psychiatric clinic patients and psychiatric evaluation and disposition (Doctoral dissertation, Columbia University, 1965). *Dissertation Abstracts*, 1966, *27*, 610B–611B. (University Microfilms No. 66-6941).

London, P. *The modes and morals of psychotherapy.* New York: Holt, Rinehart & Winston, 1964.

Lowe, C. M. *Value orientations in counseling and psychotherapy: The meanings of mental health* (2nd ed.). Cranston, R.I.: Carroll Press, 1976.

Menninger, K. *Whatever became of sin?* New York: Hawthorn Books, 1973.

Mowrer, O. H. *The crisis in psychiatry and religion.* Princeton, N.J.: Van Nostrand, 1961.

Mowrer, O. H. (Ed.). *Morality and mental health.* Chicago: Rand McNally, 1967.

Murray, E. J. A content-analysis method for studying psychotherapy. *Psychological Monographs*, 1956, *70*(13, Whole No. 420).

Rychlak, J. F. *Discovering free will and personal responsibility.* New York: Oxford University Press, 1979.

Smith, M. B. "Mental health" reconsidered: A special case of the problem of values in psychology. *American Psychologist*, 1961, *16*, 299–306.

Smith, M. L., Glass, G. V., & Miller, T. I. *The benefits of psychotherapy.* Baltimore, Md.: Johns Hopkins University Press, in press.

Strupp, H. H., Hadley, S. W., & Gomes-Schwartz, B. *Psychotherapy for better or worse: The problem of negative effects.* New York: Aronson, 1977.

Szasz, T. S. *The myth of psychotherapy: Mental healing as religion, rhetoric, and repression.* Garden City, N.Y.: Doubleday, 1978.

Truax, C. B. Reinforcement and nonreinforcement in Rogerian psychotherapy. *Journal of Abnormal Psychology*, 1966, *71*, 1–9.

Vaughan, J. L. Measurement and analysis of values pertaining to psychotherapy and mental health (Doctoral dissertation, Columbia University, 1971). *Dissertation Abstracts International*, 1971, *32*, 3655B–3656B. (University Microfilms No. 72-1394).

NO

Albert Ellis

PSYCHOTHERAPY AND ATHEISTIC VALUES

In a previous article, Bergin contrasts theistic with "clinical-humanistic" values in psychotherapy, but because he identifies the latter with a limited view of psychological humanism, he fails to give an accurate picture of clinical-humanistic-atheistic values that are probably held by most modern psychotherapists. These atheistic values, which are distinctly different from theistic ones in many respects but also significantly different from Bergin's statements of clinical-humanistic values, are briefly described and contrasted with religious values.

Bergin (1980) has written an important article on psychotherapy and religious values, making many points with which I, as a clinician and a probabilistic atheist, can heartily agree. His six major theses on spiritual values are empirically confirmable and probably valid. Briefly stated, they hold that (a) values are an inevitable, and pervasive part of psychotherapy, (b) value-laden factors pervade professional change processes, (c) mental health professionals' values tend to exclude religious values and establish goals for change that frequently clash with theistic systems of belief, (d) values of mental health professionals often contrast with those of a large proportion of their more religious clients, (e) clinicians had better acknowledge that they are implementing their own value systems via their professional work and be more explicit about what they believe while respecting the value systems of others, and (f) professionals had better translate what they perceive and value intuitively into something that can be openly tested and evaluated.

My objection to Bergin's article is that he does not properly represent the views of probabilistic atheist clinicians like myself who, unlike absolutistic atheists such as Branden (1965) and Rand (1961, 1967), believe that since there is an exceptionally high probability that no gods or superhuman entities of any kind exist, we had better assume that they do not and live our lives according to this assumption (Russell, 1965). Probabilistic atheists, who may well constitute the majority of modern psychotherapists, also tend to believe that human disturbance is largely (though not entirely) associated with and springs from absolutistic thinking—from dogmatism, inflexibility, and devout shoulds, oughts, and musts—and that extreme religiosity, or what Eric Hoffer (1951) called true believerism, is essentially emotional disturbance (Ellis, 1971, 1973; Horney, 1965; Murray, 1974; Tholen, 1978).

When Bergin contrasts theistic and clinical-humanistic values, his description of the latter leaves much to be desired. As a clinician and a humanist, I find that what he calls clinical-humanistic values are certainly not my values or those of any other probabilistic atheist that I know (Ellis, 1973; Kurtz, 1976, 1977; Lazarus, 1971). Bergin has included some "humanistic" values that are subscribed to by many members of the Association for Humanistic Psychology, many of whom are themselves deeply religious in their own transcendental way, but has omitted the equally humanistic values that are subscribed to by most members of the American Humanist Association, who tend to be probabilistic atheists. The latter, moreover, tend to be considerably more "clinical" than the former, since they are practical rather than romantic.

I have revised Bergin's Table 1 and added a third column representing what I consider to be clinical-humanistic-atheistic views that are much more typical of contemporary professional therapists. The first two columns in the present Table 1 are Bergin's, and the last column contains my additions. . . .

Finally, I present below a few additional hypotheses that will briefly outline some of the main points of the probabilistic atheist position on psychotherapy and religion that, as Bergin (1980) notes, may well "be contemplated with deliberation and not emotional dismissal. They have been presented in sincerity, with passion tempered by reason, and with a hope that our profession will become more comprehensive and effective in its capacity to help all of the human family" (p. 103).

1. Devout, orthodox, or dogmatic religion (or what might be called religiosity) is significantly correlated with emotional disturbance. People largely disturb themselves by believing strongly in absolutistic shoulds, oughts, and musts, and most people who dogmatically believe in some religion believe in these health-sabotaging absolutes. The emotionally healthy individual is flexible, open, tolerant and changing, and the devoutly religious person tends to be inflexible, closed, intolerant, and unchanging. Religiosity, therefore, is in many respects equivalent to irrational thinking and emotional disturbance.

2. What is often called religion, theism, or ultimate concern may be compatible with mental and emotional health as long as it is not absolutistic or dogmatic. People can believe, for example, that some kind of god created the universe, that he or she exerts a mild control over human affairs, that this god unconditionally accepts or gives grace to all humans just because they are human, that they have some kind of immortal soul that continues to exist in some kind of afterlife, that they are at one with the universe, and so forth. As long as they do not hold these beliefs too dogmatically or are not absolutely certain that their god, fate, or other superhuman force completely rules their lives, and as long as they do not connect this superhuman force with some kind of intrinsic deservingness, universal judgment, or total damnation or deification of themselves and others, they can probably lead

Table 1

Theistic, Clinical-Humanistic, and Clinical-Humanistic-Atheistic Values

Theistic (Bergin, 1980)	Clinical-Humanistic (Bergin, 1980)	Clinical-Humanistic-Atheistic
God is supreme. Humility, acceptance of (divine) authority, and obedience (to the will of God) are virtues.	Humans are supreme. The self is aggrandized. Autonomy and rejection of external authority are virtues.	No one and nothing is supreme. To aggrandize or rate the self is to be disturbed. A balance between autonomy and living cooperatively with others and a balance between rejecting and over-conforming to external authority are virtues.
Personal identity is eternal and derived from the divine. Relationship with God defines self-worth.	Identity is ephemeral and mortal. Relationships with others define self-worth.	Personal identity is ephemeral and mortal. Relationships with others often provide increased happiness but never define self-worth. Nothing does. Self-worth, self-esteem, or rating one's "self" globally is a (theological) mistake, leading to disturbance. Self-acceptance can be had for the asking, independent of any god or human law.
Self-control in terms of absolute values. Strict morality. Universal ethics.	Self-expression in terms of relative values. Flexible morality. Situation ethics.	Basically the same as clinical-humanistic.
Love, affection, and self-transcendence are primary. Service and self-sacrifice are central to personal growth.	Personal needs and self-actualization are primary. Self-satisfaction is central to personal growth.	Personal desires and self-actualization are to be sought within a social context. Increasing self-satisfaction, including social satisfaction and love, is central to personal growth.
Committed to marriage, fidelity, and loyalty. Emphasis on procreation and family life as integrative factors.	Open marriage or no marriage. Emphasis on self-gratification or recreational sex without long-term responsibilities.	Choice of no marriage, conventional marriage, or open marriage. Emphasis on sex gratification with mutually chosen partners, with or without long-term responsibilities. Family life optional; often desirable but not necessary for health and happiness.
Personal responsibility for own harmful actions and changes in them. Acceptance of guilt, suffering, and contrition as keys to change. Restitution for harmful effects.	Others are responsible for our problems and changes. Minimizing guilt and relieving suffering before experiencing its meaning. Apology for harmful effects.	Personal responsibility for own harmful actions and changes in them. Maximizing responsibility for harmful and immoral acts and minimizing guilt (self-damnation in addition to denouncing one's acts). No apology or "cop-out" for effects of one's unethical behavior. Restitution for harmful effects.
Forgiveness of others who cause distress (including parents) completes the therapeutic restoration of self.	Acceptance and expression of accusatory feelings are sufficient.	Forgiveness of others who cause needless distress (including parents) but no condonation of their acts. Unconditional acceptance or positive regard for all humans at all times, but clear-cut condemnation of their immoral behavior. Acceptance of self helped by unconditional acceptance of others.
Knowledge by faith and self-effort. Meaning and purpose derived from spiritual insight. Intellectual knowledge inseparable from the emotional and spiritual. Ecology of knowledge.	Knowledge by self-effort alone. Meaning and purpose derived from reason and intellect. Intellectual knowledge for itself. Isolation of the mind from the rest of life.	Knowledge by self-effort and the efforts of others. Meaning derived largely from personal desire, validated for results by empiricism, reason, and intellect. Intellectual knowledge mainly for the purpose of survival and enjoyment but also enjoyable in its own right. Intellectual knowledge inseparable from emotional and behavioral. Ecology of knowledge.

Note: The first two columns in the table are from Table 1 of "Psychotherapy and Religious Values" by Allen E. Bergin, *Journal of Consulting and Clinical Psychology*, 1980, *48*, 95–105. Copyright 1980 by the American Psychological Association. Reprinted by permission.

happy lives and not seriously impair their emotional and mental functioning.

3. The elegant therapeutic solution to emotional problems is to be quite unreligious and have no degree of dogmatic faith that is unfounded or unfoundable in fact. If people would acknowledge the possibility of superhuman entities but refuse to believe in them on probabilistic grounds because there is no evidence and probably never will be any evidence to support their existence, they would tend to give up all absolutistic thinking and stop making themselves emotionally disturbed. Since it is their biological as well as sociological nature to invent absolutes and musts, they had better minimize these tendencies, even if they cannot totally eliminate them. The less religious they are, the more emotionally healthy they will tend to be.

4. Although most religions adopt moral rules of conduct, there is no intrinsic connection between religion and morality, and one can easily be a highly moral atheist or a distinctly immoral religionist (or vice versa). Moral laws are made by humans for better human living, and it is preferable, though not necessary, that they be divorced from religious values.

5. There are some individuals who, because of their innate and/or acquired inability to think nonabsolutistically, may benefit from certain kinds of religious views, such as the views of those religions that undogmatically emphasize the freedom of the individual, the desirability of unconditional self-acceptance, the toleration and forgiveness of others who act poorly, and other forms of "liberal" religion. These individuals would benefit more without their belief in the intervening variable of religion or god, but since they will often refuse to surrender this belief, they may live comfortably and healthfully with it.

CONCLUSION

Humanistic psychology (or psychotherapy) is not the same as humanistic philosophy (or ethical humanism). Contrasting theistic with "clinical-humanistic" values in psychotherapy, as Bergin (1980) has done, does not give an accurate picture of clinical-humanistic-atheistic values. These atheistic values, which are distinctly different from theistic ones in many respects but also significantly different from Bergin's outline of clinical-humanistic values, have been briefly described and contrasted with religious values in this article.

REFERENCES

Bergin, A. E. Psychotherapy and religious values. *Journal of Consulting and Clinical Psychology*, 1980, 48, 95–105.
Branden, N. *Who is Ayn Rand?* New York: Paperback Library, 1965.
Ellis, A. *The case against religion: A psychotherapist's view.* New York: Institute for Rational Living, 1971.
Ellis, A. *Humanistic psychotherapy: The rational-emotive approach.* New York: Crown, 1973.
Hoffer, E. *The true believer.* New York: Harper, 1951.
Horney, K. *Collected writings.* New York: Norton, 1965.
Kurtz, P. Gullibility and nincompoopery. *Religious Humanism*, Spring 1976, pp. 1–6.
Kurtz, P. *Exuberance.* New York: Prometheus Books, 1977.
Lazarus, A. A. *Behavior therapy and beyond.* New York: McGraw-Hill, 1971.
Murray, M. *Why I am an atheist.* Austin, Tex.: American Atheist Press, 1974.
Rand, A. *For the new intellectual.* New York: New American Library, 1961.
Rand, A. *Introduction to objectivist epistemology.* New York: The Objectivist, 1967.
Russell, B. *The basic writings of Bertrand Russell.* New York: Simon & Schuster, 1965.
Tholen, G. More psychiatric implications of religion. *American Atheist*, 1978, 20(12), 15.

CHALLENGE QUESTIONS

Should Psychotherapy Include Religious Values?

1. If values are as pervasive in psychotherapy as these authors describe, how might you counsel someone in finding a compatible psychotherapist? What questions would you advise they ask, and why?

2. Ellis is the founder of a major school of psychotherapy—rational-emotive therapy. Find a description of this therapy and discuss how Ellis's own atheistic values might influence his formulation of this therapy.

3. Bergin maintains that values pervade even the testing of psychotherapy's effectiveness. Discuss what effect values might have on this type of research.

4. What do you think would be the strengths and weaknesses of a therapy based upon Bergin's theistic value system?

ISSUE 17

Is Electroconvulsive Therapy Safe?

YES: Raymond R. Crowe, from "Electroconvulsive Therapy: A Current Perspective," *The New England Journal of Medicine* (July 19, 1984)

NO: Leonard Roy Frank, from "Electroshock: Death, Brain Damage, Memory Loss, and Brainwashing," *The Journal of Mind and Behavior* (Summer/ Autumn 1990)

ISSUE SUMMARY

YES: Psychiatrist Raymond R. Crowe argues that ECT is not only safe and effective, but it also acts quickly after many other treatments have failed.
NO: Former ECT patient Leonard Roy Frank asserts that ECT only seems effective because of the brain damage it causes and that many practitioners of ECT underestimate its risks.

Electroconvulsive therapy (ECT) has been controversial since it was first introduced in 1938. Despite continued questions, approximately 100,000 people in the United States are treated with ECT each year. ECT is used for a variety of problems, including depression, schizophrenia, and obsessive-compulsive disorder. During ECT treatments, electrical current is applied to the patient's brain for one-half to two seconds, which produces a seizure. The number of seizures induced during a course of treatment varies from 6 to 35, depending on the disorder and the severity of the symptoms.

The controversy surrounding ECT originates from both its side effects and its questionable effectiveness. Common side effects include memory loss, confusion, disorientation, apathy, dizziness, and headaches. While most of these seem to subside several hours after treatment, critics of ECT argue that some of these effects—especially memory loss—are permanent and compromise its effectiveness. Proponents of ECT claim that this is an outmoded view. They argue that changes in technology have reduced the side effects and risks formerly associated with the procedure, and outcome research has indicated its effectiveness as a treatment strategy.

Raymond R. Crowe argues that ECT is often the most effective treatment available. In treating depression, for example, ECT is especially useful to individuals who do not respond to medication. He cites evidence that 75 to 85 percent of depressed patients respond positively to this type of treatment.

He also claims that the mortality rate for ECT is very low and that ECT is considered one of the safest medical procedures requiring general anesthesia. Part of the reason why ECT is now considered a relatively safe treatment is the introduction of new procedures—side effects have been dramatically reduced. Memory loss remains the most common complaint, but this can be at least partially a function of depression itself. Crowe reports that the majority of ECT patients proclaim the helpfulness of ECT and that most would undergo it again if it were recommended.

Leonard Roy Frank contends that ECT is just as harmful today as it was when it was first introduced. He describes his own experience with ECT and the long-term effects of this experience. He claims that the use of ECT is increasing due to the financial gains it provides the people who administer it. He further claims that the "effectiveness" of ECT comes from brain damage that is induced by the seizures. Following ECT, patients have symptoms similar to those found in persons with head injuries. Psychiatrists simply redefine these symptoms as signs of improvement. Frank cites evidence indicating that the death rate from ECT is much higher than is claimed by Crowe. In addition, other adverse effects are much more serious and occur more frequently than is typically reported by ECT practitioners. He concludes that ECT is analogous to brainwashing, because both ECT and brainwashing produce changes in one's perception of reality.

POINT	COUNTERPOINT
• Electroconvulsive therapy is often more effective than drugs in treating depression.	• ECT's "effectiveness" is actually brain damage that is caused by the procedure.
• Electroconvulsive therapy is among the safest of all medical procedures that require general anesthesia.	• Evidence suggests that those who administer ECT underestimate its dangers.
• Complaints of memory loss among depressed patients are the result of the depression.	• Memory loss is a common complaint after ECT, regardless of the diagnosis.
• Recent modifications in treatment technique have reduced the occurrence of side effects.	• While modifications have been made, the underlying destructive potential remains the same.
• The majority of ECT patients feel they were helped.	• ECT changes an individual's perception of reality.

YES

Raymond R. Crowe

ELECTROCONVULSIVE THERAPY:
A CURRENT PERSPECTIVE

Electroconvulsive therapy has become a national issue. Attacks on it have appeared in movies and television documentaries, as well as in the popular and professional press. These criticisms have resulted in legislation restricting its use in several states and, more recently, in an attempt to ban its use altogether in Berkeley, California. Because of growing public concern, physicians are likely to be consulted by the public about the treatment; thus, it is surprising that a current review of the subject is not available in a major general medical journal. A considerable body of research has been carried out on electroconvulsive therapy and several comprehensive reviews have been published, but they appear in books and specialty journals that may not be readily available to the nonpsychiatrist. The purpose of this article is to review the current status of this type of treatment for the nonspecialist.

Electroconvulsive therapy induces a grand mal seizure by means of an electric current applied across scalp electrodes. In current practice a series of 8 to 12 treatments is given at a rate of 2 to 3 treatments per week. Although the mechanism of action is unknown, most investigators agree that the seizure rather than the electricity produces the therapeutic benefit.

INDICATIONS AND EFFECTIVENESS

The primary indication for electroconvulsive therapy is severe depression, with this diagnosis accounting for 77 per cent of cases in which the treatment is used in this country. Since electroconvulsive therapy is often more effective than drugs, it is indicated in depressions that are refractory to medication, and since it acts more rapidly, it is indicated in cases involving a serious risk of suicide.

In the early 1960s two large trials of treatment for depression included a comparison of electroconvulsive therapy with placebo. In the American study, electroconvulsive therapy resulted in "marked improvement" in 76 per cent of 63 depressed patients, as compared with a 46 per cent response

From Raymond R. Crowe, "Electroconvulsive Therapy: A Current Perspective," *The New England Journal of Medicine*, vol. 311, no. 3 (July 19, 1984), pp. 163-166. Copyright © 1984 by the Massachusetts Medical Society. Reprinted by permission. References omitted.

rate among 39 controls given placebo. The difference between electroconvulsive therapy and placebo was even larger in patients who were manic–depressive or had involutional depression: 78 to 85 per cent of such depressions responded to electroconvulsive therapy, and 25 to 37 per cent responded to placebo. This difference contrasts with the usually milder and more chronic "neurotic" depressions, 78 per cent of which responded to either treatment. In the British investigation 84 per cent of 58 patients treated with electroconvulsive therapy improved, and 71 per cent were rated as having "no or only slight symptoms." In contrast, the respective rates for 51 controls receiving placebo were 45 and 39 per cent.

Although these large studies were conducted in different countries by different investigators using different diagnostic criteria, the agreement in results is striking, and the findings are consistent with those of other studies comparing electroconvulsive therapy with a placebo. In short, the evidence suggests that 75 to 85 per cent of depressed patients will respond to this type of treatment, as compared with a placebo response rate of 25 to 45 per cent. Moreover, acute endogenous depressions are likely to show the largest effects from the treatment.

The effectiveness of electroconvulsive therapy in depression is further supported by 10 trials employing a sham-treatment group. Nine were double-blind and the same number used random assignment to treatment groups and objective outcome ratings. Nine of the 10 studies found electroconvulsive therapy to be superior to sham treatment at a statistically significant level. Two of the studies deserve further comment. The only study with negative results used low-energy stimulation, which may be less effective than stimulation with higher levels of electrical energy. Another study found electroconvulsive therapy to be superior to sham treatments at the end of the treatment course, but one month later no difference was evident. However, many of the patients in both groups received antidepressant drugs after the trial; therefore, the question this study raises is whether electroconvulsive therapy is superior to conventional antidepressant therapy.

The effectiveness of electroconvulsive therapy as compared with standard antidepressants can be judged from the results of the American and British trials of antidepressant therapy cited above. Both studies administered two classes of antidepressant medication (tricyclic antidepressants and monoamine oxidase inhibitors) in therapeutic doses over an adequate trial period. The American study was an eight-week trial of imipramine (200 to 250 mg), phenelzine (60 to 75 mg), isocarboxazid (40 to 50 mg), and electroconvulsive therapy (nine or more treatments). Marked improvement was observed in 49 per cent of the 73 patients receiving imipramine, in 50 per cent of the 38 receiving phenelzine, and in 28 per cent of the 68 receiving isocarboxazid, as compared with 76 per cent of the group treated with electroconvulsive therapy. The difference between the latter and every other treatment group was statistically significant at the 0.05 confidence level, by a Yates chi-square analysis.

In the British study 58 patients received a minimum of four weeks of imipramine treatment in doses adjusted up to 200 mg, 50 received up to 60 mg of phenelzine, and 58 received four to eight electroconvulsive treatments. The percentage of patients with "no or only slight symptoms" was 52 per cent in the imipramine group and 30 per cent in the phenelzine group, as compared with 71 per cent of those receiving electroconvulsive therapy. The difference between imipramine and electroconvulsive treatment was just short of statistical significance (P = 0.056) but the difference between phenelzine and electroconvulsive therapy was significant (P<0.001).

Differences in the response rates between active treatments are more difficult to demonstrate than treatment– placebo differences, and it is not surprising that some studies have failed to show a difference between electroconvulsive therapy and either tricyclic antidepressants or monoamine oxidase inhibitors, although others have found such a difference. Assuming that the true response rates are 75 per cent for electroconvulsive therapy and 50 per cent for drugs, a power analysis reveals that at least 43 patients in each treatment group would be necessary to achieve a 50 per cent probability of detecting the difference at the 0.05 level of significance. Indeed, all four studies with sample sizes exceeding this minimum have shown a statistically significant superiority of electroconvulsive therapy over drug. Perhaps more telling, however, is the fact that no study has found drugs to be more effective than electroconvulsive treatment.

Thus, electroconvulsive therapy is clearly as effective as antidepressant medication; moreover, it has two advantages over drugs: its rapid onset of action and its effectiveness when drugs have failed. In a recent double-blind trial comparing electroconvulsive therapy and imipramine (150 mg), 11 patients received sham imipramine and electroconvulsive therapy, and 13 received imipramine and sham electroconvulsive therapy. Both groups responded well after four weeks, but the response to electroconvulsive therapy was significantly greater during the first three weeks. This rapid response has been noted by others as well. The effectiveness of electroconvulsive therapy in cases in which drugs have failed is illustrated by an investigation of 437 depressed patients who were treated with 200 to 350 mg of imipramine per day; when the 190 patients who did not respond after one month received electroconvulsive therapy, a 72 per cent improvement rate was observed.

Schizophrenia accounts for only 17 per cent of cases treated with electroconvulsive therapy. Common indications include unresponsiveness to drugs in an illness of less than 18 months' duration, the presence of a secondary depression, and a superimposed catatonic state. Manic excitement responds well to electroconvulsive therapy but is the indication in only 3 per cent of patients receiving this therapy, since it has largely been replaced by medication in the treatment of mania. Finally, catatonic stupor is a rare condition in which electroconvulsive therapy is often effective even when drug therapy fails. . . .

Mortality
The mortality rate from 3438 courses of electroconvulsive therapy administered in Denmark during 1972–1973 was 4.5 deaths per 100,000 treatments, or 2.9 deaths per 10,000 patients treated. Complications included six instances of endotracheal intubation due to secretions, several cases of laryngospasm, and a tooth fracture. The largest reported series of deaths included 62 from the years 1947 to 1952. The cause was cardiovascular in 55 per cent of the cases, pulmonary in 31 per cent, and cerebrovascular in 6

per cent, with miscellaneous causes accounting for the remaining 8 per cent. Although the mortality statistics are from Scandinavia, the treatment technique was comparable to current American practice; therefore, the findings should also be representative of experience in the United States. If they are, these figures place electroconvulsive therapy among the safest of all medical procedures requiring general anesthesia.

Adverse Effects

Adverse effects can be divided into those occurring during treatment, those appearing on recovery from each treatment, and those persisting after the course of treatments is over.

Adverse effects occurring during treatment may result either from the seizure or from the drugs used to modify it. Examples of the former include hypotension, hypertension, and bradyarrhythmias and tachyarrhythmias. Although frequent, they are rarely serious. Fractures, the most frequent complication of unmodified electroconvulsive therapy, have practically been eliminated by the use of muscle-paralyzing agents. Prolonged seizures are rare and easily terminated with intravenous diazepam. Adverse effects secondary to medication include laryngospasm and prolonged apnea due to pseudocholinesterase deficiency.

In the immediate post-treatment period, all patients experience transient postictal confusion. The next most frequently reported effects are memory disturbance and headache, which were mentioned by 64 and 48 per cent, respectively, of patients interviewed about previous electroconvulsive therapy. Less frequent effects after treatment are nausea and muscle pain.

The most frequently reported long-term effect of electroconvulsive therapy is memory disturbance, which has led to concern that the treatment may cause permanent brain damage. The apparent simplicity of investigating this question is deceptive. Patients with depression often perform at an impaired level on cognitive testing, and their performance improves with electroconvulsive therapy, masking any cognitive impairment that may have resulted from the treatment. Conversely, patients who have a relapse or do not improve may perform poorly on follow-up testing, leading to an erroneous assumption of persistent deficits secondary to electroconvulsive therapy. Thus, the importance of an appropriate control group cannot be overstressed, and in this respect, much of the earlier research is inadequate. Fortunately, renewed concerns over possible brain damage have led to a number of properly controlled studies, so that the question can be answered more firmly today than it could a few years ago.

In a recent follow-up study 55 per cent of patients who had received bilateral electroconvulsive therapy reported memory loss three years later. However, memory complaints are common in depression, and many patients who report memory disturbance after electroconvulsive therapy are clinically depressed; thus, it may be misleading to attribute these complaints entirely to the treatment. Nevertheless, considerable evidence indicates that electroconvulsive therapy does affect memory. First of all, complaints after treatment differ from those voiced before treatment and are therefore not entirely due to depression. Secondly, the nature of the memory disturbance differs as well. Depressed patients have poor registration and normal retention, but after electroconvulsive therapy they have normal registration and poor retention. Finally, reports of memory disturbance are more frequent after bilateral than after unilateral electroconvulsive therapy.

Reports of memory disturbance can be verified objectively. Memory tests conducted seven months after a course of bilateral electroconvulsive therapy indicate that memory of events immediately before and during the course of treatments remains impaired, memory of events up to two years before treatment shows minimal impairment, and more remote memory returns to normal. On the other hand, anterograde memory tested six months after electroconvulsive therapy demonstrates no impairment, as compared with the performance of controls with affective disorders.

In contrast to retrograde memory, other cognitive functions return to normal after electroconvulsive therapy. Weeks et al. conducted a prospective study of 51 depressed patients who received electroconvulsive therapy, 51 depressed patients receiving other treatments, and 51 normal controls. The groups were assessed before and after treatment and again after four and seven months, with a battery of 19 cognitive tests. Before treatment the group receiving electroconvulsive therapy scored below the patient-controls on 9 of the 19 tests; no test score deteriorated with treatment, and after four months performance on only one test separated the two groups. By seven months the electroconvulsive-therapy group outperformed the patient-controls on one test, but both patient groups performed at a level somewhat below that of the normal controls on several tests, presumably because of persistent depression in some patients. The North-

wick Park trial also found that by six months groups that had received electroconvulsive therapy or sham therapy did not differ on cognitive testing.

How are these findings to be reconciled with the frequent reports of memory disturbance by patients treated with electroconvulsive therapy? First of all, continuing depression undoubtedly accounts for some of the complaints, although it cannot explain all of them. Secondly, continuing retrograde amnesia for events around the time of treatment may sensitize the patient to the normal process of forgetting. These two explanations are supported by the finding that patients who have undergone electroconvulsive therapy perform as well on objective memory tests as patients with depression who have not undergone such therapy. Finally, it is possible that anterograde memory may be impaired after treatment in a small number of patients. One study enrolled patients on the basis of subjective memory impairment that had persisted after electroconvulsive therapy, and administered a battery of 19 cognitive tests on them. The patients scored significantly below controls on three tests of verbal and nonverbal anterograde memory, after the confounding effects of medication and residual depression had been eliminated. However, because of the way in which these patients were identified, it is difficult to attribute their memory impairment to electroconvulsive therapy. Moreover, as already noted, the same investigators prospectively administered an identical battery of tests to carefully matched groups of patients with affective disorders receiving electroconvulsive therapy or other treatments and found no difference on any memory functions seven months after treatment.

MODIFICATIONS

The fear and adverse effects associated with unmodified electroconvulsive therapy have led to a number of modifications in treatment technique, with the aim of reducing morbidity without sacrificing effectiveness.

First of all, pharmacologic modifications have been used, including a short-acting anesthetic such as methohexitol for general anesthesia, oxygen to prevent hypoxia, atropine to reduce secretions and bradyarrhythmias, and succinylcholine to attenuate the convulsion.

Secondly, unilateral electrode placement on the nondominant hemisphere has been found to reduce the volume of brain tissue exposed to electricity and to spare the language functions located in the dominant hemisphere. A large number of studies comparing unilateral with bilateral electrode placement have reported less memory impairment with the former, but the findings with respect to treatment effectiveness are less clear. The majority of studies have found the two forms of treatment to be equally effective, but a minority have found unilateral placement less effective.

Finally, brief-stimulus therapy has been used. This form of treatment uses a stimulus consisting of a train of brief electrical pulses rather than a continuous sinusoidal wave form. The brief stimulus is capable of inducing a seizure with half the electrical energy of a sine-wave stimulus, and often less. The hypothesis that a brief stimulus causes less cognitive impairment has been difficult to substantiate statistically, although two recent studies have found a trend in that direction. However, the therapeutic efficacy of this therapy has generally equalled that of sine-wave treatment.

PATIENT ACCEPTANCE

Perhaps the ultimate judge of a treatment should be the person who receives it. How do patients who have received a course of electroconvulsive therapy regard the experience? A recent survey found that 40 per cent remembered approaching the treatment with some degree of anxiety, but in retrospect 82 per cent considered it no more anxiety-provoking than a dental appointment. The most unpleasant aspects were premedication, waiting for treatment, waking up, and recovery—each considered unpleasant by 15 to 20 per cent of patients. Seventy-eight per cent felt they were helped by electroconvulsive therapy, and 80 per cent said they would not be reluctant to have it again.

CONCLUSION

Electroconvulsive therapy is a safe and effective treatment for severe depression. Its advantages are its rapid onset of action and its effectiveness when other treatments have failed. Recent follow-up investigations have found no evidence of damage to the central nervous system. The most troublesome adverse effect is a transient amnestic syndrome in some patients, which clears but leaves a mild deficit in retrograde memory. The frequency of this disorder can be reduced by treatment modifications, but its occurrence cannot be eliminated altogether. Although the majority of patients with amnestic symptoms do not find them bothersome, some do, and patients should be apprised of the common adverse effects, as well as the benefits, of electroconvulsive therapy.

NO

Leonard Roy Frank

ELECTROSHOCK: DEATH, BRAIN DAMAGE, MEMORY LOSS, AND BRAINWASHING

Since its introduction in 1938, electroshock, or electroconvulsive therapy (ECT), has been one of psychiatry's most controversial procedures. Approximately 100,000 people in the United States undergo ECT yearly, and recent media reports indicate a resurgence of its use. Proponents claim that changes in the technology of ECT administration have greatly reduced the fears and risks formerly associated with the procedure. I charge, however, that ECT as routinely used today is at least as harmful overall as it was before these changes were instituted. I recount my own experience with combined insulin coma-electroshock during the early 1960s. . . . I report on who is now being electroshocked, at what cost, where, and for what reasons. . . . I examine assertions and evidence concerning ECT's effectiveness and ECT-related deaths, brain damage, and memory loss. Finally, I . . . [draw] a parallel between electroshock and brainwashing.

In October 1962, at the age of 30, I had a run-in with psychiatry and got the worst of it. According to my hospital records (Frank, 1976), the "medical examiners," in recommending that I be committed, wrote the following: "Reportedly has been showing progressive personality changes over past 2 or so years. Grew withdrawn and asocial, couldn't or wouldn't work, & spent most of his time reading or doing nothing. Grew a beard, ate only vegetarian food and lived life of a beatnik—to a certain extent" (p. 63). I was labeled "paranoid schizophrenic, severe and chronic," denied my freedom for nine months and assaulted with a variety of drugs and 50 insulin-coma and 35 electroshock "treatments."

Each shock treatment was for me a Hiroshima. The shocking destroyed large parts of my memory, including the two-year period preceding the last shock. Not a day passes that images from that period of confinement do not float into consciousness. Nor does the night provide escape, for my dreams bear them as well. I am back there again in the "treatment room"; coming

From Leonard Roy Frank, "Electroshock: Death, Brain Damage, Memory Loss, and Brainwashing," *The Journal of Mind and Behavior,* vol. 11, nos. 3 & 4 (Summer/Autumn 1990), pp. 489-504, 506. Copyright © 1990 by the Institute of Mind and Behavior, P.O. Box 522, Village Station, New York, NY 10014. Reprinted by permission. The original article includes 58 references and is also available from the author; address: 2300 Webster Street, San Francisco, CA 94115.

out of that last insulin coma (the only one I remember); strapped down, a tube in my nose, a hypodermic needle in my arm; sweating, starving, suffocating, struggling to move; a group of strangers around the bed grabbing at me; thinking—where am I, what the hell is happening to me?

Well into the shock series, which took place at Twin Pines Hospital in Belmont, California, a few miles south of San Francisco, the treating psychiatrist wrote to my father:

> In evaluating Leonard's progress to date, I think it is important to point out there is some slight improvement but he still has all his delusional beliefs regarding his beard, dietary regime and religious observances that he had prior to treatment. We hope that in continuing the treatments we will be able to modify some of these beliefs so that he can make a reasonable adjustment to life. (p. 77)

During the comatose phase of one of my treatments, my beard was removed—as "a therapeutic device to provoke anxiety and make some change in his body image," the consulting psychiatrist had written in his report recommending this procedure. He continued, "Consultation should be obtained from the TP [Twin Pines Hospital] attorney as to the civil rights issue—but I doubt that these are crucial. The therapeutic effort is worth it—inasmuch that he can always grow another" (p. 76). Earlier, several psychiatrists had tried unsuccessfully to persuade me to shave off my beard. "Leonard seems to attach a great deal of religious significance to the beard," the treating psychiatrist had noted at the time. He had even brought in a local rabbi to change my thinking (p. 75), but to no avail. I have no recollection of any of this: it is all from my medical records. . . .

One day, about a week after my last treatment, I was sitting in the "day room," which was adjacent to the shock-treatment wing of the hospital building. It was just before lunch and near the end of the treatment session (which lasts about five hours) for those being insulin-shocked. The thick metal door separating the two areas had been left slightly ajar. Suddenly, from behind the door, I heard the scream of a young man whom I had recently come to know and who was then starting an insulin course. It was a scream like nothing I had ever heard before, an all-out scream. Hurriedly, one of the nurses closed the door. The screams, now less audible, continued a while longer. I do not remember my own screams; his, I remember.

> [The insulin-coma patient] is prevented from seeing all at once the actions and treatment of those patients further along in their therapy. . . . As much as possible, he is saved the trauma of sudden introduction to the sight of patients in different stages of coma—a sight which is not very pleasant to an unaccustomed eye. (Gralnick, 1944, p. 184)

During the years since my institutionalization, I have often asked myself how psychiatrists, or anyone else for that matter, could justify shocking a human being. Soon after I began researching my book *The History of Shock Treatment* (1978) I discovered Gordon's (1948) review of the literature in which he compiled 50 theories purporting to explain the "healing" mechanism of the various forms of shock therapy then in use, including insulin, Metrazol, and electroshock. Here are some excerpts:

> Because prefrontal lobotomy improves the mentally ill by destruction, the improvement obtained by all the shock

therapies must also involve some destructive processes. . . .
They help by way of a circulatory shake up. . . .
It decreases cerebral function. . . .
The treatments bring the patient and physician in closer contact. . . .
Helpless and dependent, the patient sees in the physician a mother. . . .
Threat of death mobilizes all the vital instincts and forces a reestablishment of contacts with reality. . . .
The treatment is considered by patients as punishment for sins and gives feelings of relief. . . .
Victory over death and joy of rebirth produce the results. . . .
The resulting amnesia is healing. . . .
Erotization is the therapeutic factor. . . .
The personality is brought down to a lower level and adjustment is obtained more easily in a primitive vegetative existence than in a highly developed personality. Imbecility replaces insanity. (pp. 199–401)

One of the more interesting explanations I found was proposed by Manfred Sakel, the Austrian psychiatrist who in 1933 introduced insulin coma as a treatment for schizophrenia. According to Sakel (cited in Ray, 1942, p. 250),

with chronic schizophrenics, as with confirmed criminals, we can't hope for reform. Here the faulty pattern of functioning is irrevocably entrenched. Hence we must use more drastic measures to silence the dysfunctioning cells and so liberate the activity of the normal cells. This time we must *kill* the too vocal dysfunctioning cells. But can we do this without killing normal cells also? Can we *select* the cells we wish to destroy? I think we can. (italics in original)

Electroshock may be considered one of the most controversial treatments in psychiatry. As I document below, the last decade has witnessed a resurgence of ECT's popularity, accompanied by assertions from proponents concerning its effectiveness and safety—assertions which deny or obscure basic facts about the historical origins of ECT, the economic reasons behind its current popularity, as well as its potential for destroying the memories and lives of those subjected to it. . . .

ELECTROSHOCK FACTS AND FIGURES

Since 1938 between 10 and 15 million people worldwide have undergone electroshock. While no precise figure is available, it is estimated that about 100,000 people in the United States are electroshocked annually (Fink, cited in Rymer, 1989, p. 68). Moreover, the numbers appear to be increasing. Recent media accounts report a resurgence of ECT interest and use. One reason for this is the well-publicized enthusiasm of such proponents as Max Fink, editor-in-chief of *Convulsive Therapy*, the leading journal in the field. Fink was recently cited as saying that "[ECT should be given to] all patients whose condition is severe enough to require hospitalization" (Edelson, 1988, p. 3).

A survey of the American Psychiatric Association (APA) membership focusing on ECT (APA, 1978) showed that 22% fell into the "User" category. Users were defined as psychiatrists who had "personally treated patients with ECT," or "recommended to residents under their supervision that ECT be used on patients," during the last six months (p. 5). If valid today, this figure indicates that approximately 7,700 APA members are electroshock Users.

A survey of all 184 member hospitals of the National Association of Private

Psychiatric Hospitals (Levy and Albrecht, 1985) elicited the following information on electroshock practices from the 153 respondents (83%) who answered a 19-item questionnaire sent to them in 1982. Fifty-eight percent of the respondents used electroshock (3% did not use electroshock because they considered it to be "inappropriate treatment for any illness"). The hospitals using ECT found it appropriate for a variety of diagnoses: 100% for "major depressive disorder," 58% for "schizophrenia," and 13% for "obsessive-compulsive disorder." Twenty-six percent of the ECT-using hospitals reported no contraindications in the use of the procedure. Darnton (1989) reported that the number of private free-standing psychiatric hospitals grew from 184 in 1980 to 450 in 1988. In addition, nearly 2,000 general hospitals offer inpatient psychiatric services (p. 67). While the use of ECT in state hospitals has fallen off sharply over the last 20 years, the psychiatric wards of general hospitals have increased their reliance on ECT in the treatment of their adult inpatients (Thompson, 1986).

In cases of depression, an ECT series ranges from six to 12 seizures—in those of schizophrenia, from 15 to 35 seizures—given three times a week, and usually entails four weeks of hospitalization. In 72% of the cases, according to the APA (1978, p. 8) survey cited above, electroshock costs are paid for by insurance companies. This fact led one psychiatrist to comment, "Finding that the patient has insurance seemed like the most common indication for giving electroshock" (Viscott, 1972, p. 356). The overall cost for a series of electroshock in a private hospital ranges from $10,000 to $25,000. With room rates averaging $500 to $600 a day,

and bed occupancy generally falling, some hospitals have obtained considerable financial advantage from their use of ECT. A regular ECT User can expect yearly earnings of at least $200,000, about twice the median income of other psychiatrists. *Electroshock is a $2–3 billion-a-year industry.*

More than two-thirds of electroshock subjects are women, and a growing number are elderly. In California, one of the states that requires Users to report quarterly the number and age categories of electroshock subjects, "the percentage 65 and over" being electroshocked increased gradually from 29% to 43% between 1977 and 1983 (Warren, 1986, p. 51). More recently, Drop and Welch (1989) reported that 60% of the ECT subjects in a recent two-year period at the Massachusetts General Hospital in Boston were over 60 years and 10% were in their eighties (p. 88). There are published reports of persons over 100 years old (Alexopoulos, Young, and Abrams, 1989) and as young as 34 1/2 months (Bender, 1955) who have been electroshocked. In the latter case, the child had been referred in 1947 to the children's ward of New York's Bellevue Hospital "because of distressing anxiety that frequently reached a state of panic. . . . The child was mute and autistic." The morning after admission he received the first of a series of 20 electroshocks and was discharged one month later. "The discharge note indicated a 'moderate improvement,' since he was eating and sleeping better, was more friendly with the other children, and he was toilet trained" (pp. 418–419).

Children continue to be electroshocked. Black, Wilcox, and Stewart (1985) reported on "the successful use of ECT in a prepubertal boy with severe depression."

Sandy, 11 years old, received 12 unilateral ECTs at the University of Iowa Hospitals and Clinics in Iowa City. He "improved remarkably" and "was discharged in good condition. Follow-up over the next 8 years revealed five more hospitalizations for depression" (p. 98). . . .

In the early 1970s electroshock survivors—together with other former psychiatric inmates/"patients"—began forming organizations aimed at regulating or abolishing electroshock and other psychiatric practices which they believed were harmful. In 1975 one group, the Network Against Psychiatric Assault (San Francisco/Berkeley), was instrumental in the passage of legislation that regulated the use of electroshock in California. Since then more than 30 states have passed similar legislation.

In 1982 the Coalition to Stop Electroshock led a successful referendum campaign to outlaw ECT in Berkeley, California. Although the courts overturned the ban six weeks after it went into effect, this was the first time in American history that the use of any established medical procedure had been prohibited by popular vote.

The Committee for Truth in Psychiatry (CTIP), all of whose members are electroshock survivors, was formed in 1984 to support the Food and Drug Administration (FDA) in its original (1979) classification of the ECT device in the high-risk category of medical devices, Class III, which earmarks a device or its related procedure for a safety investigation. To prevent an investigation of ECT, the APA had petitioned the FDA in 1982 for reclassification of the ECT device to Class II, which signifies low risk. After many years of indecision, the FDA proposed in 1990 to make this reclassification—but has not yet done so. . . .

CLAIMS OF ELECTROSHOCK EFFECTIVENESS

Virtually all the psychiatrists who evaluate, write about and do research on electroshock are themselves Users. This partially explains why claims regarding ECTs effectiveness abound in the professional literature—while the risks associated with the procedure are consistently understated or overlooked. User estimates of ECT's effectiveness in the treatment of the affective disorders (i.e., depression, mania, and manic-depression) usually range from 75% to 90%. Two important questions, however, need to be addressed: What is meant by effectiveness and how long does it last?

Breggin (1979, p. 135; 1981, pp. 252–253) has proposed a "brain-disabling hypothesis" to explain the workings of electroshock. The hypothesis suggests that ECT "effectiveness" stems from the brain damage ECT causes. As happens in cases of serious head injury, ECT produces amnesia, denial, euphoria, apathy, wide and unpredictable mood swings, helplessness and submissiveness. Each one of these effects may appear to offset the problems which justified the use of ECT in the first place. Amnesia victims, having forgotten their problems, tend to complain less. Denial serves a similar purpose: because of their embarrassment, ECT subjects tend to discount or deny unresolved personal problems as well as ECT-caused intellectual deficits. With euphoria, the subject's depression seems to lift. With apathy, the subject's "agitation" (if that had been perceived as part of the original problem) seems to diminish. Dependency and submissiveness tend to make what may have been a resistive, hostile subject more cooperative and friendly. In hailing the wonders of electroshock, psychiatrists often simply redefine the symptoms of psychiatrogenic brain damage as signs of improvement and/or recovery.

Electroshock advocates themselves unwittingly provide support for the brain-disabling hypothesis. Fink, Kahn, and Green (1958) offered a good example when describing a set of criteria for rating improvement in ECT subjects: "When a depressed patient, who had been withdrawn, crying, and had expressed suicidal thoughts, no longer is seclusive, and is jovial, friendly and euphoric, denies his problems and sees his previous thoughts of suicide as 'silly,' a rating of 'much improved' is made" (p. 117). . . .

On the question of duration of benefit from ECT, Weiner (1984)—in one of the most important review articles on ECT published during the last decade—was unable to cite a single study purporting to show long-term, or even medium-term, benefits from ECT. Opton (1985) drew this conclusion from the Weiner review: "In this comprehensive review of the literature, after fifty years of research on ECT, no methodologically sound study was found that reported beneficial effects of ECT lasting as long as four weeks" (p. 2). Pinel (1984), in his peer commentary on the Weiner article, accepted Weiner's conclusion that "the risks of ECT-related brain damage are slight" and then added, "it is difficult to justify any risks at all until ECT has been shown unambiguously to produce significant long-term therapeutic benefits" (p. 31). . . .

The underlying assumption of this approach ["maintenance" ECT] is that affective disorders are for the most part chronic and irreversible. There is a popular saying among psychiatrists, "Once a schizophrenic, always a schizophrenic." While not a maxim, "Once a depressive,

always a depressive," is nevertheless a core belief among many ECT Users. It "explains" so much for them. From this perspective, there are hardly any ECT failures, only patients with recurring depressive episodes who require ongoing psychiatric treatment, intensive and maintenance by turns.

Proponents also claim, but cannot demonstrate, that ECT is effective in cases of depression where there is a risk of suicide. They often cite a study by Avery and Winokur (1976) to support their position. But this study makes no such claim, as we can see from the authors' own conclusion: "In the present study, treatment [ECT and antidepressants] was not shown to affect the suicide rate" (p. 1033). Nevertheless, Allen (1978), in the very first paragraph of his article on ECT observed, "Avery and Winokur showed that suicide mortality in patients afflicted with psychotic depression was lower in patients treated with ECT than in those who were not" (p. 47).

DEATH FROM ELECTROSHOCK

Proponents claim that electroshock-caused death is rare. Alexopoulos et al. (1989) cited studies published in 1979 and 1985 indicating that the death rate from ECT was between 1 and 3 per 10,000 persons treated (0.01%–0.03%)—considerably lower than estimates for the early years of ECT and, according to the authors, "probably related to the introduction of anesthesia and muscular relaxants" (p. 80). On the other hand, Kalinowsky (1967), who reported a death rate of up to 1 per 1,000 for the period before the premedicative drugs were being routinely used, had "the definite impression that the anesthesia techniques increased the number of fatalities" (p. 1282). Crowe (1984a, p. 164) cited a study conducted during 1972–1973 in Denmark which reported a rate of 2.9 deaths per 10,000 cases (0.029%).

Can any of these figures be relied upon? In researching my book on shock treatment (Frank, 1978, p. 153–156), I found reports of 384 electroshock-related deaths published between 1941 and 1977 in English-language sources, among which were a number of reports and studies with much higher death rates than those cited above. For example: three deaths in 150 cases—2% (Lowinger and Huddleson, 1945); four deaths in 276 cases—1.4% (Gralnick, 1946); five deaths in 356 cases—1.4% (Martin, 1949); two deaths in 18 cases—11.1% (Weil, 1950); three deaths in 700 cases—0.4% (Gaitz, Pokorny, and Mills, 1956); three deaths in 90 cases—3.3% (Kurland, Hanlon, Esquibel, Krantz, and Sheets, 1959); three deaths in 1,000 cases—0.3% (McCartney, 1961); two deaths in 183 cases—1.1% (Freeman and Kendell, 1980).

In the broadest and most informative study on ECT-related deaths, Impastato (1957) reported 254 deaths: 214 from published accounts and 40 previously unpublished. Most of the fatalities had received unmodified ECT. He estimated an overall death rate of 1 per 1,000 (0.1%) and 1 per 200 (0.5%) in persons over 60 years of age. Impastato was able to determine the cause of death in 235 cases. There were 100 "cardiovascular deaths" (43%), 66 "cerebral deaths" (28%), 43 "respiratory deaths" (18%), and 26 deaths from other causes (11%) (p. 34).

Impastato's estimate of an ECT death rate among elderly persons five times higher than the overall death rate—coupled with his finding that cardiovascular failure was responsible for 43% of the deaths—should be very troubling in light of the growing tendency toward shocking the elderly. To justify this practice,

Users usually point to the serious risks of cardiac complications and death involved in treating the elderly depressed—particularly those with heart disease—with antidepressant drugs. In current standard psychiatric practice, these drugs constitute basically the only alternative to electroshock.

Whether ECT or antidepressants offer less risk of fatality for these persons remains an open question, but Users assume ECT is less risky. . . .

The Impastato findings have embarrassed the electroshock camp. As a result, this essential research has been largely neglected in the literature on electroshock since then. Thus, in three key review books authored or co-authored by Kalinowsky (Kalinowky, 1959; Kalinowsky and Hippius, 1969; Kalinowsky and Hoch, 1961), the Impastato study was nowhere mentioned, although Impastato's other works were frequently cited. Kalinowsky is not alone in this regard. Crowe's (1984a) ECT-review article—because it was published in the influential *New England Journal of Medicine*—must be considered among the most important of the 1980s. Citing a paper by Maclay (1953), Crowe wrote that "the largest reported series of deaths included 62 from the years 1947–1952" (p. 164), but Crowe neither referred to the Impastato study in his ECT mortality section nor cited it among his 80 references. . . .

BRAIN DAMAGE FROM ELECTROSHOCK

One does not need a medical degree to recognize the destructive potential of passing 100 to 150 volts of electricity through the human brain. The same amount of current used to produce a seizure in ECT, if applied to the chest, would be fatal (Task Force, 1977, p. 1).

Fifteen years before the Impastato study (1957) which reported 66 "cerebral deaths," and four years after the introduction of ECT, Alpers and Hughes (1942) commented on their findings in an autopsy performed on a woman who had died following electroshock:

> The foregoing case is the first reported instance, so far as we know, of hemorrhages in the brain attributable to electrical convulsion treatment. . . . [T]he importance of the case lies in that it offers a clear demonstration of the fact that electrical convulsion treatment is followed at times by structural damage of the brain. (p. 177)

Hoch (1948), a well-known ECT proponent, likening electroshock to lobotomy, claimed that the brain damage each produced was beneficial:

> This brings us for a moment to a discussion of the brain damage produced by electroshock. . . . Is a certain amount of brain damage not necessary in this type of treatment? Frontal lobotomy indicates that improvement takes place by a definite damage of certain parts of the brain. (pp. 48–439)

Psychiatrist and neurophysiologist Pribram commented in a 1974 interview:

> I'd much rather have a small lobotomy than a series of electroconvulsive shocks. . . . I just know what the brain looks like after a series of shocks—and it's not very pleasant to look at. (p. 9)

The American Psychiatric Association's (1978) ECT survey, cited earlier, reported that 41% of the psychiatrist-respondents agreed with the statement, "It is likely that ECT produces slight or subtle brain damage." Only 26% disagreed. In their review of the literature,

Templer and Veleber (1982) concluded "that ECT caused and can cause permanent brain pathology" (p. 65). Sament (1983), a neurologist, published his views on ECT's brain-damaging effects in a letter to the editor of a professional journal:

> I have seen many patients after ECT, and I have no doubt that ECT produces effects identical to those of a head injury. After multiple sessions of ECT, a patient has symptoms identical to those of a retired, punch-drunk boxer.
>
> After one session of ECT the symptoms are the same as those of a concussion (including retrograde and anterograde amnesia). After a few sessions of ECT the symptoms are those of a moderate cerebral contusion, and further enthusiastic use of ECT may result in the patient functioning at a subhuman level. (p. 11)

Sackeim (1986) also describes in a straightforward manner the effects of ECT:

> The ECT-induced seizure, like spontaneous generalized seizures in epileptics and most acute brain injury and head trauma, results in a variable period of disorientation. Patients may not know their names, their ages, etc. When the disorientation is prolonged, it is generally referred to as an organic brain syndrome. (p. 482) . . .

Despite evidence of ECT-caused brain damage, most fully documented by Breggin (1979), proponents continue to claim that ECT does not cause brain damage. . . .

In a recent 216-page document, *The Practice of ECT: Recommendations for Treatment, Training and Privileging*, the Task Force on ECT (APA, 1989) dismissed the critical issue of electroshock-caused brain damage with two sentences. The first, "Cerebral complications are notably rare" (p. 63), is false. The second, which concluded the Task Force's recommendations for information to be provided in the formal consent document for ECT—"In light of the available evidence, 'brain damage' need not be included as a potential risk" (p. 77)—is falsely premised. From this latter statement we see that the report's authors not only denied the possibility of ECT-caused brain damage, but found the very notion of such damage so *unthinkable* that they placed the term in quotation marks.

MEMORY LOSS FROM ELECTROSHOCK

The most serious and common effect of electroshock as reported by survivors is memory loss. The loss stretching backward in time from the treatment period is called retrograde amnesia and may cover many months or years. The memory loss from the treatment period forward in time is called anterograde amnesia and usually covers several months, often including the treatment period itself. The amnesia may be global or patchy; some memories return, others are permanently lost. These losses affect one's entire personality and are often experienced as a diminution of self. They not only impair one's ability to function in everyday affairs but also higher realms of spiritual and creative activity.

Herskovitz (cited in Philadelphia Psychiatric Society, 1943) reported finding memory defects among 174 people treated with ECT at the Norristown State Hospital, Pennsylvania, "to be rather general and often prominent. Therefore, patients whose occupation requires intellectual ability are selected for treatment with caution" (p. 798). In 1973, at the age of 49 Marilyn Rice (cited as Natalie Parker, a

pseudonym, in Roueché, 1974) underwent a series of eight ECTs at the Psychiatric Institute of Washington. Soon afterwards, ECT-caused disability forced her into early retirement from her job as an economist. She described her return to work following electroshock:

> I came home from the office after that first day back feeling panicky. I didn't know where to turn. I was terrified. All my beloved knowledge, everything I had learned in my field during twenty years or more was gone. I'd lost the body of knowledge that constituted my professional skill. . . . I'd lost my experience, my knowing. But it was worse than that. I felt I'd lost myself. (pp. 95–96)

Andre (1988) described her memory losses following a series of 15 ECTs at New York Hospital in New York City in 1984 when she was 24 years old:

> My behavior was greatly changed; in a brain-damaged stupor, I smiled, cooperated, agreed that I had been a very sick girl and thanked the doctor for curing me. I was released from the hospital like a child just born. I knew where I lived, but I didn't recognize the person I lived with. I didn't know where I had gotten the unfamiliar clothes in the closet. I didn't know if I had any money or where it was. I didn't know the people calling me on the phone. . . . Very, very gradually—because you can't know what you don't remember—I realized that three years of my life were missing. Four years after shock, they are still missing. (p. 2) . . .

Abrams (1988a) summarized his chapter on memory functioning after ECT as follows: "A remarkable amount has been learned in the past decade about the effects of ECT on memory, and the day is now past when the physician administering bilateral ECT can blithely assure his patient that 'the memory-loss will only be temporary' " (p. 153). Abrams favors unilateral ECT, claiming that it causes little or no "memory disturbance" and that "whatever dysmnesia does occur will be transient and probably undetectable 6 months later" (p. 154).

Over the years, ECT Users have tried to discount the significance of amnesia reports from electroshock survivors. Kalinowsky and Hoch (1952) gave an early explanation: "All patients who remain unimproved after ECT are inclined to complain bitterly of their memory difficulties" (p. 139). Implicit in this remark is the suggestion to Users that an ECT series should continue until the subject's memory "complaints" cease. In the same vein, the APA's 1978 report on ECT lent its weight to the notion that ECT "might lead many individuals . . . to have persistent illusion of memory impairment" (p. 68).

More recently, Users have been arguing that the culprit responsible for memory problems is more likely to be the depression, not the electroshock (Crowe, 1984a). They assert that memory loss is a component of depression. Where the ECT subject is elderly, Users are likely to regard reports of memory loss as a normal sign of the aging process and, in the more severe cases, as symptomatic of senility. It is interesting to note that the Janis (1950) study—which concluded that ECT caused persistent amnesia (p. 372)— included very few depressed persons (only 3 of 30 subjects). More significantly on this point, the control group of 19 "depressed patients" who had not undergone ECT in the Squire (1983) study . . . "reported no memory problems at all at follow-up" (p. 6). . . .

ELECTROSHOCK AND BRAINWASHING

The term "brainwashing" came into the language during the early 1950s. It originally identified the technique of intensive indoctrination developed by the Chinese for use on political dissidents following the Communist takeover on the mainland and on American prisoners of war during the Korean War. The method involves the systematic application of sleep and food deprivation, prolonged interrogation, brow-beating, and physical punishment to force captives to renounce their beliefs. Once "brainwashed," they are reprogrammed to accept the beliefs of their captors.

While electroshock is not overtly used against political dissidents, it is used against cultural dissidents, social misfits and the unhappy, whom psychiatrists diagnose as "mentally ill" in order to justify ECT as a medical intervention. Indeed, electroshock is a classic example of brainwashing in the most meaningful sense of the term. Brainwashing means washing the brain of its contents. Electroshock destroys memories and ideas by destroying the brain cells in which memories and ideas are stored. A more accurate name for what is now called electroconvulsive therapy (ECT) would be electroconvulsive brainwashing (ECB). . . .

While electroshock cannot, of course, be used to reshape reality, it—like brainwashing—can and has been used to reshape the subject's perception of reality. Warren (1988) reported on interviews with ten married women 26–40 years old, from the San Francisco Bay Area who had undergone ECT between 1957 and 1961. The salient feature of ECT for these women was memory loss: "Troubling life-events and relationships commonly forgotten by these women included the existence of their husbands and children, their own names, and their psychiatrists" (p. 292). Some of the husbands, Warren reported, "used their wives' memory loss to establish their own definitions of past situations in the marital relationship." Other relatives found they "could freely re-define past situations without challenge" (p. 294). Warren comments: "When the recollections of one [marital] partner are to some degree erased, the dynamic reconstruction of reality shifts a little, or a lot" (p. 297).

Those who define reality usually control it. What had shifted here was power—away from the electroshock survivor. Without referring to brainwashing as such, Warren shows that electroshock and brainwashing serve similar ends. Electroconvulsive brainwashing is psychiatry's cleansing ritual; its method for controlling painful, unhappy memories and false or unpopular beliefs by destroying them.

CONCLUSION

Mystification and conditioning have undoubtedly played an important role in shaping the public's tolerant attitude toward electroshock. But it is not only the uninformed and misinformed public that has stood by silently during the electroshock era. There has hardly been a voice of protest from the informed elite—even when one of its own has been victimized.

While undergoing a series of involuntary electroshocks at the famed Mayo Clinic in 1961, Ernest Hemingway told visitor A. E. Hotchner, "Well, what is the sense of ruining my head and erasing my memory, which is my capital, and putting me out of business? It was a brilliant cure but we lost the patient. It's a bum turn, Hotch, terrible . . ." (cited in Hotchner, 1967, p. 308). A few days after his release from the Mayo Clinic following a second course of ECT, Hemingway killed himself with a shotgun. With all that has been written about him since his death, no recognized figure from the world of literature, academia, law, religion or science has spoken out against those responsible for this tragedy. As might have been expected, the psychiatric profession has also been silent. Not only did the psychiatrist who electroshocked Hemingway escape the censure of his colleagues, but a few years later they elected him president of the American Psychiatric Association. . . .

ECT User Robert Peck titled his book *The Miracle of Shock Treatment* (1974). Antonin Artaud (cited in Sontag, 1976), the French actor and playwright, who was electroshocked in the early 1940s, wrote afterwards: "Anyone who has gone through the electric shock . . . never again rises out of its darkness and his life has been lowered a notch" (p. 530). In which perspective—or at what point between these two perspectives—is the truth to be found? This is no trivia question. For some, it will be the gravest question they will ever have to answer.

CHALLENGE QUESTIONS

Is Electroconvulsive Therapy Safe?

1. If you or a close family member were severely depressed and had not responded to other treatments, would you support the use of ECT? Are the benefits worth the risks of treatment?

2. How can you evaluate and make sense of the widely varying claims and the supporting evidence cited in reference to this issue? Crowe is a medical professional, while Frank is a former mental health patient. Does this affect your interpretation of the data in any way? Why or why not?

3. Is ECT a form of brainwashing? Why or why not?

4. Frank states that signs of "effectiveness" are really symptoms of brain damage. Do you agree with this position? What evidence supports your position?

5. Frank quotes a psychiatrist as saying that the most common reason for administering ECT is the patient's having health insurance to cover its cost. Why might this be the case? Describe how economic considerations might be weighed into recommendations for treatment.

PART 6

Social Issues

One issue that seems to permeate all of society is the use of drugs. In this section, debate revolves around very different ways in which drugs constitute a problem.

A recent concern for psychologists is whether or not the privilege to prescribe medications to their patients would benefit the psychological profession. Though many psychologists favor such privileges, others feel that the ability to prescribe drugs would have negative effects on certain political issues that are important to psychology.

Illegal drugs, and the present war against them, constitute a tremendous burden on society. Could legalizing drugs, as some assert, lift that burden and actually benefit society?

Should Psychologists Be Allowed to
　Prescribe Drugs?

Would Legalizing Drugs Have
　Beneficial Effects on Society?

ISSUE 18

Should Psychologists Be Allowed to Prescribe Drugs?

YES: Ronald E. Fox, from "Prescription Privileges: Their Implications for the Practice of Psychology," *Psychotherapy* (Winter 1988)

NO: Garland Y. DeNelsky, from "Prescription Privileges for Psychologists: The Case Against," *Professional Psychology: Research and Practice* (vol. 22, no. 3, 1991)

ISSUE SUMMARY

YES: Clinical psychologist Ronald E. Fox argues that prescription privileges for psychologists is a logical extension of psychological practice and that allowing those privileges is in the public interest.
NO: Clinical psychologist Garland Y. DeNelsky argues that such privileges would make psychology a medical specialty and remove psychology's uniqueness as a discipline.

The general public often confuses the practices of psychology and psychiatry, partly because both disciplines treat many of the same patients. Most of the time this working relationship is quite harmonious, but once in a while—particularly during hard economic times—battles break out between the disciplines over the mental health "turf." Psychiatry may encroach upon the behavioral elements of mental health, which are normally held by psychology. And psychologists may wish to invade the turf traditionally held by psychiatry.

A recent and currently ongoing turf battle concerns the privilege of prescribing drugs. Traditionally, one of the main distinctions between psychology and psychiatry is that only the psychiatrist can prescribe drugs. Psychiatrists are medical doctors who have their primary training in the anatomy and physiology of the human body. Psychologists, on the other hand, are experts in human relations. Although some receive considerable education in pharmacology (the study of medications) and related topics, few have the training necessary to enable them to competently prescribe drugs. However, the question arises: What if an appropriate level of training were obtained? Should psychologists, then, be able to prescribe drugs to their patients?

Ronald E. Fox argues that the prescription privilege is a logical extension of the practice of psychology. Other fields related to medicine (such as dentistry and optometry) have recently obtained prescription privileges for use with their patients. Why not psychology? The traditional distinction between psychology and psychiatry, according to Fox, stems from the outmoded concept that mind and body are independent entities. Fox, however, argues that hardly anyone accepts this dualistic concept anymore. Mind and body are inextricably interwoven; any intervention into one is an intervention into the other. Consequently, the traditional dichotomy between psychological and psychiatric factors is false. Moving away from this false dichotomy would better serve the public interest, and allowing psychologists the privilege of prescribing drugs would help accomplish this.

In opposition, Garland Y. DeNelsky asks, "Where would [this] lead psychology?" Would this make psychology a medical specialty? Psychiatrists have increasingly moved away from psychotherapy and toward medication as a treatment for economic reasons. If psychologists could prescribe drugs, DeNelsky predicts that they would do the same, which would shortcircuit important psychotherapy strategies. DeNelsky contends that a large portion of the public prefers nonmedication treatment. With the inevitable economic pressures to move away from psychotherapeutic strategies, psychology would lose its hard-earned distinction from psychiatry, as well as a significant portion of the patient population. Moreover, the inevitable costs of a "war" with psychiatry would remove needed resources from many other worthy projects.

POINT	COUNTERPOINT
• Other health-related fields have obtained prescription privileges.	• No other field duplicates a specialty of medicine like psychology does psychiatry; the two disciplines must remain separate.
• Psychiatry has no difficulty encroaching upon psychology's "turf."	• Psychiatry has increasingly moved toward medication treatments only.
• To protect its market, psychology has no choice but to move toward prescription privileges.	• The market share of psychiatry has actually decreased, while that of psychology has increased.
• Prescription privileges are a logical extension of psychological practice.	• The uniqueness of psychology is its psychotherapy treatments.
• Psychologists need drugs to care for their patients properly.	• Prescription privileges will result in a decrease of psychotherapeutic treatment.

YES

Ronald E. Fox

PRESCRIPTION PRIVILEGES: THEIR IMPLICATIONS FOR THE PRACTICE OF PSYCHOLOGY

The practice of psychology has never been a secure occupation, but in the past few years the profession has been subjected to new pressures that are threatening to erode its very foundations. As the nation has struggled to contain spiraling health care costs, new forms of health delivery have emerged that typically either ignore or are antagonistic to the needs of psychology practitioners. In addition to various prepaid plans and closed-panel options, the medical profession and hospitals have developed a series of specialized medical treatment programs for problems that also are treated independently by psychologists. Hospital-operated inpatient and outpatient programs for the treatment of alcoholism, for the management of chronic pain, for various behavior disorders of children and adolescents, for sleep disorders, for rehabilitation programs, and for geriatric day care programs (to name just a few) are growing rapidly in number as hospitals and physicians seek to expand their markets by providing programs that are less expensive alternatives to traditional hospital care. Typically, such programs are designed for physicians with little or no provision for psychologists as autonomous or equal partners. Despite the fact that the major problems being addressed in the new programs are behavioral, and without regard for the fact that the interventions of choice for many of the target symptoms are psychological treatments developed by psychologists, the medical profession shows no hesitancy in coopting such treatments as "medical" or hospital services.

As psychology has grown in knowledge and sophistication its practitioners have felt increasingly hampered by several constraints that make the full use of their knowledge and skills difficult to exercise: lack of appropriate hospital privileges, inability to control restricted drugs used in treating their patients' emotional or behavioral problems, and restrictions in the use of some physical intervention devices developed and/or commonly used by psychologists. . . . In 1985 the Division of Independent Practice of APA [American Psychological Association] established a committee for limited medical privileges to formulate recommendations regarding psychologists' use of psychopharmacological drugs and easier access to hospital care for their patients. While it is too early to determine the final outcome of such efforts, the existence of such groups indicates the seriousness which practitioners attach to these issues.

This article focuses on issues and implications regarding the use of prescription drugs as a part of psychological practice as one aspect of the use of physical interventions by psychologists.

RATIONALE

Psychologists should seek prescription privileges for several reasons: 1) use of medications is a logical extension of psychological practice; 2) current practice and regulations governing practice are based on the false concept of a mind-body dichotomy; and 3) prescription privileges for some psychologists would serve the public interest. The arguments supporting these reasons and some implications of the proposed change follow.

Logical Extension of Practice

. . . [T]he ultimate concerns of professional psychologists are those problems involving human coping skills and human coping effectiveness. Attempts to define the profession by types of client complaints addressed (e.g., mental or emotional problems), or techniques utilized (e.g., behavior modification or psychoanalysis), or by organizational setting in which services are delivered (e.g., clinic or school), are actually definitions of subdomains or specialties of professional

practice and should not be confused with a general definition of professional practice. The value of the psychologist to the public does not hinge on the use of psychotherapy, or on an emphasis on nonphysical interventions, but rather on the fact that it is grounded in the science of human behavior and encompasses extensive knowledge about how to enhance or improve coping skills.

Using the proposed definition, a psychologist treating a patient whose behavior was severely disrupted by acute anxiety attacks could use whatever techniques were available, including anxiolytic drugs, to help the client to cope more effectively. The use of drugs in such a situation would be a logical extension of the psychologists' role as an expert in helping clients to enhance their behavioral coping skills.

The BPA [The American Psychological Association's Board of Professional Affairs] task force on psychologists' use of physical interventions (BPA, 1981), after reviewing and summarizing the large number of physical procedures developed and/or used by psychology practitioners, defined the practice of psychology as

> the observation, assessment or the alteration of behavior and/or concomitant physiological functioning through behavioral procedures. The techniques available to effect such alterations include both physical as well as purely psychologic interventions. (p. 14)

This definition, based on current psychological practice and knowledge, supported the task force's conclusion that psychologists using physical interventions are practicing within the scope of their profession provided that such use 1) is in the domain of health care and designed to improve the quality of assessment or treatment; 2) is within the scope of the practitioner's competence (formal and appropriately supervised training and experience); and 3) is primarily determined by a decision based on consumer welfare. With respect to the issue of the use of controlled substances (medications) in psychological practice, the task force went on to note that "psychologists have made substantial contributions in the field of chemotherapeutic intervention and that it probably would be unwise for psychology as a science and as a profession to accept an indefinite 'proscription' of prescriptive intervention" (BPA, 1981).

Clearly, how the profession defines itself has major implications as to whether the prescription of controlled substances is viewed as falling within the purview of psychological practice. Given definitions such as those discussed above, it is clear that prescription privileges represent a logical extension of current professional practice. Adams (1986) argues that we should not be debating the issue of seeking prescription privileges for all practitioners; rather, we should be seeking to make such privileges a viable practice option for those subspecialty practitioners who wish to exercise it. As Adams correctly points out, options are routinely available for practitioners in other disciplines for using procedures that specific individuals may or may not choose to exercise.

Other professions have been considerably less timid than psychology in seeking the privilege to prescribe drugs. Nurse midwives, optometrists, podiatrists, and dentists have sought and obtained such rights. Psychologists' inability to prescribe drugs makes them an exception among most health care providers which in turn helps contribute to an erroneous public perception that psychologists do not deal with real or serious problems. Psychologists are in direct competition with medicine, for example, and the ability to use drugs (and hospital-based care) has permitted psychiatry to exercise marketing advantages in the treatment of such disorders as anorexia, bulimia, panic disorders, phobic reactions, sleep difficulties, and nicotine addiction, to name but a few. If we continue to sit idly by, our practice base may be taken from us.

Mind–Body Dichotomy
Much of current professional practice, education, and regulation is based on the concept of a mind–body dualism that is widely recognized as invalid. Forty years ago, when efforts were being made to pass the first licensing laws, it doubtless was prudent and politically expedient to accept a dualism that placed all hands-on interventions beyond the scope of the practice of psychology (BPA, 1981). However, it is now undeniably evident to even the casual observer that biomedical and behavioral factors are inextricably interwoven and that no one can adequately treat or understand the one without simultaneously affecting the other.

It seems evident that any profession that is conceptually based on an untenable premise is doomed in the long run. It is no longer intellectually honest to subscribe to the increasingly evident misconception that it is possible to distinguish meaningfully between mind–body units. The mind and body are interacting parts of a single whole, and just as there are physical concomitants of psychological events, so too are there psychological concomitants of physical events. As a science, as an academic discipline, and as a profession, psychology must shed adherence to a dualism that is patently false and free itself to deal with the physical concomitants, components, and consequences of psychological events. The only limits that are acceptable are those imposed by competence, not those imposed by erroneous concepts. . . .

The Public Interest

Prescription privileges for psychologists would serve the public interest in several ways. First, the research training of psychologists uniquely qualifies them to evaluate the efficacy of psychopharmacological interventions. As a profession, psychology has an enviable research record in evaluating the effectiveness of various drugs and their impact on behavior. While research investigations conducted on comparatively homogeneous samples of patients who frequently receive intensive preliminary workups is an entirely different professional activity from the process of routine engagement in the everyday management of a heterogeneous population, a solid foundation for further development has been established.

Second, the predominant symptoms in many diseases of major societal concern are psychological and behavioral in nature. Problems of senility in an increasing population of elderly citizens is one example. Many troublesome conditions and states of aging and/or senility can be materially diminished or ameliorated through psychological intervention, and associated psychopharmacological treatment. Restricting those interventions to one set of providers restricts the availability of needed services and increases costs since free-market conditions cannot prevail.

Third, it is generally acknowledged by practitioners with relevant experience that general practice physicians are, as a rule, less able to evaluate the consumer's response to psychotropic medication than are psychologists (Adams, 1986). While psychologists are capable of learning to prescribe psychoactive drugs at least as well as the average physician in general practice, such a standard of performance may not be ideal and may not be better for consumers (Brandsma & Frey, 1986). Psychologists can be sufficiently prepared by education and training to prescribe drugs in a more appropriate and sophisticated manner than now characterizes the state of the art, and it can be argued that the public interest would be better served by such training.

Fourth, with prescription privileges, psychologists may find it easier to work with nonpsychiatric physicians in meeting the needs of some patients. Many physicians already have formal working relationships with psychologists but find themselves in a less than optimal position when there is a need for psychopharmacological intervention or hospitalization (Adams, 1986). In the author's experience, nonpsychiatric physicians tend to make two types of mistakes in prescribing antianxiety and antipsychotic drugs: 1) insufficient dosage to achieve a therapeutic effect or 2) excessive dosage for the condition being treated. The typical nonpsychiatric physician may not routinely use some of the medications in the course of practice and in addition is unfamiliar with the nature and course of most emotional disorders. In the author's opinion, it is better for the physician, for the psychologist, and for the patient when the medication is handled by the person assuming overall responsibility for the treatment program of the behavioral problem at hand (i.e., the psychologist). While some argue that inappropriate use of medication may simply reflect inter-professional strife and/or poor judgment on the part of psychologists regarding when or how to make needed referrals (Brandsma & Frey, 1986), the author's experience in working with nonpsychiatric physicians over the past 25 years does not support such a conclusion. Many physicians prefer working with a psychologist rather than a psychiatrist, but such physicians do not always want to play a partnership role in the careful management of difficult emotional problems that often involve experimentation with dosages and types of medication and the careful monitoring of the effects. It simply seems more efficacious, and less expensive, for the practitioner who is most knowledgeable about the emotional problem being treated (i.e., the psychologist) also to prescribe and manage the drugs used as a part of the treatment.

Fifth, many psychological disorders can be directly and effectively managed by psychopharmacological approaches. Adams (1986) noted that recent research has demonstrated that rapid and direct intervention through drugs for problems such as sleeping, eating, and panic disorders is a highly efficacious and cost-effective treatment. Given that drugs may be the treatment of choice for some of these problems in some instances, psychologists may well anticipate a day when they could be held legally liable for failure to arrange medication for a particular client. Brandsma & Frey have argued that psychoactive drugs are not panaceas and that proper referral could handle any potential threats regarding failure to prescribe. However, it may be somewhat specious to argue that drugs are not panaceas, since the same may be said about all treatments for emotional disorders and, as stated earlier, referral

to another practitioner for medication is not always an efficient or effective solution. In any event, there is no denying the fact that drugs can play an important and highly effective role in the treatment of many behavioral problems. In the final analysis, it may be unwise for psychologists to accept restrictions of their roles that ultimately may limit their ability to serve the public.

Ethical Considerations

The current APA ethical code (APA, 1981) was not developed to provide guidance for psychologists who are prescribing drugs. Consequently, several major changes would be needed. The preamble to the *Ethical Principles of Psychologists* enjoins psychologists to use their knowledge and skills only for the promotion of human welfare, a statement that obviously would apply equally to drug prescription and to current modes of practice.

It is the section on competence and consumer welfare that would need the most revision in order to provide proper guidance for the practitioner as well as protection for clients. In terms of competence, the current principles state that psychologists "recognize the boundaries of their competence and the limitations of their techniques. They only provide services and only use techniques for which they are qualified by training and experience." Education, training, and supervised expoeriences would need to be developed for that subset of providers who would be prescribing medications and the ethical principles may well have to be strengthened with respect to psychologists' obligations to obtain the necessary training and experience. Special care would need to be taken to ensure that psychologists are made aware of their own limitations and the limitations of their techniques. While the development of a proper knowledge base (and the attendant attitudes and skills) would properly fall to the education and training components of the profession, there also are serious ethical implications regarding how the principles discussed above are codified and implemented.

The ethical code section on competence further states that psychologists must "maintain knowledge of current scientific and professional information related to the services they render." With the advent of prescription privileges, this statement would assume a whole new meaning. If properly and professionally enforced, the implications of such a principle are enormous. Continuing education offerings would have to be expanded exponentially just to provide updates on a rapidly expanding field. Because the changes in psychopharmacology are so rapid, a practitioner who wishes to remain informed will have to devote significantly more time to some form of continuing education than currently is the case. Current ethical principles and guidelines governing the definition of practitioner competence and the maintenance of competence would have to be thoroughly revised and carefully written to cover the many possibilities that increased responsibilities and vulnerabilities would create.

The section on consumer welfare would need special attention and extensive revision. Current standards simply call for the psychologist to fully inform consumers as to the purpose of treatments or procedures being used. The use of medications in diagnosis and treatment would dictate a much more detailed and fully explicated set of rules. Among the myriad consumer protection issues that would be raised is the matter of informed consent. The BPA Task Force warned that if psychologists are to use physical interventions (including controlled substances) they must be required to subscribe fully to informed consent procedures that include providing clients with reliable and accurate knowledge of the purposes, value, and risks of the proposed intervention (BPA, 1981).

REFERENCES

Adams, D. B. (1986). A prescription for psychologists. *Georgia Psychologist*, 39, 13–15.

American Psychological Association (1981). Ethical principles of psychologists. *American Psychologist*, 36, 633–638.

Board of Professional Affairs Task Force Report (1981). *Psychologists' Use of Physical Interventions*. Washington, D.C.: American Psychological Association.

Brandsma, J. M. & Frey, J. III. (1986). Caveats regarding psychologists' prescribing drugs. *Georgia Psychologist*, 39, 16–19.

NO

Garland Y. DeNelsky

PRESCRIPTION PRIVILEGES FOR PSYCHOLOGISTS: THE CASE AGAINST

Several prominent psychologists have argued forcefully in favor of prescription privileges for psychologists (Burns, DeLeon, Chemtob, Welch, & Samuels, 1988; DeLeon, 1988; Fox, 1988a). Only a few authors have opposed this position, despite surveys that indicate that a majority of practicing psychologists are not in favor of psychologists obtaining prescription privileges (Boswell, Litwin, & Kraft, 1988; Piotrowski & Lubin, 1989). The purpose of this article is to provide a reasonably comprehensive exposition of the arguments against psychologists seeking prescription privileges, followed by a critical examination of those arguments that have been proposed in favor of such privileges for psychologists.

CONCEPTUAL ISSUES: WHERE WOULD IT LEAD PSYCHOLOGY?

Prescription privileges could change the direction in which professional psychology evolves. Clinical psychology began in the late 19th century as the application of psychological techniques to the individual (Garfield, 1974). As it developed it focused on assessment, behavioral interventions of various sorts, consultation, and applied research (Kilburg, 1988). The acquisition of prescription privileges could move psychology from a predominantly behavioral field toward one increasingly similar to a medical specialty.

Although no consensus has yet emerged as to a single definition of professional psychology, one definition that has been widely circulated comes from Fox, Barclay, and Rodgers (1982). They proposed that "professional psychology is that profession which is concerned with enhancing the effectiveness of human functioning" (Fox et al., 1982, p. 307). Consistent with this definition, psychology produces a large number of well-trained practitioners who spend much of their professional lives doing psychotherapy and other types of psychological and behavioral interventions.

Before the widespread use of psychoactive medications, psychiatry also emphasized the practice of psychotherapy. It may be more than coincidence

From Garland Y. DeNelsky, "Prescription Privileges for Psychologists: The Case Against," *Professional Psychology: Research and Practice*, vol. 22, no. 3 (1991). Copyright © 1991 by the American Psychological Association. Reprinted by permission. References omitted.

that as psychiatry moved toward increased reliance on psychoactive medications it turned more and more away from psychotherapy. It can be argued that psychoactive medications frequently produce "quick fixes"—reductions in symptoms, with little if any lasting changes in behavior or perception. In the short run, medications are quicker, easier, and more profitable than the demanding work of psychotherapy. When a patient reports a condition such as anxiety, depression, a panic attack, or a sleep disorder, it is both easier and faster to turn to a prescription pad than to those behavioral and psychotherapeutic techniques that have been shown to be effective and lasting. The therapist feels that he or she is doing something now, and the patient may gain some immediate symptomatic relief.

The immediate reinforcement of both therapist and patient can begin a pattern with far-ranging implications. For the therapist the message is that medications provide a quick way to produce some symptomatic relief. Over time, it is possible that some therapists may gradually become influenced by another pattern of reinforcement—that regular use of medications yields greater profits because less time is needed per patient, which results in shorter appointments and hence more available appointment times per day. This could gradually lead to a short circuiting of psychotherapeutic efforts, an effect that may have already influenced many in the field of psychiatry. Perhaps psychologists would like to believe that they are above such temptations, but the profit motive combined with a genuine desire to intervene immediately in a manner that makes the patient feel better are strong forces to overcome.

The use of medications also has some significant messages for the patient. Some of these messages may actually interfere with the processes of personal change and growth. Medications can subtly undercut psychotherapeutic efforts by implying that benefit comes from external agents, not from one's own efforts at change and growth. As Handler (1988) noted, "medication is a temporary solution which has powerful and sometimes peculiar control over consciousness; it teaches the patient little or nothing enduring about self-control" (p. 47).

A large proportion of the population seems to sense the limitations of medications and prefers the nonmedication orientation of psychology (Handler, 1988). If psychologists in large numbers began prescribing medications their patients, many of whom may be seeking bona fide alternatives to medications, may turn to social workers, counselors, and other nonmedical therapists. There can be little question that psychologists' obtaining prescription privileges could have profound effect on the future directions of the profession.

EFFECTS OF PRESCRIPTION PRIVILEGES ON TRAINING

Prescription privileges could have a major impact on the training of psychologists. It is highly likely that training would have to be substantially longer than it is now. Training to prescribe medications will require more than a basic understanding of dosage and side effects, information that many practicing psychologists currently know. Professional education will need to focus a great deal more on basic physiology, neuroanatomy, pharmacology, and physical diseases. This could result in increasing the length of graduate study by a full year or more. Although one proponent of prescription privileges (Fox,

1988b) asserted that "addition of a special tract [to teach medications] would neither seriously distort our basic education in psychology nor necessarily require an extension in the length of time to earn the doctorate" (p. 27), it is hard to imagine how this could be achieved unless there is a great deal of unessential material in current doctoral programs. It is more likely that one or more years of postdoctoral training would be dedicated to acquiring competence in prescribing (Buie, 1988).

When considering training implications, it must be noted that psychologists who prescribe medications will be held responsible for any and all complications that arise from their use. Medication education will need to include, for example, knowledge about how to deal with hypertensive patients, patients on hormone therapy, and diabetics, to mention but a few. Although most patients may present few if any such complications, psychologists will have to learn how to deal with the difficult, medically complex patient. Because psychology will be "the new kid on the block," and a nonmedical one at that, psychologists may be held to higher standards than are customary for physicians. Those standards will no doubt carry over to the courts. Substantially higher malpractice insurance rates can be expected for psychologists who prescribe and those who train others to prescribe; psychiatric malpractice insurance rates are currently 3 to 24 times higher than psychological malpractice coverage, depending on the state (Dörken, 1990).

The basic emphasis in psychology graduate education would shift. At present, the emphasis is on psychologists becoming the preeminent specialists in human behavior change and psychotherapy. By necessity, training would shift from an exclusive emphasis on behavioral change and personal growth through psychological interventions to, at best, a dual emphasis on psychological and medical interventions. This change would carry over into postgraduate continuing education programs as well. Because there is a new crop of medications each year or so, and because the malpractice risk is greater with medical than psychological interventions, it is likely that the preponderance of continuing education programs would be devoted to medication rather than to psychotherapy, behavioral change, assessment, or other psychologically oriented topics. Practicing psychologists would devote less time to keeping up with new developments in psychology and more to acquiring new information about medications.

POLITICAL CONSIDERATIONS: A MAJOR WAR AHEAD?

Even the strongest backers of prescription privileges for psychologists acknowledge that the struggle to secure such privileges would be a major one (Fox, 1988b). It is likely that such a war would indeed be monumental. It is true that an independent profession does not allow other professions to determine its boundaries; nevertheless, the political implications and the potential costs involved must be considered.

The effort to obtain medication privileges would mire psychology in a full-scale war with both psychiatry and medicine. Psychiatry and medicine have issued vehement protests against psychologists prescribing medications in the Indian Health Service (Staff, 1989a). Psychiatrists have denounced a proposed pilot demonstration training program in the military to instruct psychologists in the use of psychoactive medications (Staff, 1989b). The American Medical Association (AMA) has formally gone on record opposing prescription privileges for psychologists (Staff, 1989c).

In all likelihood, the battles that psychology has fought in the past and is currently engaged in over licensure, third-party reimbursement inclusion in Medicare, and even hospital privileges, would be eclipsed. Medicine seems more grimly committed than ever to resisting all efforts to encroach on what it defines as its turf. It is true that other professionals such as dentists, podiatrists, optometrists, pharmacists, nurse practitioners, and physician assistants have secured prescription privileges (Burns et al., 1988). Yet, most of these professions obtained prescription privileges at a time when organized medicine was not as rigidly committed to resisting further incursions into what it defines as its prerogatives. Even more significantly, psychologists with prescription privileges would probably not be viewed as *limited practitioners*, as are those other providers with prescription privileges. If psychologists were able to prescribe medications they would be capable of duplicating virtually everything that psychiatrists do—or at least that is how psychiatry and organized medicine would perceive them. None of the other non-medical professions that have obtained prescription privileges pose such a complete threat to their analogous medical specialities. In short, if organized psychology decided to push ahead for the right to prescribe, it would find itself locked in an enormous struggle.

The financial cost of such a struggle would be immense. It has been estimated that in Massachusetts alone upwards of $4 million would be needed to fight the battle for prescription privileges (Tanney,

1987). If that figure is extrapolated to all 50 states it would not be an overstatement to estimate that the battle could exhaust all of organized psychology's current assets and much more.

Closely related to the issue of financial cost is the question of energy expenditure. If organized psychology decided to seriously pursue prescription privileges, other issues would almost certainly receive diminished emphasis (Kovacs, 1988). Issues such as inclusion of psychological services in health maintenance organizations (HMOs), hospital privileges, minimum mental health benefits, closing the Employment Retirement Income Security Act of 1974 (ERISA) loopholes, and marketing of psychological services would all have to assume reduced priority. When a field is fighting a major war that requires all of its resources, there is a limit to how many other battles can be undertaken simultaneously.

The war could even cost psychology many of its hard-earned gains of the past two or three decades. All current psychology licensing laws preclude prescription of medications, and would have to be revised or amended (Fox, 1988b). These licensing laws would be opened up at a time when psychology's opponents were mobilized against it. It is not too difficult to imagine attempts to eviscerate existing psychology licensing laws and strip away many of the significant gains of the past. Psychology could end up with much less than it started with.

Psychology could also end up with more divisiveness than now exists. If psychologists do obtain prescription privileges, initially there will be a few psychologists who are able to prescribe and many who are not. In view of the strong feelings that are likely to emerge on both sides of this issue, major discord could develop.

For example, after having fought so hard and at such cost to earn the right to prescribe, at least some psychologists will probably exercise that right rather freely. That behavior is likely to draw considerable criticism from others in the field. It is also possible that those psychologists with the right to prescribe may consider themselves "full practitioners" in comparison with their peers who cannot prescribe, which could result in animosities in psychology like those that frequently emerge between psychologists and psychiatrists. For example, if gaining prescription privileges really does lead to broader third-party reimbursement and full hospital privileges for those qualified to prescribe (as has been argued by some), then psychologists unable to prescribe may feel that they have been relegated to a second-class status in their own profession.

MARKETING PSYCHOLOGY: EASIER OR MORE DIFFICULT?

Some proponents of prescription privileges have argued that not securing the right to prescribe keeps psychology at a competitive disadvantage with psychiatry (Fox, 1988a). Although this may be true in some instances, the overall record of psychology in the marketplace does not support this contention. Figures from the Civilian Health and Medical Program for Uniformed Services (CHAMPUS) reveal that in 1987 psychologists provided services for 34% of outpatient behavioral health visits compared with less than 22% for psychiatrists (Buie, 1989a). Five years earlier the figures were reversed, with psychiatrists providing service for 36% of the visits and psychologists for 28%. In short, without prescription privileges, psychologists have become the leading providers of outpatient mental health services. Psychiatry, on the other hand, has been steadily losing its market share over the past five years.

Handler (1988) asserted that the main reason that clinical psychology has prospered is that it has built a reputation as being different from psychiatry. He pointed out that there has been a steady growth, averaging more than 10% per year, in the number of clinical psychologists from 1966 to 1983. He attributed these gains to psychology being "independent and innovative in our training, our research, and in our service delivery . . . to ape psychiatry in providing biological answers when our psychologically based answers are far more adequate for psychotherapeutic intervention is ill advised" (Handler, 1988, p. 45).

Psychology is a vigorous, growing field that is perceived by many as a favorable alternative to the increasingly biological orientation of organized psychiatry. Psychologists should not attempt to blur the differences between psychology and psychiatry in the public's mind; Handler (1988) has argued that "the more the public understands the differences between the two professions the more they will choose a psychologist for the tasks of assessment and psychotherapy" (p. 48). It would be curious logic to engage in a monumental struggle to acquire a tool (prescription privileges) that seems to be leading those who have it to a diminishing share of their market.

CHALLENGE QUESTIONS

Should Psychologists Be Allowed to Prescribe Drugs?

1. Both authors discuss the definition of the psychology profession. Why is this important, and how might different definitions influence the outcome of this issue?

2. Describe how a philosophic question such as the mind/body relationship affects the discussion of this issue.

3. How does a profession like psychology balance the sometimes competing interests of market share and the good of the public?

4. DeNelsky claims that most people prefer a nonmedication treatment when they experience emotional disturbances. Would this be true of you, if you were to experience emotional problems? Why or why not?

ISSUE 19

Would Legalizing Drugs Have Beneficial Effects on Society?

YES: Richard J. Dennis, from "The Economics of Legalizing Drugs," *The Atlantic* (November 1990)

NO: James Q. Wilson, from "Against the Legalization of Drugs," *Commentary* (February 1990)

ISSUE SUMMARY

YES: Richard J. Dennis, chairman of the Advisory Board of the Drug Policy Foundation, argues that legalizing most drugs would reduce crime, save money, and not increase the number of addicts.
NO: Professor of management and public policy James Q. Wilson feels that legalizing drugs would lead to an increase in use, accidents, and drug-related violence.

Drug abuse and drug trafficking have become a national travesty. In fact, many people perceive the problems to be getting worse, rather than better. General frustration with current governmental policies has led many to consider alternative approaches. One such alternative is controlled legalization, or the decriminalization of drugs. This would mean not only that drugs could be bought and sold legally, but that drugs could also be regulated and taxed like alcohol and tobacco (which are also drugs).

Proponents of legalization vary in the extent to which drugs should be permitted. Some advocate that all drugs be legalized, while others lobby for the legalization of marijuana only. All such proponents, however, argue that the cost to our society would be dramatically reduced. Currently the federal government spends billions of dollars a year on antidrug law enforcement. Proponents propose that the money saved could be used to educate and treat drug addicts. Drug offenses account for about 23 percent of all convicted felons. If drugs were legalized, then fewer people would need to violate laws to obtain drugs.

This is essentially the argument of Richard J. Dennis, who writes in favor of legalizing drugs. He suggests that the drug problem is not a moral issue and that most Americans are not morally opposed to substances that alter one's mind or mood. Most believe, for example, that adults should be allowed to use the drug of alcohol as they see fit, as long as others are not harmed in the process. *Excessive* use of drugs is, of course, harmful, but this is also the case with alcohol and tobacco. Dennis does argue that laws protecting children should be retained. He also believes distinctions should be made between certain drugs, such as crack and marijuana, because crack is harmful in ways that marijuana is not. However, the same rules that apply to drugs such as alcohol and tobacco should also apply to other drugs that are of comparable danger.

James Q. Wilson, on the other hand, is opposed to drug legalization. He argues that drug laws increase prices and reduce supplies, which leads to fewer drug users. Legalization, however, would have the opposite effect. If drugs were more readily available, the result would be lower prices and increased drug usage. Wilson uses Great Britain's experience with the legalization of heroin as a case in point. When doctors could legally prescribe heroin to addicts, the number of addicts increased thirtyfold in 10 years. Wilson also decries the "social experimentation" that legalization would entail. Social experiments of this sort have risks that far outweigh their potential benefits. The time and money involved in such experiments would be better spent on drug treatment and education. Wilson warns that there is no way to predict the effects of legalization on our society. However, he believes an increase in drug use and a greater number of crimes are the likely result.

POINT	COUNTERPOINT
• If drugs were legalized, they could be taxed and regulated as alcohol is now.	• Drug enforcement limits the number of users by limiting the drug supply.
• The benefits of legalization would be great enough to offset any resulting increase in the number of users.	• Great Britain's legalization experiment dramatically increased the number of addicts.
• Legalizing drugs would reduce crime and corruption and save society money.	• Legalizing drugs is a social experiment with many possible risks.
• The money saved through legalization could be used to treat addicts.	• Efforts should be aimed solely at more effective treatment programs.
• The drug problem is not a moral issue.	• Dependency on mind-altering drugs is a moral issue.

YES   Richard J. Dennis

THE ECONOMICS OF LEGALIZING DRUGS

Last year federal agents in southern California broke the six-dollar lock on a warehouse and discovered twenty tons of cocaine. The raid was reported to be the largest seizure of illegal narcotics ever. Politicians and law-enforcement officials heralded it as proof not only of the severity of our drug problem but also of the success of our interdiction efforts, and the need for more of the same. However, in reality the California raid was evidence of nothing but the futility and irrationality of our current approach to illegal drugs. It is questionable whether the raid prevented a single person from buying cocaine. Addicts were not driven to seek treatment. No drug lord or street dealer was put out of business. The event had no perceptible impact on the public's attitude toward drug use. People who wanted cocaine still wanted it—and got it.

If the raid had any effect at all, it was perverse. The street price of cocaine in southern California probably rose temporarily, further enriching the criminal network now terrorizing the nation's inner cities. William Bennett, the director of national drug-control policy, and his fellow moral authoritarians were offered another opportunity to alarm an already overwrought public with a fresh gust of rhetoric. New support was given to a Bush Administration plan that is meant to reduce supply but in fact guarantees more money to foreign drug lords, who will soon become the richest private individuals in history.

Indeed, Americans have grown so hysterical about the drug problem that few public figures dare appear soft on drugs or say anything dispassionate about the situation. In a 1989 poll 54 percent of Americans cited drugs as the nation's greatest threat. Four percent named unemployment. It is time, long past time, to take a clear-eyed look at illegal drugs and ask what government and law enforcement can really be expected to do.

Drug illegality has the same effect as a regressive tax: its chief aim is to save relatively wealthy potential users of drugs like marijuana and cocaine from self-destruction, at tremendous cost to the residents of inner cities. For this reason alone, people interested in policies that help America's poor

From Richard J. Dennis, "The Economics of Legalizing Drugs," *The Atlantic* (November 1990). Copyright © 1990 by Richard J. Dennis. Reprinted by permission of the author.

should embrace drug legalization. It would dethrone drug dealers in the ghettos and release inner-city residents from their status as hostages.

Once the drug war is considered in rational terms, the solution becomes obvious: declare peace. Legalize the stuff. Tax it and regulate its distribution, as liquor is now taxed and regulated. Educate those who will listen. Help those who need help.

Arguments for the benefits of drug legalization have appeared frequently in the press, most of them making the point that crime and other social hazards might be reduced as a result. This article presents an economic analysis of the benefits of legalizing drugs.

SOME WRONG WAYS TO DISCUSS THE DRUG PROBLEM

In order to make any sort of sane argument about drugs, of course, we have to decide what the problem is. That isn't as simple as it might seem, Bennett's thirty-second sound bites notwithstanding. It's easier to say what the drug problem is not.

The drug problem is not a moral issue. There's a streak of puritanism in the national soul, true, but most Americans are not morally opposed to substances that alter one's mind and mood. That issue was resolved in 1933, with the repeal of Prohibition. There is no question that drugs used to excess are harmful; so is alcohol. Americans seem to have no moral difficulty with the notion that adults should be allowed to use alcohol as they see fit, as long as others are not harmed.

The drug problem is not the country's most important health issue. The use of heroin and cocaine can result in addic-

tion and death; so can the use of alcohol and tobacco. In fact, some researchers estimate the yearly per capita mortality rate of tobacco among smokers at more than a hundred times that of cocaine among cocaine users. If the drug-policy director is worried about the effect on public health of substance abuse, he should spend most of his time talking about cigarettes and whiskey.

The drug problem is not entirely a societal issue—at least not in the sense that it is portrayed as one by politicians and the media. Drug dealing is a chance for people without legitimate opportunity. The problem of the underclass will never be solved by attacking it with force of arms.

So what is the problem? The heart of it is money. What most Americans want is less crime and less profit for inner-city thugs and Colombian drug lords. Less self-destruction by drug users would be nice, but what people increasingly demand is an end to the foreign and domestic terrorism—financed by vast amounts of our own money—associated with the illegal drug trade.

This, as it happens, is a problem that can be solved in quick and pragmatic fashion, by legalizing the sale of most drugs to adults. Virtually overnight crime and corruption would be reduced. The drug cartels would be shattered. Public resources could be diverted to meaningful education and treatment programs.

The alternative—driving up drug prices and increasing public costs with an accelerated drug war—inevitably will fail to solve anything. Instead of making holy war on the drug barons, the President's plan subsidizes them.

Laws protecting children should obviously be retained. Some might question the effectiveness of combining legal drug use by adults with harsh penalties for the sale of drugs to minors. But effective statutory-rape laws demonstrate that society can maintain a distinction between the behavior of adults and that of minors when it truly believes such a distinction is warranted.

Legalization would require us to make some critical distinctions among drugs and drug users, of course. The Administration's plan approaches the drug problem as a seamless whole. But in fact crack and heroin are harmful in ways that marijuana is not. This failure to distinguish among different drugs and their consequences serves only to discredit the anti-drug effort, especially among young people. It also disperses law-enforcement efforts, rendering them hopelessly ineffective. Instead of investing immense resources in a vain attempt to control the behavior of adults, we should put our money where the crisis is. Why spend anything to prosecute marijuana users in a college dormitory when the focus should be on the crack pusher in the Bronx schoolyard?

The appropriate standard in deciding if a drug should be made legal for adults ought to be whether it is more likely than alcohol to cause harm to an innocent party. If not, banning it cannot be justified while alcohol remains legal. For example, a sensible legalization plan would allow users of marijuana to buy it legally. Small dealers could sell it legally but would be regulated, as beer dealers are now in states where beer is sold in grocery stores. Their suppliers would be licensed and regulated. Selling marijuana to minors would be criminal.

Users of cocaine should be able to buy it through centers akin to state liquor stores. It is critical to remove the black-market profit from cocaine in order to destabilize organized crime and impoverish pushers. Selling cocaine to minors would be criminal, as it is now, but infractions could be better policed if effort were concentrated on them. Any black market that might remain would be in sales of crack or sales to minors, transactions that are now estimated to account for 20 percent of drug sales.

Cocaine runs the spectrum from coca leaf to powder to smokable crack; it's the way people take it that makes the difference. Crack's effects on individual behavior and its addictive potential place it in a category apart from other forms of cocaine. The actual degree of harm it does to those who use it is still to be discovered, but for the sake of argument let's assume that it presents a clear danger to people who come in contact with the users. A crack user, therefore, should be subject to a civil fine, and mandatory treatment after multiple violations. Small dealers should have their supplies seized and be subject to moderate punishment for repeat offenses. Major dealers, however, should be subject to the kinds of sentences that are now given. And any adult convicted of selling crack to children should face the harshest prison sentence our criminal-justice system can mete out.

The same rules should apply to any drug that presents a substantial threat to others.

A serious objection to legalizing cocaine while crack remains illegal is that cocaine could be bought, turned into crack, and sold. But those who now buy powder cocaine could take it home and make it into crack, and very few do so. Moreover, legal cocaine would most likely be consumed in different settings and under different circumstances than still-illegal crack would be. Researchers believe that more-benign settings reduce the probability of addiction. Legalization could make it less likely that cocaine users will become crack users. In addition, an effective dose of crack is already so cheap that price is not much of a deterrent to those who want to try it. No price reduction as a result of the legalization of cocaine, then, should lead to a significant increase in the number of crack users.

As for heroin, the advent of methadone clinics shows that society has realized that addicts require maintenance. But there is little practical difference between methadone and heroin, and methadone clinics don't get people off methadone. Heroin addicts should receive what they require, so that they don't have to steal to support their habit. This would make heroin unprofitable for its pushers. And providing addicts with access to uninfected needles would help stop the spread of AIDS and help lure them into treatment programs. . . .

SOME OBJECTIONS CONSIDERED

The fear that legalization would lead to increased drug use and addiction is not, of course, the only basis on which legalization is opposed. We should address other frequently heard objections here.

Crack is our No. 1 drug problem. Legalizing other drugs while crack remains illegal won't solve the problem. Although crack has captured the lion's share of public attention, marijuana has always commanded the bulk of law-enforcement interest. Despite de facto urban decriminalization, more than a third of all drug arrests occur in connection with marijuana—mostly for mere possession. Three fourths of all violations of drug laws relate to marijuana, and two thirds of all people charged with violation of federal marijuana laws are sentenced to prison (state figures are not available).

Crack appears to account for about 10 percent of the total dollar volume of the drug trade, according to National Institute on Drug Abuse estimates of the number of regular crack users. Legalizing other drugs would free up most of the law-enforcement resources currently focused on less dangerous substances and their users. It's true that as long as crack remains illegal, there will be a black market and associated crime. But we would still reap most of the benefits of legalization outlined above.

Legalization would result in a huge loss in productivity and in higher health-care costs. In truth, productivity lost to drugs is minor compared with productivity lost to alcohol and cigarettes, which remain legal. Hundreds of variables affect a person's job performance, ranging from the consumption of whiskey and cigarettes to obesity and family problems. On a purely statistical level it can be demonstrated that marital status affects productivity, yet we do not allow employers to dismiss workers on the basis of that factor.

If legal drug use resulted in higher social costs, the government could levy a tax on the sale of drugs in some rough proportion to the monetary value of those costs—as it does now for alcohol and cigarettes. This wouldn't provide the government with a financial stake in addiction. Rather, the government would be making sure that users of socially costly items paid those social costs. Funds from the tax on decriminalized drugs could be used for anti-drug advertising, which could be made more effective by a total ban on drug advertising. A government that licenses the sale of drugs must actively educate its citizens about their dangers, as Holland does in discouraging young people from using marijuana.

Drug legalization implies approval. One of the glories of American life is that many things that are not condoned by society at large, such as atheism, offensive speech, and heavy-metal music, are legal. The well-publicized death of Len Bias [a potential professional basketball star who died of a crack overdose] and other harrowing stories have carried the message far and wide that drugs are dangerous. In arguing that legalization would persuade people that drug use is safe, drug warriors underestimate our intelligence.

Any restriction on total legalization would lead to continuing, substantial corruption. Under the plan proposed here, restrictions would continue on the sale of crack and on the sale of all drugs to children. Even if black-market corruption continued in those areas, we would experience an immediate 80 percent reduction in corruption overall.

Legalization is too unpredictable and sweeping an action to be undertaken all at once. It would be better to establish several test areas first, and evaluate the results. The results of such a trial would probably not further the case of either side. If use went up in the test area, it could be argued that this was caused by an influx of people from areas where drugs were still illegal; if use went down, it could be argued that the area chosen was unrepresentative.

Even if current drugs are legalized, much more destructive drugs will be developed in the future. The most destructive current drug is crack, which would remain illegal. Many analysts believe that the development of crack was a marketing strategy, since powder cocaine was too expensive for many users. If cocaine had been legal, crack might never have been marketed. In any case, if a drug presents a clear danger to bystanders, it should not be legal.

No matter how the government distributes drugs, users will continue to seek greater quantities and higher potency on the black market. If the government restricts the amount of a drug that can be distributed legally, legalization will fail. It must make drugs available at all levels of quantity and potency. The government should regulate the distributors but not the product itself. The model should be the distribution of alcohol through state-regulated liquor stores.

Legalizing drugs would ensure that America's inner cities remain places of hopelessness and despair. If drugs disappeared tomorrow from America's ghettos, the ghettos would remain places of hopelessness and despair. But legalization would put most drug dealers out of business and remove the main source of financing for violent gangs. At the least, legalization would spare the inner cities from drug-driven terrorism.

Marijuana in itself may be relatively harmless, but it is a "gateway drug." Legalization would lead its users to more harmful and addictive drugs. While government studies show some correlation between marijuana use and cocaine addiction, they also show that tobacco and alcohol use correlate with drug addiction. Moreover, keeping marijuana illegal forces buyers into an illegal market, where they are likely to be offered other drugs. Finally, 60 million Americans have tried marijuana, and there are one million cocaine addicts. If marijuana is a gateway drug, the gate is narrow.

Legalizing drugs would aggravate the growing problem of "crack babies." The sale of crack would remain illegal. Even so, it is difficult to believe that anyone ignorant or desperate enough to use crack while pregnant would be deterred by a law. Laws against drug use are more likely to deter users from seeking treatment. Crack babies probably would have a better chance in a less censorious environment, in which their mothers had less to fear from seeking treatment.

Drug use in the United States can be seen as a symptom of recent cultural changes that have led to an erosion of traditional values and an inability to replace them. There are those who are willing to pay the price to try to save people from themselves. But there are surely just as many who would pay to preserve a person's right to be wrong. To the pragmatist, the choice is clear: legalization is the best bet.

NO

James Q. Wilson

AGAINST THE LEGALIZATION OF DRUGS

In 1972, the President appointed me chairman of the National Advisory Council for Drug Abuse Prevention. Created by Congress, the Council was charged with providing guidance on how best to coordinate the national war on drugs. (Yes, we called it a war then, too.) In those days, the drug we were chiefly concerned with was heroin. When I took office, heroin use had been increasing dramatically. Everybody was worried that this increase would continue. Such phrases as "heroin epidemic" were commonplace.

That same year, the eminent economist Milton Friedman published an essay in *Newsweek* in which he called for legalizing heroin. His argument was on two grounds: as a matter of ethics, the government has no right to tell people not to use heroin (or to drink or to commit suicide); as a matter of economics, the prohibition of drug use imposes costs on society that far exceed the benefits. Others, such as the psychoanalyst Thomas Szasz, made the same argument.

We did not take Friedman's advice. (Government commissions rarely do.) I do not recall that we even discussed legalizing heroin, though we did discuss (but did not take action on) legalizing a drug, cocaine, that many people then argued was benign. Our marching orders were to figure out how to win the war on heroin, not to run up the white flag of surrender.

That was 1972. Today, we have the same number of heroin addicts that we had then—half a million, give or take a few thousand. Having that many heroin addicts is no trivial matter; these people deserve our attention. But not having had an increase in that number for over fifteen years is also something that deserves our attention. What happened to the "heroin epidemic" that many people once thought would overwhelm us?

The facts are clear: a more or less stable pool of heroin addicts has been getting older, with relatively few new recruits. In 1976 the average age of heroin users who appeared in hospital emergency rooms was about twenty-seven; ten years later it was thirty-two. More than two-thirds of all heroin users appearing in emergency rooms are now over the age of thirty. Back in the early 1970's, when heroin got onto the national political agenda, the typical heroin addict was much younger, often a teenager. Household surveys show the same thing—the rate of opiate use (which includes heroin) has been flat for the better part of two decades. More fine-grained studies of inner-city neighborhoods confirm this. John Boyle and Ann Brunswick found that the percentage of young blacks in Harlem who used heroin fell from 8 percent in 1970–71 to about 3 percent in 1975–76.

Why did heroin lose its appeal for young people? When the young blacks in Harlem were asked why they stopped, more than half mentioned "trouble with the law" or "high cost" (and high cost is, of course, directly the result of law enforcement). Two-thirds said that heroin hurt their health; nearly all said they had had a bad experience with it. We need not rely, however, simply on what they said. In New York City in 1973–75, the street price of heroin rose dramatically and its purity sharply declined, probably as a result of the heroin shortage caused by the success of the Turkish government in reducing the supply of opium base and of the French government in closing down heroin-processing laboratories located in and around Marseilles. These were short-lived gains for, just as Friedman predicted, alternative sources of supply— mostly in Mexico—quickly emerged. But the three-year heroin shortage interrupted the easy recruitment of new users.

Health and related problems were no doubt part of the reason for the reduced flow of recruits. Over the preceding years, Harlem youth had watched as more and

more heroin users died of overdoses, were poisoned by adulterated doses, or acquired hepatitis from dirty needles. The word got around: heroin can kill you. By 1974 new hepatitis cases and drug-overdose deaths had dropped to a fraction of what they had been in 1970.

Alas, treatment did not seem to explain much of the cessation in drug use. Treatment programs can and do help heroin addicts, but treatment did not explain the drop in the number of *new* users (who by definition had never been in treatment) nor even much of the reduction in the number of experienced users.

No one knows how much of the decline to attribute to personal observation as opposed to high prices or reduced supply. But other evidence suggests strongly that price and supply played a large role. In 1972 the National Advisory Council was especially worried by the prospect that U.S. servicemen returning to this country from Vietnam would bring their heroin habits with them. Fortunately, a brilliant study by Lee Robins of Washington University in St. Louis put that fear to rest. She measured drug use of Vietnam veterans shortly after they had returned home. Though many had used heroin regularly while in Southeast Asia, most gave up the habit when back in the United States. The reason: here, heroin was less available and sanctions on its use were more pronounced. Of course, if a veteran had been willing to pay enough—which might have meant traveling to another city and would certainly have meant making an illegal contact with a disreputable dealer in a threatening neighborhood in order to acquire a (possibly) dangerous dose—he could have sustained his drug habit. Most veterans were unwilling to pay this price, and so their drug use declined or disappeared.

RELIVING THE PAST

Suppose we had taken Friedman's advice in 1972. What would have happened? We cannot be entirely certain, but at a minimum we would have placed the young heroin addicts (and, above all, the prospective addicts) in a very different position from the one in which they actually found themselves. Heroin would have been legal. Its price would have been reduced by 95 percent (minus whatever we chose to recover in taxes.) Now that it could be sold by the same people who make aspirin, its quality would have been assured—no poisons, no adulterants. Sterile hypodermic needles would have been readily available at the neighborhood drugstore, probably at the same counter where the heroin was sold. No need to travel to big cities or unfamiliar neighborhoods—heroin could have been purchased anywhere, perhaps by mail order.

There would no longer have been any financial or medical reason to avoid heroin use. Anybody could have afforded it. We might have tried to prevent children from buying it, but as we have learned from our efforts to prevent minors from buying alcohol and tobacco, young people have a way of penetrating markets theoretically reserved for adults. Returning Vietnam veterans would have discovered that Omaha and Raleigh had been converted into the pharmaceutical equivalent of Saigon.

Under these circumstances, can we doubt for a moment that heroin use would have grown exponentially? Or that a vastly larger supply of new users would have been recruited? Professor Friedman is a Nobel Prize-winning economist whose understanding of market forces is profound. What did he think would happen to consumption under his legalized regime? Here are his words: "Legalizing drugs might increase the number of addicts, but it is not clear that it would. Forbidden fruit is attractive, particularly to the young."

Really? I suppose that we should expect no increase in Porsche sales if we cut the price by 95 percent, no increase in whiskey sales if we cut the price by a comparable amount—because young people only want fast cars and strong liquor when they are "forbidden." Perhaps Friedman's uncharacteristic lapse from the obvious implications of price theory can be explained by a misunderstanding of how drug users are recruited. In his 1972 essay he said that "drug addicts are deliberately made by pushers, who give likely prospects their first few doses free." If drugs were legal it would not pay anybody to produce addicts, because everybody would buy from the cheapest source. But as every drug expert knows, pushers do not produce addicts. Friends or acquaintances do. In fact, pushers are usually reluctant to deal with non-users because a non-user could be an undercover cop. Drug use spreads in the same way any fad or fashion spreads: somebody who is already a user urges his friends to try, or simply shows already-eager friends how to do it.

But we need not rely on speculation, however plausible, that lowered prices and more abundant supplies would have increased heroin usage. Great Britain once followed such a policy and with almost exactly those results. Until the mid-1960's, British physicians were allowed to prescribe heroin to certain classes of addicts. (Possessing these drugs without a doctor's prescription remained a criminal offense.) For many years this policy worked well enough because the addict patients were typically middle-class people who had become dependent on opiate painkillers while undergoing hospital treatment. There was no drug culture. The British system worked for many years, not because it prevented drug abuse, but because there was no problem of drug abuse that would test the system.

All that changed in the 1960's. A few unscrupulous doctors began passing out heroin in wholesale amounts. One doctor prescribed almost 600,000 heroin tablets—that is, over thirteen pounds—in just one year. A youthful drug culture emerged with a demand for drugs far different from that of the older addicts. As a result, the British government required doctors to refer users to government-run clinics to receive their heroin.

But the shift to clinics did not curtail the growth in heroin use. Throughout the 1960's the number of addicts increased—the late John Kaplan of Stanford estimated by fivefold—in part as a result of the diversion of heroin from clinic patients to new users on the streets. An addict would bargain with the clinic doctor over how big a dose he would receive. The patient wanted as much as he could get, the doctor wanted to give as little as was needed. The patient had an advantage in this conflict because the doctor could not be certain how much was really needed. Many patients would use some of their "maintenance" dose and sell the remaining part to friends, thereby recruiting new addicts. As the clinics learned of this, they began to shift their treatment away from heroin and toward methadone, an addictive drug that, when taken orally, does not produce a "high" but will block the withdrawal pains associated with heroin abstinence.

Whether what happened in England in the 1960's was a mini-epidemic or an epidemic depends on whether one looks at numbers or at rates of change. Compared to the United States, the numbers were small. In 1960 there were 68 heroin addicts known to the British government; by 1968 there were 2,000 in treatment and many more who refused treatment. (They would refuse in part because they did not want to get methadone at a clinic if they could get heroin on the street.) Richard Hartnoll estimates that the actual number of addicts in England is five times the number officially registered. At a minimum, the number of British addicts increased by thirtyfold in ten years; the actual increase may have been much larger.

In the early 1980's the numbers began to rise again, and this time nobody doubted that a real epidemic was at hand. The increase was estimated to be 40 percent a year. By 1982 there were thought to be 20,000 heroin users in London alone. Geoffrey Pearson reports that many cities—Glasgow, Liverpool, Manchester, and Sheffield among them—were now experiencing a drug problem that once had been largely confined to London. The problem, again, was supply. The country was being flooded with cheap, high-quality heroin, first from Iran and then from Southeast Asia.

The United States began the 1960's with a much larger number of heroin addicts and probably a bigger at-risk population than was the case in Great Britain. Even though it would be foolhardy to suppose that the British system, if installed here, would have worked the same way or with the same results, it would be equally foolhardy to suppose that a combination of heroin available from leaky clinics and from street dealers who faced only minimal law-enforcement risks would not have produced a much greater increase in heroin use than we actually experienced. My guess is that if we had allowed either doctors or clinics to prescribe heroin, we would have had far worse results than were produced in Britain, if for no other reason than the vastly larger number of addicts with which we began. We would have had to find some way to police thousands (not scores) of physicians and hundreds (not dozens) of clinics. If the British civil service found it difficult to keep heroin in the hands of addicts and out of the hands of recruits when it was dealing with a few hundred people, how well would the American civil service have accomplished the same tasks when dealing with tens of thousands of people?

BACK TO THE FUTURE

Now cocaine, especially in its potent form, crack, is the focus of attention. Now as in 1972 the government is trying to reduce its use. Now as then some people are advocating legalization. Is there any more reason to yield to those arguments today than there was almost two decades ago?*

I think not. If we had yielded in 1972 we almost certainly would have had today a permanent population of several million, not several hundred thousand,

*I do not here take up the question of marijuana. For a variety of reasons—its widespread use and its lesser tendency to addict—it presents a different problem from cocaine or heroin. For a penetrating analysis, see Mark Kleiman, *Marijuana: Costs of Abuse, Costs of Control* (Greenwood Press, 217 pp., $37.95).

heroin addicts. If we yield now we will have a far more serious problem with cocaine.

Crack is worse than heroin by almost any measure. Heroin produces a pleasant drowsiness and, if hygienically administered, has only the physical side effects of constipation and sexual impotence. Regular heroin use incapacitates many users, especially poor ones, for any productive work or social responsibility. They will sit nodding on a street corner, helpless but at least harmless. By contrast, regular cocaine use leaves the user neither helpless nor harmless. When smoked (as with crack) or injected, cocaine produces instant, intense, and short-lived euphoria. The experience generates a powerful desire to repeat it. If the drug is readily available, repeat use will occur. Those people who progress to "bingeing" on cocaine become devoted to the drug and its effects to the exclusion of almost all other considerations—job, family, children, sleep, food, even sex. Dr. Frank Gawin at Yale and Dr. Everett Ellinwood at Duke report that a substantial percentage of all high-dose, binge users become uninhibited, impulsive, hypersexual, compulsive, irritable, and hyperactive. Their moods vacillate dramatically, leading at times to violence and homicide.

Women are much more likely to use crack than heroin, and if they are pregnant, the effects on their babies are tragic. Douglas Besharov, who has been following the effects of drugs on infants for twenty years, writes that nothing he learned about heroin prepared him for the devastation of cocaine. Cocaine harms the fetus and can lead to physical deformities or neurological damage. Some crack babies have for all practical purposes suffered a disabling stroke while still in the womb. The long-term consequences of this brain damage are lowered cognitive ability and the onset of mood disorders. Besharov estimates that about 30,000 to 50,000 such babies are born every year, about 7,000 in New York City alone. There may be ways to treat such infants, but from everything we now know the treatment will be long, difficult, and expensive. Worse, the mothers who are most likely to produce crack babies are precisely the ones who, because of poverty or temperament, are least able and willing to obtain such treatment. In fact, anecdotal evidence suggests that crack mothers are likely to abuse their infants.

The notion that abusing drugs such as cocaine is a "victimless crime" is not only absurd but dangerous. Even ignoring the fetal drug syndrome, crack-dependent people are, like heroin addicts, individuals who regularly victimize their children by neglect, their spouses by improvidence, their employers by lethargy, and their co-workers by carelessness. Society is not and could never be a collection of autonomous individuals. We all have a stake in ensuring that each of us displays a minimal level of dignity, responsibility, and empathy. We cannot, of course, coerce people into goodness, but we can and should insist that some standards must be met if society itself—on which the very existence of the human personality depends—is to persist. Drawing the line that defines those standards is difficult and contentious, but if crack and heroin use do not fall below it, what does?

The advocates of legalization will respond by suggesting that my picture is overdrawn. Ethan Nadelmann of Princeton argues that the risk of legalization is less than most people suppose. Over 20 million Americans between the ages of eighteen and twenty-five have tried cocaine (according to a government survey), but only a quarter million use it daily. From this Nadelmann concludes that at most 3 percent of all young people who try cocaine develop a problem with it. The implication is clear: make the drug legal and we only have to worry about 3 percent of our youth.

The implication rests on a logical fallacy and a factual error. The fallacy is this: the percentage of occasional cocaine users who become binge users *when the drug is illegal* (and thus expensive and hard to find) tells us nothing about the percentage who will become dependent when the drug is legal (and thus cheap and abundant). Drs. Gawin and Ellinwood report, in common with several other researchers, that controlled or occasional use of cocaine changes to compulsive and frequent use "when access to the drug increases" or when the user switches from snorting to smoking. More cocaine more potently administered alters, perhaps sharply, the proportion of "controlled" users who become heavy users.

The factual error is this: the federal survey Nadelmann quotes was done in 1985, *before* crack had become common. Thus the probability of becoming dependent on cocaine was derived from the responses of users who snorted the drug. The speed and potency of cocaine's action increases dramatically when it is smoked. We do not yet know how greatly the advent of crack increases the risk of dependency, but all the clinical evidence suggests that the increase is likely to be large.

It is possible that some people will not become heavy users even when the drug is readily available in its most potent form. So far there are no scientific grounds for predicting who will and who will not become dependent. Neither socioeconomic background nor personality traits differentiate between casual and intensive users. Thus, the only way to settle the question of who is correct about the effect of easy availability on drug use, Nadelmann or Gawin and Ellinwood, is to try it and see. But that social experiment is so risky as to be no experiment at all, for if cocaine is legalized and if the rate of its abusive use increases dramatically, there is no way to put the genie back in the bottle, and it is not a kindly genie. . . .

THE BENEFITS OF ILLEGALITY

The advocates of legalization find nothing to be said in favor of the current system except, possibly, that it keeps the number of addicts smaller than it would otherwise be. In fact, the benefits are more substantial than that.

First, treatment. All the talk about providing "treatment on demand" implies that there is a demand for treatment. That is not quite right. There are some drug-dependent people who genuinely want treatment and will remain in it if offered; they should receive it. But there are far more who want only short-term help after a bad crash; once stabilized and bathed, they are back on the street again, hustling. And even many of the addicts who enroll in a program honestly wanting help drop out after a short while when they discover that help takes time and commitment. Drug-dependent people have very short time horizons and a weak capacity for commitment. These two groups—those looking for a quick fix and those unable to stick with a long-term fix—are not easily helped. Even if

we increase the number of treatment slots—as we should—we would have to do something to make treatment more effective.

One thing that can often make it more effective is compulsion. Douglas Anglin of UCLA, in common with many other researchers, has found that the longer one stays in a treatment program, the better the chances of a reduction in drug dependency. But he, again like most other researchers, has found that dropout rates are high. He has also found, however, that patients who enter treatment under legal compulsion stay in the program longer than those not subject to such pressure. His research on the California civil-commitment program, for example, found that heroin users involved with its required drug-testing program had over the long term a lower rate of heroin use than similar addicts who were free of such constraints. If for many addicts compulsion is a useful component of treatment, it is not clear how compulsion could be achieved in a society in which purchasing, possessing, and using the drug were legal. It could be managed, I suppose, but I would not want to have to answer the challenge from the American Civil Liberties Union that it is wrong to compel a person to undergo treatment for consuming a legal commodity.

Next, education. We are now investing substantially in drug-education programs in the schools. Though we do not yet know for certain what will work, there are some promising leads. But I wonder how credible such programs would be if they were aimed at dissuading children from doing something perfectly legal. We could, of course, treat drug education like smoking education: inhaling crack and inhaling tobacco are both legal, but you should not do it because it is bad for you. That tobacco is bad for you is easily shown; the Surgeon General has seen to that. But what do we say about crack? It is pleasurable, but devoting yourself to so much pleasure is not a good idea (though perfectly legal)? Unlike tobacco, cocaine will not give you cancer or emphysema, but it will lead you to neglect your duties to family, job, and neighborhood? Everybody is doing cocaine, but you should not?

Again, it might be possible under a legalized regime to have effective drug-prevention programs, but their effectiveness would depend heavily, I think, on first having decided that cocaine use, like tobacco use, is purely a matter of practical consequences; no fundamental moral significance attaches to either. But if we believe—as I do—that dependency on certain mind-altering drugs *is* a moral issue and that their illegality rests in part on their immorality, then legalizing them undercuts, if it does not eliminate altogether, the moral message.

That message is at the root of the distinction we now make between nicotine and cocaine. Both are highly addictive; both have harmful physical effects. But we treat the two drugs differently, not simply because nicotine is so widely used as to be beyond the reach of effective prohibition, but because its use does not destroy the user's essential humanity. Tobacco shortens one's life, cocaine debases it. Nicotine alters one's habits, cocaine alters one's soul. The heavy use of crack, unlike the heavy use of tobacco, corrodes those natural sentiments of sympathy and duty that constitute our human nature and make possible our social life. To say, as does Nadelmann, that distinguishing morally between tobacco and cocaine is "little more than a transient prejudice" is close to saying that morality itself is but a prejudice.

THE ALCOHOL PROBLEM

Now we have arrived where many arguments about legalizing drugs begin: is there any reason to treat heroin and cocaine differently from the way we treat alcohol?

There is no easy answer to that question because, as with so many human problems, one cannot decide simply on the basis either of moral principles or of individual consequences; one has to temper any policy by a common-sense judgment of what is possible. Alcohol, like heroin, cocaine, PCP, and marijuana, is a drug—that is, a mood-altering substance—and consumed to excess it certainly has harmful consequences: auto accidents, barroom fights, bedroom shootings. It is also, for some people, addictive. We cannot confidently compare the addictive powers of these drugs, but the best evidence suggests that crack and heroin are much more addictive than alcohol.

Many people, Nadelmann included, argue that since the health and financial costs of alcohol abuse are so much higher than those of cocaine or heroin abuse, it is hypocritical folly to devote our efforts to preventing cocaine or drug use. But as Mark Kleiman of Harvard has pointed out, this comparison is quite misleading. What Nadelmann is doing is showing that a *legalized* drug (alcohol) produces greater harm than *illegal* ones (cocaine and heroin). But of course. Suppose that in the 1920's we had made heroin and cocaine legal and alcohol illegal. Can anyone doubt that Nadelmann would now be writing that it is folly to continue our ban on alcohol because cocaine and heroin are so much more harmful?

And let there be no doubt about it—widespread heroin and cocaine use are associated with all manner of ills. Thomas Bewley found that the mortality rate of British heroin addicts in 1968 was 28 times as high as the death rate of the same age group of non-addicts, even though in England at the time an addict could obtain free or low-cost heroin and clean needles from British clinics. Perform the following mental experiment: suppose we legalized heroin and cocaine in this country. In what proportion of auto fatalities would the state police report that the driver was nodding off on heroin or recklessly driving on a coke high? In what proportion of spouse-assault and child-abuse cases would the local police report that crack was involved? In what proportion of industrial accidents would safety investigators report that the forklift or drill-press operator was in a drug-induced stupor or frenzy? We do not know exactly what the proportion would be, but anyone who asserts that it would not be much higher than it is now would have to believe that these drugs have little appeal except when they are illegal. And that is nonsense.

An advocate of legalization might concede that social harm—perhaps harm equivalent to that already produced by alcohol—would follow from making cocaine and heroin generally available. But at least, he might add, we would have the problem "out in the open" where it could be treated as a matter of "public health." That is well and good, if we knew how to treat—that is, cure—heroin and cocaine abuse. But we do not know how to do it for all the people who would need such help. We are having only limited success in coping with chronic alco-

holics. Addictive behavior is immensely difficult to change, and the best methods for changing it—living in drug-free therapeutic communities, becoming faithful members of Alcoholics Anonymous or Narcotics Anonymous—require great personal commitment, a quality that is, alas, in short supply among the very persons—young people, disadvantaged people—who are often most at risk for addiction.

Suppose that today we had, not 15 million alcohol abusers, but half a million. Suppose that we already knew what we have learned from our long experience with the widespread use of alcohol. Would we make whiskey legal? I do not know, but I suspect there would be a lively debate. The Surgeon General would remind us of the risks alcohol poses to pregnant women. The National Highway Traffic Safety Administration would point to the likelihood of more highway fatalities caused by drunk drivers. The Food and Drug Administration might find that there is a non-trivial increase in cancer associated with alcohol consumption. At the same time the police would report great difficulty in keeping illegal whiskey out of our cities, officers being corrupted by bootleggers, and alcohol addicts often resorting to crime to feed their habit. Libertarians, for their part, would argue that every citizen has a right to drink anything he wishes and that drinking is, in any event, a "victimless crime."

However the debate might turn out, the central fact would be that the problem was still, at that point, a small one. The government cannot legislate away the addictive tendencies in all of us, nor can it remove completely even the most dangerous addictive substances. But it can cope with harms when the harms are still manageable.

SCIENCE AND ADDICTION

One advantage of containing a problem while it is still containable is that it buys time for science to learn more about it and perhaps to discover a cure. Almost unnoticed in the current debate over legalizing drugs is that basic science has made rapid strides in identifying the underlying neurological processes involved in some forms of addiction. Stimulants such as cocaine and amphetamines alter the way certain brain cells communicate with one another. That alteration is complex and not entirely understood, but in simplified form it involves modifying the way in which a neurotransmitter called dopamine sends signals from one cell to another. . . .

Whatever the exact mechanism may be, once it is identified it becomes possible to use drugs to block either the effect of cocaine or its tendency to produce dependency. There have already been experiments using desipramine, imipramine, bromocriptine, carbamazepine, and other chemicals. There are some promising results.

Tragically, we spend very little on such research, and the agencies funding it have not in the past occupied very influential or visible posts in the federal bureaucracy. If there is one aspect of the "war on drugs" metaphor that I dislike, it is its tendency to focus attention almost exclusively on the troops in the trenches, whether engaged in enforcement or treatment, and away from the research-and-development efforts back on the home front where the war may ultimately be decided.

I believe that the prospects of scientists in controlling addiction will be strongly influenced by the size and character of the problem they face. If the problem is a few hundred thousand chronic, high-dose users of an illegal product, the chances of making a difference at a reasonable cost will be much greater than if the problem is a few million chronic users of legal substances. Once a drug is legal, not only will its use increase but many of those who then use it will prefer the drug to the treatment: they will want the pleasure, whatever the cost to themselves or their families, and they will resist—probably successfully—any effort to wean them away from experiencing the high that comes from inhaling a legal substance.

IF I AM WRONG . . .

No one can know what our society would be like if we changed the law to make access to cocaine, heroin, and PCP easier. I believe, for reasons given, that the result would be a sharp increase in use, a more widespread degradation of the human personality, and a greater rate of accidents and violence.

I may be wrong. If I am, then we will needlessly have incurred heavy costs in law enforcement and some forms of criminality. But if I am right, and the legalizers prevail anyway, then we will have consigned millions of people, hundreds of thousands of infants, and hundreds of neighborhoods to a life of oblivion and disease. To the lives and families destroyed by alcohol we will have added countless more destroyed by cocaine, heroin, PCP, and whatever else a basement scientist can invent.

Human character is formed by society; indeed, human character is inconceivable without society, and good character is less likely in a bad society. Will we, in the name of an abstract doctrine of radical individualism, and with the false comfort of suspect predictions, decide to take the chance that somehow individual decency can survive amid a more general level of degradation?

I think not. The American people are too wise for that, whatever the academic essayists and cocktail-party pundits may say. But if Americans today are less wise than I suppose, then Americans at some future time will look back on us now and wonder, what kind of people were they that they could have done such a thing?

CHALLENGE QUESTIONS

Would Legalizing Drugs Have Beneficial Effects on Society?

1. How would drug legalization affect you personally? Would you or your friends be more likely to try drugs? Why or why not?

2. Do you feel that most people who refrain from using drugs do so for moral or legal reasons? Poll your class to investigate your hypothesis.

3. Do you believe that legal drugs, such as alcohol and tobacco, are more or less harmful than illegal drugs? Support your position.

4. Marijuana use has been called a "victimless crime." Do you agree that this drug has no harmful effects on persons other than the user? How might your position change if marijuana were legalized?

CONTRIBUTORS
TO THIS VOLUME

EDITORS

BRENT SLIFE is an associate professor of psychology at Baylor University, where he teaches and currently serves as director of clinical training. A fellow of the American Psychological Association, he has authored over 60 books and articles. His most recent book, *Time and Psychological Explanation* (SUNY Press, scheduled for 1992), describes the overlooked influence of linear time on mainstream psychology. Professor Slife was recently designated the "Outstanding Research Professor" of Baylor University. He is the editor of *Theoretical and Philosophical Psychology* and serves in editorial capacities on the *Journal of Mind and Behavior* and *Theory and Psychology*. He received his Ph.D. from Purdue University, where he helped start the dialogue approach to psychology that is the basis of this volume.

JOSEPH RUBINSTEIN is professor emeritus of psychology in the Department of Psychological Sciences at Purdue University. As director of the introductory psychology program, he became known for his teaching contributions and was awarded the designation of Master Teacher. He received his Ph.D. in physiological psychology from the University of Michigan in 1960 and completed postdoctoral training in clinical psychology at the U.S.V.A. in Palo Alto, California, where he served as staff clinical psychologist. He is a fellow of the American Psychological Association, elected through the Division of the Teaching of Psychology.

STAFF

Marguerite L. Egan   Program Manager
Brenda S. Filley   Production Manager
Whit Vye   Designer
Libra Ann Cusack   Typesetting Supervisor
Juliana Arbo   Typesetter
David Brackley   Copy Editor
David Dean   Administrative Assistant
Diane Barker   Editorial Assistant
David Filley   Graphics

AUTHORS

ALAN C. ACOCK is a professor in and the chair of the Department of Human Development and Family Sciences at Oregon State University in Corvallis, Oregon.

APA INTERDIVISIONAL COMMITTEE ON ADOLESCENT ABORTION was appointed by the American Psychological Association to review the state of knowledge relevant to behavior assumptions on adolescent abortion and to provide guidelines to psychologists in light of the legal standards. The committee was chaired by Gary B. Melton, Adolph Happold Professor of Psychology and Law at the University of Nebraska at Lincoln, and included Nancy E. Adler, University of California, San Francisco; Henry P. David, Transnational Family Research Institute; Jeanne Marecek, Swarthmore College; Roberta A. Morris; Nancy Felipe Russo; Elizabeth S. Scott; Lois A. Weithorn; and Kathleen Wells.

MAHZARIN R. BANAJI is an assistant professor of psychology at Yale University in New Haven, Connecticut. Her research interests are in social recognition and interpersonal processes, which are reflected in her article "Alcohol and Self-Inflation: Can a Social Cognition Approach Be Beneficial?" in *Social Cognition* (1989), coauthored with C. M. Steele.

ALLEN E. BERGIN is a professor of and director of clinical psychol-

ogy at Brigham Young University in Provo, Utah. He is a former president of the Society for Psychotherapy Research and received the 1989 Distinguished Professional Contributions to Knowledge award from the American Psychological Association.

JAMES T. BERRY recently graduated from Virginia Commonwealth University in Richmond, Virginia.

MALVIN W. BRUBAKER was an attorney in private practice in Richmond, Virginia, when he coauthored the article that is featured in this edition of *Taking Sides: Psychological Issues.*

GEORGE A. CLUM is a professor in the Department of Psychology at Virginia Polytechnic Institute and State University in Blacksburg, Virginia.

JOHN R. COLE is an anthropologist at the University of Massachusetts at Amherst and the assistant director of the Massachusetts Water Resources Research Center. He has long been an advocate of improved science education and a critic of creationist "science."

CHERYL COLECCHI is a professor in the Department of Psychology at Virginia Commonwealth University in Richmond, Virginia.

ROBERT G. CROWDER is a professor of psychology and the director of undergraduate studies at Yale University. His research interests involve auditory memory or, more broadly, auditory cognition.

RAYMOND R. CROWE is a clinical psychiatrist and a professor in the Department of Psychiatry at the University of Iowa College of Medicine in Iowa City, Iowa.

DAVID H. DEMO is an associate professor in the Department of Sociology at Virginia Polytechnic Institute and State University in Blacksburg, Virginia. His research focuses on the influences of family structure and family relations on parents and children.

GARLAND Y. DeNELSKY is the head of the section of psychology and the director of the Psychology Training Program at the Cleveland Clinic, where he provides training and supervision for both psychology fellows and psychiatry residents. His clinical and research interests include the enhancement of coping skills, smoking cessation, and treating performance anxiety.

RICHARD J. DENNIS is the president of *New Perspectives Quarterly* magazine, a publication of the Center for the Study of Democratic Institutions; the president of the Chicago Resource Center, a grant-making foundation concerned with civil liberties; and the chairman of the Advisory Board of the Drug Policy Foundation.

BERNARD DIXON is the European editor of *The Scientist* magazine. His publications include *From Creation to Chaos: Classic Writings in Science* (Basil Blackwell, 1989).

ALBERT ELLIS, founder of rational-emotive therapy, is president of the Institute for Rational-Emotive Therapy, located in New York City. He received his Ph.D. in clinical psychology from Columbia University and has authored and coauthored more than 600 articles and over 50 books on psychotherapy, marital and family therapy, and sex therapy, including *Why Some Therapies Don't Work: The Dangers of Transpersonal Psychology* (Prometheus Books, 1989), with Raymond Yaeger.

CYNTHIA FUCHS EPSTEIN is a professor in the Department of Sociology, Graduate Center, of the City College of New York, where she has been teaching since 1975. She is an editor of *Sex Roles*, a quarterly journal, and the author of *Deceptive Distinctions: Sex, Gender, and the Social Order* (Yale University Press, 1988).

HERBERT FINGARETTE is a professor of philosophy at the University of California, Santa Barbara. He has also served as an alcoholism and addiction consultant to the World Health Organization.

RONALD E. FOX is a professor in and the dean of the School of Professional Psychology at Wright State University in Dayton, Ohio, where he has been teaching since 1977. He has recently completed nine years of service on the Board of Directors of the American Psychological Association.

LEONARD ROY FRANK, since his involuntary commitment to the Twin Pines Psychiatric Hospital in Belmont, California, has been an outspoken advocate against psychiatric shock therapy and involuntary commitment to psychiatric hospitals. He is a cofounder of the Network Against Psychiatric Assault (NAPA) in San Francisco and Berkeley, California, and a member of Concerned Citizens Opposing Electroshock, which is also in San Francisco.

STEVEN GOLDBERG is an associate professor and the acting chair of the Department of Sociology at City College of the City University of New York, where he has been teaching since 1970. He is a contributor for the magazines *Psychiatry, Ethics, Yale Review,* and *Saturday Review* and the author of *Inevitability of Patriarchy* (William Morrow & Co., 1973).

C. E. M. HANSEL is a psychologist at the University of Wales and the author of many articles on ESP.

ARTHUR R. JENSEN is a professor of educational psychology at the University of California, Berkeley.

DAVID B. LARSON is an assistant secretary of planning at the Department of Health and Human Services in Washington, D.C.

DAVID LOYE is a psychologist and a codirector of the Institute for Futures Forecasting.

WILLIAM MADSEN is a professor of anthropology at the University of California, Santa Barbara. His specialties include primitive religion, psychological anthropology, and addiction. He is an Honorary Life Member of the Board of Directors for the National Council on Alcoholism–Santa Barbara chapter.

STANLEY MILGRAM (1933–1984) was an experimental social psychologist and a professor of psychology at the Graduate School and University Center of the City University of New York. He is especially well known for his series of controversial investigations regarding obedience to authority, which were done at Yale University from 1960 to 1963. His publications include *Obedience to Authority: An Experimental View* (Harper & Row, 1975).

DAVID MORROW, a graduate student of psychology at Virginia Commonwealth University, is currently serving as an intern in psychology with the Federal Correctional Institute at St. Petersburg, Virginia.

THOMAS H. MURRAY is the director of the Center for Biomedical Ethics in the School of Medicine at Case Western Reserve University in

Cleveland, Ohio. He is the coeditor of *Feeling Good, Doing Better* (Humana, 1984) and, with Arthur L. Caplan, *Which Babies Shall Live?* (Humana, 1985).

ULRIC NEISSER is the Robert W. Woodruff Professor of Psychology at Emory University in Atlanta, Georgia. A member of the National Academy of Sciences, Neisser is best known for three books on cognition: *Cognitive Psychology* (W. H. Freeman, 1967), which helped to establish that field in 1967; *Cognition and Reality: Principles and Implications of Cognitive Psychology* (W. H. Freeman, 1976), which helped to reorient it in 1976; and *Memory Observed: Remembering in Natural Contexts* (W. H. Freeman, 1982), which introduced the ecological approach to the study of memory in 1982.

JOANNE CURRY O'CONNELL is an associate director of research at the Institute for Human Development and an associate professor of educational psychology at Northern Arizona University in Flagstaff, Arizona.

RICHARD RESTAK is a neurologist in Washington, D.C. He is the author of *The Brain: The Last Frontier* (Bantam Books, 1985) and *The Mind* (Bantam Books, 1988).

D. L. ROSENHAN is a professor of law and psychology at Stanford University and a social psychologist who has been focally concerned with clinical and personality matters. He has also been a faculty member at Princeton University, the University of Pennsylvania, and Swarthmore College.

JOSEPH F. RYCHLAK holds the Maude C. Clark Chair of Humanistic Psychology at Loyola University of Chicago. He has written numerous journal articles on humanistic psychology and is the author of *The Psychology of Rigorous Humanism*, 2d ed. (New York University Press, 1987).

HERBERT A. SIMON is the Richard King Mellon University Professor of computer science and psychology at Carnegie Mellon University in Pittsburgh, Pennsylvania. He has studied decision-making and problem-solving processes for 30 years, using computers to stimulate human thinking, and was awarded the 1978 Nobel Prize in economics for his pioneering work on the decision-making process within organizations.

ROBERT L. SPITZER is affiliated with the New York State Psychiatric Institute in New York City. He is a former chairman of the American Psychiatric Association and its Task Force on Nomenclature and Statistics.

ROBERT J. STERNBERG is a professor of psychology at Yale University and a consultant to the Thinking Skills Project, Urban Development Component, at Research for Better Schools, Inc.

ELLEN SWITZER is a free-lance writer who specializes in medicine, psychology, and law.

THOMAS SZASZ is a psychiatrist, a psychoanalyst, and a professor emeritus in the Department of Psychiatry at State University of New York Health Science Center in Syracuse, New York, where he has been teaching since 1956. He is the senior and visiting scholar for the Faculty Improvement Program of the Eli Lilly Foundation and a member of the Board of Governors of the International Academy of Forensic Psychology. His most recent publications include *Our Right to Drugs: The Case for a Free Market* (Praeger, 1992).

JUDITH S. WALLERSTEIN is a lecturer in social welfare at the University of California, Berkeley, the senior consultant to Marin County Community Mental Health Center, and the executive director of the Center for the Family in Transition.

BURTON L. WHITE is the director and trustee of the Center for Parent Education in Newton, Massachusetts.

JAMES Q. WILSON is the James Collins Professor of Management and Public Policy at the University of California, Los Angeles, where he has been teaching since 1985. He has studied and advised on issues in crime and law enforcement for nearly 25 years and has authored, coauthored, and edited numerous books on crime, government, and politics. He is the chairman of the board of directors of the Police Foundation and a member of the American Academy of Arts and Sciences. His publications include *Bureaucracy: What Government Agencies Do and Why They Do It* (Basic Books, 1989).

EVERETT L. WORTHINGTON, JR., is a professor in the Department of Counseling Psychology at Virginia Commonwealth University in Richmond, Virginia. His most recent works include *Psychotherapy and Religious Values* (Baker Book House, 1992).

STEVEN ZAK is a research attorney for the California Superior Court in the County of Los Angeles. He received his B.A. in psychology from Michigan State University in 1971, his M.S. from Wayne State University School of Medicine in 1975, and his J.D. from the University of Southern California Law School in 1984. He has written about animals in relation to ethics and the law for numerous publications.

INDEX